Beginning Bioethics

Beginning Bioethics

A TEXT WITH INTEGRATED READINGS

Aaron Ridley

University of Southampton
England

Bedford/St. Martin's

Boston ◆ *New York*

Editor-in-chief: Steve Debow
Development editor: Natalie Hart
Manager, Publishing services: Emily Berleth
Senior editor, Publishing services: Douglas Bell
Project management: Pine Tree Composition
Production supervisor: Scott Lavelle
Cover design: Evelyn Horovicz
Cover photo: Reginald Wickham

Library of Congress Catalog Card Number: 97-065376

Manufactured in the United States of America.

6
f e

For information, write: Bedford/St. Martin's, 75 Arlington Street,
Boston, MA 02116 (617-399-4000)

ISBN: 0-312-13291-3

Acknowledgments

Page 76: Mark Lipkin, "On Lying to Patients" from *Newsweek* (June 4, 1979). Copyright © 1979 by Mark
Lipkin. Reprinted by permission.

Page 91: Mark Siegler, "Confidentiality in Medicine: A Decrepit Concept" from *The New England Journal of
Medicine* 307 (1982): 1518–1521. Copyright © 1982 by The Massachusetts Medical Society. Reprinted
with the permission of *The New England Journal of Medicine.* All rights reserved.

Page 117: Don Marquis, "Why Abortion Is Immoral" from *The Journal of Philosophy* LXVIII, no. 4 (April
1989): 183–202. Reprinted with the permission of the author and *The Journal of Philosophy.*

Page 127: Judith Jarvis Thomson, "A Defense of Abortion" from *Philosophy and Public Affairs,* 1, no. 1
(1971): 47–66. Copyright © 1971. Reprinted with the permission of Princeton University Press.

Page 165: James Rachels, "Active and Passive Euthanasia" from *The New England Journal of Medicine* 292, no.
2 (January 9, 1975): 78–80. Copyright © 1982 by The Massachusetts Medical Society. Reprinted with
the permission of *The New England Journal of Medicine.* All rights reserved.

Page 183: Aaron Ridley, "Ill-Gotten Gains: On the Use of Results from Unethical Experiments in Medicine"
from *Public Affairs Quarterly* 9, no. 3 (July 1995). Reprinted with the permission of the publishers.

Page 195: Tom Regan, "The Case against Animal Research" from *The Case for Animal Rights,* pp. 84–86,
327–328, 376–383, 384–385, 387–394, and 416. Copyright © 1995 by The Regents of the University of
California. Reprinted with the permission of University of California Press.

Page 212: Thomas Szasz, "The Myth of Mental Illness" from *The American Psychologist* (1960). Copyright ©
1960 by Thomas Szasz. Reprinted with the permission of the author and the American Psychological Association.

Page 223: Paul Chodoff, "The Case for Involuntary Hospitalization of the Mentally Ill" from *The American
Journal of Psychiatry* 133 (1976). Copyright © 1976 by the American Psychiatric Association. Reprinted
with the permission of the publishers.

Page 249: Kai Nielsen, "Autonomy, Equality, and a Just Health Care System" from *The International Journal
of Applied Philosophy* 4 (1989). Copyright © 1989 by Indian River Community College. Reprinted by permission.

Page 268: L. M. Purdy, "Genetic Diseases: Can Having Children Be Immoral?" from John J. Buckley, Jr.,
ed., *Genetics Now: Ethical Issues in Genetics Research.* Copyright © 1978. Reprinted with the permission of
University Press of America.

To Melissa and Anil

Table of Contents

Part Two: The Basic Issues of Bioethics   69

Preface

Beginning Bioethics is intended as a general introduction to bioethics for readers with little or no background in philosophy. It is organized into two parts. Part One gives students the background they need in the basics of ethical discussion. They learn about the advantages and disadvantages of the three major ethical theories-deontology, act and rule utilitarianism, and rights. They also discover the roles of various ethical principles and general methods of argument.

In Part Two we grapple with six major topics in bioethics. Each chapter starts with a general discussion of the main issues involved, then moves to one or two articles by professional ethicists, followed by a critical discussion of their arguments. The purpose behind this strategy is three-fold. First, it will introduce the reader to a diversity of thought-provoking and interesting arguments. Second, it will show what a reflective engagement with philosophically diverse views looks like in practice. And third, it will promote a conception of ethical thought that takes seriously the value of debate over dogmatism. The chapter concludes with four "Study Questions" that readers might like to reflect upon.

I do not, of course, aim to provide definitive answers to bioethical problems, because bioethical problems, like problems in ethics of every kind, admit of no final solution. A philosophy that pretended to clear up ethical problems once and for all would, by definition, be guilty of over-simplifying and misrepresenting the sort of problems that ethical problems pose. This book contains no answers, only strategies, approaches, clarifications, and discussions.

Because bioethics deals with concrete, specific cases, and not merely discussion of issues, this book has been constructed so it can be used alongside *Cases in Bioethics*, third edition, edited by Bette Jane Crigger. *Cases in Bioethics* contains discussion of cases presented to readers of *The Hastings Center Report*. For those who wish to use the two books in conjunction, the chapter organization is the same in each, and at the end of every chapter in Part Two I have indicated which of Crigger's cases bear most directly on the issues that chapter has attempted to clarify and discuss.

As advances are made in medical technology, new techniques and capabilities often run into conflict with various moral and religious convictions. The debates that have stormed around abortion, euthanasia, surrogate motherhood, and buying organs for transplantation are only some examples, not to mention the conflicts among hospitals, doctors, patients, and health care insurers about the allocation of shrinking resources. Since these debates do not seem likely to go away, it is in our best interests as citizens to learn how to participate in them in a helpful, intelligent manner. In this book I aim to demonstrate how philosophical discussion can help clarify our thoughts on bioethical problems.

I have been challenged critically by a number of people in the course of writing this book. I am grateful to them for it and the book is better as a result. I'd like to thank Victoria S. Wike, Loyola University Chicago; Albert Flores, California State University at Fullerton; Fran Silvernail, College of Staten Island, City University of New York; Gary Fuller, Central Michigan University; Glenn McGee, University of Pennsylvania Center for Bioethics; Nick Fotion, Emory University; Don Marquis, The University of Kansas; Bette-Jane Crigger, The Hastings Center; Robert T. Pennock, The University of Texas at Austin. Thanks, too, to Ann Spencer for providing the excellent illustrations that appeared in the original manuscript version of the book: I miss them. Above all, though, I'd like to thank the physical therapy students to whom I taught bioethics at Ithaca College in the early 1990s. They, more than anyone, showed me just what was involved in the attempt to take bioethics seriously — and the fruits of what they taught me are to be found in the following pages.

Aaron Ridley

About the Author

Aaron Ridley is a lecturer in philosophy at the University of Southampton in England. In the United States, he has taught medical ethics at Ithaca College. He has published articles in *Analysis, Philosophy and Literature,* the *Journal of Aesthetics and Art Criticism,* and the *British Journal of Aesthetics,* as well as a book, *Music, Value, and the Passions* (1995).

PART ONE

The Basics
of Ethical Argument

INTRODUCTION

It is perhaps no accident that the medical profession was the first profession in history to provide itself with a code of ethics. The Hippocratic oath represents the earliest serious attempt to come to grips with the unique and difficult ethical problems that the practice of medicine raises. Members of the health care professions face moral and ethical dilemmas as a routine part of their working lives, to a degree unequalled by any other profession. As medical science grows more sophisticated, and the range of treatments, procedures, and options increases, the ethical aspects of medicine become ever more complex, and ever more difficult to resolve. These dilemmas are problems in bioethics.

New technologies produce new ethical problems. Only very recently have we been able to keep people alive on life-support systems, for instance, or transplant organs from one person to another. Our ability to do these things brings great benefits. But this ability also creates deep and unfamiliar ethical difficulties that are important for us, as a society, to address. The age at which a fetus is able to survive outside of the mother's womb decreases almost yearly. We are gaining a better understanding of human genetics, to the point where we will soon be able to manipulate and modify the genetic make-up of our descendants. These technologies, too, raise disturbing questions about what we ought, or ought not, to do—they raise ethical questions about the limits and purposes of the practice of medicine.

These new problems have of course only added to the ethical problems that have surrounded medicine and the health care professions from the very beginning. Questions about confidentiality, for example, or about the duty to save lives at any cost, are as relevant today as they ever were. Traditional questions, such as those surrounding abortion and euthanasia, are not only still with us, but are now made even harder by the complexities and developments of the modern health care setting.

The process of resolving or trying to make sense of ethical problems is one with which we are all familiar from our everyday lives and relationships. Should we tell our friend the truth when we know that the truth will hurt her? Should we break a promise we have made if breaking it will help someone? Such questions, as we all know, can be extremely difficult to answer. But the attempt to provide strategies for thinking about them is one of the central tasks of moral philosophy or, as it is sometimes called, philosophical ethics. Philosophers are fascinated by the nature of moral thought and by the difficulties of arriving at acceptable solutions to ethical problems. By increasingly focusing on real-life practical issues, moral philosophers have tried to change the common picture of philosophy as an abstract subject with little relevance to our everyday concerns. The contribution which moral philosophers have made, and continue to make, to the clarification of practical problems in ethics is encouraging. Nowhere is that contribution more in evidence than in the areas of bioethics and medical ethics.

The characteristic method of philosophy is *argument*—the development and reasoned criticism of positions and perspectives on particular issues. Whenever we argue about ethics, then, or attempt to explore alternative standpoints on issues that we care about or that confuse us, we are engaging in an activity that is thoroughly philosophical. The purpose of this book is to help make that activity as productive as it can be, especially in connection with issues in bioethics.

In order to realize that purpose, however, we must first understand why it is important to argue philosophically about ethics, and we must also assemble some of the nuts and bolts from which philosophical arguments are constructed. In Part One, then, we explore the motivations for arguing philosophically about ethics, lay out some of the materials useful in making and understanding such arguments, and outline the methods by which philosophical arguments about ethics can most successfully be developed and pursued.

CHAPTER ONE

Motivations

It is all very well to talk about ethical argument and to make claims about the virtues of arguing philosophically. But suppose you simply don't *want* to argue about ethics. Or suppose you think it's pointless to argue about ethics. Unless we can come up with a good set of reasons for engaging in ethical argument and can agree, at least roughly, on what such arguments are meant to achieve, we shall get off to a very poor start. As with any kind of argument—indeed, as with any human activity—a shared set of suppositions and objectives is an essential requirement. Imagine, for example, trying to play a game without understanding any of the rules or what you have to do to win. You'd quickly get bored. You'd quickly decide that the game was pointless. So what are the motivations for arguing about ethics? Why should we bother?

1.1 AVOIDING BLOODSHED

Everyone knows that disagreements about ethical matters can arouse strong emotions. You only have to look at the protesters outside an abortion clinic, or at the marchers in an anti-war demonstration, to realize how heated ethical differences can get. Unfortunately, when strong emotions are aroused, it is always only a short step to something worse.

If two people are reduced to a shouting match, we know that the chances of their reaching a sensible agreement about anything is practically zero. And if they end up coming to blows, then a resolution of their dispute will be achieved only by one of them knocking the other out, or else by the timely intervention of the police. None of these outcomes is at all constructive. None of them furthers an ethical case. And none of them gets us any closer to finding out what the proper resolution of a disagreement should be. In fact, the more an issue fuels tempers, the more likely a dispute about it will be futile.

Ethics calls for a cool head. If we can substitute reason for passion, and argument for violence, then at the very least this will be good for our health. More fundamentally, it will be good for our thinking and for our decision-making. The challenge is to move the center of ethical engagement from the guts to the head, so that we come to rely more and more on dispassionate reflection and less and less on impassioned conviction. The attempt to discover a language within which ethical disagreements can be worked through productively is essential to the study of ethics. It is also essential if we wish to move away from mere stubbornness and bad temper and towards a more creative approach to our problems. Given human nature, of course, it would be unrealistic to hope that every ethical dispute can be settled by reasoned argument. But that doesn't mean that it is pointless to try. One of the prime motivations for developing the habit of ethical argument, then, is that it is a lot better, and better in a lot of ways, than some of the common alternatives.

1.2 RESISTING RELATIVISM

Someone might agree that it is better to talk things through than to fight about them, but he or she may still suggest that it is a waste of time to *argue* about ethics. This line of reasoning might go like this: ethics is subjective; ethical values (what you consider right and wrong) depend upon how you feel about something; all people have their own ethical feelings and values, all of which are equally valid; you can't change the way someone feels about something by arguing with him or her; indeed it would be wrong to try to impose your own feelings on somebody else; so it is bound to be pointless, and maybe even wrong, to try to persuade someone to change his or her mind through ethical argument. The name for this kind of position—which claims that we should respect the diversity of people's ethical beliefs, and not try to tell them what they should think—is ethical relativism.

Almost everyone has been tempted at some time or another by ethical relativism. It sounds so tolerant, so harmless. Indeed, what could be nicer? But when you stop to think about it, relativism turns out to be nearly impossible to defend. For one thing, it conflicts with many of our deeply held intuitions about ethics. Imagine a man who thought it was ethically fine to rape children or poke out the eyes of the elderly. Wouldn't such a person be making a *mistake* of some kind? Wouldn't we think there was something simply wrong with his ethical feelings and values? It is doubtful that we would just shrug our shoulders and say, "Well, I suppose those are his own personal views. Who are we to tell him what he should do or think?" If people responded like that, we would surely conclude that there was something wrong with their ethical values too!

By the same token, if someone was a *true* relativist, he or she would have to say that what the Nazis did to the Jews in World War II, for instance, was simply an expression of one of the many equally valid feelings one might have about genocide (after all, the Nazis seemed to feel that what they were doing was ethically acceptable). Wouldn't this be mad? Moreover, a *true* relativist couldn't approve of Amnesty International's efforts to draw attention to and to prevent human rights abuses around the world, for instance in the context of female circumcision. After all, the relativist would have to say, who are we to tell other nations and cultures what they should do? If, for example, the rulers of a certain country feel that it's ethically fine to mutilate young women, that's their prerogative. This kind of response, surely, is not so much tolerant and harmless as callous and awful. Yet it is just the response that follows from ethical relativism.

The point is that we do think that some ethical values are straightfor-wardly wrong, and that some ethical perspectives should be discouraged. But this is just what relativism denies. The relativist's reasons for taking this posi-tion don't stand up to scrutiny, however. The relativist claims that ethical values are subjective, that they are based on feelings. But even if this were true, it still wouldn't follow automatically that all ethical points of view are equally valid. We can make mistakes about subjective matters, just as we can make mistakes about objective matters. For example, someone who is terri-fied of paper clips, or of small cardboard cartons, has clearly made an error of some kind, even though his or her response is undoubtedly a subjective one. We would probably try to persuade such a person that paper clips, or small cardboard cartons, did not really pose any danger. If we succeeded in this, we have succeeded in changing the way the person felt. He or she ought no longer be terrified of clips or cartons. The mere fact that a response involves feeling, then, doesn't show that it is immune to error, or that it lies in some way beyond the reach of argument. Thus if ethical values depend upon feel-ings, as the relativist claims, it might still be worth arguing about them, and it might still be worth holding on to the intuition that certain ethical values can be mistaken.

There are other reasons for objecting to ethical relativism. A particularly obvious one is that it contradicts itself. If the relativist were correct, in claim-ing that all ethical views are equally valid, then he or she would have no grounds for claiming that we shouldn't criticize the ethical values of others, or that we should respect ethical diversity. For in making the latter claim, the relativist appears to suggest that we should recognize certain ethical val-ues, such as tolerance of, and refusal to interfere with, the ethical beliefs of others, regardless of our own personal feelings. In other words, the relativist seems to defend two incompatible claims. The first claim holds that all ethical positions are equally valid, so that no claim is absolutely right or absolutely wrong. The second claim holds that because everyone has their own ethical values, it is absolutely wrong for people to interfere with or to criticize ethi-cal values that are different from their own. But you can't have it both ways. Either there are absolutes in ethics, for instance that it is absolutely wrong to interfere with the ethical beliefs of others, or there aren't absolutes in ethics. And obviously it is the second claim—that there aren't absolutes in ethics—which represents the relativist's true position. But this means that the rela-tivist's defense of tolerance goes out the window. Tolerance might accord well with the relativist's own personal feelings, but other less tolerant people might very well feel differently. Thus the superficially attractive quality of relativism—its apparent tolerance of the views of others—depends upon an outright contradiction, and crumbles as soon as you look at it. (We will re-turn to this contradiction in 4.1.)

Ethical relativism is well worth resisting, even in versions more sophisti-cated than that presented here. It turns out to be less attractive than it seems at first sight. It also turns out to be quite incompatible with the intuition that some people can be ethically mistaken, regardless of the sincerity of their feelings to the contrary. Far from promoting tolerance, relativism in fact pro-

motes an attitude of callous indifference to suffering and injustice. By denying that some ethical views are more valid than others, the relativist refuses
in the end to take ethical problems seriously enough. One very compelling
reason to engage in ethical argument, therefore, is that by doing so we do acknowledge the seriousness of ethical problems, and we signal our determination to make progress toward resolving them. In opening such problems up
for debate, we give substance to our antirelativist intuition that some ethical
positions are better than others. Indeed, we make an effort to find out which
positions those are. Serious ethical issues, such as those surrounding the life
and death decisions in bioethics, are simply too important to be left up to the
relativist.

1.3   SIDESTEPPING RELIGION

We sometimes talk about "preaching to the converted." What we mean is
that someone is expressing views that appeal to an audience already sharing
those views but are not found persuasive by anybody else. If we wish to
avoid deadlock, standoff, bad temper, or worse, in our efforts to face difficult
ethical problems, then we will do well to avoid preaching to the converted.

As the phrase suggests, the chances of preaching to the converted are
particularly immediate in a religious context. If we base our ethical views
solely on theological considerations, we will find it very difficult to engage in
pointful discussion with anyone who happens not to share the same theological position. If one person claims, for example, that abortion is wrong because the Pope says it is wrong, such a claim is clearly not going to carry
weight with non-Catholics. Similarly, if I derive my ethical views from the
Koran, then my efforts to persuade you of the truth of some ethical position
by quoting the Koran will meet with failure, unless, of course, you too happen to derive your ethical views from the Koran. Indeed, human history illustrates all too well the futilities and dangers of relying solely upon religious
principle to settle disputes between peoples of differing religious persuasions.

A powerful motivation for engaging in philosophical argument about
ethical matters, therefore, is the desire to avoid the deadlock and futility
characteristic of religious disagreement. In philosophical argument, we try to
discover or to describe ethical principles which speak to, and which can be
used by, people of any religious persuasion, or of none. We attempt to find a
common language which will allow ethical problems to be addressed from a
variety of perspectives. We try to promote a constructive approach to ethics,
rather than an approach—such as the religious approach—certain to produce a breakdown in communication and then a standoff.

This doesn't mean that religious insights are unimportant for ethics.
Quite the reverse. But it does mean that we must find ways to express such
insights in terms that are intelligible and persuasive to people whose religious perspective is different. Now clearly the task envisaged here is a demanding one. But it is an important one, too, and all the more important in
the culturally diverse context of a modern society. Philosophical argument,

in attempting to sidestep explicitly religious concepts and concerns, represents our best chance of dealing productively with the ethical problems confronting us all, whatever our religious convictions might be. Philosophical argument about ethics is secular, and that is one of its major strengths and one of the major motivations for engaging in it.

1.4 CLARIFYING YOUR POSITION

One of the real advantages of arguing philosophically about ethics is that it can help us discover what we really think about a particular problem. Too often we rest content with some vague intuition about an issue that we never trouble to explore or to go through properly. When we discuss and argue about the issue, by contrast, we are forced to confront it head-on, and we are obliged to subject our intuitions to close scrutiny. An unexpected argument or example from the person we are talking to can surprise us out of our complacency, and can lead us to expand, abandon, or modify views that we hadn't really bothered to think about carefully before. We can approach ethical problems more deeply when we agree to discuss them, and we can arrive at ever clearer conceptions of what those problems truly involve, and of how they can most fruitfully be addressed.

Any ethics teacher will be able to tell you how his or her views have been altered by discussing ethical issues in class with students (it happens to me all the time!). And anyone who has engaged in philosophical argument about ethics will confirm that they have benefitted not only in reaching a clearer conception of specific issues in ethics, but also in reaching a clearer conception of themselves as actors in an ethically complex world.

1.5 PERSUASION AND PUBLIC POLICY

It is clear by now that many of the advantages that I am claiming for the activity of arguing philosophically about ethics derive from the capacity of that activity to get us around the dead ends that plague other ways of engaging with ethical issues. One of the reasons why that is a good thing, of course, is that if we are condemned always to run into a dead end with our ethical disagreements and perplexities, then we will never be able to persuade anyone of anything. When I recommended that we resist ethical relativism (see 1.2), I suggested that we hold on to our intuition that some ethical views are more valid than others. For instance, we should hold on to the intuition that Hitler's ethical views were less valid than those of, say, Amnesty International. If we can engage people in philosophical argument about ethics, we have at least some hope of persuading them to embrace those more valid views (and, indeed, of coming to recognize and to embrace more valid views ourselves). There is no need to be squeamish about "forcing your views on others," for in philosophical argument no one is forced to do anything—except to examine an issue closely and rationally. If the result of a philosophical argument is that people come to accept the view that you have advanced, then the reason for that is not that you have "forced" your view upon them, but that the force of your argument has had its due effect.

A good reason for arguing philosophically about ethics, then, is that we hope to make a difference to the ethical views of others, as well as improve our own views. This applies to the views of our friends, families, and acquaintances. But also, and very importantly, it applies to the ethical views of those who frame and vote on public policy. One of our most significant duties as citizens of a democracy is to engage critically with the ethical dimensions of public policy-making.

A major concern of public policy is of course the law; and it is very important for us, as we think about ethics, to be clear about the difference between ethics and the law, between what is ethically acceptable and what is legally acceptable. We quite often hear people saying that such-and-such must be ethically okay because it isn't against the law. Or we hear someone claim that so-and-so is surely unethical because it is, as a matter of fact, illegal. But remarks like these reveal a confusion. Ethics and the law are quite different things. Murder may be wrong, both legally and ethically; and contributing to certain charities may be ethically good and also legal. But consider adultery: Adultery is surely unethical. Yet there are no laws against it. Or think about jay-walking. In some states it is illegal to step out onto an empty street if the pedestrian crossing sign says Stop. But is there anything unethical about crossing an empty street? One and the same action can be both ethically wrong and legally fine, or both ethically fine and legally wrong. The Lord Chancellor in Gilbert and Sullivan's *Iolanthe* sings:

> The law is the true embodiment
> Of everything that's excellent
> It has no kind of fault or flaw
> And I, my Lords, embody the law.

But it would only be in some strange Utopia that ethics and the law coincided so perfectly. In practice, they tend to diverge quite widely from each other. Which means, first, that in the real world the legal status of an action has little or no bearing upon its ethical status. Second, we can deduce nothing about what is legal simply by reflecting upon what is ethical. What we can do, however, and this is the important point, is reflect ethically upon the law in an attempt to discover whether the law is as it ought to be. In other words, we can ask ourselves whether existing laws are ethically acceptable; and we can try to envisage or to work out what a more ethically acceptable set of laws might be like. If we begin to do this, then we take our first step towards engaging productively and critically with an important aspect of the ethics of public policy.

A democratic people gets the laws it deserves; and if we refuse to argue about our ethical priorities, and to argue reasonably about them, then the laws that we get will not be the best ones. They may even be ethically offensive (think of the slavery laws before the Civil War, or the laws discriminating against women before the introduction of universal suffrage). Some very important questions in public policy are exactly the questions with which bioethics is concerned. Is abortion acceptable? Is it acceptable to harm research subjects in medical experiments? Who can become an organ donor? In arguing philosophically about these and other issues we contribute to the public discussion essential to the formation and criticism of policy in a democracy.

1.6   RECAP: REASONS FOR ARGUING ABOUT ETHICS

I hope that this chapter encourages you to engage in argument about ethical issues. I hope, too, that it persuades you that such argument should be *reasoned* argument—that it should be philosophical. Only by engaging in argument of this kind can we hope to minimize the uglier effects of ethical disagreement. Reason is the best defense we have against anger and violence. It is also our best safeguard against the temptations of relativism—the doctrine that all ethical views are equally valid, that no one's views can be criticized. Only reason can underwrite the tolerance that relativism appears to recommend; and only reason can dispel the indifference that relativism in fact entails. The public, nonsectarian language of reasoned debate represents our best hope of overcoming ethical deadlock and our best response to dogmatism of every kind. If we refuse to engage in this activity, we surrender any chance we have of making a positive contribution to the many difficult ethical questions facing us, and we give up any hope we have of influencing the values by which our society lives. In addressing the ethical problems that the practice of modern medicine raises, we embark upon a serious attempt to improve our ethical understanding of the world, and hence to improve the quality of what is done and thought in that world. Arguing about ethics is a very important activity indeed.

CHAPTER TWO
Materials: Theories in Ethics

In this section we will assemble some of the basic tools needed to understand and engage in philosophical arguments about ethics. There isn't very much jargon—and you'll find that what there is can be learned quickly, making things a lot easier and more convenient later on. It's essentially a matter of getting together a common language. The concepts and terms employed in this section are the ones that figure most commonly and prominently in the philosophical literature. They should be useful to you when framing your own arguments about issues in bioethics.

2.1 WHAT IS AN ETHICAL THEORY?

As people have reflected upon and struggled with ethical issues, they have found it useful to develop general perspectives from which particular ethical issues can be contemplated. These general perspectives are called ethical theories. An ethical theory indicates a distinctive way of looking at ethical issues —a distinctive way of making sense of them and of attempting to resolve them. Such theories are *prescriptive* theories. This means that they set out to tell us how we ought to address and resolve ethical difficulties. They set out to tell us how things should be.

We can bring out the kind of thing that an ethical theory is with an example. Suppose that instead of facing a problem in ethics, you are facing a problem in sport—how to win a tennis match. Now there are a number of ways in which you might resolve this problem. You might decide, for instance, that the most fruitful approach would be to play an out-and-out baseliner's game—staying as much as possible in the backcourt and only approaching the net when absolutely necessary. You have then adopted a certain theory about winning tennis matches—a "baseline" theory. Alternatively, you might think that being a serve-and-volleyer is the best approach —you come to the net whenever you can and only stay on the baseline when you have no other option. In this case, you have adopted a "serve-and-volley" theory. Both the baseline theory and the serve-and-volley theory indicate an overall perspective you might take if your goal is to win a tennis match. Ethical theories are just the same. They suggest which perspective on an ethical problem you *ought* to take if you want to resolve the problem in an ethically successful way.

In this section, then, we will survey some of the most important ethical theories that have been developed as approaches to ethical problems. The theories we will look at are: deontology, act utilitarianism, and rule utilitarianism. We will then look at a subsidiary theory—the theory of rights—which, although it cannot be used on its own, can be used as part of a wider perspective in ethics.

2.2 DEONTOLOGY

Deontology is an ethical theory whose name is derived from the Greek word *deon*, meaning duty or obligation. That, in a nutshell, is what deontology is all about. Deontology holds that people act in an ethically acceptable way whenever they act in accordance with their duties and obligations. An unacceptable action, by contrast, will violate some duty or obligation that the person in question has. For the deontologist, then, the most important task that people have when they face an ethical issue is to decide which duties or obligations are relevant to the case. Having settled that, they will then be in a position to perform an ethically acceptable action, or else to recommend to others what an ethically acceptable action would be.

A very simple example of someone taking a deontological perspective on an issue is a person who thinks that you should always keep your promises, however inconvenient it might be to do so. Thus, if I have promised you that I will mail a letter today, and then find that it is pouring rain and the last thing I want to do is to go out, the deontologist will tell me that I have an obligation to go out and mail your letter (I promised you, after all), and that if I fail to go out and mail it I will have acted unethically. In a case like this, the deontologist will say that the only ethically acceptable course of action is to keep my promise, even if it means that I will get soaked to the skin. Only an action undertaken in accordance with my duties and obligations is ethically correct.

But how do I know what my duties and obligations are—or what anyone else's are, for that matter—beyond simple things like keeping promises? Well, that depends on what *kind* of deontology is adopted. Just as there are different ways of being a baseliner in tennis—for instance, you might hit every ball hard and with lots of topspin, or else you might mix the pace with slices and drop-shots—so there are different ways of being a deontologist. A deontologist who is in the army, for example, might claim that his duties and obligations are whatever his superior officers say they are, and thus ethically acceptable behavior on his part consists simply in following orders. A deontological judge, by contrast, might hold that it is the duty of everyone to obey the laws of the land, no matter what their superiors might order them to do. In fact, professional codes of conduct very often provide good examples of the different kinds of duty that might figure within a deontological theory. Doctors, for instance, are expected to act in accordance with a code of conduct that is very different from the ones that might apply to teachers, for example, or to politicians. While it may be the duty of a policeman to tell people that they have the right to remain silent, it would not normally be the duty of a nurse to inform people of the same thing. A deontological perspective, then, is one that identifies the ethically correct course of action as that which is in accordance with whichever are the relevant duties and obligations. And different deontological theories will arise as different sets of duties and obligations are marked out as the relevant ones.

Now let us explore some of the features, as well as some of the problems, that are distinctive of deontology. (All ethical theories have their problems!) We'll start with the positive features.

2.2a   Deontology and Consistency

One very important quality of deontology is its consistency. A deontologist will tend to act in a predictable and reliable way. A deontologist can be relied upon to take his or her promises seriously, for instance; the deontological soldier will predictably and reliably follow orders; the deontological teacher will predictably and reliably attempt to teach his or her students things that are true; and so on. Because deontologists believe in honoring their duties and obligations, their behavior can in principle be foreseen by anyone who knows what those duties and obligations are. And it isn't hard to see why consistency of this kind is valuable. Imagine living in a world where people's behavior was completely *in*consistent—where people only kept their promises when they felt like it, where judges only enforced the law at whim, or where doctors only tried to save lives if they happened to wake up in an especially good mood. Apart from being frightening and chaotic, such a world would also be an impossible world for you to act in. Just think how many of your actions each day depend upon other people behaving more or less as you expect them to; just imagine how difficult it would be to decide what to do if you had absolutely no idea what anyone else was about to do next. Life would be impossible! It is only in a world where other people's behavior is at least somewhat consistent that any of us can hope to behave at all consistently ourselves. So the consistency of behavior entailed by deontology is certainly both an important feature and an advantage—an advantage not shared by every other ethical theory (see 2.3h). Only where others are consistent can we hope to be consistent ourselves.

2.2b   Deontology and Special Obligations

Another strength of deontology is that it can take account of what is often felt to be an extremely important kind of obligation—a "special" obligation. A special obligation is an obligation someone has as a result of standing in a certain relationship to someone or something else. Examples of special obligations would be: the obligations parents have to their children; the obligations employers have to their employees; the obligations company directors have to their shareholders; the obligations nurses have to their patients; the obligations priests or ministers have to their flocks; and so on. Obligations of this kind are special in the sense that they are limited. Parental obligation, for instance, is something that only parents can have, and it is something that parents can only have towards their own children. Similarly —and while there is no doubt that all of us have some general obligation towards someone who is ill—only members of the relevant health care team can have a *special* obligation towards that person as a patient. Special obligations, then, are created by the relationships that people stand in, and they are limited to cover only the people defined by those relationships. Many ethical theories have a hard time taking special obligations into account (again, see 2.3f), but deontology, with its emphasis on taking obligations seriously, is not one of them. Indeed, of all ethical theories, deontology is best able to accommodate those obligations that many of us think that our relationships—both personal and professional—impose upon us.

2.2c Deontology and Supererogation

The final strength of deontology that we will explore is that it has room for "supererogation"—which sounds either like a farming term or something very complicated. Happily, though, it is neither. Supererogation actually means acting above and beyond the call of duty, or exceeding one's obligations. We know that deontology is very closely concerned with duties and obligations. We also know, if we think for a moment, that any sensible and workable set of duties will have to be quite moderate: After all, a set of duties and obligations that demands from people an unrealistic degree of courage or of self-sacrifice will never work in practice. Therefore, any sensible deontological theory must not require *too* much—it must ask only as much of people as they might reasonably be expected to comply with. This is not to say that a deontological theory has to be weak or forgiving. It is only to say that such a theory must not be unrealistically or foolishly demanding. This means that from the perspective of deontology there will always be room for the peculiarly generous or courageous person to act not merely correctly— by fulfilling his or her duties and obligations—but to act superbly. Such a person will go above and beyond the call of duty and do things that no one could reasonably require them to do, or require anyone else to do. Such a person does things that no one could possibly be blamed for not doing.

Suppose a hand-grenade is tossed into the middle of a crowded room. Clearly no deontological theory could sensibly claim that it was anybody's duty to spring upon it and protect others from the blast with his or her own body—for hardly anyone would have the courage to comply with such an obligation. Such an obligation, then, could not play a part in a realistic or workable set of deontological duties. Therefore, if someone does fling himself firmly upon the grenade—with all of the results, both good and bad, that action might have—his action would count as a clear case of supererogation. Such a person would have acted superbly and have done something that no one could reasonably have blamed him for not doing. The fact that deontology has room for the category of supererogation is a definite point in its favor. For our intuitions tell us that there are indeed some actions that no one can reasonably be required to perform (such as leaping onto a hand-grenade), but that are some of the most ethically valuable actions imaginable. Because our intuitions work like this, we think of some people as "saints" and of others as "heroes"; because our intuitions work like this we might find it difficult to be convinced by any ethical theory which cannot make room for the idea of supererogation. (For examples of theories that have problems in this respect, see 2.2.)

We have seen, then, that deontology has some real strengths. But it also has some rather serious weaknesses.

2.2d Deontology and Rational Justification

One of deontology's weaknesses is that there is nothing strikingly *rational* about it. In all of the examples I cited, the duties and obligations involved were reasonable enough. We discussed doctors trying to save lives and judges attempting to enforce the law. But it's not difficult to imagine a set of duties and obligations that would be unreasonable in the extreme but perfectly compatible with a deontological perspective. Imagine a code of duties requiring fish-sellers to collect gravel, for instance, or demanding that senators ride around in bright orange baby strollers. While quite amusing to contemplate, it isn't clear that obligations of this kind would have anything much to do with ethics. Would it really be ethically wrong for a fish-seller to fail to collect gravel, or for a senator to choose a stroller of the most violent pink? Presumably not.

The important point here is that deontology requires a justification for the duties and obligations it imposes. And the difficulty is that it is not clear where that justification is supposed to come from. In practice, religious texts of various kinds have very often been at the bottom of specific deontologies. The Ten Commandments, for example, provide a model set of duties and obligations, and the Sermon on the Mount, interpreted to the same end, yields a deontological set of duties and obligations. Examples can be drawn from other religions too—even the U.S. Constitution functions like a religious text at times! But we have already noted the drawbacks of bringing religion into ethical contexts (see 1.3); deontology will be a less attractive ethical position the more it depends upon religious considerations.

Whenever we encounter a deontological perspective in bioethics, then, we will do well to ask ourselves, "Where have these duties and obligations come from? How are they being justified?" And where we cannot come up with satisfactory answers to these questions, we will do well to remain a little skeptical. The point here is not that deontology is hopelessly flawed, or that it cannot represent a workable perspective in ethics. The point is only that the problem of rational justification is particularly acute for deontology, and that we, in our exploration of the various ethical issues in this book, should remain alert to that fact.

2.2e Deontology and Conflicting Duties and Obligations

A second problem for deontology can be stated more quickly. Because deontological ethics is concerned with sets of duties and obligations, usually of a fairly rigid kind, and because the real world tends to produce some rather complicated situations, it often turns out that in those situations a person's duties and obligations will come into conflict with each other. For example, suppose you are a doctor. Suppose you have an obligation to keep secret the things that patients tell you in your consulting room; but suppose that you also have an obligation to safeguard the health of the general public. A patient tells you in your consulting room that he intends to poison the city's water supply. What do you do? Your obligations have come into conflict with each other. If you honor your obligation to keep secret the things that you have been told in your consulting room, you must ignore your obligation to safeguard the health of the general public. But if you honor your obligation towards the general public (by alerting the police), you must break your obligation to keep your patients' secrets. You are in a position where you can honor only one of the conflicting obligations laid upon you, and you must somehow decide which of the two obligations is the more important.

The example I have given here is no doubt rather extreme. But we can all imagine more down-to-earth examples of conflicting obligations, where the essential pattern will be much the same. From a deontological perspective, such conflicts, however down-to-earth, obviously raise a real problem. How are dilemmas of this kind to be resolved? The deontologist needs a procedure for deciding between conflicting obligations if the deontological perspective is to have a hope of working as a practical ethical theory. Such procedures can often be rather difficult to find or to agree upon.

2.2f Deontology and Indifference to Consequences

A final major problem for deontology must be mentioned. The deontological perspective appears to be completely indifferent to the consequences that actions undertaken in accordance with duties and obligations might have. Remember, from a deontological point of view, an action is ethically acceptable if it accords with a duty or obligation, and an action is ethically unacceptable if it violates a duty or obligation. It is only the relation which an action has to a duty or an obligation that determines its ethical standing. There is no mention of, or room for, the results that an action has. This leads many people to think that something is seriously wrong with deontology as an ethical perspective. Such people suggest that if an action is perfectly in accord with a duty or obligation, but nevertheless leads to the most disastrous consequences, it simply cannot be an ethically unproblematic action. If I have promised you $100, and later learn that you mean to spend it on a gun with which to shoot your parents, then, from a deontological point of view, I ought to go ahead and give you $100. By promising to give you the money, I entered into an obligation to you; and only by giving you $100 will I satisfy that obligation. From a deontological perspective, then, it would be unethical of me to break my promise to you, to go back on my obligation, *whatever the consequences might be.* Can this be right? Can this really be an ethically sound position? The emphasis that deontology places upon acting in accordance with duties and obligations at the expense of any consideration for consequences makes it very vulnerable to examples of this kind, and gives it a definite credibility problem. It also, we should note, makes it impossible for the deontologist to appeal to the consequences of actions when trying to decide between conflicting obligations of the kind we discussed here. The option of not giving you $100, which might on the face of it have looked attractive, is not one that the deontologist can consistently choose. Deontology is about acting in accordance with obligations; it is not about acting in order to avoid bad results, or to achieve good ones.

More than any other factor, the indifference of deontology to the consequences of actions has led to the development of alternative ethical perspectives, perspectives which *do* give weight to the results that actions have. But we will see in 2.3 and 2.4 that these alternatives have difficulties of their own, and also that they lack some of the characteristic strengths of deontology.

In summary, deontology is all about acting in accordance with duties and obligations. Good things about this perspective include consistency, and the ability to make sense of special obligations and of supererogation. Bad things include a problem with rational justification, a problem with conflicting duties and obligations, and a complete indifference to the consequences of actions. Of course, deontology has other characteristics, both positive and negative, than those mentioned here. Some of them will emerge by contrast during the discussions of other theories in the next several sections. And in 2.7 there is a summary of the strengths and weaknesses of each of the ethical theories covered in this chapter. However, the characteristics of deontology that we have looked at in this section are certainly some of the most important ones. They are also some of the most helpful characteristics to bear in mind when later examined deontological ethical theories in practice.

Selected Bibliography

Kant, Immanuel, *The Moral Law: Groundwork of the Metaphysic of Morals,* Routledge, 1991.
Sullivan, Roger J., *An Introduction to Kant's Ethics,* Cambridge University Press, 1994.
Ross, William D., *The Right and The Good,* Oxford University Press, 1930.

2.3   ACT UTILITARIANISM

We saw in 2.2f that a weakness of deontology is its indifference to the consequences of actions. The opposite of deontology in this respect is the ethical theory known as act utilitarianism, which takes account of nothing except the consequences of actions. For this reason, act utilitarianism is sometimes called a consequentialist theory of ethics.

The central idea behind act utilitarianism is very simple, and it is captured perfectly in the slogan "Act for the greatest good of the greatest number." For the act utilitarian, the "good" is measured in terms of happiness or of satisfaction; the "bad" is measured in terms of suffering or of dissatisfaction. Thus the act utilitarian seeks in every action to maximize the overall amount of happiness in the world and to minimize the overall amount of suffering. The best possible action will be that which produces the greatest quantity of happiness at the expense of the smallest quantity of suffering; the worst possible action will be one that gets the balance the other way around. The act utilitarian, then, is concerned only with the results or consequences of actions; so that only an action which has good consequences, or which has the least bad consequences, will qualify as an ethically good action.

How does the act utilitarian decide which is the best action to perform in any given situation? In three stages. The first stage is to survey all of the possible courses of action. The second stage is to predict what consequences, in terms of happiness and suffering, each of those courses of action will have. The third stage is to calculate which course of action's consequences represent the best balance of good results over bad results. Only now, having surveyed, predicted, and calculated, will the act utilitarian know which action is ethically the best—which action is the one that will lead to the best overall balance of consequences, to the most happiness at the expense of the least suffering.

Take a very simple example. Suppose that an expedition of ten botanists, led by an act utilitarian, is captured by bandits in a place far from help. Suppose that the bandit-chief tells the expedition that they will all be shot unless the leader of the expedition agrees personally to shoot four of the botanists. If the expedition leader agrees to shoot four of the botanists, then the surviving six members of the expedition will be allowed to go free. Suppose in addition that the bandit-chief clearly means exactly what he says; suppose that there is no hope of escape; and suppose that there is no hope of rescue. What does the act utilitarian expedition leader do?

The first part is easy. A swift survey of the possible courses of action reveals that there are only two: either accept the bandit-chief's deal and shoot four colleagues; or reject the deal and allow all ten members of the expedition to be shot. The second part is also fairly simple. To accept the bandit-chief's deal will predictably lead to very bad consequences for four people (death) and to reasonably good consequences for six people (life and freedom). To reject the bandit-chief's deal, on the other hand, will predictably lead to very bad consequences for ten people (death) and to good consequences for no one. The act utilitarian's third stage is to calculate which course of action will produce the best overall balance of consequences. Now in this case *both* of the available alternatives will have bad consequences. Nevertheless, it is clear that the second course of action—rejecting the bandit-chief's deal—will have worse overall consequences than the first course of action. To accept the bandit-chief's deal will save six lives at the cost of four deaths (you might describe this as a score of + 2); to reject the bandit-chief's deal will save no lives at the cost of ten deaths (a score of −10). Thus the first course of action represents the most positive balance available, given the situation. Therefore the act utilitarian leader of the expedition will conclude that the ethically proper course of action is to shoot four botanical colleagues in order to save the lives of the rest, and that is what he will proceed to do. This is no doubt rather an extreme example, but it illustrates exactly what kind of decision-making process the act utilitarian perspective requires.

Several things need to be emphasized. One is that, from the act utilitarian perspective, no one individual's happiness or suffering is intrinsically more important than anyone else's. If an action of mine will cause a certain amount of misery to me, but produce a greater amount of satisfaction for you, then the action will be a good one. The fact that the misery is mine is irrelevant. There is nothing self-centered about act utilitarianism; the important thing is only that there be the best available balance of good consequences over bad, no matter to whom those consequences happen.

Another point to note is that because the act utilitarian is concerned with the overall balance of consequences, the ethical value of an action may only be determined by consequences that are very remote from the action itself. For instance, an action that is performed in one place may have repercussions thousands of miles away, so its consequences may be remote in space. Also, and more importantly, an action which is performed now may initiate a chain of results stretching far into the future (like the domino effect), so the consequences of an action may be remote in time. This means that while an action viewed here and now might seem to have one balance of consequences, the same action viewed from a more remote perspective in space and time might have a quite different balance of consequences. Which means, in turn, that the ethical value of an action—which depends upon the balance of consequences that it brings about—may be determined only by calculating the most remote of consequences.

When we looked at deontology, we examined its good points first, and we will follow that pattern in our discussion of act utilitarianism. Essentially the theory has three main strengths: it is well-meaning; it is rational; and it is situational. We will look at these advantages in turn. (Don't be misled by the relative brevity of the discussion, by the way. The reason for it is not that act utilitarianism's advantages are trivial. The discussion is short because those advantages are straightforward enough to require little explanation.)

2.3a   Act Utilitarianism and Benevolence

Act utilitarianism is well-meaning or benevolent. I should think that the truth of this claim is obvious. The central idea behind act utilitarianism, afterall, is to maximize happiness, to act in every case so as to bring about the greatest amount of happiness at the expense of the smallest amount of suffering. The act utilitarian values nothing more than human happiness and seeks wherever possible to produce it; the act utilitarian deplores nothing more than human misery and tries whatever possible to alleviate it. Even when the act utilitarian behaves in ways that many would consider appalling (see 2.3i), the motive for the behavior is always the desire to increase the amount of happiness in the world and to reduce the amount of suffering. So there can be no doubt that act utilitarianism is a well-meaning ethical theory. There can be no doubt, either, that being well-meaning is an advantage. Ethical theories suggest perspectives from which ethical problems involving ourselves and other people can be addressed, and a benevolent approach to such problems, and to other people, is clearly preferable to a malicious approach.

But aren't *all* ethical theories benevolent? Not necessarily, no. There is nothing necessarily well-meaning about deontology, for instance. The duties and obligations that a deontological theory lays down *may* be well-meaning, to be sure. But there is no reason why they must be. For example, there is nothing evidently well-meaning about the deontological approach of a soldier who only follows orders. Clearly, then, some ethical theories may not be benevolent—indeed they may be quite indifferent to the question of human happiness. It is a strength of act utilitarianism, then, that it is not such a theory. Act utilitarianism is always well-meaning, and it is less indifferent to the question of human happiness than any other ethical theory.

2.3b Act Utilitarianism and Rationality

The second advantage of act utilitarianism is that it is rational. Again, I think it is quite easy to see what is meant. The act utilitarian tries to decide which action to perform on the basis of a calculation. The good consequences of each possible action are added together; the total of bad consequences is then set against the good consequences, to yield a "score"; the "scores" of all the possible actions are compared with each other; whichever action "scores" the highest is identified as the best action to perform. The procedure is a model of rational decision-making. Whenever an act utilitarian makes an ethical decision in accordance with the act utilitarian decision-making procedure, he or she is in a position to offer a rational defense of the decision that has been made. One of the reasons why it is possible for the act utilitarian to do this is that his or her theory has just one overarching principle: act for the greatest good of the greatest number. Every decision that the decision-making procedure yields can be traced back, in a rational way, to this principle.

The contrast with deontology is again instructive. We saw in 2.2d, above, that the deontologist has a problem with rational justification. A deontologist often has difficulty saying just where a given set of duties and obligations came from, and it is often even harder to say just why we should adopt this set of duties and obligations rather than some other. Deontology, in other words, enjoys far fewer of the benefits of rationality than act utilitarianism does.

2.3c Act Utilitarianism and Situational Decision-Making

The final strength of act utilitarianism that we will discuss in this section is that it is situational. What this means is that the act utilitarian addresses ethical difficulties on a case-by-case basis. Because the act utilitarian attempts in every situation to assess the balance of good and bad consequences that will follow from each possible course of action, no two situations will ever be treated in quite the same way. After all, no two situations will offer quite the same range of possible actions, and in no two situations will those possible actions lead to quite the same consequences. Thus the act utilitarian makes different decisions for different situations, each based on the unique features of the situation in question. Any decision that the act utilitarian decision-making procedure yields, then, is tailor-made to the exact qualities of the situation at hand. This is clearly an advantage.

It is not an advantage shared by every ethical theory. Deontology, for instance, lacks it. Duties and obligations are necessarily rather general, designed to cover classes of cases, rather than highly specific, individual situations. Thus deontology is unable to take into account those unique features of particular cases that might set them apart from the cases that the duties or obligations were designed to cover. For instance, if I promise to meet you at six, then that promise, for the deontologist, should be binding. If I fail to show up because I have been helping rescue my neighbors from a fire, then the deontologist will say that I acted wrongly in breaking my promise. But surely this is far too rigid. In taking the view that "promises are promises," the deontologist has failed to give due consideration to those special features that make this case unusual, even unique, and completely unlike a normal case of promise-breaking. That's the problem, if you like, of too much consistency. The act utilitarian, however, will never suffer from such a problem. Because an act utilitarian's decisions are, by definition, tailor-made to specific situations, the act utilitarian will never fail to give due consideration to those features of a situation that make it unusual or unique. To consider such features is an absolutely essential part of the act utilitarian's decision-making procedure. The theory is situational, then, and this is a quality that allows it to cope exceptionally well with the variations and complexities of the real world.

Those, then, are the principal strengths of act utilitarianism. But what of its weaknesses? These, as we shall see, are rather formidable.

2.3d   Act Utilitarianism and Predicting the Future

One drawback of the act utilitarian perspective is that the ethical value of an action can only be determined by calculating the most remote consequences. For remote consequences are often almost entirely unpredictable. Everyone will have heard something about chaos theory. Chaos theory states that the tiniest variations in starting conditions can lead to the most radically different results—results that are, in practice, impossible to predict. This is why the weather forecast is often so much better at producing irritation than enlightenment. And act utilitarianism suffers from chaos in a similar way.

Imagine that I have an unusually eventful week, during which I save one small boy, John, from death on Monday, and a second small boy, Mike, from death on Thursday. Now viewed in the short term, and from an act utilitarian perspective, it seems clear that both of my actions are ethically good and probably that they are equally good. John and Mike are alive rather than dead, and their parents have been spared a considerable amount of suffering. Now suppose that, a few years later, John gets involved in all sorts of petty crime, while Mike excels at school, is a pleasure to know, and spends his spare time helping out at the local soup-kitchen. My original actions now take on a slightly different ethical character. Presumably both of my actions are still ethically good. But my action on Thursday, when I saved Mike, is beginning to look like a better action than my action on Monday, when I saved John. John's involvement in petty crime, which produces unhappiness (for his victims), and Mike's involvement in good works, which produces happiness (for those he helps), are both results of my having saved their lives. So the happiness brought about by Mike and the unhappiness brought about by John are included among the remote consequences of the actions that I performed all those years ago.

But let's suppose finally that John reforms, and goes on to lead a normal and relatively harmless life; while Mike, who seemed to be such a nice person, turns out to have been a wolf in sheep's clothing. Indeed, suppose that Mike becomes a serial killer and claims a large number of victims before he is caught. For the act utilitarian, everything has once again changed. Monday's action, when I saved John, now looks much better. But Thursday's action—saving Mike—no longer looks even like a good action. In fact it now looks like a very bad action indeed. The overall balance of consequences that I brought about by saving Mike has become overwhelmingly negative. On the plus side, there is the fact that Mike's life was saved, that his parents were spared the suffering of his death, and that during his sheep's clothing days he caused a certain amount of happiness. But on the minus side there are all of those deaths, all of the suffering inflicted on the friends and relatives of Mike's victims, and—to add insult to injury—the suffering that Mike himself must now undergo as punishment for his crimes. This lot gives us a pretty negative score! The original action of saving the young Mike's life turns out, on the act utilitarian calculation, to have been a real ethical blunder. I acted wrongly in saving this small boy's life. The circumstances may have seemed identical to those in which I saved the life of the other boy—there may have been no discernible differences between the cases—and yet this action turns out to have had the worst consequences imaginable.

But how was I to know what would happen? The answer is, I wasn't. However, that is not the point from the act utilitarian perspective. For the act utilitarian, the consequences of an action are all that determine its ethical value. The fact that I didn't know—indeed, couldn't know—that Mike would grow up to be a serial killer is unimportant. He did grow up to be a serial killer; if I hadn't saved his life when he was a small boy he wouldn't have grown up to be a serial killer; therefore my action had his crimes among its consequences; therefore my action was, ethically, very bad indeed.

The problem for act utilitarianism is surely obvious. For if there is no way of knowing in advance what the long-range consequences of an action will be, then there is no way of using act utilitarianism as a means for deciding which action, in any given circumstance, is the right action to perform. Remember: the second stage in the act utilitarian decision-making process is to predict what consequences, in terms of happiness and suffering, each of the available courses of action will have. But the utilitarian chaos-factor—the fact that small boys can grow up to be serial killers, for instance—makes this second stage a practical impossibility. The act utilitarian's decision-making procedure assumes that you can accurately predict the future. But you can't, which makes the act utilitarian's decision-making procedure more or less useless. Act utilitarianism, you might say, suffers from an exaggerated faith in predictability, and so falls victim to chaos.

Does the act utilitarian have any way out of this problem? To an extent, yes, for the act utilitarian's position can be modified. Instead of assuming God-like powers of prediction, the act utilitarian's demands can be reduced somewhat, so that only what is reasonably foreseeable is taken into account. In this model, the person who has reached stage two of the act utilitarian decision-making procedure will only be concerned with what can be predicted with reasonable certainty. The ethical value of an action will no longer be determined by *all* of the consequences an action has, however remote, but only by those consequences that lie within the scope of what might reasonably have been predicted. Thus, on this modified account, my action in saving the young Mike's life will remain the ethically good action that it first seemed to be, for the action's good consequences were reasonably foreseeable (in other words, it wasn't surprising that Mike's parents were happier with him alive than dead). This means its terrible consequence (that the young Mike would now live to become a monster) was the most dreadful bad luck, that no one could reasonably have been expected to see coming.

So the remote consequences of an action now count simply as bad luck or as good luck; they no longer contribute to the ethical value of the action. Certainly this seems to be more in tune with our intuitions (would it really be fair to *blame* me for Mike's serial killings?). It also saves the act utilitarian position from some of the worst effects of chaos. But only at a price. For it is now possible to imagine someone who scrupulously follows the modified act utilitarian decision-making procedure, who performs actions that are all ethically good according to the modified act utilitarian standards, but who never succeeds in acting so as to bring about the greatest good for the greatest number of people (which, you will recall, is what act utilitarianism was supposed to be all about). So we now have the concept of a "perfect" act utilitarian who never once manages to maximize happiness. (Just bad luck, I guess. But then, isn't that what you expect when you place too much faith in the future?)

2.3e   Act Utilitarianism and Incommensurability

We've seen that exaggerated faith in predictability is one problem with act utilitarianism. Another, which I think is sometimes felt to be more serious than it really is, goes under the daunting name of incommensurability. A pair of things are said to be incommensurable when they cannot be compared with each other, when they cannot be measured on the same scale. When someone says "You can't put a price on happiness," for instance, or "Money can't buy you love," they are making a point about incommensurability. They are saying that you cannot compare happiness, or love, with money, that you cannot measure happiness or love on the scale of monetary value. What they are saying, then, is that happiness and money, or love and money, are incommensurable values.

But what has this got to do with act utilitarianism? Quite a lot, actually. One of the most important things that an act utilitarian tries to do, remember, is to calculate which action will lead to the most happiness at the expense of the least suffering. And the word "calculate" is the point here. For, in essence, what the act utilitarian has to do is add up the various happinesses, to get a happiness-total; add up the various sufferings, to get a suffering-total; and then subtract the suffering-total from the happiness-total, to find out what the net amount of happiness/suffering produced by a given action will be. Now clearly it will only be possible to do this if the various kinds of happiness and suffering involved are commensurable—if they can be measured on the same scale. If you think back to the example of the ill-fated botanists, you will see that there was no problem there with incommensurability. The expedition leader had to compare four deaths with ten deaths, six lives with no lives. At each stage he was comparing like with like, and that is why it was comparatively easy to assign "scores" (of + 2 and −10) to the courses of action open to him. But such examples are really the exception. It is altogether more common to find the things that have to be weighed against each other are incommensurable.

Imagine the following. You have to decide whether to tell your highly sensitive friend that he is extremely ugly—so ugly, in fact, that he has just been voted the ugliest person in town, for which he can claim a fifty dollar prize. If you decide not to tell your friend, then he won't learn of his achievement, and he will forfeit his winnings. So what do you do? Clearly if you tell him what has happened it will hurt his feelings; but if you don't tell him, it will cost him fifty dollars. How do you compare the value of fifty dollars plus deeply wounded feelings to the value of no dollars plus feelings left unhurt? Which comes to the question: How do you compare dollars with feelings? How do you put a price on happiness? The decision you have to make has run straight into the problem of incommensurable values. If you are an act utilitarian, this problem will arise for you all the time. How do you compare the pleasure of a thick, juicy steak with the pleasure of a good night's sleep? How do you weigh the pain of a broken toe against the satisfaction of a job well done? How do you choose between baldness and heartburn? Between fame and fortune? Between peace and the peace that surpasseth understanding? There are incommensurable values lurking everywhere.

But this problem isn't as serious as it is sometimes portrayed. Certainly it's a problem, and it won't just go away. Yet it's the kind of problem that we run into every day. Deciding between incompatible benefits, choosing which of two nuisances to avoid, wondering if something's worth the hassle—we do it all the time. And the point here is that we do it. We do decide, we do choose, we do manage to overcome the incommensurability of the many benefits and pains that the world offers us or threatens us with. Sometimes, to be sure, we'll think later that we got it wrong, that we chose the wrong thing. But often we won't think that. Indeed, we may even think that our judgment about such matters is rather good. And so, to be honest, it should be. For even if the value of a good party is incommensurable with the value of a good result in an examination, it's pretty obvious which is the more important—which, in the long run (let alone the morning after), is likely to produce greater benefits. If we choose the party we'll be annoyed with ourselves later. We'll know that we got it wrong. More often than not a certain amount of thought will tell us what we ought to do, even if we then go on to do something different.

The fact that act utilitarianism is committed to comparing, and to calculating, incommensurable values puts it squarely in the real world of decision-making. And our day-to-day experience of deciding between incommensurable goods, or between incommensurable harms, tells us that such decisions can usually be made—even if they do sometimes involve a judgment call. The incommensurability of values is a nuisance for act utilitarianism: The theory would work much more neatly if all values were commensurable. But an act utilitarian would probably claim, and with some reason, that the theory has no more difficulty with this than any theory attempting to address real-world problems. The act utilitarian would probably say that incommensurable values come with the territory.

2.3f   Act Utilitarianism and Special Obligations

Two other drawbacks of act utilitarianism can be dealt with swiftly. We saw earlier that deontology could make sense of special obligations such as those between parent and child, or those between preacher and parish. Act utilitarianism, by contrast, cannot. As noted earlier, no one's happiness or suffering is intrinsically more important than anyone else's from an act utilitarian perspective. This means that an act utilitarian mother will accord to her own child's happiness no more importance than she will accord to the happiness of someone she has scarcely met. If acting for the greatest good of the greatest number means sacrificing her child for strangers, then that is what the act utilitarian mother will do. Special obligations have no place in the act utilitarian scheme of things.

2.3g   Act Utilitarianism and Supererogation

Supererogation—acting above and beyond the call of duty—also has no place in the act utilitarian scheme of things. After all, the only act utilitarian obligation is to act for the greatest good of the greatest number of people. This means it is not possible for anyone to act above and beyond this one basic obligation. The very best consequences are what the act utilitarian thinks you should always be aiming for. There is nothing above and beyond them. There is nothing better than the best. From the act utilitarian perspective, supererogation is completely meaningless. Saints and heroes do no more than they should do, and people who fling themselves on handgrenades in order to save their companions are simply doing what they ought to do. It would be wrong of them *not* to do it.

Now that we are aware of these two additional difficulties for act utilitarianism—that it can accommodate neither special obligations nor the concept of supererogation—the final and most serious problem for act utilitarianism must be addressed. This comes in two parts. The first is that act utilitarianism is inconsistent in the actions it recommends. The second is that act utilitarianism has no concern for justice. These two parts fit together, but we will consider them in the order just mentioned.

2.3h   Act Utilitarianism and Inconsistency

Deontology, you will remember, is consistent because a deontologist will always honor his or her obligations (conflict between obligations allowing). A deontologist's behavior is consistent because, quite predictably, a deontologist will do what he or she has undertaken to do. The value of consistent behavior is obvious (see 2.2a). But the act utilitarian is quite different. Will an act utilitarian keep a promise? Well, it depends. If keeping the promise will bring about the most happiness, then yes. But if not, then no. In other words, an act utilitarian will sometimes keep a promise, sometimes not, depending on what consequences keeping or not keeping a promise seem likely to have. The act utilitarian's behavior is not consistent. This is the flipside of the fact that act utilitarianism is situational (see 2.3c, above). His or her behavior is not reliable enough for you to build your own plans and actions around. From this point of view, then, the act utilitarian is a real nuisance.

Inconsistency is by no means a problem confined to the act utilitarian's way with promises. For instance, an act utilitarian's way with *you* might also be startlingly inconsistent. If the pursuit of the greatest happiness for the greatest number appears to indicate that being nice to you is a good idea, then the act utilitarian will be nice to you. But two hours later, if the likely balance of consequences seems to have changed, then the act utilitarian might treat you extremely unpleasantly—and not because of anything you've done in the meantime. Indeed, when his or her calculations do indicate that it's best to inflict some suffering on you, the act utilitarian will even try to inflict that suffering callously. After all, the act utilitarian is seeking the best possible consequences overall. If he or she finds it painful to inflict suffering on you, then his or her pain will have to figure in the calculation too, making the overall balance of consequences worse. How much better, then, if the suffering can be inflicted coldly! (Or better still, with pleasure: Someone once remarked that a utilitarian paradise would contain no one but sadists being vile to masochists.)

The fact is that the act utilitarian's pursuit of the greatest sum total of human happiness, regardless of whose happiness it happens to be, requires a very flexible attitude towards particular instances of human happiness, or of human suffering. And this "flexibility" is signalled in the unpredictable, inconsistent behavior resulting from the act utilitarian doctrine. Keep your promises sometimes; betray your friends if that seems best; be nice if the greatest good demands it (but not otherwise). With the act utilitarian, you never know where you are.

2.3i   Act Utilitarianism and Injustice

Inconsistent behavior is a problem in act utilitarianism. But inconsistent behavior produces unfairness and injustice as well as confusion. Suppose that I borrow some money from you and some from another friend, and then pay the other friend back, but I give the money that I owe you to a charity because that will lead to more happiness. Or suppose that a teacher gives two equally good pieces of work completely different grades because one of the students has been having a hard time lately and needs cheering up. Or suppose that an eminent surgeon murders someone and is given a suspended sentence so that he can carry on saving lives, whereas an ordinary murderer simply gets life in prison. None of these pieces of behavior appears to be motivated by a concern for justice, or by the slightest feeling for what's fair. Yet each of these pieces of behavior might be recommended by an act utilitarian. We will look at the philosophical use of the concept of justice in more detail later (see 3.5); but for the moment it is enough to notice that the kinds of inconsistency that can result from act utilitarianism are quite incompatible with our ordinary, everyday notions of justice or fair play. An ethical theory that ignores such basic ethical concepts as these is certainly, and to say the least, a strange one.

This problem for act utilitarianism is highlighted in its acutest form by the "punishing-the-innocent" example. This example goes as follows. A number of dreadful crimes have been committed in a large city. The inhabitants of the city are terrified to think what will happen next; the police can't catch the criminal; pressure is mounting on them to do something; there is a grave threat to public order; the affairs of the city grind to a halt; there are further crimes, and further demands for police action. The situation, from an act utilitarian perspective, is about as bad as it could be, with the quantities of suffering and dissatisfaction far exceeding the quantities of happiness.

So what is the solution? One solution would be to carry on trying to catch the criminal, while the situation deteriorates further. But beyond a certain point this solution is unlikely to appeal to an act utilitarian. What an act utilitarian might instead suggest is that the police should arrest someone who is innocent—and preferably also of little value to the community: a homeless person, for instance—and announce that they have caught the criminal. This will produce pleasure and relief throughout the city. The innocent person should then be put on trial in the most dramatic way possible. This will have all of the positive effects of theater. The innocent person should then be found guilty and sentenced to the severest possible punishment, preferably death. This will satisfy the city's longing for vengeance. The innocent person should then be executed. This will have the advantage of destroying the evidence of the hoax (the hoax only works if the population is fooled by it), and also of squeezing out from the city's inhabitants the very last ounce of vengeful pleasure. When and if the crimes continue, the police should simply announce that they have been committed by someone else, by a new criminal, and the whole thing can begin again.

The utilitarian's case here is pretty strong. Even if not one fewer crime is committed as a result of the hoax, the sum total of human happiness among the population has risen. Every member of the population has experienced relief, pleasure, entertainment, and vengeful satisfaction; in a sizeable city, with a large number of inhabitants, that represents a lot of happiness. Of course, some unhappiness has been generated too—most notably in the person arrested, vilified, tried, and executed for crimes that he did not commit. But even here there are compensations. The sum total of unhappiness in the population at large has been reduced by the false belief that the "criminal" has been captured and is no longer to be feared; it has been reduced by the fact that the population is no longer angry with the police; since the victim of the hoax was selected carefully, no one apart from the victim himself has been made unhappy by the fate which befell him. Thus the many individuals who make up the population of the city have all benefitted from the hoax, they have all had an increase in happiness. (Even if the crimes continue, they'll be no worse off than they were before, and they'll have been a lot better off in the meantime.) And what is the price of this considerable gain in human happiness? The suffering of just one individual. The balance of consequences is clear. The act utilitarian's hoax has significantly increased the total of human happiness, at the expense of a relatively trifling amount of suffering. The greatest good for the greatest number of people has been achieved.

Now exactly what does this mean for the act utilitarian? It obviously means that the hoax is desirable (just look at those lovely consequences!). But it doesn't mean that the hoax is merely practically desirable, or merely politically desirable. No. It means that the hoax is ethically desirable. The consequences, remember, are the only things that matter to the act utilitarian. So this hoax—this gross perversion of justice, in which a person is deliberately framed and punished for a crime he did not commit—turns out to be ethically correct, to be good, to be praiseworthy! That, surely, is an extraordinary result. Many people believe that the ability of act utilitarianism to deliver such judgments disqualifies it altogether as an ethical theory. No truly ethical theory, they argue, could possibly show so little concern for justice as to recommend the deliberate punishment of innocent people (no matter how unusual the case). According to this argument, when the ends justify the means (as in act utilitarianism), justice is the loser, and without justice there can be no ethics.

This is a very substantial charge indeed. I think that the act utilitarian's only response to it is to bite the bullet. The act utilitarian will have to say: "Justice has been overrated. It doesn't matter as much as people think. Our ethical system aims to make people happy. If that means that occasionally, in some very unusual cases, we think it acceptable to punish the innocent—well, so it goes." This tells you that you'll need to have a very strong stomach if you want to become a card-carrying act utilitarian.

We have now surveyed all of the most important strengths and weaknesses of act utilitarianism. On the plus side, there is the fact that act utilitarianism is well-meaning, the fact that it is rational, and the fact that it is situational. Set against these on the negative side, there is the theory's excessive faith in the predictability of the future; there is the problem of incommensurable values; there is the failure to make sense of special obligations and of supererogation; there is the inconsistency of behavior, and there is a disregard for the demands of justice.

2.4   RULE UTILITARIANISM

It is clear from our discussion of act utilitarianism (see 2.3) that it suffers from a number of significant weaknesses. It has some strengths, to be sure, but it is often felt that those strengths are not powerful enough to compensate for the weaknesses. So is it possible to preserve the good points of act utilitarianism—particularly its attention to consequences—while getting rid of most of its bad points? The attempt to answer "yes" to this question has resulted in a modified utilitarian perspective called rule utilitarianism. Indeed rule utilitarianism can be seen as a kind of halfway house between act utilitarianism and deontology. It is a theory that sets out to have the best of both worlds.

The central idea behind rule utilitarianism is this: You should act in accordance with rules that, if you and everyone else always acted upon them, would produce the greatest amount of happiness for the greatest number of people. Or, to put it more simply: You should act in accordance with good-maximizing rules. A good action, in this theory, is an action in accordance with such a rule; a bad action is an action that breaks such a rule. You can see the influence of deontology in this with the emphasis laid on rules: A rule is pretty much like a duty or an obligation, after all. The influence of act utilitarianism is also clear: The greatest good for the greatest number is still the overall goal. Indeed, because rule utilitarianism seeks good results, in terms of human happiness, this theory, just like act utilitarianism, may be described as a consequentialist theory of ethics.

So rule utilitarianism states that one should act in accordance with good-maximizing rules. But how exactly has this formula been devised? Suppose you wanted to come up with an ethical theory that enjoyed the best points of both act utilitarianism and deontology. How would you work it out? Perhaps you'd reason something like the following.

The worst aspect of act utilitarianism is its lack of concern for justice (see section 2.3i above) which is part-and-parcel of the inconsistent behavior that tends to result from act utilitarianism (see section 2.3h, above). Therefore, it would be good to get rid of the element of inconsistent behavior. But the tendency to recommend inconsistent behavior is the flip-side of one of the good points of act utilitarianism: its situational decision-making procedure. So if we want to get rid of the possible injustices act utilitarianism may cause, we will have to get rid of its inconsistency *and* its situational decision-making procedure. Act utilitarianism is situational in the sense that it makes its decisions on a case-by-case basis, so that even very similar cases may be treated in different ways (in other words, they may be treated inconsistently). Therefore, if we want to remove inconsistency we have to ensure that similar cases are always treated in similar ways. In other words, instead of deciding each individual case on a situational basis, we need some set procedure —or some rule—for dealing with cases of each particular kind. If we do that, then every case falling under a given rule will be treated in the same way as every other case falling under that rule; the danger of inconsistency will have been removed. This is one sense in which rule utilitarianism is similar to deontology.

But how do we decide which rules to have? You might argue that one of the desirable things about act utilitarianism was its benevolence—its well-meaning desire to promote human happiness. So perhaps we can use that for choosing our rules. Perhaps we can choose rules that, if we all adopted them, would promote human happiness—would lead to the greatest amount of good for the greatest number of people. If we did that, we'd also manage to retain the other advantage of act utilitarianism—the advantage of rationality. For just as the act utilitarian has a rational procedure for deciding which action to perform, we now have a rational procedure for deciding which rule to adopt. It goes like this: we consider a potential rule—for example, the rule "Don't punish the innocent"; we predict whether the consequences of everyone following this rule would be better than the consequences of everyone breaking it (in this case, presumably, the consequences would be better); if the consequences of everyone following the rule would be better, we adopt the rule as one of the rules of rule utilitarianism. In this example, we adopt the rule "Don't punish the innocent." Because it's a rule, we adopt it without exceptions. Even if there *is* the odd, bizarre case in which it would produce more happiness to punish innocent people (see the example given in 2.3i, above), we will still behave consistently. Even in the unusual case, we will still refuse to punish the innocent; we will refuse to punish them because we have predicted that punishing the innocent is not in general a good way to achieve the greatest amount of happiness for the greatest number of people. We can justify our selection of rules, then, by appealing to the greatest happiness principle. We can do this without getting into the kinds of difficulty about justice that were such a problem for the act utilitarian.

In our ethical theory, our improved utilitarian perspective, we recommend that one should act in accordance with rules that, if followed by everyone, will maximize human happiness. We select those rules by predicting which rules will, as a matter of fact, have happiness-maximizing effects. As such, the theory does seem to occupy a position somewhere between act utilitarianism and deontology. Indeed, it seems like a blend of the two. This impression will be reinforced when we survey the strengths and weaknesses of rule utilitarianism, because those strengths and weaknesses are a fairly predictable mix of the ones we have already met in the contexts of act utilitarianism and deontology.

2.4a   Some Strengths of Rule Utilitarianism

I have already mentioned most of the important advantages of rule utilitarianism. This theory shares with act utilitarianism the advantages of benevolence and rationality. Rule utilitarianism is benevolent, or well-meaning, because it recommends adopting rules that will, if generally followed, promote human happiness. Just as it is for the act utilitarian, the main goal for the rule utilitarian is to bring about good consequences, measured in terms of human happiness. The rule utilitarian differs from the act utilitarian in that the rule utilitarian tries to select *general* rules whose adoption will lead to good consequences; whereas the act utilitarian tries to identify individual actions that will produce good consequences.

Rule utilitarianism is rational in the sense that its rules are adopted on the basis of calculating which rules will, if adopted by people in general, lead to the best results. This means that any rule-utilitarian rule can, in principle, be traced back in a rational way to the objective of maximizing the overall quantity of human happiness.

But we have seen that rule utilitarianism also has a good deal in common with deontology. Specifically, rule utilitarianism—like deontology—has the advantages of being consistent and of having room for the demands of justice. Rule utilitarianism is consistent because it recommends the adoption of rules that should be followed in all situations of a similar kind. So, for example, if it is a rule-utilitarian rule to "Keep your promises" (as it well might be: consider the consequences of wholesale promise-breaking), then all promises will fall under the rule. Thus all promises will consistently be treated in accordance with the happiness-maximizing rule "Keep your promises".

Such consistency, as we saw in section 2.3i, above, fits nicely with the demands of justice. If someone follows a set of rules consistently, they will treat similar cases similarly; they will treat similar cases *fairly*. They will not, for instance, repay some debts while choosing not to repay others; they won't give different grades for assignments of the same standard; they won't allow famous surgeons to get away with murder, while sentencing ordinary murderers to life in prison. The contrast with act utilitarianism is enormous. In addition, the rule utilitarian has, as we have already seen, a good reply to any objection based on the "punishing-the-innocent" example. The rule utilitarian can make a persuasive case for the claim that, in general, punishing the innocent will not promote happiness. (Imagine the general misery that would be caused by knowing that one might, at any time, and for no reason that had anything to do with what one had done, be punished: This would definitely be happiness-minimizing!) Therefore, the rule utilitarian would claim, the correct rule would prohibit such actions: A rule would say "Don't punish innocent people." Indeed, the rule utilitarian can argue with some plausibility that *no* piece of grossly unjust behavior can be squared with any properly thought-out set of rule-utilitarian rules. The general knowledge that one might, at any moment, be treated unfairly or unjustly would cancel out the very occasional benefits of treating someone in an unfair or an unjust way. So the rule utilitarian, like the deontologist, can accommodate the demands of justice.

A strength of rule utilitarianism that we haven't touched upon so far is that, again like deontology, rule utilitarianism can make sense of special obligations—those obligations that one individual (or group of individuals) has as a result of standing in a particular relationship to another individual (or group of individuals). Parents often feel a special obligation—a parental obligation—to their children. Children often feel a special obligation towards their parents—a filial obligation. Members of the health care professions often feel a special obligation—a professional or vocational obligation—towards their parents. And so on. Rule utilitarianism can acknowledge these obligations by appealing to the greatest happiness principle. The rule utilitarian can argue that the world will, overall, be a happier place if these obligations are generally honored—if parents do their best for their children, if children respect their parents, if health care professionals try to help their patients. One could plausibly argue that these special obligations are instances of rules that, if everyone who stood in the relevant relationships adopted them, would promote human happiness. Such obligations might be regarded as rule-utilitarian rules, in other words.

2.4b   Some Weaknesses of Rule Utilitarianism

Most of the weaknesses of rule utilitarianism have already emerged from the discussion—even though the only weakness I mentioned explicitly is that rule utilitarianism is not situational. The situational decision-making procedure that is characteristic of act utilitarianism had to be discarded in order to achieve consistency of behavior, and in order to make rule utilitarianism compatible with the demands of justice. Any theory that establishes sets of rules (or of duties and obligations) to cover general classes of situation is bound to be nonsituational. After all, if a rule applies to a case, then the rule must be followed; if it applies to another case, then it must be followed there too. Similar cases are treated similarly, and there is no scope for deciding cases on a case-by-case basis. There is no room for exceptions. So the price that rule utilitarianism pays for its consistency, and for its compatibility with the demands of justice, is that it cannot employ situational decision-making procedures.

But can't the theory be more situational than I have made it out to be? Can't the rule utilitarian be a bit more cunning in designing his or her rules? Instead of simply having a rule which says "Keep your promises," for example, why doesn't the rule utilitarian have a rule with an escape-clause? An appropriate escape-clause might be a rule which says "Keep your promises—*except* when breaking them will save lives." That way the rule utilitarian can respond flexibly to situations that are out of the ordinary—to cases that have features that set them apart from the cases the rule was really meant to cover. (After all, no one would honestly say that you should keep a minor promise rather than save a life.) Indeed, you might think, if the rule utilitarian were cunning enough, the rules might contain so many escape-clauses that the theory would become wholly situational. Every case would be treated on its own unique merits, courtesy of all the exceptions the rules allow.

This suggestion is fine within limits. There is no reason why the rule utilitarian can't include the odd escape-clause among his or her rules, and so make the theory a little more situational. But there are limits. For one thing, if you put in too many excape-clauses the rules will be so complicated that they will be just about impossible to use in practice. Imagine . . . every rule would look something like this: "Do such-and-such; except when a; or except when b; or except when c; or d; . . . or except when z." No one could be expected to remember or to apply such rules.

More importantly, if you put in all these escape-clauses, so as to make rule utilitarianism situational, you'll end up losing the benefits that the theory was designed to have in the first place. You'll lose consistency. For example, your rules about keeping promises will be so complex, and so full of exceptions, that it will never be certain whether any particular promise will actually be kept—even apparently similar cases may no longer be treated similarly. You'll also lose touch with justice. After all, it will only be a matter of time before your rule about not punishing innocent people acquires an escape-clause, for instance, "Don't punish innocent people—except when, as it happens, to do so will maximize happiness." In short, the effort to make rule utilitarianism situational will really result in a theory that is exactly like act utilitarianism, except a great deal more clumsy. Rule utilitarianism plus multiple escape-clauses equals act utilitarianism minus the simplicity. So the rule utilitarian can have some escape-clauses designed to meet the more predictable kinds of exceptions to the general rules. But the theory can't have too many escape-clauses, or else it will collapse under their weight and become indistinguishable from act utilitarianism. Thus, if rule utilitarianism is to remain a distinctive ethical theory, with its own distinctive advantages, the fact that it is essentially nonsituational will have to be taken on board and tolerated.

The remaining disadvantages of rule utilitarianism can be explored quickly. The theory has exactly the same problems with predicting the future as act utilitarianism has (see 2.3d, above). It is impossible to predict with perfect certainty what consequences, in terms of human happiness and human suffering, the adoption of any given rule will actually have. Therefore, the rule utilitarian must be limited in his or her selection of rules to considering only those consequences that are reasonably foreseeable. This means, in effect, that the rules adopted by a rule utilitarian may not actually be happiness-maximizing. (Remember, small boys can grow up to be serial killers.) Just like the act utilitarian, then, the rule utilitarian is vulnerable to the effects of chaos.

Rule utilitarianism also shares with act utilitarianism a difficulty over incommensurable values, those values that cannot be compared with each other directly, or measured on the same scale. A rule utilitarian tries to find rules that, if generally followed, will maximize happiness and minimize suffering. But happiness and suffering come in many different forms, and not all of those forms are commensurable. So the rule utilitarian is committed to the strictly impossible task of comparing, and calculating with, values that cannot be compared or measured along the same scale. This is certainly a problem for the rule utilitarian. But I suggested in section 2.3e, above, how the act utilitarian might respond to the problem of incommensurable values;

the rule utilitarian's response to the problem should be the same. Incommensurability is a nuisance for rule utilitarianism rather than a fatal handicap.

Supererogation poses a problem for rule utilitarianism, too. Since the rule utilitarian is always supposed to be acting in accordance with the very *best* rules—the rules that will bring about the greatest amount of happiness, at the cost of the least amount of suffering—there doesn't seem to be any possibility of acting above and beyond the call of duty. The rule utilitarian's duty, just like the act utilitarian's duty, is the ultimate anyway. There is nothing above and beyond the ultimate. So supererogation does not make sense from the rule utilitarian perspective. Our everyday intuition that some people behave better than anyone could be expected to behave—that some people are saints or heroes—finds no echo in this particular ethical theory.

The final drawback of rule utilitarianism that we will explore in this section is a drawback that it shares with deontology. We saw in section 2.2e, above, that deontological duties and obligations sometimes come into conflict with one another. The same is true of the rule utilitarian's rules. It will often be the case that two incompatible rules apply to the same situation, so that only one of the two rules can actually be followed. For example, suppose that a rule utilitarian doctor has a rule that says, "Respect your patients' confidences" and another rule that says, "Safeguard the public health." If a patient tells the doctor in confidence that he or she has a murderous plan afoot, then these two rules clearly come into conflict. The doctor can either respect the patient's confidence (by keeping quiet) or safeguard the public health (by informing some appropriate authority of the patient's plan).

So how does a rule utilitarian decide which of two conflicting rules is the more important? It's easy enough in principle. The rule utilitarian must calculate which of the two rules has the stronger link to the greatest happiness principle. In other words, the rule utilitarian must calculate which of the two rules, if generally followed, would result in more happiness. Whichever rule that is will then be the more important rule, because it will be the rule which is, in general, better at maximizing human happiness. Easy enough in principle, as I say. But in practice such calculations will often be very difficult to make for some of the reasons mentioned earlier: The future cannot be predicted with great accuracy; the competing rules may well have been designed to produce incommensurable kinds of happiness. What this means is that there will sometimes be serious and perhaps unresolvable disagreements between rule utilitarians about which of two conflicting rules really should take priority. All rule utilitarians might agree about the principle for deciding between the conflicting rules, but they may not be able to agree about the results of applying that principle in practice. So rule-conflict certainly poses a problem for rule utilitarianism.

This concludes our survey of the strengths and weaknesses of rule utilitarianism. The most important strengths are that it is benevolent, rational, consistent, compatible with the demands of justice, and capable of accommodating special obligations. The most significant weaknesses of rule utilitarianism are that it is nonsituational; it has problems with the predictability of the future and with the incommensurability of values; it can't make sense of supererogation; and its rules may sometimes come into conflict with each other.

Selected Bibliography

Lyons, David, *Forms and Limits of Utilitarianism*, Oxford University Press, 1965.
Mill, J. S., *Utilitarianism*, Fontana, 1962.
Sen, Amartya and Bernard Williams, eds., *Utilitarianism and Beyond*, Cambridge University Press, 1982.
Smart, J. C. C. and Bernard Williams, *Utilitarianism: Before and Against*, Cambridge University Press, 1973.

2.5   RIGHTS

We turn now to a kind of subsidiary ethical perspective—the theory of rights, that holds that people's rights are an essential factor to consider when addressing any ethical issue. I call it a subsidiary perspective because this theory is not of any great use by itself, but it can be used fruitfully in tandem with certain wider ethical perspectives—with deontology, for instance, or with rule utilitarianism. The reason why rights-theory requires a wider perspective will become clearer in a moment. But let us discuss it first by itself.

The view that people's rights must be taken into account when addressing ethical issues will be familiar to anyone who has ever engaged in an ethical argument. Whenever a question in ethics is discussed, it is likely that someone will talk about rights. People will be said to have "a right to decide for themselves"; prisoners will be said to have "a right to decent treatment"; babies will be said to have "a right to be looked after by their mothers"; extremists will be said to have "a right to speak freely"; and so on. Talk about rights occupies a very noticeable position in most ethical debates. But what exactly are rights? What do we mean when we say that someone has a right to something?

In the first place, when we say that someone has a right to something we are saying that there are certain ways in which other people ought or ought not to behave towards them. We are saying that the person who has the right is owed an obligation of some kind by other people. If I promise to give you all of my old LPs, for example, then I have entered into an obligation towards you. I have an obligation to give you all of my old LPs. You now have a right to be given my LPs. Your right and my obligation go hand in hand together. In fact, your right and my obligation are like opposite sides of the same coin. If it is true that I have an obligation to give you my LPs, then it is true that you have a right to be given them. Equally, if it is true that you have a right to be given my LPs, then it must be true that I have an obligation to give them to you. If you simply announced that you had a right to be given my LPs, without my having entered into any obligation to give them to you (by promising to give them to you), then your claim to have a right to them would be mistaken. In this sense, any claim about rights needs to be backed up by a claim about obligations.

So far so good. But until now we have been talking only about rights of a limited kind—rights resulting from one individual undertaking an obligation towards another. This is an important kind of right, to be sure. But it is not the kind of right that people mean when they say, for example, that everyone has a right to free speech, or a right not to be killed unjustly. These seem to be rights of a general kind. These seem to be rights of a kind that everyone has, regardless of the promises, agreements, or obligations that they have deliberately contracted with other individuals. What is going on here?

What occurs in the case of general rights is actually very much the same as what goes on in the case of the limited rights discussed a moment ago. We saw there that rights and obligations were like opposite sides of the same coin—that one person's right to something involved someone else's obligation to provide it. But if everyone has a right to a certain thing—for instance, free speech—then it clearly cannot be the case that just one other person has the obligation to provide it. If we all have the right to free speech, then it isn't up to my next door neighbor, for example, or to any other particular individual, to make sure that we can speak freely. No. The general right to free speech involves a general obligation to allows others to speak freely. It is only if all of us have an obligation not to interfere with the speech of others that all of us can have the right to free speech. A general right, therefore, depends upon a general obligation. The general right not to be killed unjustly depends upon all of us having an obligation not to kill others unjustly; a general right to health care depends upon all of us having an obligation to provide, or to contribute towards the provision of, health care for others; a general right to privacy depends upon all of us having an obligation not to go around invading other people's private spaces; and so on.

In any case where a general right is claimed to exist, the general obligation that corresponds to that right must be claimed to exist too. Thus if one group accuses another group of abusing human rights (human rights being rights of a very general kind), the first group is in fact doing two things. It is saying that there are general obligations that correspond to those general or human rights (in other words, obligations to treat all human beings decently), and it is saying that the second group is failing to honor those obligations. If the first group does not believe that such general obligations exist, then its charge that the second group is abusing human rights will be empty rhetoric. Rights and obligations always go together.

Rights, then, whether limited or general, can be seen as the flip-side of obligations. Rights entail obligations, and obligations entail rights. This is why I said at the beginning of this section that rights-theory is best used in tandem with some wider ethical perspective. Specifically, rights-theory is best used in tandem with an ethical perspective that has something distinctive to say about obligations. For it is only if we have a view about what our obligations are that we will be in any position to say what our rights are. Rights-theory, then, stands in need of the support that only an ethical perspective that is committed to the concept of obligation can provide. This means that rights-theory can be incorporated into any ethical theory that includes mention of obligations; mention of obligations implies a commitment to the rights that correspond to those obligations. So talk of rights, whether limited or general, is best confined to those contexts in which a wider, obligation-based, ethical perspective is being used.

In practice, this often means that translating talk about rights into talk about corresponding obligations is helpful if we want to clarify the theoretical perspective we are employing, or if we want to make sense of some particular claim. For instance, if I claim that I have a right to become talented, then what is involved in my (strange!) claim will become clearer if we translate what I have said into terms of obligations. For me to have a right to become talented, there must be someone who has an obligation to make me talented, or at any rate an obligation not to stand in the way of my becoming talented. But this doesn't seem to make any sense at all. No one can make another person talented. Because talent is something that you either have or you don't, no one can either stand in the way or not stand in the way of another person's becoming talented. The obligations envisaged here are simply empty. So while it might be true that I'd *like* to become talented, it doesn't seem to make a lot of sense for me to claim that I have a *right* to become talented.

Unless I can say that someone else—or everyone else—has a coherent obligation that is relevant to my acquiring talent, then it cannot be true that I have a right of the kind that I claimed. And it cannot be true, because no coherent, obligation-based ethical perspective could possibly include an obligation of the kind required. In this case, then, translating a claim about rights into a claim about obligations has helped make clear exactly what is being claimed, and has helped to establish how (un)reasonable that claim is. You will find that translating rights into obligations like this is very often the best way to assess a position that makes a claim about rights. The translation makes explicit what wider position is being adopted; it makes explicit what theoretical assumptions about obligation are being made.

Not all rights theorists would agree with the position I've just outlined. Many, for instance, would argue that the relation between rights and obligations is more complex than I've suggested, or that rights may in some sense be more basic than obligations. So I won't insist that the outline I've given is the only one possible. But for the remainder of this book the concept of rights will be treated in the way I have suggested because it assigns a place to rights talk that doesn't make such talk pointless and mystifying. Speaking of rights only in relation to obligations brings rights talk properly into the reciprocal relationships of health care provider and patient that characterize issues in bioethics. In summary, a right depends upon a corresponding obligation. Someone has a limited right only if someone else has a corresponding limited obligation. We all have a general right only if we all have a corresponding general obligation. Because rights depend in this way upon obligations, talk of rights can always be translated into talk of obligations. Hence, talk of rights can be incorporated into any ethical theory that assigns a significant role to the concept of obligation. Let's look at how talk of rights fits with the ethical theories we've discussed.

2.5a   Rights and Deontology

Clearly, deontology is one theory that can incorporate rights, for deontology emphasizes duties and obligations above everything else. Therefore, when a deontological theory lays down duties and obligations of a certain kind it inevitably lays down whatever rights correspond to those duties and obligations. For instance, if a deontological theory states that we all have an obligation to tell others the truth, then the theory is claiming at the same time that all of us have the right to be told the truth. So deontology and rights go together very neatly. Indeed, it might be said that it is within the wider perspective of deontology that the theory of rights finds its natural home.

2.5b   Rights and Act Utilitarianism

Act utilitarianism is completely incompatible with the theory of rights—it can never incorporate rights into its perspective. The reason for this is very simple. Act utilitarianism recognizes only *one* obligation—the obligation to act in every case for the greatest good of the greatest number of people. Therefore the only right entailed by act utilitarianism is the right to have your own happiness taken into account together with everybody else's, and to have it accorded no less (but no more) weight then theirs. Which, I suppose, is a kind of right. But it doesn't go very far. And it certainly doesn't go far enough to grant you a right to free speech, for instance, or to privacy, or a right not to be killed unjustly. The theory's tendency to recommend inconsistent pieces of behavior does not allow rights of this kind (see 2.3h, above). Free speech? Only in those cases where it promotes happiness. Privacy? Not if it will hurt somebody's feelings. The right not to be killed unjustly? Yes, except in cases where it is desirable to punish the innocent.

Act utilitarianism and rights are like oil and water. But it's a matter of opinion whether this is an advantage or a drawback. Some would certainly think it an advantage. Jeremy Bentham, for instance, one of the founders of act utilitarianism, famously described rights as "nonsense on stilts"; so he presumably wouldn't have minded. (Whether he was correct to say this, however, is a question I'll leave to you.)

2.5c   Rights and Rule Utilitarianism

Rule utilitarianism, by contrast, is perfectly compatible with the theory of rights. It can incorporate the theory of rights effortlessly. The rules of rule utilitarianism are intended to tell us how we ought to behave towards one another. Thus the rules of rule utilitarianism lay down obligations of a certain kind; rights, as we know, are the flip-side of obligations. Therefore rule utilitarianism acknowledges whichever rights are entailed by the rules of the theory. For example, the general rule "Don't punish innocent people" entails the general right not to be punished if one is innocent; the general rule "Treat others with consideration" entails the general right to be treated with consideration; and so on. Because rule utilitarianism includes the concept of obligation, rule utilitarianism includes the concept of rights. In this sense it is exactly like deontology.

Selected Bibliography

Feinberg, Joel, *Rights, Justice and the Bounds of Liberty*, Princeton University Press, 1980.
Rawls, J., *A Theory of Justice*, Harvard University Press, 1971.
White, A. R., *Rights*, Oxford, Clarendon, 1984.

2.6   ETHICAL THEORIES IN COMBINATION

I have presented the main ethical theories (deontology, act utilitarianism, and rule utilitarianism) as if they rivaled one another. To an extent, they do. Each of them claims to introduce an especially valuable perspective on ethical issues. But I'm sure few people live their lives as strict deontologists, say, or as strict rule utilitarians, without ever trying out a different perspective. Indeed it would be quite frightening to imagine someone attempting to live in that way. Most of us won't want to be so dogmatic. So what do we do instead?

We probably recognize in each of the theories aspects that sound plausible, without thinking that any of the theories has a monopoly on the truth. For instance, consider the case of keeping promises. Most of us, I am sure, believe that one of the reasons we should keep a promise is just that we have promised—that we have said we would do something. We feel obliged to do what we have undertaken to do. This belief is clearly deontological: We feel that we should act in accordance with our obligations. But at the same time, I expect that most of us would also say that a good reason to keep a promise to someone is that by breaking it we might hurt them; we keep the promise to avoid causing pain. This thought is distinctly act utilitarian: We are trying to bring about good consequences and to avoid bad consequences. And still again, I should imagine that most of us think it is a good idea to keep a promise on the grounds that a world in which people generally keep their promises will be a happier world than one in which people generally do not. In other words, we are inclined to take a rule utilitarian view as well. We keep promises because promise-keeping accords with a good-maximizing rule. So at one and the same time we find ourselves buying into all three of the ethical theories that we have discussed. Certainly this isn't dogmatic of us. But isn't it rather confused of us? Can we really carry on like this with theories that are not, after all, compatible with one another?

The answer is: Yes, we can carry on like this as long as we don't get confused. Ethical theories, remember, indicate particular perspectives from which an ethical issue might be viewed. There is nothing wrong with looking at an ethical issue from several different angles. There is only a problem, or a danger of a problem, if we forget or if we misunderstand which perspective we are taking at any given moment.

For instance, there is no problem with taking both the deontological and the rule utilitarian perspective on promise-keeping described above, as long as we recognize that they commit us to quite different claims. It is a very different thing to claim that we should keep our promises because we should always honor our obligations than it is to claim that we should keep our promises because a generally promise-keeping world will be a happier one. These claims are not interchangeable: they involve altogether different conceptions of what makes an action right or wrong. Of course, we can believe that there is more than one kind of thing that makes an action right or wrong: Promise-breaking may be wrong for the reasons given by the deontologist and for the reasons given by the rule utilitarian, for example. An action may be wrong because it violates an obligation, and also wrong because it does not accord with a good-maximizing rule. But we sink into confusion if we fail to recognize that these reasons are distinct. Clear ethical thinking depends upon maintaining a lively sense of which perspective we are adopting, and of what claims that perspective commits us to.

Another way of bringing out this point is to refer back to the strengths and weaknesses of the various theories we surveyed. If, for example, we take the view that it might sometimes be right for a doctor to lie to patients, if that will make patients happier than telling them the truth, then we ought to recognize that we are taking an act utilitarian perspective on the issue. Recognizing this will warn us of the difficulties that such a view might face. It can prepare us for the kinds of objections that might be raised against us. For instance, act utilitarianism is vulnerable to the charge that it sometimes recommends unjust behavior. If we are aware of this then we will be better prepared to respond if such a charge is raised. We might be prepared to argue that the kinds of cases that we have in mind are so rare that no overall threat to justice is posed by our view on this issue. We might be prepared to argue that, in the cases we have in mind, it would actually be less just to tell patients the truth than it would be to tell them a comforting lie. There are a number of responses that we might make. But if we fail to recognize the possibility that some such response might be needed, we have failed to fully understand our own position on the issue at hand.

Let's take another example. If we adopt a rule utilitarian perspective on the issue of keeping a patient's confidences, we will say that a patient's confidences should always be respected because a patient's belief that whatever he or she might say will be kept confidential encourages the patient to tell the doctor more, thereby improving the doctor's chances of treating the patient effectively. Thus, we will say, keeping confidences improves treatment and so maximizes happiness. Our rule utilitarian view is plausible. But we'd better be aware that it *is* a rule utilitarian view—and that one of the problems with rule utilitarianism is rule-conflict. In other words, we'd better be prepared for the objection that other rule utilitarian rules—such as the rule to safeguard the public health—might sometimes come into conflict with the confidence-keeping rule (see 2.4b, above). We're going to need an answer to such an objection. The point here is not that having an answer is going to win us points in an argument. The point is that unless we recognize the possible need for such an answer we have failed to grasp the position which we have adopted. An awareness of the possible weaknesses of a position is usually a vital part of the process of developing a coherent view about anything at all, and it is certainly a vital part of the attempt to develop a coherent view about a problem in ethics. Our survey of the various ethical theories, and of their strengths and weaknesses, should have helped us in our efforts to arrive at ethical positions that we understand and that do make sense.

So there is nothing wrong with adopting several distinct perspectives on the same ethical issue, as long as we recognize that this is what we are doing, and as long as we don't get confused. A good exercise here is to look through the OpEd pages of the newspapers, and to try to distinguish between the various perspectives which often appear within a single article on an ethical issue (for example, on abortion). You will be surprised to find just how many changes can happen within a very few sentences. (The author of the article would probably be surprised too!) This fact underlines just how complicated even the most simple-seeming of ethical arguments can be—and therefore just how clear-headed we will need to be if we are to make sense of, and to assess, those arguments.

Consider the following passage—not a piece of OpEd, more a piece of reportage—and try to follow the shifts in perspective:

> "The guy did really well," said Lieutenant Grey. "It was a one-off situation, and he responded magnificently. He didn't consider his own safety at all. If more people in this town had his attitude then we'd soon be rid of our problems. But I guess you can't hope that everyone will be as brave as him. The guy's a hero."

The shifts in perspective here are kaleidoscopic. The first sentence is scene-setting—just a piece of general-purpose commendation. But the next two sentences definitely betray a perspective. There is the point that the situation was a "one-off"—that it was unique; there is the implication that what was done in that situation was "magnificently" well-suited to it. There is also the fact that the "guy" accorded no special significance to his own safety, to his own well-being. Taken together these considerations point fairly firmly towards act utilitarianism (even if the second consideration might also be consistent with deontology). Act utilitarianism is situational. It produces recommendations on a case-by-case basis, taking into account all the distinctive features of each situation. An act utilitarian, of course, regards his or her own happiness (well-being) as no more important than anyone else's. So the lieutenant's remarks certainly appear to start off in act utilitarian territory. But they don't stay there for long: The lieutenant converts to rule utilitarianism in the very next sentence. He regrets the fact that everyone doesn't behave in the way that the person he is praising behaved. In other words, he says it would be a good thing if that person's behavior were adopted as a model by everybody else. In other words, "Behave like that guy!" would be a good-maximizing rule. If everyone adopted the rule "Behave like that guy!" according to the lieutenant, "we'd soon be rid of our problems." So we have a spark of rule utilitarianism. This spark, however, is extinguished almost at once by a sunburst of deontology. The deontological perspective, remember, is the only perspective which is able to accommodate the concept of supererogation—of acting above and beyond the call of duty. It is the only perspective that acknowledges the possibility of saints or heroes. The lieutenant's final words unmistakably come from this perspective.

So this passage contains a little bit of everything. The lieutenant is swept by his enthusiasm from one theory to the next. Is the lieutenant confused? No, not necessarily. By itself this passage suggests nothing more sinister than the kind of perspective-shifts we discussed earlier in the context of promise-keeping. But it might be rather difficult for the lieutenant—or anybody else, for that matter—to build his remarks up into a large-scale set of recommendations about human behavior. The effort to do that, given the number of perspectives in operation at once, would almost certainly result in inconsistency and confusion.

Let us look now at a slightly more interesting example adapted from a letter written during the Civil War:

> Slavery and the forces of disunion are a barbarity which nothing can justify. This union and its government must be sustained at any and every cost. We must produce among the people of the South a thorough conviction of the personal misery which attends war, and the utter helplessness of their rulers to protect them. If that terror and grief shall help to paralyze their husbands and fathers who are fighting us it is mercy in the end. Everywhere the enemies of slavery must recognize and practice this horrible truth, that mercy in the long term is worth terror and grief in the short.

There are some distinct shifts in perspective here. The passage opens in a deontological mood. The writer says that nothing can justify slavery and the forces of disunion. And you'd never find a utilitarian making that claim. A utilitarian would say that the production of large amounts of happiness would justify slavery and the forces of disunion. If slavery and disunion turned out to be for the greatest good of the greatest number, then the utilitarian would justify slavery and disunion. So the first sentence is clearly deontological. The second sentence is deontological too. To say that something must be sustained "at any and every cost" is to say that it must be sustained regardless of the consequences; only deontology, with its indifference to consequences, could accommodate that thought. But then the perspective begins to change. The third sentence is ambiguous. It can be read deontologically, as a further expression of indifference to the human happiness or suffering that actions may cause. Or, more plausibly, it can be regarded as an introduction to the clearly utilitarian thought that follows. For the fourth sentence is explicitly consequentialist. To say that "terror and grief" might be a "mercy in the end" is to suggest that a certain amount of human happiness —"mercy"—can be bought at the cost of a certain amount of human suffering—"terror and grief." There is nothing in this sentence to tell us whether the dominant perspective is act or rule utilitarian; it could be either. But the final sentence comes down clearly on the side of rule utilitarianism. Here the writer recommends a general guideline, or rule, for unionist behavior: Unionists must inflict terror and grief. The rule-utilitarian justification for this rule is that "mercy in the long term is worth terror and grief in the short." In other words, the writer is predicting that if all unionists were to follow the rule "inflict terror and grief," then the merciful happiness of the long-term consequences will outweigh the dreadful suffering of the short-term consequences. The rule in question is being justified by an appeal to the greatest happiness principle.

So this passage moves smoothly from the most clear-cut deontological perspective, through a short transitional phase, to an unmistakably rule-utilitarian perspective. What does this mean for us? It raises a couple of questions. For instance, what exactly is the author's attitude towards consequences? At the beginning, he seems to suggest that consequences don't matter at all—that the union must be sustained "at any and every cost." (What—even at the cost of millions of people getting killed?) At the end he seems to be saying that the good long-term consequences—"mercy"— will be worth paying for with suffering in the short term. (In which case, would he reconsider if he began to suspect that the "terror and grief" caused by the war would actually outweigh the merciful consequences of a sustained union? If he's a rule utilitarian, he ought to reconsider.) The writer's position looks a little confused, in other words. He appears to be committed to two conflicting claims: that the consequences don't matter at all and that mercy is a sufficiently desirable consequence to be worth paying a high price for.

How would you respond if you were the writer of this passage? Would you water down the rhetoric at the beginning so that it squared better with the consequentialism at the end? Would you remove the references to mercy, so that the entire piece could be taken deontologically? Or would you go for something more cunning?

If I were the author, I'd go for something more cunning. I'd say that my overall perspective was a deontological one. That is, I'd say that I thought there was an absolute duty to sustain the union and to abolish slavery, and I'd say that we should honor that duty at any and every cost. But I'd say that I thought there was also a duty to make sure that that cost was as low as it could be, a duty to inflict the smallest possible amount of suffering. In an effort to honor that duty, I'd say, it might help to adopt a kind of subperspective *within* the overall perspective of deontology. That subperspective is rule utilitarianism. From the rule utilitarian point of view, there seems to be a good case for causing a large amount of suffering in the short term in the hope that the war will end more quickly. I'd predict, in other words, that a shorter, nastier war will actually cause a smaller total amount of suffering than a longer, more gentlemanly war. Therefore I'd recommend, on rule-utilitarian grounds, the adoption of the rule "Inflict great short-term suffering on the families of the South." I would emphasize, however, that this piece of rule utilitarianism is only a subperspective, and that if it ever came into conflict with my prime perspective—my deontological perspective— then the rule utilitarianism would be dropped.

Therefore, to the questions posed above I would answer: My overall attitude towards consequences is deontological, although of course I would like them to be as good as the objective of honoring an absolute duty allows. If honoring that duty requires that millions of people be killed, I'm afraid that's just too bad. If it turns out that the "terror and grief" of the war outweigh the "mercy" of a sustained union, then, no, I would not reconsider my policy: We have an absolute obligation to vanquish "slavery and the forces of disunion," and to do so "at any and every cost."

Whether the author of the quoted passage would have welcomed this interpretation of his argument is an open question. But this interpretation at least means that nothing in the passage needs to be changed (and authors are usually in favor of that!); it presents the argument as subtle, and perfectly self-consistent, rather than confused. For our purposes, moreover, the interpretation that I have given has the advantage of showing how two ethical perspectives can be taken on the same issue, and of how they can be used together without causing problems. Of course, if this is how the author of the argument intends it to be taken, he will have to keep his wits about him. For instance, he will have to be sure to remember that rule utilitarianism, for him, is strictly a subperspective, and that what really matters is the deontological duty with which he began. But then one has to be careful whenever one embarks upon a difficult argument. The main point here is that an eye to the characteristics—both good and bad—of the main ethical theories can help us chart a course through some tricky arguments in ethics, particularly when those arguments employ several different perspectives at the same time.

I hope these examples persuade you that you need to be alert if you are to pick up on the changes of perspective that can happen in even the shortest passage. I hope, too, that you have been persuaded of the value of bearing in mind the various advantages and disadvantages of the perspectives concerned.

2.7   RECAP: PLUSES AND MINUSES

Each of the ethical theories we have discussed has a distinctive view of what makes an action right or wrong. Each of these ethical theories also has a distinctive set of strengths and weaknesses. In the following Table I summarize what those views, and what those strengths and weaknesses, are. "Rights" does not have a separate heading because rights work best in conjunction with other, wider, ethical perspectives. So what I have done instead is to state in the "Essentials" column whether a particular perspective is compatible with rights or not.

The Ethical Theories

The Essentials	*Strengths*	*Weaknesses*
DEONTOLOGY		
Act in accordance with duties and obligations	Consistent	The problem of rational justification
An action that accords with a duty or an obligation is ethically good	Takes account of special obligations	Conflicting duties and obligations
An action that violates a duty or an obligation is ethically bad	Makes sense of super-erogation	Not situational
Compatible with theory of rights	Concern for justice	Not necessarily benevolent
		Indifference to consequences of actions
ACT UTILITARIANISM		
Act in every case for the greatest good of the greatest number	Rational	Exaggerated faith in predictability
An action that results in the greatest good for the greatest number is ethically good	Situational	Incommensurable values
An action that fails to result in the greatest good for the greatest number is ethically bad	Benevolent	No room for supererogation or for special obligations
Not compatible with theory of rights		Inconsistent
		No concern for justice
RULE UTILITARIANISM		
Act in accordance with good-maximizing rules	Rational	Not situational
An action that accords with such a rule is ethically good	Consistent	Incommensurable values
An action that breaks such a rule is ethically bad	Benevolent	No room for supererogation
Compatible with theory of rights	Takes account of special obligations	Conflicting rules
	Concern for justice	Exaggerated faith in predictability

Other features than those listed in the table could have been mentioned. But the features discussed here are the most important features of the most important theories in ethics. They are the features, and the theories, that we need to understand if we are to engage productively with issues in bioethics.

CHAPTER THREE
More Materials: Principles in Ethics

We have completed our survey of the main ethical theories. In the process, we have gathered a fair amount of the common vocabulary that is needed to discuss concrete issues in bioethics. But first we must introduce the remaining bits and pieces of ethical language and terminology. The most important of these bits and pieces concern ethical principles.

3.1 WHAT IS AN ETHICAL PRINCIPLE?

An ethical principle is more specific than an ethical theory. Where an ethical theory is intended to indicate some overall perspective that might be taken on an ethical problem, an ethical principle is intended to indicate a particular guideline, or a rule of thumb, that you ought to follow in your ethical reasoning—a guideline that you must follow if your ethical reasoning is to be successful. Ethical principles are always prescriptive, then (see 2.1).

I will explain how an ethical principle works by going back to the tennis example that I used to introduce the idea of an ethical theory. If the "baseline" perspective and the "serve-and-volley" perspective both represent tennis-playing theories, then more specific guidelines like "Keep your concentration up," "Play to your opponent's weaknesses," or "Don't try impossible shots" represent tennis-playing principles. These recommendations, and others like them, tell you what you simply have to do if you wish to play tennis successfully. It is important to notice that such principles are equally necessary no matter what tennis-playing theory you adopt. If you adopt the serve-and-volley theory, then it is just as vital for you to "Keep your concentration up" as it is if you adopt the baseline theory: you must "Play to your opponent's weaknesses" regardless of whether you're a baseliner or a serve-and-volleyer. Thus any given principle—for instance, "Don't try impossible shots"—will be consistent with any viable tennis-playing theory, which means that different theories will share the same principles. And the parallel with ethical theories and principles is exact. An ethical principle tells you what you simply have to take into account if you wish to reason in an ethically successful way; which means that different ethical theories, if they are to be viable, will have to acknowledge a shared set of ethical principles.

In this section, then, we will look at some of the most important ethical principles that our ethical theories must share if they are to be useful to us in addressing issues in bioethics.

3.2 BENEFICENCE

"Beneficence" comes from the Latin for "doing good," and it means exactly that. The word is therefore extremely close to "benevolence," mentioned earlier: "Benevolence" comes from the Latin for "wishing good." Benevolence, in our terminology, is a property of ethical theories such as act and rule utilitarianism. Beneficence, by contrast, is an ethical principle. The aim to "do good" is often considered an essential part of any ethical perspective that hopes to suggest acceptable solutions to ethical dilemmas, of whatever kind. But such an aim is certainly an essential part of any ethical perspective that hopes to suggest acceptable solutions to dilemmas in *bio*ethics.

A moment's reflection will show why this is. What is the goal of health care? What is the purpose of health care? What are the goals and purposes of health care professionals? Clearly the goal of health care is to help people to get healthy and to stay healthy. It exists to do people good. Health care professionals exist to do people good. The whole point of health care and of those involved in it is to do people good (and even to make them happy, to whatever extent health and happiness go together). Health care, in other words, is an essentially beneficent phenomenon. The aim to do good, to be beneficent, is intrinsic to it. Therefore, any approach to the ethical problems that the practice and the possibilities of health care raise has got to acknowledge the beneficent aims that lie at the heart of health care itself. A person who argues that abortion is acceptable simply because it is cheaper to abort fetuses than it is to bring up children might have a point, but he or she has failed to engage with abortion as an issue in bioethics. Considerations of monetary cost—however important they might, in some contexts, be—do not connect with abortion in the context of health care practices that aim to do people good. No ethical perspective that is indifferent to beneficence can hope to address bioethical problems in a way that is relevant to them. Without the desire to do good, health care would not exist; the ethical problems that it raises spring from the desire to do good; therefore those problems must be addressed from a perspective which recognizes the desire to do good —the beneficent desire—as central.

Beneficence is an ethical principle that must be included in every ethical theory relevant to our study of bioethics. How do the theories we discussed in chapter two measure up to this requirement?

Rather well, as a matter of fact. Almost nothing needs to be said about act or rule utilitarianism. Those theories present human happiness and the reduction of human suffering as the very essence of ethics. Therefore, in so far as an illness is a cause of suffering, and health is an enabling source (if not a cause) of happiness, the two utilitarian theories are automatically well-suited to address problems in bioethics. Both are intrinsically beneficent.

Deontology is slightly thornier. After all, in section 2.7 above, it was listed as a weakness of deontology that there was nothing necessarily benevolent about it—nothing necessarily well-meaning. But this needn't ring the death knell over deontology as a theory in bioethics. For deontology is the ethical theory that takes duties and obligations more seriously than any other. So why not simply include beneficence as an obligation? What could be easier than to make beneficence a deontological duty? Nor is there anything wrong with adopting this simple solution to the problem. All we need to do in the future is distinguish between those deontological theories that include beneficence and those deontological theories that don't. The former will be relevant to bioethics. The latter, however valuable they may be for other purposes, will fail to relate in an interesting way to any problem in bioethics. Thus the inclusion of an obligation to seek human good, or human happiness, or human well-being, will qualify a deontological perspective as a viable perspective in bioethics.

So all of our theories pass muster at this stage. All of them are compatible with the ethical principle of beneficence.

3.3   RESPECT FOR AUTONOMY

"Autonomy" comes from the Greek words meaning "self-governance," meaning the capacity to select your own fate, to rule yourself, to choose what you do and what is done to you. To respect people's autonomy, therefore, is to respect their capacity to choose for themselves, is to do to them only what they wish to have done, is to respect them for going their own way. As was the case with beneficence, the principle of respect for autonomy is sometimes claimed to be essential to ethical theories of every kind. But whether or not this is so, it is certainly true that the principle of respect for autonomy is essential to theories in bioethics.

What makes this principle essential? There are several factors—indeed, this is one of those questions that could be discussed at enormous length. But we need only look at one factor. For the importance of respect for autonomy in bioethics can be established simply by reflecting upon beneficence. Beneficence, remember, means "doing good," and health care, we said in the last section, has to be understood as an intrinsically beneficent phenomenon. But there are many ways of doing people good. Making people healthy, or keeping them healthy, may be doing good in a relatively uncontroversial sense. More or less everybody would rather be healthy than unhealthy, other things being equal. But often matters are more complicated, and other things aren't equal.

For example, people may have objections to the means that will have to be employed in order to make them more healthy. Certain religious factions object to the transfusion of blood, for instance. Or a person might regard the improvement of health that a certain treatment offers as insufficiently great to justify the unpleasantness or uncertainty of the treatment itself. On these grounds, someone might choose, for example, not to undergo a heart transplant. In other words, it will not always be obvious what course of action *is* the beneficent course of action, what course of action will actually count as the one that "does good." And it will only be possible to settle that question in the context of the autonomous desires, goals, and preferences of the individuals whom one hopes to benefit.

The principle of beneficence, then, cannot be applied effectively without respecting autonomy. If you want to benefit someone, you'd better find out what they want first. There's nothing beneficent in giving chocolate to confirmed chocolate-haters, or in buying the complete works of Shakespeare for someone who loathes literature. Only by applying the principle of respect for autonomy will our beneficent impulses have a chance of being exercised fruitfully. Insofar, then, as beneficence is an ethical principle that is essential to any ethical theory that is relevant to bioethics, respect for autonomy will also be an essential principle in bioethics. The two principles are tied very closely together (although, as we will see in the next section, they can sometimes come into conflict with each other). So how well do the ethical theories we discussed in Chapter Two accommodate the principle of respect for autonomy?

Again, rather well. The two varieties of utilitarianism clearly require that autonomy be respected. After all, you can only hope to maximize happiness if you know what will in fact make people happy. Not everyone likes chocolate, for example, and plenty of people would prefer to be given the cash equivalent than the complete works of Shakespeare. A utilitarian who has no interest in the autonomy of others will be a hopelessly unsuccessful happiness-maximizer. Which means that utilitarian theories are bound to take seriously the principle of respect for autonomy, and therefore that such theories are bound to be well-suited to problems in bioethics.

The case is not quite so obvious with deontology. There are some complicated historical and technical reasons for supposing that respect for autonomy is in fact an essential deontological principle, but we needn't go into those here. For our purposes it will be enough to perform the same kind of operation in this case as we did in the case of beneficence. In other words, we need only distinguish between those deontological theories that do include the obligation to respect autonomy and those deontological theories (if any) that don't. Only the former kind of theory will represent a viable perspective in bioethics.

So, once again, all of our theories measure up to requirements. All of them are compatible with the ethical principle of respect for autonomy.

3.4 CONFLICTS OF PRINCIPLE

In this section we will see how the principles of beneficence and respect for autonomy, although both vital principles in bioethics, can nevertheless come into conflict with each other. As we do so, we will begin to get a clearer idea of exactly what is involved in each of these principles.

I said a moment ago that it is essential to respect autonomy if you wish to be beneficent: Only if you are aware of other people's autonomous preferences, goals, and desires can you hope to be of service to them, to benefit them. Within limits, what I said was perfectly true. But if what I said was absolutely true, then there clearly couldn't be any conflict between beneficence and respect for autonomy: Every successful act of beneficence would necessarily involve respect for autonomy, and every successful act of respecting autonomy would necessarily be beneficent. But matters are more complicated than this.

There are two main kinds of cases in which matters are more complicated. The first kind arises when just one person's interests are at stake. What happens when someone's autonomous preferences are clearly not in his or her own best interests? What happens when, by treating people as they want to be treated, we do not treat them at all beneficently? For instance, how should we behave towards people who are determined, on utterly nonsensical grounds, to kill themselves? Or towards a person who refuses to take an important medicine because it tastes bad? Or towards people who insist that they'd sooner be ill in the street than be admitted to the hospital? In each of these cases, the principles of respect for autonomy and beneficence appear to be incompatible. If we respect the individuals' autonomy—by letting them go ahead and kill themselves, or not take their medicine, or by leaving them ill in the street—then we do not seem to be benefitting them, or to be doing them any good at all. But if instead we act beneficently—and attempt to ensure that they do not kill themselves, that they do take their medicine, or that they do get themselves admitted to hospital—then we quite blatantly ignore their wishes, and so fail to respect their autonomy. We don't seem to be able to behave in a way that is both beneficent and respectful of their autonomy: The principles are in conflict.

The second kind of case where conflict arises are those in which more than one person's interests are at stake. What happens when one person's autonomous preferences are clearly not in the best interests of some second person? What happens when, by treating one person as he or she wishes to be treated, we end up treating someone else in an unbeneficent way? For instance, how should we behave when one person wants us to keep confidential a piece of information that could be of great benefit to somebody else? Or when parents have religious objections to a form of therapy that could save the life of their child? Or when someone who poses a danger to the public would rather not seek treatment? In each case we can either respect autonomy or act beneficently. We can keep the secret, withhold the therapy, or leave the person at large, but only at the cost of beneficence. Alternatively, we can break the confidence, ignore the parent, or seek a court order, but only if we are prepared to disrespect autonomy. Again, the principles are in conflict.

There is no easy way of settling conflicts between the principles of beneficence and respect for autonomy. Such conflicts point up just how complicated even the simplest-seeming of ethical situations can be. But they also invite us to think more closely about what is really involved in the effort to "do good," or in the effort to respect the preferences of others; indeed, such thinking will be vital when we come to investigate the issues in the rest of this book. For example, we will have to consider whether a doctor's prime duty is to do whatever he or she considers is in the patient's best interests, or whether it is to do whatever the patient considers is in the patient's best interests. We will have to ask whether, for example, it is in anybody's best interests to keep a comatose person "alive" indefinitely on life-support. Do the family's preferences matter? What sort of life is worth living? We will have to decide which individuals are capable of autonomy—which individuals are capable of forming preferences that we are obliged to respect or to take into account. Are animals autonomous? Are fetuses? Small children? Mentally ill people? Senile people? Unconscious people?

These are all extremely difficult questions—and they are questions of a kind which we will have to consider before we are in any position to resolve particular conflicts between beneficence and respect for autonomy. But for the moment we can sketch out two broad approaches to such conflict. These might be labelled paternalism and libertarianism.

3.4a Paternalism

A "paternalist" position is one that tends to give precedence to the demands of beneficence over those of respect for autonomy. The paternalist believes that it is more important to do people good than it is to deal with them as they wish to be dealt with.

So, for example, a paternalist might think that it was ethically proper to ignore a patient's preferences if a doctor (who is much better informed, after all) has a different view about what treatment is likely to be most effective. A paternalist might think it proper to stop people from behaving in certain ways if those ways of behaving can be shown not to be in people's best interests (for example, drinking, smoking). A paternalist might decide that someone's life is worth living, and take steps to prolong that life, even when the person whose life it is thinks that it isn't worth living. And so on. Typical paternalist sentiments are captured in remarks such as: "Doctor knows best"; or "I know what's good for you better than you know yourself"; or "Believe me, I have your best interests at heart"; or "You need to be saved from yourself."

Clearly paternalism is an authoritarian, and even an arrogant position. But it would be wrong simply to reject it. For the paternalist's motives are good ones, remember. The desire to do good governs the paternalist's decisions. This means that it can be argued that health care, itself an intrinsically beneficent practice that strives above all to do good, is also intrinsically paternalistic. If health care exists to do good, then why, it might be asked, should the ignorant desires of uninformed people be accorded any ethical significance in a medical context? We will see in later chapters that this question can be difficult to answer. But for now let us simply note that all of us are paternalists at times: no one, surely, would think it sensible to let a two-year-old child refuse important medication because it doesn't taste good; or to let a person suffering from senile dementia wander off whenever he or she feels like it. The beneficent impulse essential to paternalism is one with which we are all familiar. All of us, at one time or another, believe that it is right to do things for a person's good even against that person's will.

3.4b Libertarianism

A "libertarian" position is one that prefers to respect autonomy at the cost of beneficence whenever the two come into conflict. The libertarian thinks that it is more important to allow people to do as they wish than it is to do them good.

So, for example, a libertarian might think it ethically proper to allow a patient to decide what his or her own course of treatment should be, even when the patient's decision does not accord with the best medical advice. A libertarian might think it proper to allow people to kill themselves with drink and cigarettes if that is what they want to do. A libertarian might think that the only person in any position to say whether a given life is worth living is the person whose life it is. Typical libertarian sentiments are captured in remarks such as: "To each his own"; or "Let them go to hell as they choose,"; or "You're mad, but I'm not going to stand in your way"; or "It's your funeral."

Clearly libertarianism has its attractions; and it certainly accords well with the instincts most of us have much of the time. But it would be a mistake simply to conclude that libertarianism is unproblematic, or that it is obviously preferable to paternalism. After all, in a health care context—where an extremely important if not overriding goal is to do people good—respect for autonomy is bound to have its limits. This is especially clear when one reflects that part of the motive people have in seeking medical advice, or in placing themselves in a health care setting, is to allow other highly trained and expert people do what they can to produce benefits. In other words, a person (for example, a patient) may autonomously choose to surrender his or her autonomy to the beneficent ambitions of somebody else (for example, a surgeon). Furthermore, an unfettered libertarian may be so unconcerned with the demands of beneficence that he or she ends up being completely indifferent to people's welfare. Someone who thinks that everyone should be allowed to do whatever they choose in any circumstance is not only being rash or unrealistic (just think of the consequences of letting everyone do exactly what they feel like!), such a person is also betraying a deep lack of interest in human happiness. And you don't have to be a committed utilitarian to think that human happiness is more important than that.

Neither full-blown libertarianism nor full-blown paternalism seems an entirely attractive position to take on conflicts between the principles of beneficence and respect for autonomy. But the attempt to strike a balance between the two—an attempt which we will have to make repeatedly when discussing the issues in the rest of this book—is a tricky one, which will require from us not only some hard thinking, but also a good deal of imagination.

3.5 JUSTICE

The final ethical principle we will look at here is the principle of justice. I have separated justice from the earlier two principles because it operates at a different level from that at which beneficence and respect for autonomy operate. The principles of beneficence and respect for autonomy invite us to ask, in particular cases, "How can I do good here? How can I give due weight to the preferences of others?" The principle of justice, by contrast, invites us to survey our ethical behavior in a broader context. It invites us to ask if our behavior is consistent; to ask if we are behaving in an even-handed way; to ask if we are treating people fairly. The principle of justice requires that our behavior—whether it is deontological or utilitarian, paternalist or libertarian —be motivated by a constant set of considerations.

Perhaps the easiest way of stating the principle of justice is to say that justice demands that like cases be treated alike. If the ethically relevant features of two cases are similar to one another, then so should be the actions that we perform in those cases. If in the first case we decide, for instance, to prefer the demands of beneficence to those of respect for autonomy, then we ought to decide similarly in the second case. If, as deontologists, we resolve a particular conflict between obligations in one way in one case, then we ought to resolve a similar conflict in a similar way in a second case, and so on. The principle of justice recommends no particular kind of action: Rather, it recommends that our actions in general be consistent with one another. Thus the principle of justice is sometimes said to be a formal principle, that is, a principle that is concerned not with the content of any particular action, but with the relationship between actions, with the pattern formed by one's actions considered *en masse.*

It is easy to see why the principle of justice is important. After all, if your behavior between cases is not consistent, then how are the differences between your various bits of behavior to be justified? Surely it's not good enough simply to say, "Well, I acted differently in that case because I felt like it." If you are ever called upon to defend apparent inconsistencies in your actions, then it is desirable to be able to come up with something better than an admission of whim or caprice. Indeed, beyond a certain point, if whim and caprice are the best justifications you can offer for your actions, then you are very likely to be deemed incompetent in a technical sense—to be thought less than fully responsible for your actions. A plea of diminished responsibility may be relevant and even desirable in certain legal contexts. But in an ethical context it is far better not to find oneself in a position where such a plea needs to be made. And the best way to avoid that position is to pay due regard to the principle of justice.

So how should you respond if called upon to defend apparent inconsistencies in your actions? The answer is obvious from the question. You should show that the inconsistencies in your actions are indeed only apparent. The best way of doing that is to show that the cases in which you appeared to have acted inconsistently are themselves only apparently similar. For example, if someone asks you why you gave one small child a bar of chocolate when the child asked for it, but refused to give a second child chocolate under seemingly similar circumstances, then the fact that the second child is diabetic will explain your behavior. The two cases were only apparently similar (there was at least one important difference between them); therefore, your actions were only apparently inconsistent (there was at least one good reason for treating the cases in dissimilar ways). By showing what the difference between the cases is, you successfully defend yourself against charges of inconsistent behavior. You show that you did not, after all, behave unjustly.

These considerations suggest a second way of expressing the principle of justice. The principle of justice requires that differences in treatment must be justified by appeal to relevant differences between cases. Only where cases are relevantly different (for example, where one of two children is diabetic and chocolate is being given out) can a difference in treatment, or behavior, be justified. Of course the cases must indeed be *relevantly* different. If you decided not to give one child a bar of chocolate because you objected to the color of the child's hair, your behavior would not be justified. Hair color is not a relevant factor in the capacity to desire, benefit from, or to enjoy chocolate. To treat cases differently on grounds such as this is to discriminate (in a bad sense), and it is to ignore completely the requirements of justice. Of course there is room for legitimate disagreement about what differences between cases do count as relevant differences. Indeed, we will see in Chapter Ten that such disagreements can lead to very different conceptions of the principle of justice, and I defer detailed consideration of most of the issues until then. But for the moment we need only recall that justice requires that like cases be treated alike; we need only remember that trivial or frivolous differences should not prevent cases from being regarded as "like" cases.

So how do the ethical theories we surveyed in Chapter Two measure up to the demands of justice? We already know the answer to that. In 2.7 we listed as a strength of deontology and rule utilitarianism the fact that they could accommodate the demands of justice. But we listed as a weakness of act utilitarianism the fact that it could not. Does this mean that act utilitarianism is now of no further interest to us, that its difficulties with justice make it a redundant theory in bioethics? I think that if we were extremely strict about it, then probably we would say that it did. But there are two reasons to be more lenient.

In the first place, as we noted in 2.3i, the act utilitarian can simply bite the bullet over justice, and claim that the principle is an overrated one. Indeed, it is possible for the act utilitarian to go one step further. The act utilitarian can claim that the actions recommended by his or her theory, although not consistent in the way that the actions recommended by deontology or by rule utilitarianism are consistent, are nevertheless only *apparently* inconsistent in a damaging sense. After all, the act utilitarian does justify differences in treatment by appealing to differences between cases. Two very similar cases may be treated differently in virtue of the different consequences that those treatments are predicted to yield. Thus, although one innocent person may be punished while a second innocent person is not, the act utilitarian can explain this discrepancy by pointing to the unique factors about the first person's circumstances that make punishing that person acceptable, in terms of the act-utilitarian calculation of consequences, where punishing the second person would not be acceptable. If two apparently similar cases lead to different consequences, then that certainly counts as a relevant difference from the act utilitarian perspective. In other words, the act utilitarian can claim that the principle of justice does, in one highly literal sense, fit in with his or her theory (even if many would argue that the mere possibility that it might condone the punishment of innocent people shows that act utilitarianism is unable to accommodate the true spirit of the principle of justice). Some of the features of this position are explored further in 10.1c.

A second reason to be lenient over act utilitarianism's strange relationship to justice is that act utilitarianism is, as we have seen, the only one of the ethical theories capable of being situational—of making decisions on a case-by-case basis. This might be thought important because the kinds of issue that arise in bioethics—and especially in some of the more complicated areas of bioethics—can be so unusual. The thought here is that, for some issues, only a perspective capable of addressing each case strictly on its own distinctive merits will be able to make sense of the problems involved. Now this thought may or may not be a correct one. But we will find it useful at least to suspend judgment for the time being. For it may turn out that in certain extraordinary—even extreme—cases, act utilitarianism will have a contribution to make that cannot be made by exploiting the resources of deontology or of rule utilitarianism.

3.6   RECAP: PRINCIPLES IN OUTLINE

Ethical principles are intended to indicate guidelines that you must follow if you wish your ethical reasoning to be successful. These guidelines are or ought to be compatible with any viable ethical perspective (the compatibility of justice with act utilitarianism is a possible exception here). The principle of beneficence indicates a guideline that will be relevant to any and every case in which there is a possibility of doing or of failing to do good. The principle of respect for autonomy indicates a guideline that will be relevant to any and every case in which there is a possibility of respecting or of failing to respect the interests and preferences of others. These two principles may sometimes conflict with one another. The principle of justice is more general than either of the other two principles. The principle of justice gives no indication of how any particular case is to be settled; rather, it provides a recommendation about the way in which particular ethical decisions should be related to one another. The following table gives a brief summary of each of the three main ethical principles.

Beneficence	*Respect for Autonomy*	*Justice*
The principle that one should attempt to do good; that one should attempt to benefit others	The principle that one should attempt to give due weight to the goals, preferences, and interests of others	The principle that one should treat like cases alike: Differences in treatment must be justified by appeal to relevant differences between cases

A good deal more could have been said about each of these principles. But for the moment it will be enough if we have a general idea of what each of them stands for. As we go on to explore particular bioethical issues in the remainder of this book, our conceptions of beneficence, of respect for autonomy, and of justice will inevitably become richer; we will find that many of those issues will themselves become richer, and more complex, as we bring ethical principles to bear upon them.

Selected Bibliography

Beauchamp, T. and J. Childress, *Principles of Biomedical Ethics*, Oxford University Press, 1989.
Lindley, Richard, *Autonomy*, Humanities Press, 1986.
Shelp, Earl, ed., *Justice and Healthcare*, D. Reidel, 1981.

CHAPTER FOUR

Methods

In Chapter One, we examined some powerful motivations for engaging in ethical argument. In Chapters Two and Three, we explored some of the materials useful in conducting such arguments. In this section, we will briefly survey some of the methods by which ethical arguments may most effectively be advanced and assessed. The purpose of this section is not to provide a kind of crash course on critical thinking (for that, you will need to sign up for a crash course on critical thinking); rather, the purpose is to provide an overview, or a series of snapshots, of the methods most commonly employed in this book, and indeed in ethical argument in general. The intention is to give the reader some hints and some reference points that may be helpful in discussing the issues raised in future chapters.

4.1 RATIONAL ARGUMENT

It may seem odd to describe rational argument as a method, or at least as a distinctive method. For isn't *all* argument rational? Isn't it the whole point of argument to be rational? Yes, in a way that is the point of argument. But it certainly isn't true that all argument is rational. We have all taken part in hot-tempered shouting matches, or in futile altercations with people who refuse to consider any point of view but their own (most us of have also been guilty of this ourselves). These might be described as arguments. But by no stretch of the imagination could they be described as rational arguments. Indeed, we saw in 1.1 and 1.3 that one of the main reasons for engaging philosophically with problems in ethics is that by doing so we may hope to avoid exactly these kinds of fruitless disputes.

But what precisely is involved in rational argument? What sets a rational argument apart from other, less desirable, kinds of argument? There is no simple answer to these questions. There is no single feature that one can point to in an argument, and say "There—that's what makes it rational." But it is possible to give some general guidelines, nevertheless.

For instance, a rational argument always proceeds step-by-step. One step leads to the next; there is no step that does not follow from the steps that come before it. Sometimes, of course, these steps will not be spelled out in an explicit way. There may be phases that are simply too obvious to need explicit treatment. But even in these cases, it will always be true that the missing steps could, in principle, be filled in. Very often it will be necessary to fill them in. If someone misses the point of your argument, or fails to follow it clearly, then it is possible that you have made a jump which, although it seems obvious to you, may not after all be that straightforward. If this is what has happened then it is essential that you be willing and able to make explicit those steps which, earlier, you glided over or dealt with too quickly. The step-by-step nature of rational argument enables others to understand your position and how you have arrived at it. It also allows them to assess your position. After all, if the steps which you go through do not actually follow on from each other, there will be good reason to doubt whether your argument is genuinely able to establish the conclusions you draw. The soundness of your eventual position will depend, then, upon the quality of the arguments that got you there.

There are two main ways in which an argument can fail to establish a conclusion satisfactorily. One way, which I have just mentioned, is to include steps that do not in fact follow on from each other. The other way is to make or to imply inconsistent, or even contradictory, claims. It is an axiom of rational thought that two contradictory propositions cannot both be true. "Murder is evil," "Murder is not evil." Provided that the words in these propositions are being used to mean the same things in each case, these two claims cannot possibly both be true. Either murder is evil, or it isn't. Thus an argument containing contradictory propositions must inevitably include at least one proposition that is false and an argument that includes false propositions is clearly not going to be a satisfactory argument.

This point seems almost too obvious to be worth making and certainly it would be a very bad argument that contained a contradiction as blatant as the one mentioned a moment ago. But that's just the point. Most contradictions or inconsistencies are not very blatant: they may be very deeply concealed. However, you will not be inclined to look for the unobvious contradictions unless you appreciate exactly how fatal *every* contradiction is. And every contradiction is exactly as fatal to an argument as a blatant contradiction is—like the blatant contradiction between "Murder is evil" and "Murder is not evil." None of us wants to advance an argument containing a contradiction as obvious as that, but we should be precisely as reluctant to advance an argument that contains a subtle or a concealed contradiction. For the damage is as serious either way: We commit ourselves to at least one false claim.

What this means in practice is that you need to be tremendously alert for lurking contradictions, even in the most innocent-seeming of arguments. We have already seen at least one example of a hidden contradiction. When we looked at relativism in 1.2, we encountered the following argument.

1. All ethical views are equally valid; therefore
2. It is wrong to criticize the ethical views of others.

Now on the face of it, this argument does not look contradictory. It even looks quite reasonable. But a closer inspection reveals what's wrong. Proposition 1 implies that, since all ethical views are equally valid, no ethical view can be regarded as better than any other. No ethical view, therefore, can be regarded as absolutely right or as absolutely wrong. We now have a third proposition.

3. No ethical view is absolutely right or wrong.

Proposition 2, however, says that it is wrong to criticize the views of others. This, surely, implies that there is at least one ethical view that is absolutely right: the ethical view expressed in proposition 2. This gives us a fourth proposition:

4. There is at least one ethical view that is absolutely right.

Now proposition 4 clearly contradicts proposition 3. But proposition 4 is implied by proposition 2, and proposition 3 is implied by proposition 1. Therefore proposition 2 contradicts proposition 1. Therefore the relativist argument consisting of 1 and 2 is a contradictory argument that cannot survive scrutiny. (Notice, however, that had the second proposition simply said that it is *pointless* to criticize the ethical views of others, the contradiction would have been avoided: 2 would not have implied 4; so 4 would not have contradicted 3, so 2 would not have contradicted 1.) The contradiction in this case is certainly not as blatant as the murder-is-evil/murder-is-not-evil example—it must be unearthed. But most of the contradictions in arguments about ethics are like that. You have to keep your eyes open for them.

We have now looked at two of the hallmarks of successful rational arguments: Such arguments proceed step-by-step, and they don't contradict themselves. But above all rational argument is reasoned argument. It proceeds—and it must proceed, if it is to be effective—by offering reasons for each of the assumptions made and reasons for each of the steps taken. In the absence of such reason-giving, argument is doomed never to persuade, and never to shed light on the issues it addresses. Only by arguing rationally—by giving reasons—can we hope to improve our understanding of the issues that interest us, or hope to persuade others to take our views on such issues seriously.

4.2   THE ROLE OF INTUITION

The emphasis given in the last section may appear to suggest that there is no place in ethics for anything except rational argument. In particular, it may appear to suggest that there is no place for intuition. But that would be a misleading impression. For intuition does have a significant role to play, and it plays that role within the context of rational argument.

The two points during a rational argument when an appeal to intuition is most likely to be helpful is right at the beginning and right at the end. You can't simply embark upon a rational argument out of the blue, with nothing to build on or to leap off from. You need to start with something. That something will very often be an intuition of some kind, or perhaps a set of loosely related intuitions. So, for example, a rational argument about abortion might begin with an intuition that there is something inherently valuable about life, and an intuition that there is something about fetuses that makes them importantly different from fully fledged human beings. The argument itself might then proceed to try to make sense of these intuitions, to explore their implications, and to discover whether either or both of them are really rationally sustainable. Such an argument might also attempt to establish whether these intuitions, or refined versions of them, are compatible with one another. It might conclude by relating these findings explicitly to some aspect of the abortion debate. Thus our intuitions will often function as a kind of fuel for rational argument. When they do function like this, it will be part of the function of rational argument to assess and to refine our intuitions.

So intuition can get a rational argument going. But it may also feature at the end of such an argument. For if an argument produces a conclusion, we will clearly be interested to know whether that conclusion deserves to be taken seriously. One way of trying to settle this is to assess the argument itself. Does it satisfy the requirements of rationality? If it does then there will be good grounds for taking the conclusion seriously. But these considerations may not be conclusive. Often we will have to take another step. We will have to ask ourselves whether the conclusion squares with our intuitions.

Do we believe the conclusion? Do we find it convincing? Does it, in the end, tell us something we think might be true? If the answer to these questions is No—if we simply cannot bring ourselves to believe that the conclusion of the argument is plausible—then we have good reason to go back to the argument and to try to discover what, if anything, has gone wrong. Is the argument really a rational one? Were the intuitions from which the argument started really all that intuitive? It is possible that our distrust of the conclusion will sharpen our critical faculties so that we are able to discover a previously overlooked shortcoming in the argument. On the other hand, it is possible that it won't. In which case we will either have to bite the bullet— and accept a conclusion which clashes with our intuitions—or else suspend judgment, and assume that sooner or later a flaw in the argument will come to light. Either way, the match—whether good or bad—between the conclusion of an argument and our intuitions is likely to affect our attitude towards the conclusion. Our intuitions often function, then, as a standard against which we test the outcome of an argument.

This role is an important one. But of course we must be careful in our use of intuition. After all, there is no guarantee that our intuitions are right, or even that they are especially sensible. It would be a mistake, then, to assume that the deliverances of intuition are sacrosanct or beyond criticism. But if we are suitably cautious and moderate in our use of intuition as a standard against which to test the conclusions of ethical argument, then there is little question that our arguments will gain as a result. Nor is there much question that, over time, our intuitions will themselves adjust in subtle ways so as to reflect more closely the conclusions of rational argument. Rational argument and intuition need to be held in a delicate balance, then. When the balance is right, argument and intuition will regulate one another and feed into each other, so that our ethical thought becomes richer and better suited to the subtleties and complexities of the ethical issues with which we are concerned.

4.3   THE USE OF EXAMPLES

In ethical argument there is hardly anything more important than the use of examples. Indeed it is virtually impossible to have too many examples. In this introduction I have tried to illustrate arguments with examples at more or less every stage, and in the remainder of the book you will encounter an almost limitless number of them.

But why is this? Aren't examples really rather like the icing on the cake—very welcome, perhaps, but essentially a sideshow? Surely, you might suggest, if the argument were made clearly enough then there wouldn't be any need for examples. Someone who followed the argument could imagine their own, if that was what they wanted to do.

There is a grain of truth to this suggestion. But only a grain. Certainly it is true that examples ought not to substitute for clarity of argument. If you find that examples are actually carrying the main burden of your argument, then it is probably time to go back and start your argument again. But there are essential uses for examples nonetheless. For instance, you can never be entirely sure that your argument *is* ideally clear. It may be clear to you; it may be clear to a lot of people; yet there may be people who, for one reason or another, fail to get the drift of your argument as you have stated it. These people will find the presence of examples an enormous help. There is almost no one who will not find the presence of examples at least somewhat helpful. A well-chosen example can encapsulate a point more economically than the most careful paraphrase of an argument. The use of examples, then, can be a vital aid to the successful communication of your point.

But there is another reason why the use of examples is important. Examples can not only help to get your point across better, but also to make sure that your point is worth getting across at all. Consider: Arguments in ethics are supposed to address real-world problems. They are supposed to engage with practical issues of certain kinds. The use of examples, therefore, derived from various practical contexts, serves to anchor an ethical argument more closely to those real-world problems with which it is meant to be concerned. Thus it will always be a test of your ethical argument to see whether you can think of good examples to illustrate it with. If you can, then there is every reason to suppose that your argument, whatever its other virtues, does at least have the virtue of engaging with practical ethical concerns. If you cannot think of good examples, however hard you try, it indicates that your argument has become altogether too abstract. The argument itself may be impeccably rational and utterly logical from beginning to end. But if there seems to be no way of illustrating it with real-world examples, then it is highly unlikely that the argument will succeed in addressing any genuinely practical problem in ethics. (Notice how I refrain from illustrating this point with an example!) Thus attempting to illustrate your argument with suitable examples is, at the same time, attempting to ensure that your argument is relevant to the issues with which it deals. In fact, you will discover in the course of this book that arguments in bioethics revolve around particular cases that are usually real, and not merely hypothetical. Therefore, an argument in bioethics that does not include examples fails to address the fact that health care professionals are practicing in the midst of highly specific circumstances. Examples aren't just the icing on the cake, then. They can also function as an indicator that the cake beneath the icing is in good, healthy shape.

4.4 ARGUMENT BY ANALOGY

You will often find it useful when making or exploring an argument in bioethics to argue by analogy. An analogy is an example which, although it is not an example of the phenomenon that you are primarily interested in, does share important features with that phenomenon. A well-chosen analogy highlights those common features in a way that makes it easier to investigate them. Thus, a well-chosen analogy helps you understand the phenomenon in which you are primarily interested more clearly. And when you argue by analogy, you exploit the similarities between that phenomenon and the analogy to suggest that what is true of the analogy is also true of the phenomenon itself.

Argument by analogy can be either constructive or critical. It is constructive when the analogy is used to make or to clarify a case. One of the most famous analogies in bioethics, invented by Judith Jarvis Thomson (and discussed more fully in Chapter Six), is an example of constructive analogy. The phenomenon Thomson is primarily interested in is abortion. But her analogy could not, at first sight, seem further removed from that. She asks us to imagine that you are kidnapped, and that you wake up back-to-back in bed with another person. The other person's blood is filtering through your kidneys, via an arrangement of tubes. You are told that this procedure, which will continue for nine months, will do you no long-term harm. You are also told that if you do not stay in bed with the other person for nine months, filtering their blood, they will certainly die. Would it be ethically acceptable for you to decide to unplug yourself from the other person and to return to your everyday life?

It isn't hard to work out what's going on here. The person who requires the use of your body in order to stay alive is the equivalent of a fetus. You are the equivalent of a pregnant woman. Nine months is how long pregnancies last. Pregnancies do not typically inflict long-term harm. The fact that you were kidnapped suggests the equivalent of rape (in other words, you found yourself in your present situation against your will). To unplug yourself from the other person would be the equivalent of having an abortion. The analogy highlights the features of abortion (in the context of rape) that Thomson believes are the most important ones. She uses the analogy to draw certain ethical conclusions and she varies the analogy so that she can discuss the abortion of fetuses not conceived through rape. Thomson's hope is that by isolating what she claims are the most important features of abortion from their usual context, and by expressing them in an analogy, we will be able to discuss and to try to understand what abortion really involves without getting entangled in the confusing, and often highly emotive, aspects of the abortion debate itself. In other words, Thomson hopes that her analogy will allow us to approach the abortion debate in a more dispassionate and intelligent way than we might otherwise approach it. She claims that her analogy will also help us to see what we ought to say about abortion. The intended function of the analogy is wholly *constructive*, then.

When an argument by analogy is used critically, by contrast, the idea is to try to suggest where an argument has gone wrong. Suppose that one person argues that you have no responsibility for a pregnancy if you attempted to avoid it by using a contraceptive that was almost certain to work (after all, the odds against pregnancy were very high). A second person might object to this argument with an analogy. Imagine, the second person might say, that you point a gun at someone and pull the trigger, being "almost certain" that it isn't loaded. However, suppose that it *is* loaded; surely you are responsible now for the fact that you have shot someone (after all, you didn't have to point the gun or pull the trigger).

The point of the second person's analogy suggests that the relation between the probability of an outcome and someone's responsibility for that outcome is more complicated than the first person's argument recognizes. The first person's argument assumes that if the risk of a certain outcome is very small, you cannot be held responsible for that outcome if it arises. But the analogy shows—or it strongly suggests—that things are less simple. For if one chooses to run a risk, when one could perfectly well have avoided it, then it seems reasonable to suppose that one must bear at least some responsibility for whatever consequences follow. This is not the place to try to assess these claims. But the example does show how an analogy can be employed to highlight a potential weakness in an ethical position. When analogies are used to this end, then, they are used critically.

We have looked at examples of both of the main uses of argument by analogy. In both kinds of use, the function of the analogy is to highlight certain essential features of a problem so that those features can be more clearly appreciated, and so that the problem can be more fruitfully addressed. Sometimes this will mean that the analogy is quite far-fetched (as in the case of Thomson's analogy). But it is important not to be put off by exotic or extreme analogies. If they succeed in highlighting the relevant features of an issue then they are doing their job effectively. It is not necessary that they also be realistic, probable or down-to-earth. To object to an analogy merely because it seems far-fetched or unlikely is most usually to miss the point. In arguing by analogy you have a lot of license: You can invent all kinds of wonderful stories. But even so, a successful analogy needs to be designed with great care. If an analogy fails to highlight the essential features of a case, or of an issue, then it is bound to be quite useless, and may even be misleading. Undertaken carelessly, then, argument by analogy can be a menace. But done properly it can be a tremendously valuable method in ethics.

4.5 SLIPPERY-SLOPE ARGUMENTS

Suppose someone makes the following argument: "I don't think we should use brain-dead people as organ donors. The demand for organs will always outstrip supply—there will never be enough brain-dead donors. So what will happen is that someone will decide, sooner or later, that we need more of them, or that we need a different kind of donor. They'll begin classifying comatose people as potential donors; they'll start using people on death row; they'll even be tempted by orphanages. Before you know it, they'll be commandeering organs from perfectly healthy people in order to transplant them into 'more deserving' people. I think we should stop this particular problem before it gets started."

This is a classic "slippery-slope" argument (and such arguments are common in bioethics). It begins by considering one quite narrow proposal (that brain-dead people should be used as organ donors); it goes on to suggest ways in which that proposal might conceivably, or even quite likely, be widened, so that it would eventually include some clearly unacceptable course of action (such as using healthy orphans as organ donors). It concludes that the wider proposal is so appalling that it renders unacceptable even the narrower proposal with which the argument began.

We are all familiar with slippery-slope arguments: "Let the government get away with *this* tax rise, and pretty soon they'll be taxing away every cent we earn"; "Any more TV channels and no one will remember how to read"; "Make it illegal to own a machine gun, and next thing you know you'll need a license to buy a steak-knife"; "Just one puff on a cigarette and you'll be addicted, and probably hooked on heroin, too." You know the kind of argument. In each case, the initial proposal—however harmless it might seem— is portrayed as the first step on an extremely steep decline into awfulness. And the implication is that you cannot avoid the awfulness once you've taken that first step. Do *A*, the argument goes, and you'll inevitably find yourself doing *B*, and then *C*, *D*, and *E*, until you finally end up doing *N*— which everyone agrees would be a dreadful thing. So don't do *A*.

What ought we to make of slippery-slope arguments? The first thing to say is that they are not, by themselves, conclusive, or even particularly compelling. The successive steps on the slippery-slope are rarely, if ever, related to one another with the degree of inevitability that the arguments appear to suggest. For instance, the organ donor argument give above clearly doesn't prove anything. It is conceivable that people who think it a good idea to use brain-dead people as organ donors might come to think it is a good idea to use healthy orphans as well. However, there is no reason to suppose that they have to come to think that; nor is there any reason to suppose it likely that they will come to think that. Brain-dead people and healthy orphans are quite distinct kinds of individuals. There is no necessary connection between a proposal concerning one of those kinds of individual and a proposal concerning the other. Perhaps there is a sort of "slope" between them. But there is nothing forcing you to slide down it.

So slippery-slope arguments don't actually prove anything. Specifically, they don't prove that there is anything necessarily wrong with the first step (for example, in the arguments sketched above, with using brain-dead people as organ donors, with some particular tax rise, with outlawing machine-guns, etc.). One can always, in principle, take the first step without slipping any further down the slope. So are slippery-slope arguments a mistake—just a waste of time?

If it's proof you want, then the answer is yes. But there can be more to an argument than its capacity to prove. In the case of slippery-slope arguments, there is a capacity to warn. By portraying one proposal, perhaps a comparatively innocent one, as being related by a series of loose connections to some clearly horrible proposal, the slippery-slope argument alerts us to what needs to be avoided—to what needs to be defended against. Of course no necessary connection exists between using brain-dead people as organ donors and using orphans as organ donors. But the warning of the slippery-slope argument is that having taken the first step, deciding to transplant organs from one category of defenseless individual, we might find it that much easier in the future to extend our procurement policy so as to include other categories of defenseless individuals. In other words, the slippery-slope argument invites us to specify as closely as possible the kinds of individual from whom it will be permissible to remove organs, so that we avoid accidentally or carelessly drawing the line in a way that we might later regret.

In what is usually a very graphic way, then, slippery-slope arguments alert us to the dangers of framing our own arguments sloppily, or without due caution; as such they represent a useful method in ethics. They are not useful, however, when they are offered, or are taken, as proofs that certain proposals are intrinsically unacceptable. A slippery-slope argument regulates debate. It can never settle debate.

4.6   THE JOYS OF COMPROMISE

Many people, especially likeable people, instinctively want to resolve all differences of opinion by compromise. They strive to identify the middle way in an argument, and to persuade others whose positions fall on either side to bury their differences in the no-man's-land lying between them. This instinct is a praiseworthy one for the most part. It is the instinct of the natural peacemaker and diplomat. Very often the middle way will indeed make more sense than the extremes lying on either side of it.

But even so one needs to be careful. If you seek compromise blindly, without first investigating a question from every side, you are likely sometimes to find yourself straddling a most uncomfortable fence. For compromise can slide easily into loss of principle. (Although it needn't do that: This point, like any other derived from a slippery-slope argument, serves merely as a warning—see the preceding section.)

The danger is this: A person who automatically assumes that the truth is likely to lie between the opposing positions in an argument runs the risk of failing to notice that one of those opposing positions might be perfectly plausible as it stands. In other words, such a person risks messing up an entirely reasonable position by watering it down with a competing unreasonable position, so that the compromise position ends up being less reasonable than one of the initial alternatives.

For example, suppose you were present at an antebellum debate about slavery. One side argues that the institution of slavery is natural, proper, and just, and that it would be wrong to abolish it or to reduce it in any way. The other side argues that the institution of slavery is unnatural, obscene, and unjust, and that it should be abolished in its entirety. Suppose you are an instinctive compromiser. What will your middle way look like? Presumably like this: Slavery is somewhat natural, neither entirely proper nor wholly obscene, and is, at least to a degree, relatively just; thus slavery ought certainly not be extended, but then neither ought it to be entirely abolished; perhaps we could all agree just to limit it a bit?

I'm sure you'll agree that this compromise, this piece of fence-sitting, does not result in an ethically acceptable position. The example should make it clear that the compromising instinct, however estimable it may in certain cases be, is not to be trusted to resolve all ethical arguments in a wise or satisfactory way. Before you contemplate compromise, then, be sure that you have investigated the alternative positions thoroughly. For if one of those positions is perfectly sound as it stands, there is no need to compromise; indeed, it will be wrong to compromise. As always, the point here is to tread carefully, and to subject every stage of your own argument, and of the arguments of others, to the closest scrutiny.

4.7 DEVIL'S ADVOCACY

One way of subjecting an argument to close scrutiny is to "play the devil's advocate"—to adopt a stance deliberately at odds with what you actually believe. Suppose that you have come up with an argument. How can you be sure that it's a good argument? The best way is to pretend to be your own opponent—to come up with the best objections you can to your own position. This way, if you are honest, and if you work hard at being an effective devil's advocate, you will discover your argument's most serious weaknesses. You will then be well placed either to improve your argument, so that it is immune to the very best criticisms that you can think of, or, in the worst-case scenario, to abandon your argument and to think of another (ideally better) one. For an example of devil's advocacy at work, see Chapter Eight, 8.1e.

At times it can be quite difficult to play the devil's advocate well. If, for instance, you feel very strongly about your conclusion then you might be reluctant to examine your arguments too closely. But it is at exactly these times that there is the greatest need for serious devil's advocacy. After all, if your conclusions are important to you then you ought to want to make the arguments that support them as strong as you can. You will only be able to do that if you are prepared to examine your own arguments extremely carefully, and even dispassionately. If you are not prepared to do this—to play the devil's advocate against yourself—then you cannot hope to state your case in a fully persuasive way, no matter how strongly you feel that your case is a good one. Every heavenly argument needs the devil somewhere along the way.

The same goes for other people's arguments. If you want to discover whether other people's arguments are good ones, then it is essential to play the devil's advocate against them. You must probe their arguments closely, discover whether they involve illogical steps, sniff out any hidden contradictions in them, and so on. Only in this way can you be sure that you are behaving sensibly when accepting or rejecting other people's arguments. Only in this way can you hope to learn from other people's arguments.

4.8   RECAP: ON BEING PERSUASIVE

In this section I have tried to give some indication of what methods can be fruitful in making and assessing arguments in ethics. The most important recommendation to emerge from this section is that all such arguments should be rational arguments: They should proceed in a careful, step-by-step fashion, and every step should be backed up by reasons, or at least by a willingness to give reasons. Arguments will often have intuitions as their starting points. Intuition will also play a role in regulating the progress of an argument and in assessing the conclusions of an argument. An argument that is conducted rationally, and that gives due weight to intuition, will tend to be more persuasive than other kinds of argument. But rationality and intuition may not be enough by themselves to make an argument fully persuasive. For that, it will often be necessary to illustrate the argument with carefully chosen examples. Examples can make the progress and the process of an argument clearer and easier to follow; they can also serve to anchor the argument more firmly to the real-world practical problems that the argument is intended to address.

Within the scope of well-illustrated, well-regulated, and rational argument, there are several techniques that can, if used properly, further enhance an argument's power. The acute use of analogy is one such technique. A well-chosen analogy can highlight the vital features of an issue in a more immediate and helpful manner than can be achieved by any other means. Persuasive warnings about the dangers of embarking upon a particular ethical policy can be given by means of slippery-slope arguments (although these should never be used to try to prove or to demonstrate anything). You can set out to achieve a compromise between competing positions—a compromise that will ideally prove convincing to members of all competing factions—through a judicious pursuit of the middle way (although it is essential to make sure that the compromise position is more reasonable than the positions lying on either side of it).

Whatever techniques are adopted for the purposes of a particular argument, though, one technique will always be essential—the technique of devil's advocacy. You should always be prepared to subject your own arguments to the closest criticism and scrutiny. For if, in the final assessment, your own arguments do not have the power to persuade even *you*, then what is the hope that they will persuade anybody else? A successful, well thought-out argument will always have been attacked first, and most vigorously, by the person whose argument it is. An argument that has not undergone sustained assault from its inventor is unlikely to improve anybody's understanding of anything. And that, ultimately, is what the art of argument is supposed to achieve. A well-organized, imaginative, and rational argument ought to engender improved understanding of the issue it addresses. In seeking to produce such arguments, then—in seeking to argue well—we hope to understand better the issues we think are important enough to be worth arguing about at all.

CONCLUDING REMARKS

If you think that issues in bioethics are important, then you will be keen to argue about them rationally and well. I hope that Part One of this book, has gone some way towards making that task a less forbidding one. I hope too that it has emphasized how pressing that task should be. We saw in 1.5 that taking part in philosophical and rational argument about ethics is the best way we have of ensuring that the society we live in embraces the most acceptable values possible. "Philosophy," of course, means "the love of wisdom." By arguing philosophically, then, we attempt to increase the sum total of wisdom. By arguing philosophically about ethics, we attempt to increase the sum total of ethical wisdom. Surely we want our society to be as *wise* in matters of ethics as it can be. An excess of ethical wisdom, after all, sounds like something it would be impossible to have. So let's start arguing—philosophically, rationally, well—but, above all, with a sense of just what is at stake.

PART TWO

The Basic Issues of Bioethics

CHAPTER FIVE

Professional Responsibility and the Rights of Patients

INTRODUCTION

The relationship between the health care professional and the patient is the foundation upon which the whole practice of medicine rests. No matter how advanced our knowledge, or how spectacular our technological or clinical capacities become, the practice of medicine must always begin and end with the professional–patient relationship. If this relationship is not placed on a sound ethical footing, then ethical difficulties will multiply throughout the realm of health care, perhaps with terrible results. There are many dimensions to the professional–patient relationship. For instance, it is clearly best if each party treats the other with courtesy: Good manners never hurt, and habits such as punctuality and reliable timekeeping are of benefit to all concerned. Similarly, matters will run much more smoothly if each party responds to communications and requests from the other as promptly as possible. These are important aids to good relations, as everyone understands (even if not everyone behaves accordingly). Of course, these requirements are not peculiar to relations between health care professionals and patients: Decent, considerate behavior is desirable in any professional context. What is distinctive of the relations between health care professionals and patients is the degree to which the latter are dependent on the former. For most people, being returned to—or maintained in—a reasonable state of health is extremely important, and if anyone is capable of bringing this about then it is the health care professional. This confers upon physicians, therapists, and others an unusual prestige and authority. The means by which this prestige and authority are earned lie in the expertise that these individuals have acquired.

Of course, one expects any professional to be an expert. If your attorney doesn't know more about the law than you do, you need a new attorney. But because our health is so important to us, the particular expertise that the health care professional has is unusually significant to us, unusually worthy of respect. It is in this that the distinctive ethical issues surrounding the relationship between health care professionals and patients are found. Because the health care professional knows so much more than the patient does—this is, after all, the professional's value to the patient—the professional is in a position of relative power over the patient. He or she can use that power wisely or badly, responsibly or rashly, courteously or without consideration for the preferences of the patient. That is why this chapter is called Professional Responsibility and the Rights of Patients. Patients have responsibilities too, of course, and health care professionals have rights. But the professional is the comparatively powerful party to the relationship, and power brings responsibility, while the patient is the comparatively vulnerable party, and the interests of the vulnerable require protection. The issues that will occupy us in this chapter, then, all swing on the ways in which the imbalance of power implicit in the professional–patient relationship should be negotiated. Since that imbalance is brought about by the expertise of the professional, it is not surprising that most of these issues concern the proper and ethical management of information.

5.1   TELLING THE TRUTH

Most of us believe that it is a good thing to tell the truth and a bad thing to lie. If so, then one might suppose that any issues about truth-telling in a medical context would be easily settled: Professionals and patients should tell one another the truth. But we also know that matters are not so simple, in or out of a medical context. What is it to tell the truth? Think of the oath that witnesses swear in court: I swear to tell the truth, the whole truth, and nothing but the truth. This sounds straightforward enough, but in order literally to tell the *whole* truth—about anything at all—a person would have to live forever. This isn't a frivolous point. The whole truth about anything is limitless, and no one could ever tell it all. That means that truth-telling must always be selective. In telling the truth, we concentrate on what we think is relevant, on what we think the person we are telling it to wants or needs to know, on what is interesting. We filter out all sorts of things that we know to be true; we highlight whatever we judge to be to the point. The result of this is that the truth we tell, even if it *is* nothing but the truth, is never the whole truth. This inevitably raises questions about our criteria for filtering things out. With the best will in the world, we may choose to leave out information that later turns out to be crucial; we may, at the price of considerable tedium, leave in too much. Telling the truth isn't simple, then. And deciding how to tell it—in or out of a medical context—always raises ethical issues. Nor is lying simple. When does deliberately withholding information count as lying? Is lying always wrong? Is it wrong to tell a lie in order to spare someone suffering? What about so-called "white" lies—are they harmless? These are general ethical issues. But because of the crucial role played by information in the professional–patient relationship, they are issues that take on a peculiar importance in bioethical contexts.

5.1a   Knowledge and Autonomy

It is best to start at the beginning, with the question: Why is it good to tell the truth? What's so important about imparting accurate information? From the truth-teller's point of view, there may be nothing good, important, or advantageous about being honest. So the answer must refer to the interests of those who are being told the truth. Let's rephrase the question, then: Why does it matter to me that I am told the truth? What value does accurate information have for me? The answer has to do with my autonomy. My autonomy, remember, is my capacity for self-governance—my capacity to choose what actions to perform, to conceive and to pursue goals and ambitions, to form and to follow preferences. If I am to exercise my autonomy effectively, it is important that a good many of my beliefs be true. If I am choosing between courses of action, for example, then it is useful if I know what options are open to me, and what is likely to follow as a result of adopting them. If the information I have is false, my ability to act in accordance with my goals and preferences will be much diminished. The more true information I have, the better I understand my position, and the more able I will be to make sensible judgments about what to do next. The truth, then, or accurate information, is important to me because it allows me to pursue my own interests autonomously. This means that telling the truth is important because it allows others to pursue their interests. Truth-telling, in other words, is one form of the ethical principle of respect for autonomy. That is why it is good to tell the truth.

The relevance of this to the question of truth-telling in a medical context is clear. I noted earlier that the professional–patient relationship is characterized by an imbalance of power. The professional has an advantage over the patient in the sense that he or she knows so much more than the patient does. In a medical context, then, the professional's capacity for autonomous action is naturally greater than the patient's. The professional understands the medical situation in a way that the patient does not; hence the capacity of the professional to take charge of the situation is much greater than the patient's—especially if the patient has little or no information, or has few or muddled beliefs about his or her medical condition. An obvious way, then, to reduce the power imbalance inherent in the professional–patient relationship is to encourage professionals to help patients understand the true nature of their condition, and of the options and prospects before them. If we all have an obligation to respect one another's autonomy, then the autonomy of a patient is no exception; it must be a prime part of the professional's responsibility to give the patient accurate information. This much seems straightforward. Professionals clearly do have some sort of obligation to tell patients the truth. But we have seen that truth-telling must always be selective. So although we can all agree that telling patients "the truth" is a good thing, there is still scope for much disagreement about which bits it is legitimate to leave out. Or, to put it another way, we now know why truth-telling in general is a good thing, but we do not yet know what specific truths we ought to tell. We can perhaps best approach this issue by looking at the nature of dishonesty.

5.1b Dishonesty

I act dishonestly when I deliberately attempt to get someone to believe or to continue believing something that I believe is not true. Such attempts can be made in various ways, so there are many forms of dishonesty. Here are some examples: telling you that my mother is in the garden when I know this is not the case; not contradicting you when you assert that Arkansas is in India and I know that it is not; failing to mention my trip to the bar when you ask me how I have spent my day; pretending I didn't hear you call my name; shrugging when asked a question I know the answer to; putting on a cheerful expression when I'm miserable; setting off in one direction and then doubling back when I'm out of sight; trying to make you flinch by pretending to hit you; forging your signature; not leaving a party the minute I get bored. Everyone can add to this list (the human capacity for dishonesty is truly impressive!), but I've made it long enough to suggest something of the variety of forms in which dishonesty can come. Dishonesty can consist of saying something, staying silent, doing something, or doing nothing at all. Any of the ways we have for communicating with one another—speech, tone of voice, body language, etc.—can be exploited for dishonest purposes. But what all of these cases have in common is intent to mislead. (Notice that this can backfire: If I tell you that Joan of Arc was French, feeling perfectly certain that she was not, I have unwittingly told you the truth. But I was still being dishonest, because I meant to get you to believe something that I believed was false.)

Not every case of dishonesty is unethical. If you ask me how I am, and I say "Pretty good," when as a matter of fact I feel tired, my back hurts, my knee aches, I'm fed up about my pension arrangements, and I've got a rotten day ahead of me, I'm clearly being dishonest. But we've all had that sinking feeling when you ask someone how they're doing—and they actually tell you! Telling people the truth can, at times, be inconsiderate and unbeneficent. There seems to be nothing wrong with this kind of attempt to mislead. Nor is there anything wrong with dishonesty when people have agreed that attempts should be made to mislead them. The audience at a conjuring show, for instance, have implicitly agreed that attempts may be made to make them believe that doves live up people's noses and that someone who has been sawed in half can be abracadabra'd back together again. Poker players consent to their opponents' attempts to mislead them through bluffing, or through the notorious "poker-face." Boxers feint with the left before throwing the right; tennis players disguise their drop-shots. In all of these cases, participants have, as it were, waived their normal objections to being treated dishonestly. Dishonesty under these circumstances does not appear to be ethically problematic.

We saw in Chapter Three that the principle of respect for autonomy lays a general obligation upon us to tell the truth. But now it seems that dishonesty can be fine too. So what's going on? The answer must lie in what makes dishonesty unethical in the cases where it *is* unethical. When is it wrong to be dishonest?

If truth-telling is generally required by the principle of respect for autonomy, then dishonesty must be wrong (when it is wrong) in virtue of violating that principle. In other words, the wrongness of unethical acts of dishonesty must lie in a failure to respect the autonomy of others. It is easy to see how this is so. If it is generally valuable for you to have true beliefs, inasmuch as true beliefs assist you in the autonomous pursuit of your interests, then some false beliefs must be such as to interfere with that pursuit. If I tell you that nothing is wrong when in fact I know that the building you're in is even now filling with poison gas, I am attempting to get you to believe something that I believe to be false, and which it is clearly not in your interests to believe to be true: by getting you to believe that all is well, I am deliberately compromising your autonomy. An act is dishonest, then, if it constitutes an attempt by one person to get a second person to believe what the first person believes to be false. A dishonest act is wrong when it is contrary to the interests of the second person to acquire that belief. This is the sense in which unethical dishonesty violates the principle of respect for autonomy.

This analysis of the wrongness of dishonesty allows us to see why some dishonest acts are not unethical. By pretending to enjoy your party, when actually I'm bored out of my mind, I do not get you to believe anything that will interfere with your legitimate pursuit of whatever goals and ambitions you have: Your autonomy is unaffected. Similarly, I do not interfere with your interests by refraining from telling you how I really feel when you ask me how I am. This explains the concept of a white lie. A white lie is a lie, sure enough, but one believed not to harm the interests of the person to whom it is told. Needless to say, a lot swings on how well-placed the liar is to assess the interests of the person lied to—but more on that in a moment. The case is slightly different when a person has effectively agreed to be misled. It is certainly not in a poker player's interests to be misled by another player's bluff (a lot of money might be at stake), but by consenting to play poker in the first place, each participant waives the right to have this particular interest respected by the other players. That is what it is to play poker. Cases of this kind, however, are not very common outside of recreations and entertainments; there's no need, I think, to add a clause to our analysis about people not having waived their rights to have their interests respected. In a medical context, after all, the interests of the patient must be paramount. So let's stick with the thought that dishonesty is wrong when it encourages people to believe what it is not in their interests to believe.

We are now in a position to see why it is that, even though some acts of dishonesty may not be unethical, there is a general presumption in favor of telling the truth. An autonomous person, after all, is assumed to be the best judge of his or her own interests. Therefore, inasmuch as true beliefs tend to promote autonomy and false beliefs tend to undermine it, the default option must be to tell people the truth. In behaving dishonestly towards someone in what we hope is a harmless way (for instance, by telling him or her what we believe to be a white lie), we presume to judge where that person's interests lie. We are not giving that person the opportunity to judge how (or whether) his or her own pursuit of his or her own best interests might be affected by acquiring a false, as opposed to a true, belief. In this way, given that we can never be omniscient about another person's interests and preferences, we take a gamble with his or her autonomy: and that, on the face of it, is not a respectful thing to do.

Truthfulness, then, must always be our first priority. When we believe that we have grounds for acting dishonestly, the burden of proof lies squarely with us. We must have excellent reasons for supposing that it is not in a person's autonomous interest to acquire a true belief, and that it is not contrary to their interests to acquire a false one. Where the beliefs concerned are trivial, these reasons may be quite easy to come by—as, for instance, in the boring party example, or in cases where I refrain from telling an acquaintance how I really feel. But as the information becomes less trivial, so the reasons for dishonesty become harder to defend. The more it seems likely that a piece of dishonesty connects with the interests of the person being misled, the more likely it is that a dishonest act goes against the principle of respect for autonomy, and the more difficult it will be to justify. The value we place on our health, of course, suggests that information regarding it connects very closely with our interests: this means that professional acts of dishonesty towards patients are, on the face of it, indefensible. It would seem that any attempt by a health care professional to mislead a patient must constitute a violation of that patient's autonomy. Possible exceptions to this claim are discussed in the next three sections.

5.1c Paternalism and Beneficence: Lipkin's Argument: "On Lying to Patients"

A health care professional who wishes to mislead a patient will need some very good reasons for doing so. The principle of respect for autonomy is an important ethical principle, after all, and it will almost certainly be contravened by a professional act of dishonesty. The usual excuse for not respecting someone's autonomy is to appeal to the principle of beneficence. The thought, in such cases, is that it is not always in people's interests to have their autonomy respected: It will accord better with their *real* interests to have their autonomy overridden. In the present context, such a defense depends on the claim that a particular act of dishonesty is not unethical because it is not against a patient's interests to acquire a certain false belief, or to fail to acquire a certain true one. For the reasons given in the last section, the arguments in favor of misleading patients on these paternalist grounds will need to be strong. Mack Lipkin, late professor of medicine at the University of North Carolina School of Medicine at Chapel Hill, puts forth a case for dishonesty.

ON LYING TO PATIENTS
Mack Lipkin

Should a doctor always tell his patients the truth? In recent years there has been an extraordinary increase in public discussion of the ethical problems involved in this question. But little has been heard from physicians themselves. I believe that gaps in understanding the complex interactions between doctors and patients have led many laymen astray in this debate.

It is easy to make an attractive case for always telling patients the truth. But as L. J. Henderson, the great Harvard physiologist-philosopher of decades ago, commented:

> To speak of telling the truth, the whole truth and nothing but the truth to a patient is absurd. Like absurdity in mathematics, it is absurd simply because it is impossible. . . . The notion that the truth, the whole truth, and nothing but the truth can be conveyed to the patient is a good specimen of that class of fallacies called by Whitehead "the fallacy of misplaced concreteness." It results from neglecting factors that cannot be excluded from the concrete situation and that are of an order of magnitude and relevancy that make it imperative to consider them. Of course, another fallacy is also often involved, the belief that diagnosis and prognosis are more certain than they are. But that is another question.

Words, especially medical terms, inevitably carry different implications for different people. When these words are said in the presence of anxiety-laden illness, there is a strong tendency to hear selectively and with emphases not intended by the doctor. Thus, what the doctor means to convey is obscured.

Indeed, thoughtful physicians know that transmittal of accurate information to patients is often impossible. Patients rarely know how the body functions in health and disease, but instead have inaccurate ideas of what is going on; this hampers the attempts to "tell the truth."

Take cancer, for example. Patients seldom know that while some cancers are rapidly fatal, others never amount to much; some have a cure rate of 99 percent, others less than 1 percent; a cancer may grow rapidly for months and then stop growing for years; may remain localized for years or spread all over the body almost from the beginning; some can be arrested for long periods of time, others not. Thus, one patient thinks of cancer as curable, the next thinks it means certain death.

How many patients understand that "heart trouble" may refer to literally hundreds of different abnormalities ranging in severity from the trivial to the instantly fatal? How many know that the term "arthritis" may refer to dozens of different types of joint involvement? "Arthritis" may raise a vision of the appalling disease that made Aunt Eulalee a helpless invalid until her death years later; the next patient remembers Grandpa grumbling about the damned arthritis as he got up from his chair. Unfortunately but understandably, most people's ideas about the implications of medical terms are based on what they have heard about a few cases.

The news of serious illness drives some patients to irrational and destructive behavior; others handle it sensibly. A distinguished philosopher forestalled my telling him about his cancer by saying, "I want to know the truth. The only thing I couldn't take and wouldn't want to know about is cancer." For two years he had watched his mother die slowly of a painful form of cancer. Several of my physician patients have indicated they would not want to know if they had a fatal illness.

Most patients should be told "the truth" to the extent that they can comprehend it. Indeed, most doctors, like most other people, are uncomfortable with lies. Good physicians, aware that some may be badly damaged by being told more than they want or need to know, can usually ascertain the patient's preferences and needs.

Discussions about lying often center about the use of placebos. In medical usage, a "placebo" is a treatment that has no specific physical or chemical action on the condition being treated, but is given to affect symptoms by a psychologic mechanism, rather than a purely physical one. Ethicists believe that placebos necessarily involve a partial or complete deception by the doctor, since the patient is allowed to believe that the treatment has a specific effect. They seem unaware that placebos, far from being inert (except in the rigid pharmacological sense), are among the most powerful agents known to medicine.

Placebos are a form of suggestion, which is a direct or indirect presentation of an idea, followed by an uncritical, i.e., not thought-out, acceptance. Those who have studied suggestion or looked at medical history know its almost unbelievable potency; it is involved to a greater or lesser extent in the treatment of every conscious patient. It can induce or remove almost any kind of feeling or thought. It can strengthen the weak or paralyze the strong; transform sleeping, feeding, or sexual patterns; remove or induce a vast array of symptoms; mimic or abolish the effect of very powerful drugs. It can alter the function of most organs. It can cause illness or a great sense of well-being. It can kill. In fact, doctors often add a measure of suggestion when they prescribe even potent medications for those who also need psychologic support. Like all potent agents, its proper use requires judgment based on experience and skill.

Communication between physician and the apprehensive and often confused patient is delicate and uncertain. Honesty should be evaluated not only in terms of a slavish devotion to language often misinterpreted by the patient, but also in terms of intent. *The crucial question is whether the deception was intended to benefit the patient or the doctor.*

Physicians, like most people, hope to see good results and are disappointed when patients do poorly. Their reputations and their livelihood depend on doing effective work; purely selfish reasons would dictate they do their best for their patients. Most important, all good physicians have a deep sense of responsibility toward those who have entrusted their welfare to them.

As I have explained, it is usually a practical impossibility to tell patients "the whole truth." Moreover, often enough, the ethics of the situation, the true moral responsibility, may demand that the naked facts not be revealed. The now popular complaint that doctors are too authoritarian is misguided more often than not. Some patients who insist on exercising their right to know may be doing themselves a disservice.

Judgment is often difficult and uncertain. Simplistic assertions about telling the truth may not be helpful to patients or physicians in times of trouble.

5.1d   Responding to Lipkin

Lipkin is certainly right to insist that "Simplistic assertions about telling the truth may not be helpful," and he does much to explain the motivation toward paternalist (or "authoritarian") behavior that health care professionals may feel. Few will quarrel with Lipkin's point about placebos (placebos are discussed in section 5.1e). But here I want to concentrate on his claim, *"The crucial question is whether the deception was intended to benefit the patient or the doctor."*

Certainly this is *a* crucial question. But is it the only one? Lipkin seems to assume that well-intentioned dishonesty is always justifiable. A critic of Lipkin, however, may dispute this. For instance, a professional might have quite different priorities from a patient. A professional might believe that the greatest benefit it is possible to bring to a patient is the restoration or preservation of as much physiological function as possible. A patient may well agree that this is a hugely important benefit, so it seems reasonable to suppose that maximal physiological function will be a priority for both patient and physician. But the patient may also have an eye on other interests. For example, it may be important that the envisaged treatment is not disfiguring, mobility-reducing, or unduly protracted (whatever its overall physiological benefits). It may also be important to a patient to be treated with the respect due to an autonomous person who is capable of judging where his or her best interests really lie. In other words, a physician who misleads a patient with beneficent intent may indeed have correctly identified one of the things—maximal physiological function—that the patient values; but there is no reason to think that the physician is in a position to judge that this is what the patient values most.

For example, suppose I am a keyboard player, and imagine that I have an accident that severs the top joint of my index finger. The nature of the injury indicates to my surgeon that an attempt to sew the top of my finger back on will probably fail—perhaps, owing to the likelihood of gangrene, at the cost of the next joint of the finger too. In the surgeon's opinion, then, it will be best to forget about the top joint and simply concentrate on saving the remainder of the finger. Now this may very well accord with one of my interests—that is, my interest to retain maximal physiological function. But the surgeon must not just assume that this is my highest priority. After all, if I am a very committed keyboard player, the loss of two joints of the finger won't be much worse than the loss merely of the top one: Either loss will seriously impair my ability to play. Hence, it may be in my own autonomous interests to have the surgeon at least attempt to restore the whole finger to me—even against best medical opinion, and even at the risk of losing an extra joint. To withhold from me the information that such an attempt might be possible, and that it might succeed, would be to play fast and loose with my interests—even though the deception involved in withholding this information may be motivated by the best of intentions.

Depending on a patient's priorities, then, it may or may not be in his or her autonomous interests to achieve the best available level of physiological function at any price: Some prices, for some patients, may be higher than they are willing to pay. Simply to assume, then, that the physician's own conception of "greatest benefit" must be shared by the patient is to devalue the patient's autonomy. To mislead a patient in accordance with this assumption, therefore, is to fail to meet the conditions required to justify a dishonest act. "Doctor knows best" may well be true in the context of specifically medical questions, but there is no reason to assume that it's true in the context of questions that a patient might care about more. A critic might conclude that Lipkin's defense of paternalist deception pays insufficient attention to the wider interests of patients—especially those interests that are not primarily physiological.

Lipkin makes much of the fact that patients are often unable to understand or to assess the information they are given. But what does this show? Of course one wouldn't expect a person without medical expertise to have the same grasp of complex, technical information that a health care professional would have. But this doesn't mean that it's okay simply to withhold information. It means rather that the information is not being given in an appropriate and helpful way. If experts actually *want* to convey information to a layperson, they will normally be able to find a way to do so. The fact that this may require good communication skills and a certain amount of effort is not a reason for not trying. Indeed, many would argue that qualities such as the ability and the willingness to communicate are an essential part of the expertise that a health care professional ought to have. Or, to put the point another way, the ethical constraints of the situation require more effort from the professional than Lipkin seems to recognize. His own examples about cancer and arthritis actually show how easily an expert like himself can get the relevant information across when he wants to.

Lipkin also suggests that certain pieces of information may distress a patient and cause unnecessary suffering. No doubt this is sometimes true. But a critic might argue that the "unnecessary" nature of the suffering is most likely due to the way in which the information is imparted. Saying to a patient "Not a hope, I'm afraid—going to get real nasty, too" may indeed cause distress. But the tactless and insensitive style of communication must take much of the blame for that. Health care professionals who wish to avoid causing their patients distress need not take refuge in dishonesty; instead, they should work on more humane ways of telling the truth. Even if this still leads to some suffering for the patient, the reasons given earlier in favor of truth-telling remain relevant. One of a patient's interests may indeed be the avoidance of suffering. But one cannot guarantee that this will be the patient's only or highest priority. Therefore, the fact that some information may be distressing even when tactfully imparted does not by itself justify withholding that information.

The principle of respect for autonomy, then, suggests that patients should not be misled or left uninformed. Common sense and experience suggest that the relative ignorance of the patient compared to the health care professional does not pose an impossible obstacle to communication; common sense also suggests that there are ways of passing on painful information that do not cause unnecessary suffering. Thus a critic might decide that the argument for treating patients dishonestly on paternalist grounds has not succeeded.

Lipkin also discusses a quite different kind of case, in which a patient requests that information be withheld. This is clearly distinct from straightforward cases of deception: After all, a patient is now autonomously waiving his or her right to be told the truth. On the face of it, then, it seems that a patient's autonomy is being respected if the health care professional complies with the patient's sincere request and withholds information. Many will agree with Lipkin that nothing untoward is going on in such cases—provided, of course, that the patient's request appears to be seriously meant. A critic might claim against Lipkin that everyone, including patients, ought always to face up to the truth; hence a patient's request to be kept in the dark should be ignored. However, it's hard to know what might be said in defense of such a claim. If I really don't want to know the truth, and if no one's interests but my own are at stake, it is quite unclear why anyone else should feel obliged to enlighten me. Of course there may be exceptions. In other words, while it may not be true that everyone ought always to face up to the truth, it may be true that everyone ought sometimes to face up to the truth. A fairly clear example of such a situation would be when a patient's request not to know the facts conflicts with the legitimate interests of others. For instance, it may be important to relatives that patients put their affairs in order. Much less clear are cases in which there is reason to believe that a patient's ignorance may jeopardize his or her own interests in ways the patient does not suspect. For example, if I ask my physician not to tell me how long he or she believes I have left to live, I may underestimate the time remaining to me and so not bother to attempt to realize one last ambition. Cases such as these require tactful and imaginative decision-making on the part of health care professionals with an eye to a whole range of possibly conflicting interests.

It is impossible to generalize about matters of this kind. Sometimes withholding information is the best course, sometimes not. The overall principle, I think, is still clear. If a patient asks to be kept in the dark, that request ought to be honored unless the legitimate interests of someone else are threatened by the patient's ignorance, or unless the patient's ignorance threatens to compromise the patient's own interests in ways he or she has not foreseen. The guiding consideration, then, remains respect for autonomy —whether it is the patient's autonomy or the autonomy of those affected by the patient's decisions and preferences.

5.1e Placebos

A placebo is something—usually a pill—that the patient believes contains an active ingredient relevant to the condition from which he or she is suffering, when in fact it contains no such ingredient (it might be a piece of chalk or a candy). The patient believes, then, that he or she is receiving treatment (of a pharmaceutical nature) for his or her condition; it is this false belief, rather than the contents of the placebo, that has a therapeutic effect when the placebo works. Placebos are often very successful. Of course their success depends upon misleading the patient—if you know you're being given a placebo, you won't have the relevant false belief, and no therapeutic advantage will be gained. Since placebos are clear instruments of deception, then, it might be suggested that the use of placebos is ethically problematic, or even that it is straightforwardly wrong. Should we go along with either of these suggestions?

The first suggestion does seem sound. Because the use of placebos centers around a deliberate act of deception, such use is clearly not unproblematic. Dishonesty always requires justification of some kind. But perhaps in this case the justification can be provided quite easily. Remember, an act of dishonesty is wrong when it induces someone to believe something false that is not in his or her autonomous interests to believe. On these grounds, would giving someone a placebo be wrong? Normally not, one would think. If I agree to take medication, I do so because I think it might do me some good. This shows that I have an interest in getting better. If my physician judges that this interest is served most effectively by giving me a placebo, he or she is certainly trying to mislead me. However, it would seem that I am not, as a result of this deception, led to a false belief that conflicts with any of my other interests. The deception, in other words, affects only my health (if it affects anything at all), and I have shown, by my willingness to take medication, that my health is indeed of interest to me. For most people this would be a sufficient justification for the use of a placebo.

But suppose that I am a rather volatile person, and that I become indignant when I find out I've been duped. I feel I've been made a fool of. If so, then this suggests that some of my other interests have been affected after all —such as my preference not to be made a fool of. Does this show that it would be wrong to give placebos to vain and touchy people? Many would say not. The interest that is overlooked in such cases is, surely, rather trivial in the grand scheme of things, and it is far from clear that a person is "made a fool of" whenever he or she unknowingly takes a placebo. Indeed, the fact that a person who objects can plausibly be described as "vain and touchy" implies that he or she gets upset about things that ought not to be found upsetting. Thus, it might be said that the interest that is infringed does not deserve to be accorded much weight when the decision to use or not to use a placebo is taken. This is certainly quite plausible. After all, if the fact that someone might become indignant for trivial reasons were allowed to be decisive, almost every worthwhile form of human interaction would be called into question. There's no knowing what a vain and touchy person might take issue with next.

This is a plausible position, then. But there's clearly room for another view. For one thing, the fact that the touchy person's interest in not being made a fool of seems exaggerated and silly to us doesn't show that it isn't more important to that person than the interest represented by his or her health. In other words, a fully autonomous person may place more value upon not being deceived, even in this apparently innocent way, than upon effective treatment. In this case we surely violate his or her autonomous preference when we prescribe a placebo. The fact that a person's preference seems fairly stupid to us doesn't mean that we can just ignore it. Another point can perhaps be brought out by imagining the following: suppose I say to my physician, "Look, prescribe whatever's best for me—but *not* a placebo.

I can't stand being deceived." My physician could surely not justify going right ahead and prescribing me a placebo. But if this would not be justifiable, why would it be any more justifiable to prescribe me one when I haven't objected in advance? After all, we don't normally expect to have to ask someone not to lie to us. On the face of it, this seems a powerful point. But it's probably not as strong as it looks. For exactly the same point might be raised against the normal and desirable courtesy of not telling someone how you really feel when you are asked. Sure, if someone said to me, "Look, when I pass you in the street and ask you how you're doing, *tell me the truth:* I can't stand being deceived," I'd tell the truth (probably at great length!). It is safe to assume, when most people do not insist on being told, the truth about such things, that they won't mind being misled a bit. Very much the same, then, might be said about the placebo case: Only someone hypersensitive would seriously object to being misled about something that bears so little on his or her nontrivial interests.

The use of placebos does appear to be somewhat ethically problematic, then. The dishonesty involved may indeed be justifiable, but it does at least need justifying. My own view is that, in being prescribed a placebo, the false belief that a patient acquires is not such as to pose a serious threat to his or her interests. If this is right, then the use of placebos is usually justifiable. In cases where the placebo is prescribed to someone whom the physician knows to be unusually touchy or sensitive, perhaps a good, hard second thought might be in order. But you must make up your own mind.

5.1f   Recap: Full Disclosure

The analyses of truth-telling and dishonesty in 5.1a and 5.1b suggest that truth-telling is generally desirable because it constitutes one way of respecting the interests of others; dishonesty, when it is wrong, is wrong because it involves insufficient respect for those interests. Thus, issues about truth-telling are always closely bound up with the ethical principle of respect for autonomy. The importance of that principle, together with the value we normally attach to our health, strongly indicates that truth-telling in a medical context should be accorded the highest priority. There may be exceptions to this claim. Examples of possible exceptions include when a person expressly asks not to be told the truth (see 5.1c and 5.1d), or when the prescription of placebos is in question (see 5.1e), but on the whole it does seem that the health care professional has an ethical obligation to be truthful. Because of their superior expertise, health care professionals hold most of the cards in a medical context; it is only by telling the truth to patients that patients can be empowered to safeguard interests that may, to them, be as or more important than the interests to which professionals might be inclined to attach most weight.

We have seen from Mack Lipkin's article how this obligation to tell the truth may sometimes conflict with the health care professional's primary *beneficent* aims. A patient may, in the professional's view, not benefit from being told certain things. But if the discussion of Lipkin's views in 5.1d was fair, then the proper role for beneficence in the context of truth-telling does not rest in withholding information, but rather in imparting information in a sensitive and helpful way. Not even the most fanatical advocate of truth-telling would suggest that a patient should be told the horrible truth the minute he or she regains consciousness after an operation. The management of the truth calls for tact and decency, then, and the health care expert must also be an expert communicator.

However, this just underlines the main point: The beneficent communication of the truth is in the autonomous interests of the patient. Thus the principles of beneficence and respect for autonomy both point in the same direction: Health care professionals should be honest.

5.2   INFORMED CONSENT

It is widely accepted that a patient should give informed consent to any non-trivial medical procedure before it may be performed. Some patients, of course, are in no position to give consent of any kind: It would be absurd to seek consent from an infant or from an unconscious person, for instance (cases such as these are discussed in 5.2d, below). But in cases where the patient is fully autonomous, capable of understanding what is proposed, and of consenting to or refusing it, the practice of seeking informed consent is the norm. In this part of the chapter we will investigate some of the issues raised by that practice, and attempt to discover why it matters and whether there is anything problematic about it.

5.2a   The Importance of Informed Consent

What is the justification for seeking informed consent? Why is it thought to be so important? I was amazed recently when I asked this question in class: Most students answered that the practice of seeking informed consent was designed to safeguard the interests of the *professional*. By obtaining a patient's consent, after all, the professional's legal and insurance liabilities are much reduced, and the blame, if anything goes wrong, is shared by the patient. The more I thought about it, the more I thought the students were, in practice, probably right. The widespread and enthusiastic use of consent forms in hospitals does indeed suggest that the professionals (and the institutions employing them) have a lot at stake. And when one particularly cynical student suggested that this was the only reason for seeking informed consent, I was suddenly half-persuaded. But there are clearly two questions here. There is the question: Why, in practice, has the business of seeking informed consent caught on? To this question, I suspect, the students' answers were more or less on target. But there is also an ethical question: Why, from an ethical point of view, is it a good thing to obtain the patient's consent before a nontrivial medical procedure is performed? To this question I do not believe that an adequate answer can be given in terms of the professional's liabilities. If a professional is held liable for something that goes wrong when informed consent has not been obtained, then that suggests that informed consent must be independently valuable. The question here, then, is: What is independently valuable about the practice of seeking informed consent?

The answer is that the value of informed consent lies in its relation to the patient's interests, not the professional's (however great the incidental benefits to the professional might be). The grounds of that value surely lie in the patient's autonomy. When I give informed consent to a procedure, I am saying "Yes, you may go ahead and do that to me. I give you permission. As a free agent, with the preferences and goals that I have, I judge it to be in my best interests that this procedure be performed." In giving my consent, then, I exercise my autonomy, my capacity to decide for myself, my desire to have what control I can over my own destiny. In seeking that consent before proceeding, the professional respects me as someone who has that capacity and that desire. The practice of seeking informed consent, in other words, is primarily valuable as one form of the ethical principle of respect for autonomy. Professionals who neglect that principle act unethically (which is why, no doubt, they are then liable to greater legal and financial penalties).

If the importance of seeking informed consent lies in the principle of respect for autonomy, then any opposition to that practice must depend upon appeal to some other important principle—most likely beneficence. Yet this would take us straight back to the kind of paternalism discussed in 5.1c and 5.1d. It is true, surely, that the professional who proceeds without consent (from a fully autonomous patient) does so with the best of intentions—let's not question that. But if the considerations offered in 5.1c and 5.1d were fair, it does not follow from this that consent is unnecessary. For it is not the professional's place to decide where the true interests of a fully autonomous patient lie. The patient may have different priorities and preferences from the professional and may have a conception of his or her own best interests that the professional does not share or is not aware of. This means it is very hard to defend the case against seeking informed consent from fully autonomous patients.

For our present purposes, then, I'll assume that it is important to seek informed consent, and that this importance derives from the principle of respect for autonomy. We now need to ask what precisely is involved in the concept of informed consent. In the next section we'll look at the "informed" part; in the section after that we'll look at the "consent" part.

5.2b   Informing the Patient

Comparatively little needs to be said about this topic. The discussion of truth-telling in 5.1 already covered that ground quite well. But a few further details may be helpful. For instance, it is important to determine what information the patient ought to receive. We may assume that the patient knows much less than the health care professional about his or her condition, about the possible options for treatment, about the likely outcomes of the alternatives available, and about the risks. It will be about matters such as these, then, that the patient requires information. Without this information, it is not strictly possible to "consent" to any particular form of treatment. Rather, it will be possible to consent only in a very open-ended way that falls far short of giving permission for a specific type of attempted treatment. The necessary information, then, will be that which allows a patient to understand exactly what, from a range of viable alternatives, is being proposed, and why. Naturally, the kind and amount of information required to achieve this will vary from case to case. It is up to both the professional and the patient to ensure that the relevant information has been imparted and understood. A good tactic, from the professional's point of view, is to put oneself in the patient's position, and ask: If it were me for whom this treatment was being proposed, would I feel able, on the basis of the information that the patient now has, to make an informed judgement? If the answer is no, then the patient needs to be told more.

This last point brings out the necessity for dialogue between professional and patient. It is only by talking that professionals will be able to judge how well and how much patients understand of what they have been told, and it is only by talking that patients will be able to identify and fill the gaps in their understanding of the medical situation. The widespread use of written information on consent forms is a real cause for concern in this context. As a labor-saving measure for professionals the advantages are clear enough, no doubt; but it is just this sort of thing that made my students so cynical about the real purposes of seeking "informed" consent. Many patients, after all, may have difficulty understanding written information: Some, perhaps, have reading problems, and plenty of others may find the terms in the given information unhelpful and obscure. Additionally, the written information must necessarily be selective, and there may well be matters of concern to the patient that are not addressed in it. This very meager approach to communication, then, is surely not by itself sufficient to ensure that patients understand what they need to understand if they are to make an informed judgment about what treatments to permit. There is nothing wrong with written information as a supplement to dialogue, or as a basis for dialogue. But as the sole or main means of imparting information it fails to meet the ethical standards required by the principle of respect for autonomy. Hence it misses the ethical point of seeking informed consent. You do not respect someone's autonomy by giving them whatever information *you* deem necessary, in whatever form *you* think most convenient, unless you also make sure that that information has been understood and that more is not required. This may be time-consuming and tedious, but that doesn't mean that it can be ignored.

5.2c   The Patient's Consent

Signing on the dotted line may be sufficient evidence of consent for legal purposes, but it is not sufficient for ethical purposes. A person may sign on the dotted line for any number of reasons: He or she may do so out of ignorance; through fear of being a nuisance; through being pressured or coerced.

These reasons may make no difference to the legal position, but they make all the difference in the world to the ethical position. The ethical justification for seeking informed consent, after all, is to ensure that the patient's autonomy is respected. Obtaining "consent" from a patient who is ignorant, fearful, or pressured is to pay minimal heed to that requirement. From an ethical point of view, consent is only of any worth if it is freely given by an autonomous person. Only as the expression of a patient's own preferences does his or her permission to proceed with a course of treatment constitute an ethical justification for doing so.

This again highlights the inadequacy of a system centered around the use of consent forms. The mere presence of a signature on a piece of paper, after all, does not show that informed consent, in any ethically worthwhile sense, has been obtained. This is not to say that there aren't good reasons to prefer that the process of gaining consent should end with a signature on a piece of paper, for there are good reasons—most having to do with professional liability. However, the signature itself should be regarded as no more than the final stage of a much more sensitive process. The professional who has a genuine regard for the interests of the patient will wish to ensure that the patient's consent is a true expression of his or her wishes, carefully thought through in the light of the best information available. It is for this reason that many people advocate a cooling-off period before consent to serious, but nonurgent, procedures is finally given (or accepted). In the best scenario, the patient has time for as much reflection and discussion as he or she may need to arrive at a settled, considered decision. Of course, the condition of many patients is not compatible with this—a decision may be needed very quickly. But the ideal represented by the best-case scenario is still a valuable guide to the kinds of consideration that should be given to all patients, wherever that is remotely possible. The less an act of consent consists of merely signing on the dotted line, the more the ethical point of seeking informed consent will have been honored.

5.2d Patients Who Cannot Consent

So far we have only discussed cases in which the patient is fully autonomous and capable, in principle, of giving fully informed consent. We have also concentrated on situations in which seeking consent is a practical possibility. But clearly not all patients or situations are like this. For instance, if I am rushed into the emergency room after a serious accident, and require immediate treatment in order to survive, it would be madness to insist on gaining my consent before doing whatever is necessary. The reason for this is clear enough. It is not that my autonomy has suddenly become less important, or less worthy of respect. It is simply that I cannot *now* be consulted about my preferences. I suggested in 5.1d that one of the reasons for giving patients accurate information is that they themselves are the only people who are in a position to judge where their own best interests lie, even though it may be assumed that patients, like health care professionals, will regard maximal physiological function as (at least) *a* priority. But when, as in the present example, I am in no position to communicate my preferences, and treatment is extremely urgent, it is surely legitimate for emergency personnel to concentrate on the one interest that they can be reasonably sure that I do hold dear, whatever my other, more private, interests may be. That interest is maximal physiological function or, in this case, mere survival. Thus the principle of respect for autonomy is still in operation here—it is just that the extremity of the situation is such as to reduce the principle to its barest bones.

By the same token, and in a similar way, it does not seem that a patient's interests have been violated if certain things that he or she has not consented to are done during the course of a surgical procedure. For example, if I consent to an operation to sort out one problem, and another problem is discovered during surgery, it would appear that my interests will most often be served if the surgeon addresses this new problem on the spot. This will be especially so when the problem or the appropriate procedure are comparatively minor. Few would object, for instance, to the taking of a sample for biopsy when an unexpected growth is discovered during an operation intended to correct something else. Indeed most of us would be rather annoyed if the sample were not taken, and we had to recuperate from the first operation only in order to give informed consent to a second one. But clearly sensitive judgement is called for here: Unanticipated procedures that are both serious and nonurgent ought probably not to be undertaken without informed consent from the patient. The gray areas in such cases may be very wide, and it is not possible to produce hard and fast guidelines to cover every eventuality. But it is possible to say what principle should always be to the fore in the decision-making process: the principle of respect for autonomy. The patient's interests and preferences must come first, and the only justification for not consulting those interests and preferences explicitly (by obtaining informed consent) is that an unanticipated procedure is either so minor as to be compatible with almost any preferences that the patient might have (as in the case of taking a sample), or else so urgent that a failure to act now would compromise the interest in maximal physiological function that all patients, in virtue of having submitted themselves for treatment in the first place, may be presumed to share.

Explicit informed consent may not always be necessary, then, in cases where a patient is in no position, here and now, to give consent to a procedure that is either extremely urgent or extremely minor. But what about cases in which immediate decisions do not have to be made, and yet the patient is still in no position to give fully autonomous consent? Such patients may be comatose, for instance, or elderly and confused, or they may be young children. Many will say that, under such circumstances, the decision about what to do should be left to the health care professionals. They, after all, may be assumed to share with the patient at least one very important goal—that of maximal physiological function—and since the patient is not in a position to express any other, more personal preferences, it may be appropriate to leave it at that, and to go with best medical opinion.

But this route is not always the only option. Indeed, it might be seen as something of a last resort. For in many cases, the patient is fortunate enough to have family members or loved ones whose knowledge of the patient, if he or she is a confused or comatose adult, or whose relation to the patient, if he or she is a child, is such as to allow a different kind of consideration to come to the fore. This is where the idea of consent by proxy arises. Those who may reasonably be assumed to know better and to care more than anyone else where a patient's real interests lie take the patient's place in the decision-making process. Thus it is often family members or loved ones who give informed consent to procedures when the patient is, for whatever reason, unable to do so.

It is important to be clear about what is involved here. First, proxy might come in either of two forms. If I am in a position to consent-by-proxy for you, I may be your delegate or I may be your representative. As your delegate I am entitled only to report and to act upon decisions that are genuinely yours, in other words, decisions that, before you became confused or comatose, you had already made and had asked me to carry through. In this much, then, I could never be a child's delegate. As your representative, by contrast, I do not merely report those decisions you have already reported to me: I actually make the decisions, but on your behalf. Thus, whereas a delegate need only be trusted to be honest, a representative must be trustworthy in judgment too. This is where many of the difficulties associated with consent-by-proxy arise.

For instance, I may simply be mistaken about what you would have decided, had you been able to decide for yourself. Or, more seriously, my judgment may be affected by matters that have very little to do with your interests, as you might conceive them, at all. I may be looking forward to the legacy you have promised me. I may have religious scruples about medical procedures that I have no reason to think that you share. I may, indeed, be simply too upset to think clearly about where your interests lie, or about how they might best be served. It is as a result of these kinds of consideration that no system of consent-by-proxy will ever be perfect; it is in an attempt to modify the impact of such considerations that a role once again emerges for the professional.

Consent-by-proxy must be monitored and overseen: health care professionals (acting, perhaps, in concert with the hospital's ethics committee) are ideally positioned to fulfill that function for the simple reason that they may be safely assumed to have at least one of the patient's interests truly at heart —the interest in maximal physiological function. Thus consent-by-proxy may most appropriately be viewed as a kind of negotiation between the various parties concerned. Health care professionals earn their place at the table in virtue of their undoubted beneficent motives. Loved ones earn their place in virtue of the fact that if anyone is in a position to judge where a patient's overall interests lie, it is surely they. In cases where a patient is not able to give informed consent, then, it does seem that consent-by-proxy, suitably monitored, is the next best option. It is clear that the justification for consent-by-proxy lies in the principle of respect for autonomy. By transferring the authority to give informed consent to a patient's loved ones—that is, by transferring to them the patient's right to make autonomous decisions —and by ensuring as far as possible that such decisions are based on sound judgment, we come as close as we possibly can to leaving that authority where it ideally should be: with the patient. (For discussion of treatment for mentally incompetent patients, see 9.2.)

5.2e   Recap: Getting the Go-Ahead

We have seen that the practice of obtaining informed consent gains its ethical point from the principle of respect for autonomy. By obtaining a patient's consent, the health care professional acknowledges that autonomous agents must be allowed to decide what may and may not be done to them. Indeed, if the practice of seeking such consent were abandoned, it is all too easy to imagine what mayhem would ensue!

But we have also seen that the idea of informed consent is not, for all its evident virtues, a simple one. Patients begin at a disadvantage. They are not normally sufficiently knowledgeable to assess their own medical condition and prospects without expert assistance. The provision of information, therefore, needs to be flexibly and sensitively handled. Also, the notion of "consent" itself is ambiguous: Certain kinds of consent may be legally adequate without being ethically adequate. These considerations suggest that the mere use of consent forms, which patients are expected to read and sign, does not by itself guarantee that the autonomy of patients is being properly respected. Nor, as we have seen, does the principle of respect for autonomy lose its importance when patients are not able to give informed consent for themselves. In cases of emergency, or of unanticipated discoveries during surgery, a patient's autonomy may be respected by assuming that maximal physiological function is going to be at least one of his or her priorities; if no immediate decision needs to be made, still further account can be taken of a patient's autonomy by delegating powers of choice to loved ones.

In every instance, then, the focus of concern must be with the patient's own preferences. Otherwise the practice of seeking informed consent becomes ethically empty, and my students' darkest suspicions about the real purpose of seeking informed consent will be confirmed.

5.3   CONFIDENTIALITY

The idea that what a patient tells a health care professional, or what a professional discovers about a patient, should remain confidential is widely accepted. The reason for this is fairly obvious. A rule utilitarian would put it as follows: Patients may be deterred from telling a professional everything that might be relevant to their case if they fear that what they say will be shared with others; they may also be deterred from consulting a health care professional if they fear that details of their case will be made public. Fear of embarrassment, or of being compromised in some other way may well interfere with a patient's willingness or ability to seek and to receive the best health care possible. Therefore, since it is in patients' interests to receive the best health care possible, the adoption by professionals of a rule to observe confidentiality will tend to promote the greatest happiness for the greatest number of people. Hence information about, or communicated by, patients should be kept confidential.

Most, I think, would accept the broad outlines of this argument, whether or not they are committed to a rule-utilitarian perspective. It is not controversial that people are more willing to seek treatment, and to divulge any information that might be relevant to their case, when they are confident that the details will go no further; nor is it in doubt that such willingness helps health care professionals provide treatment of the highest possible standard. So the case in favor of confidentiality seems compelling. But even so there are problems. For instance, it is not clear exactly what counts as a breach of confidentiality. Nor is it clear that information should always be kept confidential: Sometimes, after all, the interests of people other than the patient may be at stake. In this part of the chapter, then, we will look at some of the problems arising from the widely accepted idea that health care professionals should keep what they know of their patients to themselves.

5.3a Modern Complexities: Siegler's Argument "Confidentiality in Medicine"

In days when the practice of medicine was simpler, so was the concept of confidentiality. The patient usually had a one-to-one relationship with his or her physician, and it was in this context that confidentiality was primarily regarded as important. The patient might occasionally also see a small number of other health care professionals, but in such cases the essential idea remained the same. The patient could be conceived as having a one-to-one relationship with each of these additional professionals, and it was up to each of them to keep information about the patient confidential. Now, however, matters are so much more complicated that, according to Mark Siegler, professor of medicine at the University of Chicago, the very *concept* of confidentiality has become problematic.

CONFIDENTIALITY IN MEDICINE—A DECREPIT CONCEPT
Mark Siegler

Medical confidentiality, as it has traditionally been understood by patients and doctors, no longer exists. This ancient medical principle, which has been included in every physician's oath and code of ethics since Hippocratic times, has become old, worn-out, and useless; it is a decrepit concept. Efforts to preserve it appear doomed to failure and often give rise to more problems than solutions.

Psychiatrists have tacitly acknowledged the impossibility of ensuring the confidentiality of medical records by choosing to establish a separate, more secret record. The following case illustrates how the confidentiality principle is compromised systematically in the course of routine medical care.

A patient of mine with mild chronic obstructive pulmonary disease was transferred from the surgical intensive-care unit to a surgical nursing floor two days after an elective cholecystectomy. On the day of transfer, the patient saw a respiratory therapist writing in his medical chart (the therapist was recording the results of an arterial blood gas analysis) and became concerned about the confidentiality of his hospital records. The patient threatened to leave the hospital prematurely unless I could guarantee that the confidentiality of his hospital record would be respected.

This patient's complaint prompted me to enumerate the number of persons who had both access to his hospital record and a reason to examine it. I was amazed to learn that at least 25 and possibly as many as 100 health professionals and administrative personnel at our university hospital had access to the patient's record and that all of them had a legitimate need, indeed a professional responsibility, to open and use that chart. These persons included 6 attending physicians (the primary physician, the surgeon, the pulmonary consultant, and others); 12 house officers (medical, surgical, intensive-care unit, and "covering" house staff); 20 nursing personnel (on three shifts); 6 respiratory therapists; 3 nutritionists; 2 clinical pharmacists; 15 students (from medicine, nursing, respiratory therapy, and clinical pharmacy); 4 unit secretaries; 4 hospital financial officers; and 4 chart reviewers (utilization review, quality assurance review, tissue review, and insurance auditor). It is of interest that this patient's problem was straightforward, and he therefore did not require many other technical and support services that the modern hospital provides. For example, he did not need multiple consultants and fellows, such specialized procedures as dialysis, or social workers, chaplains, physical therapists, occupational therapists, and the like.

Upon completing my survey I reported to the patient that I estimated that at least 75 health professionals and hospital personnel had access to his medical record. I suggested to the patient that these people were all involved in providing or supporting his health-care services. They were, I assured him, working for him. Despite my reassurances the patient was obviously distressed and retorted, "I always believed that medical confidentiality was a part of a doctor's code of ethics. Perhaps you should tell me just what you people mean by 'confidentiality'!"

TWO ASPECTS OF MEDICAL CONFIDENTIALITY

Confidentiality and Third-Party Interests

Previous discussions of medical confidentiality usually have focused on the tension between a physician's responsibility to keep information divulged by patients secret and a physician's legal and moral duty, on occasion, to reveal such confidences to third parties, such as families, employers, public-health authorities, or police authorities. In all these instances, the central question relates to the stringency of the physician's obligation to maintain patient confidentiality when the health, well-being, and safety of identifiable others or of society in general would be threatened by a failure to reveal information about the patient. The tension in such cases is between the good of the patient and the good of others.

Confidentiality and the Patient's Interest

As the example above illustrates, further challenges to confidentiality arise because the patient's personal interest in maintaining confidentiality comes into conflict with his personal interest in receiving the best possible health care. Modern high-technology health care is available principally in hospitals (often, teaching hospitals), requires many trained and specialized workers (a "health-care team"), and is very costly. The existence of such teams means that information that previously had been held in confidence by an individual physician will now necessarily be disseminated to many members of the team. Furthermore, since health-care teams are expensive and few patients can afford to pay such costs directly, it becomes essential to grant access to the patient's medical record to persons who are responsible for obtaining third-party payment. These persons include chart reviewers, financial officers, insurance auditors, and quality-of-care assessors. Finally, as medicine expands from a narrow, disease-based model to a model that encompasses psychological, social, and economic problems, not only will the size of the health-care team and medical costs increase, but more sensitive information (such as one's personal habits and financial condition) will now be included in the medical record and will no longer be confidential.

The point I wish to establish is that hospital medicine, the rise of health-care teams, the existence of third-party insurance programs, and the expanding limits of medicine all appear to be responses to the wishes of people for better and more comprehensive medical care. But each of these developments necessarily modifies our traditional understanding of medical confidentiality.

THE ROLE OF CONFIDENTIALITY IN MEDICINE

Confidentiality serves a dual purpose in medicine. In the first place, it acknowledges respect for the patient's sense of individuality and privacy. The patient's most personal physical and psychological secrets are kept confidential in order to decrease a sense of shame and vulnerability. Secondly, confidentiality is important in improving the patient's health care—a basic goal of medicine. The promise of confidentiality permits people to trust (i.e., have confidence) that information revealed to a physician in the course of a medical encounter will not be disseminated further. In this way patients are encouraged to communicate honestly and forthrightly with their doctors. This bond of trust between patient and doctor is vitally important both in the diagnostic process (which relies on an accurate history) and subsequently in the treatment phase, which often depends as much on the patient's trust in the physician as it does on medications and surgery. These two important functions of confidentiality are as important now as they were in the past. They will not be supplanted entirely either by improvements in medical technology or by recent changes in relations between some patients and doctors toward a rights-based, consumerist model.

POSSIBLE SOLUTIONS TO THE CONFIDENTIALITY PROBLEM

First of all, in all nonbureaucratic, noninstitutional medical encounters—that is, in the millions of doctor-patient encounters that take place in physicians' offices, where more privacy can be preserved—meticulous care should be taken to guarantee that patients' medical and personal information will be kept confidential.

Secondly, in such settings as hospitals or large-scale group practices, where many persons have opportunities to examine the medical record, we should aim to provide access only to those who have "a need to know." This could be accomplished through such administrative changes as dividing the entire record into several sections—for example, a medical and financial section—and permitting only health professionals access to the medical information.

The approach favored by many psychiatrists—that of keeping a psychiatric record separate from the general medical record—is an understandable strategy but one that is not entirely satisfactory and that should not be generalized. The keeping of separate psychiatric records implies that psychiatry and medicine are different undertakings and thus drives deeper the wedge between them and between physical and psychological illness. Furthermore, it is often vitally important for internists or surgeons to know that a patient is being seen by a psychiatrist or is taking a particular medication. When separate records are kept, this information may not be available. Finally, if generalized, the practice of keeping a separate psychiatric record could lead to the unacceptable consequence of having a separate record for each type of medical problem.

Patients should be informed about what is meant by "medical confidentiality." We should establish the distinction between information about the patient that generally will be kept confidential regardless of the interest of third parties and information that will be exchanged among members of the health-care team in order to provide care for the patient. Patients should be made aware of the large number of persons in the modern hospital who require access to the medical record in order to serve the patient's medical and financial interests.

Finally, at some point most patients should have an opportunity to review their medical record and to make informed choices about whether their entire record is to be available to everyone or whether certain portions of the record are privileged and should be accessible only to their principal physician or to others designated explicitly by the patient. This approach would rely on traditional informed-consent procedural standards and might permit the patient to balance the personal value of medical confidentiality against the personal value of high-technology, team health care. There is no reason that the same procedure should not be used with psychiatric records instead of the arbitrary system now employed, in which everything related to psychiatry is kept secret.

AFTERTHOUGHT: CONFIDENTIALITY AND INDISCRETION

There is one additional aspect of confidentiality that is rarely included in discussions of the subject. I am referring here to the wanton, often inadvertent, but avoidable exchanges of confidential information that occur frequently in hospital rooms, elevators, cafeterias, doctors' offices, and at cocktail parties. Of course, as more people have access to medical information about the patient the potential for this irresponsible abuse of confidentiality increases geometrically.

Such mundane breaches of confidentiality are probably of greater concern to most patients than the broader issue of whether their medical records may be entered into a computerized data bank or whether a respiratory therapist is reviewing the results of an arterial blood gas determination. Somehow, privacy is violated and a sense of shame is heightened when intimate secrets are revealed to people one knows or is close to—friends, neighbors, acquaintances, or hospital roommates—rather than when they are disclosed to an anonymous bureaucrat sitting at a computer terminal in a distant city or to a health professional who is acting in an official capacity.

I suspect that the principles of medical confidentiality, particularly those reflected in most medical codes of ethics, were designed principally to prevent just this sort of embarrassing personal indiscretion rather than to maintain (for social, political, or economic reasons) the absolute secrecy of doctor-patient communications. In this regard, it is worth noting that Percival's Code of Medical Ethics (1803) includes the following admonition: "Patients should be interrogated concerning their complaint in a tone of voice which cannot be overheard."[1] We in the medical profession frequently neglect these simple courtesies.

CONCLUSION

The principle of medical confidentiality described in medical codes of ethics and still believed in by patients no longer exists. In this respect, it is a decrepit concept. Rather than perpetuate the myth of confidentiality and invest energy vainly to preserve it, the public and the profession would be better served if they devoted their attention to determining which aspects of the original principle of confidentiality are worth retaining. Efforts could then be directed to salvaging those.[2]

Notes

1. Leake, C. D., ed., *Percival's medical ethics.* Baltimore, Williams & Wilkins, 1927.
2. Supported by a grant (OSS-8018097) from the National Science Foundation and by the National Endowment for the Humanities. The views expressed are those of the author and do not necessarily reflect those of the National Science Foundation or the National Endowment for the Humanities.

5.3b   Responding to Siegler

Siegler's case seems very strong. He is surely right that the complexity of contemporary health care has made confidentiality a less clear-cut notion than it used to be, and his claim that patients should be informed more clearly what "confidentiality" actually means in practice is persuasive. No one, I imagine, would wish seriously to quarrel with these parts of Siegler's argument.

But a critic might wonder whether Siegler really succeeds in showing, even on his own terms, that the concept of confidentially is "decrepit." A "decrepit" concept, according to him, is one that is "old, worn-out, and useless." If so, then like other old, worn-out, and useless concepts—such as alchemy, or the earth-centered picture of the universe—one would have expected it to be a concept that had lost its point, that was no longer capable of doing any work. And yet Siegler, having announced that the concept is decrepit, continues to speak of confidentiality—and of how the real point of it can be rescued—throughout the rest of his article. That strongly suggests that the concept of confidentiality is not, even in his sense, decrepit. Indeed, what he seems to be saying is that the point of confidentiality needs to be reinterpreted in the light of modern medical developments—not that it has been eliminated by them. In this much, then, saying that confidentiality is a decrepit concept is a bit like saying that "travel" is a decrepit concept because we no longer get about by horse and cart.

So what does Siegler think that the real (and rescuable) point of the concept of confidentiality is? Two things: first, "it acknowledges respect for the patient's sense of individuality and privacy"; second, it "is important in improving the patient's health care." In other words, the primary point of confidentiality is the protection and promotion of the patient's interests by the careful handling of potentially sensitive information. No one, I think, would disagree with this analysis of the point of confidentiality (indeed, it is very close to the analysis offered at the beginning of this part of the present chapter). Nor, I imagine, would anyone doubt that the existence of health care teams and complex administrative arrangements in modern hospitals calls for more sophisticated ways of maintaining confidentiality, and so of retaining the trust of patients. Given this, a critic might well wonder what the fuss is about. If we all agree what the point of confidentiality is, and if we all agree that this point can only be realized in the contemporary context if we revise our procedures for managing information, then what are we actually disagreeing about? It would seem that we are disagreeing about nothing.

To a great extent, this criticism of Siegler's position looks fair. I think that once the reader gets past his rather exaggerated (and, indeed, inaccurate) claim that the concept of confidentiality is decrepit, what remains is not so much an argument about the *possibility* of confidentiality, as it is a series of helpful suggestions about how the point of confidentiality can best be served. These suggestions will strike many as extremely sensible, especially when Siegler recommends that "patients should have an opportunity to review their medical record and to make informed choices about whether their entire record is to be available to everyone" or not. For my own part, I am very glad that Siegler does not also suggest protecting confidentiality by using numbers instead of names on patients' records. It is far harder to pick up errors when you are keying in a string of digits than it is when you key in a name. Indeed, when this procedure is used in order to ensure that students' exam papers are marked fairly, it goes wrong all the time! Students get the wrong grades, or no grades at all, and the inconvenience it causes can be immense: Just think how much more serious the consequences of a mistake might be for a patient.

In the end, then, it seems that Siegler's argument is primarily useful for highlighting the sheer complexity of the modern health care setting, and hence of the measures that may be required to maintain confidentiality within it. But nothing he says suggests that the goal of protecting and promoting patients' interests by the sensitive handling of personal information should be abandoned. Indeed, the thrust of Siegler's argument is to underline just how important that goal is. Far from being decrepit, then, the concept of confidentiality emerges from Siegler's article alive and kicking.

5.3c Gossip

Siegler briefly discusses, and disapproves of, what he calls "indiscretions"—"wanton, often inadvertent, but avoidable exchanges of confidential information that occur frequently in hospital rooms, elevators, cafeterias, doctors' offices, and at cocktail parties." These indiscretions, he suggests, can be particularly upsetting to patients. No doubt this is so. But the mere fact that someone is upset about something does not by itself show that that thing is wrong. We need to remind ourselves what the point of confidentiality is: The sensitive handling of personal information is intended to promote and to protect the patient's interests. Given this, it is clear that not every piece of gossip goes against the point of confidentiality. A piece of gossip will be wrong only if it is such as to undermine or to make vulnerable the patient's interests; an indiscretion that has neither of these effects is not objectionable.

So what kinds of gossip are ruled out? It is best, I think, to err here on the side of caution. As Siegler reminds us, indiscretions are avoidable; therefore indiscretions should be avoided whenever there is a doubt as to whether a patient's interests will be damaged. It has been a major aim of this chapter to note how varied a patient's interests may be, and to emphasize how difficult it is for someone else—such as a health care professional—to second-guess them. This suggests that any piece of gossip that may (for all one knows) affect a patient's interests should be avoided. But does that mean that *all* gossip is wrong? I don't think so. A patient's interests can only conceivably be affected if the information conveyed in a piece of gossip can be tied to him or her specifically. If the patient's identity is concealed or altered, then, it is hard to see how his or her interests could possibly be affected one way or the other. If I have seen several hundred patients over the last couple of months, and mention to you that I saw a patient the other week who . . . —you'd never be able to guess which patient I meant, and that surely means that nothing at all, from the patient's point of view, has changed. If this is right, then the patient's interests have neither been undermined nor made more vulnerable by my (careful) act of indiscretion. Of course one does need to be very careful. Merely omitting or changing a patient's name may not be enough: If I describe a patient as being six-and-a-half-feet tall, with a limp and a bright red beard, his identity may not be hard to establish. Similarly, if I am a doctor with a country practice then I probably ought to refrain from gossip: All my patients are likely to know one another, and the smallest inadvertent clue as to the identity of the person I'm talking about may be enough to give the game away. Nor is it wise to gossip about people who suffer from unusual or conspicuous conditions. In short, gossip, if it is to be justifiable at all, must be undertaken with the greatest possible care to conceal the identity of the person referred to; if that means that something of the point of the story will be lost, perhaps it is best not to tell the story at all.

I'm sure that many people will think that I'm being a bit soft on gossip here, and perhaps they're right. There's clearly a strong case to be made against any kind of gossip at all. I've assumed, arguably too optimistically, that being careful to conceal the identity of the person gossiped about will be sufficient to safeguard his or her interests. Yet all sorts of unexpected connections might be made, and there can never be a guarantee that a patient's anonymity will be preserved. So it is certainly plausible to claim that health care professionals should put the interests of their patients first, and refrain from gossiping about them under any circumstances whatever. But I have two reasons for being reluctant to go along with this claim. First, it seems almost to demand the impossible. There is nothing more natural than to chat about one's work with family and friends, and to forbid that altogether would, I suspect, place an intolerable, and probably unnecessary, burden on every health care worker. Second, I cannot see how, having disallowed all gossip on the grounds that it might somehow indirectly harm a patient's interests, one can then go on to defend the publication of case histories, or the discussion of cases at conferences or in classes. Admittedly this kind of communication is not strictly gossip, but it does appear to be problematic for exactly the same reasons. If any and every piece of gossip is held to violate the duty of confidentiality then the same must be true of the scholarly exchange and dissemination of clinical information. I'm sure that most people would agree that the scholarly exchange and dissemination of information about patients (whose anonymity is protected as far as possible) is a valuable activity to be encouraged rather than prohibited. That makes me think that one ought not to take *too* hard a line against the more everyday dissemination of information that we call "gossip."

5.3d   Harm to Others

One of the thornier problems surrounding the concept of confidentiality is whether the duty to promote and to protect patients' interests by keeping their confidences is absolutely binding. Are there exceptions? Are there cases when it is proper to break a confidence even though this will damage a patient's interests? The only imaginable justification for doing so is that the interests of others or of society at large will be harmed if the patient's confidence is kept. No one, I think, has ever advocated the breaking of confidence on any other grounds.

The rule utilitarian, with whom we began this part of the present chapter, will be keen to argue that confidences should be kept even in cases where the interests of others are at risk. The reason for this is that the rule utilitarian aims to promote the best overall results for everyone, and if the rule "Keep a patient's confidences" is conducive to this end, then it is simply too bad if, in the odd case, an innocent person's interests are jeopardized. It won't happen very often, so when it does, it's simply the price we have to pay for the good results that come from encouraging patients to trust professionals.

How convincing is this "all or nothing" picture of confidentiality? If one is a paid-up rule utilitarian, it is no doubt very convincing indeed; a deontologist, too, might hold that the duty to keep confidences is absolute and admits no exceptions. Even if one is neither of these things, there is still an appealing simplicity about the position. It is at this point, though, that people normally produce lurid and largely imaginary examples to try to force the rule utilitarian (or deontologist) to retreat. We are asked to imagine a patient who confides to her doctor that she plans to poison the city's water supply; or a patient who mentions that he plans to go home and murder his family. Should the doctor still maintain that confidentiality comes first? In cases such as these, health care professionals appear to be faced with a straightforward conflict of obligations: They can either elect to keep the patient's confidence come what may, or they can elect to safeguard the public interest, and break the confidence.

I have to confess that I have never found examples like these particularly agonizing. It seems perfectly obvious what the proper answer to the dilemma is. The health care professional (having failed, let us assume, to persuade the patient to abandon his or her plans) should report the situation to the police department right away. Where the risk to others is so extreme, the obligation to keep confidences is surely trivial in comparison. The committed deontologist may simply deny this, in which case we will have to agree to differ. The rule utilitarian will doubtless remind me that the overall point of confidentiality (the protection of the patient's interests) can only be realized if patients trust professionals *never* to divulge their secrets. But this seems highly questionable to me. After all, if I hear that my doctor has called the police about a potential mass-murderer, is this really going to deter me from discussing with him or her my own rather less dramatic problems? Am I really going to be seized by a sudden fear that news of my incontinence, for example, will be broadcast far and wide? I can't for the life of me see why I should fear this. Nothing in the doctor's conduct suggests that he or she is now any less likely to keep ordinary confidences than before. At worst, I (and others) might be deterred from revealing murderous plans to health care professionals. But it does seem rather unlikely that this would result in any general loss of trust in health care professionals, or in any consequent decline in the nation's health.

My own feeling, then, is that the general argument in favor of confidentiality is not significantly weakened by admitting that confidences should sometimes be broken. In other words, I side with those who hold that a patient's confidences should be kept except when a serious threat to the interests of others is posed by doing so. Exactly how serious that threat needs to be is debatable, and I doubt that any hard and fast rule can be given. But a rule of thumb, at any rate, might be: A threat counts as "serious" when the danger to the interests of others (posed by keeping a patient's confidence) is graver than the danger to the interests of the patient (posed by breaking the confidence). The patient, after all, considered as a person, is not intrinsically more important than anyone else; so there seems to be no reason to regard his or her interests as absolutely paramount.

How does this view operate in situations that are a little more plausible than those we have discussed so far? Consider, for instance, the case of a person with HIV. The infectiousness of the disease means that the person who suffers from it does pose a potential threat to the interests of others. However, he or she only poses an actual threat to others if he or she behaves in certain ways. The mere fact, then, that a person is HIV-positive, and wishes this to remain confidential, provides no grounds at all for breaking his or her confidence. If, on the other hand, the person declares an intention to behave irresponsibly—for instance, by having unprotected sex with as many people as possible—and he or she cannot be talked out of it, the situation changes. Now the person poses an actual threat to the interests of others. Should the confidence be broken? Many, no doubt, would say that it should: The danger posed to others is rather significant, while the danger to the patient—loss of liberty, perhaps—is comparatively slight. My own answer, however, is that the confidence should not be broken. The danger to others *is* significant, I agree, but those others can hardly be characterized as innocent bystanders. It takes two to have unprotected sex, and anyone who consents to engage in it is responsible for the risk that he or she now runs of acquiring an immune deficiency syndrome. I think it would be wrong to damage the interests of one person (the patient) in order to prevent other people from damaging their own interests (by, for instance, consenting to unprotected sex with someone whose sexual history they do not know). In cases such as this I do not believe that confidentiality should be overridden.

Nor, if the foregoing is at all plausible, is it easy to see why anyone might think it acceptable to tell employers when their employees are HIV-positive (and wish this to remain confidential). It is true that an employer's interests may be affected by the medical condition of an employee. But unless employees have agreed that every aspect of their medical condition, including aspects of it that have no bearing on their capacity to do the jobs for which they are paid, should be revealed to their employers, it would seem employers have no right to insist on disclosure. To argue otherwise is to construe the employee is a sort of possession of the employer—and no one, surely, wants to do that. So again, in cases like this I doubt that confidentiality should be overridden.

I think it *should* be overridden, however, if there are people placed in danger who have made no contribution to the risks they now run. For instance, if the patient is determined to engage in nonconsenting unprotected sex, it seems to me that his or her behavior now warrants a breaking of confidence. An example of this might be the person who is HIV-positive, but who refuses to admit this to his or her regular sexual partner. Another, nonsexual, example might be a surgeon who insists on performing invasive procedures on patients without telling them that he or she is HIV-positive. In neither case has the endangered person or persons contributed to the threat now posed to them; in both cases that threat is far greater than any threat posed to the interests of the person who is HIV-positive; I would suggest in both cases the confidence of that person might justifiably be broken.

Not everyone, I know, will agree with these conclusions. Some will believe that a patient's confidence should be broken sooner, others that it should never be broken at all. But I do hope that the discussion in this section has at least illustrated the kinds of issue that arise when the interest of a patient in having a confidence kept collides with the interests of others. I hope, too, that some of the considerations offered above will help you work out your own position on these issues.

5.3e   Recap: Keeping Secrets

The duty of the health care professional to keep a patient's confidences is one of the oldest ideas in medical ethics, dating back at least as far as the Ancient Greeks. The point of that duty, as Mark Siegler argues in 5.3a, is to protect and to promote the interests of patients. Patients simply receive better care if they feel free to consult health care professionals and to discuss their cases with them in the confidence that anything they say, or anything the health care professional discovers about them, will go no further. Nowadays that is not so easy. The contemporary health care setting is so complex that inevitably information about a patient is accessible to a large number of people. But this does not mean that the point of confidentiality cannot be maintained. So long as personal information is sensitively handled, so that the interests of patients are neither undermined nor jeopardized, confidentiality remains alive and well. For some, this implies that it can never be justifiable for a health care professional to gossip about a patient. I do not accept this, however: my own view is that gossip is fine so long as the anonymity of the patient is preserved (see 5.3c). Nor do I accept the claim that the duty of the health care professional to respect a patient's confidences is absolutely binding, with no exceptions. It seems to me that that duty should be overridden in cases where a serious threat is posed to the interests of other people if the confidence were kept (see 5.3d).

The issues raised by the concept of confidentiality are many and complex, then, and there is room for some widely divergent views. But given the importance of the relationship between the patient and the professional, and the place of trust within that relationship, it is hardly surprising that that should be so. The only thing that is certain—here, as throughout the present chapter—is that without a principled approach to the management of information in the health care setting, the aims of neither professional nor patient will be met, and all of us will be much the poorer for it.

Study Questions

1. When does a "white" lie become ethically problematic? Is there anything especially problematic about white lies told by health care professionals to patients?
2. Is a surgeon who has never successfully carried out a particular surgical procedure under an obligation to inform patients of this fact before attempting to carry out that procedure on them?
3. How might the principle of beneficence come into conflict with the principle of respect for autonomy in the context of consent-by-proxy? Can such conflicts be resolved?
4. Ought a physician to reveal medical details to a patient's insurance company against the patient's wishes? Does it matter what sort of medical details are at issue?

Related Cases in Crigger, *Cases in Bioethics,* Third Edition

Most relevant to the material in "Telling the Truth" (see 5.1) are cases 3 and 5; case 3 raises the thorny question of how honest a patient's relatives should be with health care professionals; case 5 asks us to consider whether professionals should tell the truth about one another.

"Informed Consent" (see 5.2) is represented more extensively. Case 9 concerns a patient who could consent to a procedure but doesn't; case 32 deals with the difficulties of obtaining consent from members of different cultures. There are also a number of cases about proxy consent, of which cases 6, 7, 8, 17, and 42 are perhaps the most interesting. Cases 7 and 42 concern decision-making about children; cases 6 and 17 deal with decisions made on behalf of confused or retarded patients; and case 8 invites reflection on the role of the family in consenting to treatments for patients with "locked-in syndrome." The discussion following case 8 is particularly useful.

The cases most relevant to "Confidentiality" (see 5.3) are 10, 11, and 12. Cases 10 and 11 deal with circumstances in which patients pose a direct threat to others, while case 12 involves patients who refuse to reveal the facts about their condition to family members. Case 55 brings an interesting twist to confidentiality issues, with a patient having to deal with the consequences of his employer discovering confidential information through health insurance records. The discussion following case 12 is especially helpful.

CHAPTER SIX

Reproductive Rights and Abortion

INTRODUCTION

Few things affect us more intimately than reproduction. We are all a product of it, and many, if not most of us, have either already had children or are likely in due course to do so. The family, often thought to be the basic unit of human social life, depends upon reproduction. The future, which is the focus of all of our hopes and aspirations and ambitions, will be peopled with our children, so some of our most fundamental drives are directed toward the propagation and the nurturing of generations yet to come. Given the centrality of reproduction to human life, then, it is not surprising that reproductive issues should also be of deep ethical concern to us. Few of the decisions we make are more significant than the decision to reproduce or not to reproduce; few ethical issues are capable of arousing stronger passions than those surrounding such decisions. We have all read of shootings in abortion clinics and of violent demonstrations outside them; indeed we have all witnessed directly how worked up people can get over these things. Nowhere, then, does our ethical reasoning need to be more careful or less emotive than in the context of reproductive issues. I suggested in Chapter One that one of the strongest recommendations for engaging in reasoned ethical argument was that the alternatives were uglier and worse: The abortion debate, in particular, bears this suggestion out. I also commented that specifically religious considerations were unlikely to be tremendously helpful in ethical argument, since such considerations tend to appeal only to those who already share a specific religious position: Again, the debate over reproductive matters shows how true this can be.

Indeed, I think it would not be an exaggeration to say that the standard of public debate about reproductive issues in recent years has been astonishingly low. I can think of no other context in which so much has been said, done, and written to so little effect. Our task in this chapter, then, will be to try to think much more clearly about these issues—without getting unduly worked up and without appealing to explicitly religious assumptions or preaching to the converted. Only thus, I am sure, have we any hope of reaching a civilized consensus of reasoned opinion. The first part of this chapter is devoted to issues surrounding the desire to reproduce. The second part is devoted to issues surrounding the desire not to.

6.1 REPRODUCTIVE RIGHTS

The phrase "reproductive rights" covers quite a wide spectrum of concerns, ranging from a person's right not to enter into reproductive partnerships against his or her will, to the right of a woman to act as a surrogate mother if she so wishes. A large number of the issues raised in this context do not require detailed discussion. Once one understands the ethical principle of respect for autonomy, for example, and grasps its importance, one will be in no doubt that it is wrong to force someone into a reproductive partnership against his or her will. In this part of the chapter, then, we will not concentrate on issues such as that. Rather, we will turn our attention to matters that are of general importance in bioethics, but that have specific relevance in the context of reproduction—especially now that it has become technologically possible to alter the mechanics of reproduction almost beyond recognition. Just as artificial insemination, *in vitro* fertilization, and surrogate motherhood have contributed to an opening up of our reproductive options, so have they complicated those options, and raised challenging, and sometimes unexpected, ethical questions.

6.1a Naturalness

The "natural" way of reproducing is for a male and a female to have sexual intercourse, and for pregnancy and ultimately birth to ensue. Advances in our knowledge and skills, however, have made it possible to diverge from this pattern in some surprising ways.

In artificial insemination (AI), a woman's egg is fertilized by a man's sperm, within her body, but not by means of sexual intercourse. In *in vitro* fertilization (IVF), the fertilization of the egg takes place outside the woman's body, with the resultant embryo or embryos then being transferred into her uterus (this is the process that results in so-called "test-tube" babies). In surrogate motherhood, where one woman bears a child for another (the latter often known as the "social mother"), either AI or IVF may be used: If AI is used, the surrogate mother's own egg is fertilized by the sperm of the social mother's partner; if IVF is used, the egg of the social mother is fertilized by the sperm of her partner, and the resultant embryo or embryos are transferred to the uterus of the surrogate mother. Surrogacy by AI is sometimes called "full" surrogacy; surrogacy by IVF, "partial" surrogacy. What all of these techniques have in common is a striking departure from normal reproductive patterns; it is sometimes claimed that this departure from the "natural" way of things is, in itself, ethically dubious.

The phrase "playing God" often crops up in such contexts—the idea being that we humans are somehow getting above ourselves and are tinkering around with matters better left to a higher authority. To describe a practice as "unnatural," in this sense, draws a line between those things that are perfectly "natural" and proper for human beings to do, and those that are not. But the concept of "naturalness" here is deeply problematic. How is one to decide what is and what is not natural? After all, we are natural tool-users: Surely, then, it is natural for us to use whatever tools we have. We are natural manipulators of our world: How can it be unnatural to do what comes naturally to us? The point here is that the way the word "natural" is sometimes used suggests that nothing as sophisticated as a human being could possibly count as natural; in which case, the objection that a particular human practice is "unnatural" loses its point. But clearly something a little different is normally meant when people say that a process such as IVF is "unnatural," and therefore problematic. The idea seems to be that we are employing our natural tool-using aptitudes to inappropriate, "unnatural" ends. The "unnatural" end in this case is the interference with the very processes of life itself. Behind this idea, there clearly lurks another: that the processes of life are somehow self-justifying, that they are so natural, perhaps, that no interference with them can be justified. Only if one accepts a thought such as this can one take seriously the claim that IVF, for example, is wrong because it's "unnatural."

But there is no reason at all to accept the thought in question. After all, if one did accept it, one would have to reject the whole of medicine as an illegitimate interference with life's own self-justifying processes. Cure diseases? No: Diseases are part of the natural process of life. Ease the pain of cancer? No: It's natural that cancer should be painful. Rebuild a shattered limb? No: Shattered limbs should stay naturally in bits. Almost no one believes that medicine as a whole is, simply, wrong. Therefore almost no one has any business believing that the natural processes of life itself should lie beyond the scope of human intervention. There is nothing necessarily good about what is natural. If this is right, then labeling a particular practice "unnatural" says nothing about it that is of the slightest ethical significance. Modern reproductive techniques are certainly innovative and challenging. But they are not, in an interesting sense, "unnatural"; nor, to the extent that they are "unnatural" in any sense at all, are they thereby morally wrong. We'll encounter more misplaced talk of "unnaturalness" when we discuss euthanasia in Chapter Seven.

6.1b Significant Relationships

In Chapter 5 we looked at aspects of one significant relationship—that between the patient and the health care professional. For most people, however, if they are reasonably fortunate, that relationships will not be the most important one in their lives. Our relationships with our friends, families, and loved ones ought all, ideally, to occupy us more than our dealings with health care professionals do. But the two kinds of relationship can sometimes come together—especially when reproductive matters are at stake. A mother's antenatal and postnatal care are both good examples of this. In this section, I want to focus on the relationship of motherhood, especially in the context of the new reproductive technologies we have been discussing.

I doubt that reflection on artificial insemination or *in vitro* fertilization will by itself tell us anything of great ethical significance about motherhood.

If a woman is having trouble conceiving, after all, then medically assisted fertilization seems a perfectly legitimate option. If it is successful, there seems to be no reason at all to think that she now stands in a significantly different relationship to her child than she would have done had no medical assistance been required. The situation is clouded only when one comes to consider the case of *surrogacy,* where we again run into a potential conflict between the ethical and the "natural." The potential conflict here does not arise from the fact that surrogacy itself is somehow "unnatural": rather, it arises from the fact that the relationship of motherhood is defined by both natural and ethical factors that tend to come apart when one woman bears a child for another. In the normal course of things, a woman who bears a child is quite unproblematically the child's mother. She is genetically—or "naturally"—its mother, and she has also borne it during pregnancy and given birth to it. But in cases of surrogacy the pattern is disrupted. We have all read of the legal wrangles that surrogate motherhood can cause, and these are the direct result of the disruption of that pattern. The concept of motherhood has become harder to understand than it used to be.

In a standard dispute about surrogacy, the "social" mother's right to the child is contested by the surrogate mother, who now wishes to keep the child she has borne. There are some complex legal issues at stake, but these, since we are interested in ethics, need not concern us. The question we need to ask is: When a surrogate mother and a would-be social mother both lay claim to a child, who is more appropriately to be seen as the child's "real" mother? Who has the better ethical claim to the child? This is an extraordinarily difficult question to answer. The first thing to notice is that this is not like an ordinary dispute about ownership. The child is not a possession in the way that a car or an armchair might be; rather, the child is a person to whom both women wish to stand in the ethically significant relation of motherhood. Thus the matter is not to be settled by presenting or contesting the equivalent of a bill-of-sale. Because the child is not properly to be seen as a possession, evidence of this kind of transaction is ethically irrelevant (however important it might be from a legal point of view). By the same token, then, for the would-be social mother to argue that the child is hers merely because it is her egg that has been fertilized by IVF and transferred into the surrogate mother's uterus would be beside the point. Even if she were right in saying that the *egg* was in some meaningful sense her possession (which is doubtful—see 10.2a for discussion of the "possession" of body parts), the child certainly wouldn't be her possession as a result: The child is nobody's possession. So this issue cannot be usefully discussed as if it were merely a matter of property rights.

What, then, is it to stand in the ethically significant relation of motherhood to someone? There seem to be at least two possible answers to this question. The first is that motherhood is a genetic matter: The (female) genetic progenitor of a child is its mother. The second is that motherhood is a behavioral matter: Whoever has behaved toward the child in the ways appropriate to motherhood is its mother. In cases where a surrogate mother's pregnancy has been induced by AI, it seems that the surrogate mother has a better claim to be regarded as the child's "real" mother on both counts: She is both its (female) genetic progenitor and also the one who has behaved toward the child, by bearing it and birthing it, in the obvious motherly ways. Where the pregnancy is by IVF, on the other hand, and the fertilized egg is that of the would-be social mother, it appears that both women might have a claim to be regarded as the child's "real" mother: the would-be social mother is the child's (female) genetic progenitor, while the surrogate mother has borne the child and seen it to term. Which of these claims, then, is the stronger?

Consider the following case. Suppose that your genetic mother has never behaved toward you in a motherly way; she has spent your entire childhood elsewhere, doing other things, while you have been lovingly brought up by your aunt. You might say later that your mother was never "really" a mother to you, and that your aunt was "like" a mother to you. Which of the two— your genetic mother or your aunt—stands in the more ethically significant relationship to you? It seems clear to me that your aunt does. Your aunt, who has been "like" a mother to you, has behaved in all of the ways that make motherhood *valuable*. She has nurtured, cared for, and looked after you, while your genetic mother has done none of these things. This suggests that it may be more ethically significant to be "like" a mother to a child than to be merely its (female) genetic progenitor. In most cases, of course, genetic mothers are also behaviorally "like" mothers, so no particular difficulty arises. But when one person fails to meet both conditions for motherhood, it does seem that the stronger claim to be regarded as a child's "real" mother, in an ethically significant sense, lies with the person who has been "like" a mother, rather than with the person who is, as a matter of fact, the child's genetic progenitor. If this is right, then the surrogate mother, who is the only one even to have had the chance to behave toward the child in a motherly way, by bearing it and birthing it, has a better claim to be regarded as the child's "real" mother than the would-be social mother does—no matter whose egg was fertilized at the initiation of pregnancy. If the surrogate mother chooses to give the child up to the would-be social mother, then it appears that she is not so much giving the child to its "real" mother, as giving the social mother the chance to behave in such ways as to build up an ethically significant relationship. The surrogate mother is, in other words, giving the social mother the opportunity to become the child's "real" mother. On this view, the "natural" (in other words, the genetic) fact of motherhood is ethically quite unimportant. To be "like" a mother is what counts.

The foregoing argument suggests that in cases where a surrogate mother and a would-be social mother contest custody of a child, the child ought to go to the surrogate mother. No doubt the law might, in some instances, take a different view. There is no doubt, either, that many will think I've been too dismissive of the claims of the would-be social mother. But unless someone can show that children should properly be seen as possessions (who are the appropriate objects of sale or contractual transfer), or, in the case of surrogacy by IVF, can show that the genetic facts ought to outweigh the behavioral facts, I do not see how surrogacy arrangements can be regarded as ethically binding.

But there is another question we need to ask. Surrogacy arrangements may not be ethically binding. But should they be entered into at all? In other words, whatever the outcome, ought either party to agree to this sort of arrangement in the first place? Many, no doubt, will answer: Why not? Both women are adults: both know what they are doing; whose business is it but theirs what they decide to do? No one else's interests are affected by their decision. At first sight this answer looks fairly uncontroversial. Both women are autonomous people, after all, and we ought surely to respect the decisions they make for themselves. But it may not be as simple as that. Some raise objections that surrogacy arrangements *commodify* a woman's body—in this case the surrogate's body. The thought here is that by offering or accepting payment for the use of the surrogate's uterus, both women adopt or express an inappropriate attitude towards the surrogate's body—an attitude, moreover, that is ethically suspect.

There are two closely related ways in which the inadequacy of the attitude here might be captured. The first, which is explored in more detail in 10.2a, is that both parties to the arrangement view the surrogate's uterus as a possession of hers, which she can hire out as she pleases; whereas, in truth, it is a part of her, not a part of her property. The second way is this: By hiring herself out—not for her labor, but for her very *self*—the surrogate treats herself as a marketable object rather than as a human being. She is, in effect, regarding herself as a slave (slave owners don't merely own labor, remember: they own people). By agreeing to pay her for bearing a child, the would-be social mother is regarding the surrogate in exactly the same light—as a commodity, not as a person. It doesn't, surely, take a great deal of ethical imagination to see that this is not a healthy way for people to think of themselves or of each other. If we object to the idea of a person's being seen as an object for sale, then, as a commodity with a market value, it seems that we ought to object to surrogacy arrangements on the same grounds. (In a culture like ours, however, with all its management-speak, and its talk of "human resources," it is possible that the wrongness of such attitudes is becoming increasingly invisible. Horrible thought!) If this line of thought is persuasive, it would appear that surrogacy is ethically suspect whether or not it actually leads to a dispute about who the "real" mother is.

6.1c   Recap: The Ethics of New Technologies

The discussion of this part of the present chapter suggests that reproductive technologies such as AI and IVF do not in themselves pose an ethical problem. The fact that they mark a departure from the "natural" patterns of reproduction appears to be no more significant than the fact that chemotherapy marks a departure from the natural patterns of cancer-suffering. But applied in certain ways, it does seem that these technologies can raise ethical difficulties. Specifically, it seems that surrogate motherhood—whether by AI or IVF—is deeply problematic. Both parties to a surrogacy agreement appear to have misconstrued the kind of relationship that the ethically significant relationship of motherhood is. Even if all goes according to plan—the surrogate mother surrenders the child to the would-be social mother, so that there is no dispute—we have seen reason to doubt that this is, from an ethical point of view, anything other than a happy accident. If what I've argued about commodification is correct, moreover, it seems that there is a deep moral mistake anyway in the attempt to get someone else to bear a child for you, and an identical mistake in undertaking to do so. Children aren't products like cars; a woman's uterus isn't like a rentable parking space. We sell ourselves short as human beings if we pretend otherwise.

6.2   ABORTION

I noted in the Introduction how heated and unilluminating the debate about abortion has tended to be—especially in the United States, where this issue appears to raise passions to a higher temperature than elsewhere. Why this should be so is unclear, although it is sometimes suggested that the role played by religion in American life has something to do with it. Whatever the reason, though, it is certain that no issue in contemporary bioethics stands in greater need of calm and reasoned enquiry than this one. The best start we can make with it is to cut through some of the deeply unhelpful rhetoric and labelling that has sprung up around the debate, like weeds threatening to choke sensible discussion to death. To this end, I will refer to those who defend abortion (sometimes or always) as "defenders of abortion," and to those who oppose it (sometimes or always) as "opponents of abortion." This is infinitely more constructive than the usual approach of referring to the various camps as, respectively, "pro-choice" and "pro-life." To call a defender of abortion pro-choice suggests that anyone who opposes abortion is somehow anti-choice—which, given the fact that pregnancy is voluntarily avoidable in most cases, is grossly misleading. Similarly, to refer to an opponent of abortion as pro-life conveys the impression that anyone who defends abortion is somehow anti-life or pro-death—which, again, is just pointless name-calling. An important part of the debate centers on the question of what life *is*, and of which life should be given preference when two lives come into conflict. So to begin with the neutral and far more accurate terminology of "defenders and opponents of abortion" is at once to remove one obstacle to serious debate. As this part of the chapter progresses we will have to be careful not to allow other obstacles to take its place. In what follows, I will use the single term "fetus" to refer not only to the (literal) fetus, but also to the embryo and to the conceptus: I am not aware that anything much hangs on these distinctions, and it will make the discussion far less cumbersome if we ignore them.

6.2a   The Sanctity of Life

The "sanctity of life" is one of the many phrases that tend, in the context of the abortion debate, to shed more darkness than light. "Sanctity" is the quality of being sacred or inviolable; so when one speaks of the sanctity of life, one is claiming that life itself is sacred, under no circumstances to be violated. On the face of it, this sounds reasonable enough, and people often seem to assume that once the sanctity of life is mentioned the abortion debate is as good as over. If a fetus is alive, they say, and life is sacred, then one ought not kill fetuses. But the impression of reason does tend to weaken when one pauses to think. After all, if taken literally, the phrase "the sanctity of life" might just as well be used to show that eating things—whether animals or vegetables—is morally wrong. A cabbage is alive, surely; so if life is sacred one oughtn't to eat cabbages (or anything else). Nor, of course, ought one to wash: Just think of the bacteria that die as a result. Pretty clearly these applications of the claim that life is sacred lead to nonsense. If it really were wrong to eat or to wash, it is doubtful that we'd live long enough even to *have* an abortion debate.

Proponents of the sanctity of life argument will of course claim that I have misrepresented their view. They don't just mean life in general. They mean human life, or potentially conscious life, or at any rate some narrower kind of life than that of mere cabbages or bacteria. Certainly this narrowing of the focus does succeed in disarming the objection of a moment ago. Yet it hardly moves the argument forward much. For one thing, the exclusion of other kinds of life looks a bit arbitrary: What's so special about humanity, or about potential consciousness? But even more tellingly, does anyone really believe that human life or potentially conscious life is always and everywhere inviolable? I know that I don't believe this. Like most people, I believe that it may sometimes be justifiable to kill another human being in self-defense, for example, or in defense of loved ones when their lives are unjustly threatened. Perhaps it is also justifiable to kill enemy soldiers in war, or armed hostage-takers during a siege. We may disagree about the details, but I am sure that most of us will be able to envisage a situation in which we would argue that it was justifiable to take a human life. If this is so, then it follows that most of us do not believe that human life is always and everywhere absolutely sacred. No doubt there are a small number of people who do actually believe this; perhaps for them an argument against abortion based on the sanctity of life will be compelling. But for the vast majority of people, life—although valuable and important—is not absolutely inviolable. This means that no appeal to the sanctity of life can, by itself, hope to be generally persuasive. (Exactly the same is true if, instead of the sanctity of life, one chooses to speak of the right to life.)

The real problem with the sanctity of life (or right to life) argument is that it is too vague and broad. If I am right in saying that killing may sometimes be justifiable, what we need—and what the sanctity of life argument is incapable of delivering—is an account of when and under what circumstances it may be justifiable to take a human life. We need to know when killing is not wrong, in other words, and when the sanctity of life (however important life may be) becomes less important than some other value. An attractive answer to this question might go as follows: Killing is justifiable when the person to be killed has forfeited his or her right to remain alive. Let's call this the forfeiture position on killing. Some would defend capital punishment on these grounds, for instance. It is comparatively easy to see how a person might be held to have forfeited his or her right to remain alive by, for example, wrongly threatening the life of someone else, or by joining an army that is fighting in an unjust cause. But two things need to be noted about this way of answering the question. First, all reference to the sanctity of life has become superfluous. On the forfeiture account, if it is wrong to kill someone then that is not because life is sacred, it is because the person has *not* forfeited his or her right to remain alive. Second, it provides a much better argument against abortion than the sanctity of life argument does. On the forfeiture account, after all, a human life may justifiably be taken only if the human being in question has somehow forfeited his or her right to remain alive. But a person must surely act or behave in certain ways in order to forfeit that right; and if one thing is clear it is that fetuses are in no position to act or behave in any ways at all, let alone in such ways as to forfeit the right to remain alive. It appears to follow from this that, insofar as fetuses are living humans who are wholly incapable of acting or behaving—and so of forfeiting anything—it must be unjustifiable to kill them. Hence abortion is wrong. Perhaps this is the argument that those who speak of the sanctity of life were really looking for.

A strength of the forfeiture argument is that it captures something of what is meant when people say that abortion is wrong because it involves the taking of *innocent* life. Fetuses are "innocent" on this account because, being incapable of doing anything at all, they are certainly incapable of doing whatever it is that "guilty" people are held to have done when they forfeit their right to remain alive. But the defender of abortion is unlikely to be persuaded. There are too many unexamined assumptions in the argument, some of which at least may prove to be unsustainable. For instance, the defender of abortion may claim that killing is sometimes justifiable even when a person has not acted or behaved in such a way as to forfeit his or her right to remain alive. If this is correct, then abortion may be justifiable despite the fact that fetuses are incapable of doing anything at all. An argument to this effect is presented by Judith Thomson in 6.2h, below. Alternatively, the defender of abortion may doubt that fetuses are really alive in the sense required by the forfeiture position; he or she may also doubt that fetuses are, properly speaking, human beings, and so question that fetuses have the same sort of value that you or I, for instance, have. In light of these objections, it is clearly essential to ask ourselves how fetuses are properly to be seen. What kind of things are fetuses? What value do they have?

6.2b   The Status of the Fetus

The first question to clear up is whether fetuses are to be regarded as "alive" or not, and that can be done very quickly. Obviously they are alive. Organisms and parts of organisms come in two forms—the living and the dead. Inasmuch, then, as a fetus that is capable in principle of being brought to term and born plainly isn't dead, it is alive. This hardly sounds worth saying, but it is. Far too often in the abortion debate one finds people sneaking in funny definitions of perfectly ordinary words in order to disguise controversial conclusions as harmless bits of common sense. For instance, some argue that a fetus is not really to be seen as "alive" because it is dependent for everything upon its mother (presumably newborns aren't alive either, on this definition!). Grant this weird definition of being "alive," and you'll quickly find yourself concluding that there shouldn't be a debate about abortion at all: For if the fetus isn't "alive" in the first place, it can't be killed; and if nothing is killed in an abortion, there isn't a problem to debate. Yet clearly this is just playing with words. We will, if we are wise, stick to words in their ordinary meanings. Fetuses are alive, and abortions kill them.

But merely saying this settles nothing. The fact that fetuses are alive doesn't show anything about the morality of killing them. Bacteria are alive, after all, and we kill them all the time with our soaps and bleaches and scourers. Vegetables are alive too, and they make good salads. So we need to ask whether individual fetuses have lives that are valuable in a way that individual bacterial and vegetable lives are not. (I say "individual" here because everyone agrees that a world without *any* bacterial or vegetable life would very quickly be without human life either.) Do fetuses, in other words, have lives that are deserving of ethical concern?

The opponent of abortion would answer that they do have such lives, since the lives they have are human lives, and surely if any lives are worthy of ethical concern then human lives are. This, on the face of it, looks good — and it is certainly what a proponent of the forfeiture argument against abortion needs to claim (see previous section). But it is hardly decisive. A defender of abortion might respond as follows: Let's admit that the fetus is alive; let's admit that the life it has is in some sense human. But exactly the same could be said of my appendix. That's alive, isn't it? After all, it's not dead. And given its role as a part of my body, the life it has is surely in some sense human (it doesn't have a vegetable life, or a fox life, does it?). Yet my appendix is not deserving of any particular ethical concern: Indeed it may perfectly justifiably be removed from my body whenever I choose. Thus, if appendectomies justifiably cause the death of appendixes, why can we not say on the same grounds that abortions justifiably cause the death of fetuses? The mere fact that fetuses are alive and in some sense human doesn't appear to weigh very much.

The argument here is over the kind of human life that the fetus has. The defender of abortion claims, plausibly, that fetuses have a life which is no more than genetically human—and that this puts them in the same boat as, for instance, appendixes. Whereas the opponent of abortion wishes to make a stronger claim. He or she holds that fetuses have human lives in exactly the same sense that you and I have human lives, and hence that killing a fetus would be wrong in a way that killing an appendix would not be. A lot seems to hang on which of these two positions is the more plausible. So how might one set about trying to choose between them? We'll investigate the defender of abortion's position first.

6.2c Personhood

The position taken by the defender of abortion—that while fetuses are genetically human, they are not human in the same (ethically significant) sense that you and I are human—is certainly quite persuasive. After all, the differences between you or me and a fetus are pretty striking: You can't have a chat with a fetus, or quarrel with its views, or take an interest in its projects, or hope it'll keep its promises, or laugh at its jokes, or envy its talents. In fact, you cannot interact with it in *any* of the ways in which human beings characteristically interact with one another; nor, as we have already noted, is the fetus capable of engaging in any characteristically human behavior. At first sight, then, the gulf between full-fledged human beings and fetuses seems so wide as to be unbridgeable. Indeed, some defenders of abortion have even said that dogs are more like full-fledged human beings than fetuses are. But to note the wide divergence between fetuses and ourselves is not by itself to make a lot of headway with the question whether it is justifiable to kill them. Just because an entity is not precisely like us doesn't prove that it is of no ethical importance. But noting the differences between ourselves and fetuses does have one useful consequence for the defender of abortion: It tends to spread the burden of proof around a bit. The very real differences between fetuses and ourselves show that the opponent of abortion needs an argument to demonstrate that those differences are ethically irrelevant.

In my view, the defender of abortion can hope to gain nothing more than this from the fact that fetuses and adults are different. But that is not how many defenders of abortion see the matter. I mentioned in the previous section how the abortion debate has tended to abound with idiosyncratic and self-serving definitions of perfectly ordinary words. Such definitions, I suggested, have usually been intended to disguise controversial conclusions as common sense—usually by a more or less subtle shifting of the goalposts. Nothing illustrates this better than the recent fashion of redefining the word "person" so that it means something quite different from what we ordinarily take it to mean. For most of us, the words "person" and "human being," "personhood" and "humanity," mean exactly the same: We use them interchangeably. We may not be able to agree whether a fetus *counts* as a person, but we do not normally take ourselves to be saying different things when we say "a fetus is a person," for example, and when we say "a fetus is a human being." In the abortion debate, however, the meanings of person and human being are often artificially divided, with the word person receiving a special, technical definition.

The idea goes like this. Adult humans are worthy of ethical consideration if anything is. Therefore adult humans must have certain *properties* in virtue of which this is true. The task is to identify which properties those are. If we can do that, then we will have discovered what properties an entity needs to have if it is to count as worthy of ethical consideration. We then define any entity that has those properties as a person. "Personhood," then, becomes a specifically ethical concept, intended to indicate the possession of whatever properties are held to account for the ethical significance of adult human beings. The conclusion that this redefinition of the word person is intended to generate is the comparatively reasonable-sounding one that killing persons is wrong; the flip-side, of course, being that it may not be wrong to kill "nonpersons" (where some nonpersons may actually be human).

I say that this conclusion is comparatively reasonable-*sounding* because, in the ordinary meaning of the word person, most of us would agree (other things being equal) that killing a person was wrong. But the redefinition of the crucial word makes all the difference. For now we are not being asked to accept the commonsensical position that killing people is wrong, but the far more controversial position that killing entities that possess whatever properties the philosopher in question has decided to highlight is wrong. And that is a very different matter, which becomes clear when you look at the kinds of property that these philosophers tend to highlight. Details may vary, but a standard definition of personhood normally includes properties such as autonomy, higher brain function, and a range of relatively sophisticated capacities that only a very complex and developed organism could possibly be expected to possess. It then comes as no surprise to find that, on the terms of the redefinition, fetuses do not count as persons, they count only as human beings; hence, since personhood is supposed to constitute the essence of ethical value, the conclusion follows that killing fetuses is not wrong.

But this, surely, is a cheat. If you want to make personhood into a special ethical concept, then you can define it how you like. For example, I might define person as "whatever has two legs and no feathers" (these are certainly properties enjoyed by most human adults); then go on to claim that persons and persons alone have ethical value. But this would be purely arbitrary. I have given you no reason to suppose that my definition of person captures anything of any ethical significance at all (bald ostriches would count as persons on this definition). Nor have those philosophers who redefine person in their special ways provided any such reason. Indeed, the search for special properties that give people the value they have seems mistaken from the start. I don't value you *for* your autonomy or *for* your higher brain function. I value you for being you, for being a person (whatever that involves). Thus, to insist that people's value derives from their possession of a set of independently specifiable properties is to simplify the moral picture beyond recognition, and is, in the end, to beg more questions than it is to answer. So it is that personhood theorists almost always end up by choosing their technical definition of "person" simply in order to get the conclusion they want. If the conclusion they want is that it is justifiable to kill fetuses, it is hardly surprising if they end up defining "person" in terms that no fetus could match.

The argument over abortion is debased by tactics such as these. Their purpose is not so much to promote a reasoned approach to the problem, as to define the problem away. Perhaps this would matter less were it not for a couple of effects that talk of personhood has had. One effect has been to mislead some nonphilosophers into thinking that the concept of personhood, and the alleged distinction between being a person and being a human being, is somehow the result of deep and valuable philosophical research into ethics—which it is not. It is a merely arbitrary invention. The other effect has been in the way that philosophers themselves have been misled. The favored redefinition of personhood, with its emphasis on properties like autonomy and higher neurological function, has the slightly inconvenient effect of ruling out, not merely fetuses, but also infants and certain mentally handicapped people. Now you'd have thought that this fact would have tipped the philosophers off that they were on the wrong tack. But no! So successfully have they talked themselves into taking the concept of "personhood" seriously, that some are now prepared to argue that infanticide may be morally acceptable on exactly the same grounds as (according to them) abortion is morally acceptable. This, surely, is madness. If your ethical theory leads you to conclude that it's fine, or even that it might be fine, to kill children and handicapped people, you need a new ethical theory.

6.2d   Potential Personhood

It is not only defenders of abortion who are prepared to take the redefined concept of personhood seriously, however. Opponents of abortion have been seduced by it too. Their argument goes like this: Let's agree that persons are ethically valuable (let's agree, in other words, that properties like autonomy and higher mental functioning are ethically essential); but let's add the claim that whatever is *potentially* a person also has ethical value. If this second claim is accepted, then abortion becomes morally wrong because fetuses, even if they are not persons now, surely will become persons if they are not aborted. Their potential personhood, in other words, puts them on a par ethically with actual persons.

This argument need not detain us long. First, as I've already indicated, there is no reason to take the redefined concept of personhood seriously as a contribution to ethical thought; so there is no good reason to get embroiled in this particular version of the argument. But second, even if one agrees to go along with talk of persons and personhood, the argument seems badly confused about the notion of potential. The idea is meant to be that if fetuses are potential persons, and if persons must not be killed, then fetuses must not be killed either. But the conclusion does not follow. If I am, for instance, a potential lottery-winner, and if lottery-winners have the right to receive their prizes, it certainly does not follow that I have the right to receive a prize. To be a potential lottery-winner is not to be an actual lottery-winner, and it is only actual winners who get prizes. Similarly, then, the fact that a fetus is a potential person doesn't magically entitle it to the consideration due to *actual* persons. The argument fails on every count.

I hope that I have said enough in this section and the previous one to persuade you that talk of persons and potential persons is unlikely to make a helpful contribution to the debate about abortion. For the rest of this chapter, then (and indeed for the rest of this book), I will use the word person in its ordinary, nontechnical sense—in a sense that is interchangeable with that of human being. We turn now to a far more impressive argument against abortion.

6.2e Opposing Abortion: Marquis's Argument: "Why Abortion Is Immoral"

You might have thought in the previous section that the idea of a fetus's potential was dismissed rather quickly. After all, there does seem to be something important about the thought that most fetuses, if they are not aborted, will be born and grow up into adult human beings. This fact seems to set fetuses apart rather strikingly from appendixes, for instance (to which they were compared in 6.2b, above). So is there any way of making sense of the intuition that a fetus's potential to be born and to grow up is an ethically significant fact about it, without relying on the bad argument discussed in 6.2d? According to Donald Marquis, professor of philosophy at the University of Kansas, there is.

WHY ABORTION IS IMMORAL
Donald Marquis

The view that abortion is, with rare exceptions, seriously immoral has received little support in the recent philosophical literature. No doubt most philosophers affiliated with secular institutions of higher education believe that the anti-abortion position is either a symptom of irrational religious dogma or a conclusion generated by seriously confused philosophical argument. The purpose of this essay is to undermine this general belief. This essay sets out an argument that purports to show, as well as any argument in ethics can show, that abortion is, except possibly in rare cases, seriously immoral, that it is in the same moral category as killing an innocent adult human being.

. . . In order to develop such an account, we can start from the following unproblematic assumption concerning our own case: it is wrong to kill *us*. Why is it wrong? Some answers can be easily eliminated. It might be said that what makes killing us wrong is that a killing brutalizes the one who kills. But the brutalization consists of being inured to the performance of an act that is hideously immoral; hence, the brutalization does not explain the immorality. It might be said that what makes killing us wrong is the great loss others would experience due to our absence. Although such hubris is understandable, such an explanation does not account for the wrongness of killing hermits, or those whose lives are relatively independent and whose friends find it easy to make new friends.

A more obvious answer is better. What primarily makes killing wrong is neither its effect on the murderer nor its effect on the victim's friends and relatives, but its effect on the victim. The loss of one's life is one of the greatest losses one can suffer. The loss of one's life deprives one of all the experiences, activities, projects, and enjoyments that would otherwise have constituted one's future.

Therefore, killing someone is wrong, primarily because the killing inflicts (one of) the greatest possible losses on the victim. To describe this as the loss of life can be misleading, however. The change in my biological state does not by itself make killing me wrong. The effect of the loss of my biological life is the loss to me of all those activities, projects, experiences, and enjoyments which would otherwise have constituted my future personal life. These activities, projects, experiences, and enjoyments are either valuable for their own sakes or are means to something else that is valuable for its own sake. Some parts of my future are not valued by me now, but will come to be valued by me as I grow older and as my values and capacities change. When I am killed, I am deprived both of what I now value which would have been part of my future personal life, but also what I would come to value. Therefore, when I die, I am deprived of all of the value of my future. Inflicting this loss on me is ultimately what makes killing me wrong. This being the case, it would seem that what makes killing *any* adult human being prima facie seriously wrong is the loss of his or her future.[1] . . .

The claim that what makes killing wrong is the loss of the victim's future is directly supported by two considerations. In the first place, this theory explains why we regard killing as one of the worst of crimes. Killing is especially wrong, because it deprives the victim of more than perhaps any other crime. In the second place, people with AIDS or cancer who know they are dying believe, of course, that dying is a very bad thing for them. They believe that the loss of a future to them that they would otherwise have experienced is what makes their premature death a very bad thing for them. A better theory of the wrongness of killing would require a different natural property associated with killing which better fits with the attitudes of the dying. What could it be?

The view that what makes killing wrong is the loss to the victim of the value of the victim's future gains additional support when some of its implications are examined. In the first place, it is incompatible with the view that it is wrong to kill only beings who are biologically human. It is possible that there exists a different species from another planet whose members have a future like ours. Since having a future like that is what makes killing someone wrong, this theory entails that it would be wrong to kill members of such a species. Hence, this theory is opposed to the claim that only life that is biologically human has great moral worth, a claim which many anti-abortionists have seemed to adopt. This opposition, which this theory has in common with personhood theories, seems to be a merit of the theory.

In the second place, the claim that the loss of one's future is the wrong-making feature of one's being killed entails the possibility that the futures of some actual nonhuman mammals on our own planet are sufficiently like ours that it is seriously wrong to kill them also. Whether some animals do have the same right to life as human beings depends on adding to the account of the wrongness of killing some additional account of just what it is about my future or the futures of other adult human beings which makes it wrong to kill us. No such additional account will be offered in this essay. Undoubtedly, the provision of such an account would be a very difficult matter. Undoubtedly, any such account would be quite controversial. Hence, it surely should not reflect badly on this sketch of an elementary theory of the wrongness of killing that it is indeterminate with respect to some very difficult issues regarding animal rights.

In the third place, the claim that the loss of one's future is the wrong-making feature of one's being killed does not entail, as sanctity of human life theories do, that active euthanasia is wrong. Persons who are severely and incurably ill, who face a future of pain and despair, and who wish to die will not have suffered a loss if they are killed. It is, strictly speaking, the value of a human's future which makes killing wrong in this theory. This being so, killing does not necessarily wrong some persons who are sick and dying. . . .

In the fourth place, the account of the wrongness of killing defended in this essay does straightforwardly entail that it is prima facie seriously wrong to kill children and infants, for we do presume that they have futures of value. Since we do believe that it is wrong to kill defenseless little babies, it is important that a theory of the wrongness of killing easily account for this. Personhood theories of the wrongness of killing, on the other hand, cannot straightforwardly account for the wrongness of killing infants and young children.[2] Hence, such theories must add special ad hoc accounts of the wrongness of killing the young. The plausibility of such ad hoc theories seems to be a function of how desperately one wants such theories to work. The claim that the primary wrong-making feature of a killing is the loss to the victim of the value of its future accounts for the wrongness of killing young children and infants directly; it makes the wrongness of such acts as obvious as we actually think it is. This is a further merit of this theory. Accordingly, it seems that this value of a future-like-ours theory of the wrongness of killing shares strengths of both sanctity-of-life and personhood accounts while avoiding weaknesses of both. In addition, it meshes with a central intuition concerning what makes killing wrong.

The claim that the primary wrong-making feature of a killing is the loss to the victim of the value of its future has obvious consequences for the ethics of abortion. The future of a standard fetus includes a set of experiences, projects, activities, and such which are identical with the futures of adult human beings and are identical with the futures of young children. Since the reason that is sufficient to explain why it is wrong to kill human beings after the time of birth is a reason that also applies to fetuses, it follows that abortion is prima facie seriously morally wrong.

This argument does not rely on the invalid inference that, since it is wrong to kill persons, it is wrong to kill potential persons also. The category that is morally central to this analysis is the category of having a valuable future like ours; it is not the category of personhood. The argument to the conclusion that abortion is prima facie seriously morally wrong proceeded independently of the notion of person or potential person or any equivalent. Someone may wish to start with this analysis in terms of the value of a human future, conclude that abortion is, except perhaps in rare circumstances, seriously morally wrong, infer that fetuses have the right to life, and then call fetuses "persons" as a result of their having the right to life. Clearly, in this case, the category of person is being used to state the *conclusion* of the analysis rather than to generate the *argument* of the analysis.

. . . Of course, this value of a future-like-ours argument, if sound, shows only that abortion is prima facie wrong, not that it is wrong in any and all circumstances. Since the loss of the future to a standard fetus, if killed, is, however, at least as great a loss as the loss of the future to a standard adult human being who is killed, abortion, like ordinary killing, could be justified only by the most compelling reasons. The loss of one's life is almost the greatest misfortune that can happen to one. Presumably abortion could be justified in some circumstances, only if the loss consequent on failing to abort would be at least as great. Accordingly, morally permissible abortions will be rare indeed unless, perhaps, they occur so early in pregnancy that a fetus is not yet definitely an individual. Hence, this argument should be taken as showing that abortion is presumptively very seriously wrong, where the presumption is very strong—as strong as the presumption that killing another adult human being is wrong.

How complete an account of the wrongness of killing does the value of a future-like-ours account have to be in order that the wrongness of abortion is a consequence? This account does not have to be an account of the necessary conditions for the wrongness of killing. Some persons in nursing homes may lack valuable human futures, yet it may be wrong to kill them for other reasons. Furthermore, this account does not obviously have to be the sole reason killing is wrong where the victim did have a valuable future. This analysis claims only that, for any killing where the victim did have a valuable future like ours, having that future by itself is sufficient to create the strong presumption that the killing is seriously wrong.

One way to overturn the value of a future-like-ours argument would be to find some account of the wrongness of killing which is at least as intelligible and which has different implications for the ethics of abortion. Two rival accounts possess at least some degree of plausibility. One account is based on the obvious fact that people value the experience of living and wish for that valuable experience to continue. Therefore, it might be said, what makes killing wrong is the discontinuation of that experience for the victim. Let us call this the *discontinuation account.*[3] Another rival account is based upon the obvious fact that people strongly desire to continue to live. This suggests that what makes killing us so wrong is that it interferes with the fulfillment of a strong and fundamental desire, the fulfillment of which is necessary for the fulfillment of any other desires we might have. Let us call this the *desire account.*[4]

Consider first the desire account as a rival account of the ethics of killing which would provide the basis for rejecting the anti-abortion position. Such an account will have to be stronger than the value of a future-like-ours account of the wrongness of abortion if it is to do the job expected of it. To entail the wrongness of abortion, the value of a future-like-ours account has only to provide a sufficient, but not a necessary, condition for the wrongness of killing. The desire account, on the other hand, must provide us also with a necessary condition for the wrongness of killing in order to generate a pro-choice conclusion on abortion. The reason for this is that presumably the argument from the desire account moves from the claim that what makes killing wrong is interference with a very strong desire to the claim that abortion is not wrong because the fetus lacks a strong desire to live. Obviously, this inference fails if someone's having the desire to live is not a necessary condition of its being wrong to kill that individual.

One problem with the desire account is that we do regard it as seriously wrong to kill persons who have little desire to live or who have no desire to live or, indeed, have a desire not to live. We believe it is seriously wrong to kill the unconscious, the sleeping, those who are tired of life, and those who are suicidal. The value-of-a-human-future account renders standard morality intelligible in these cases; these cases appear to be incompatible with the desire account.

The desire account is subject to a deeper difficulty. We desire life, because we value the good of this life. The goodness of life is not secondary to our desire for it. If this were not so, the pain of one's own premature death could be done away with merely by an appropriate alteration in the configuration of one's desires. This is absurd. Hence, it would seem that it is the loss of the goods of one's future, not the interference with the fulfillment of a strong desire to live, which accounts ultimately for the wrongness of killing.

It is worth noting that, if the desire account is modified so that it does not provide a necessary, but only a sufficient, condition for the wrongness of killing, the desire account is compatible with the value of a future-like-ours account. The combined accounts will yield an anti-abortion ethic. This suggests that one can retain what is intuitively plausible about the desire account without a challenge to the basic argument of this paper.

It is also worth noting that, if future desires have moral force in a modified desire account of the wrongness of killing, one can find support for an anti-abortion ethic even in the absence of a value of a future-like-ours account. If one decides that a morally relevant property, the possession of which is sufficient to make it wrong to kill some individual, is the desire at some future time to live—one might decide to justify one's refusal to kill suicidal teenagers on these grounds, for example—then, since typical fetuses will have the desire in the future to live, it is wrong to kill typical fetuses. Accordingly, it does not seem that a desire account of the wrongness of killing can provide a justification of a pro-choice ethic of abortion which is nearly as adequate as the value of a human-future justification of an anti-abortion ethic.

The discontinuation account looks more promising as an account of the wrongness of killing. It seems just as intelligible as the value of a future-like-ours account, but it does not justify an anti-abortion position. Obviously, if it is the continuation of one's activities, experiences, and projects, the loss of which makes killing wrong, then it is not wrong to kill fetuses for that reason, for fetuses do not have experiences, activities, and projects to be continued or discontinued. Accordingly, the discontinuation account does not have the anti-abortion consequences that the value of a future-like-ours account has. Yet, it seems as intelligible as the value of a future-like-ours account, for when we think of what would be wrong with our being killed, it does seem as if it is the discontinuation of what makes our lives worthwhile which makes killing us wrong.

Is the discontinuation account just as good an account as the value of a future-like-ours account? The discontinuation account will not be adequate at all, if it does not refer to the *value* of the experience that may be discontinued. One does not want the discontinuation account to make it wrong to kill a patient who begs for death and who is in severe pain that cannot be relieved short of killing. (I leave open the question of whether it is wrong for other reasons.) Accordingly, the discontinuation account must be more than a bare discontinuation account. It must make some reference to the positive value of the patient's experiences. But, by the same token, the value of a future-like-ours account cannot be a bare future account either. Just having a future surely does not itself rule out killing the above patient. This account must make some reference to the value of the patient's future experiences and projects also. Hence, both accounts involve the value of experiences, projects, and activities. So far we still have symmetry between the accounts.

The symmetry fades, however, when we focus on the time period of the value of the experiences, etc., which has moral consequences. Although both accounts leave open the possibility that the patient in our example may be killed, this possibility is left open only in virtue of the utterly bleak future for the patient. It makes no difference whether the patient's immediate past contains intolerable pain, or consists in being in a coma (which we can imagine is a situation of indifference), or consists in a life of value. If the patient's future is a future of value, we want our account to make it wrong to kill the patient. If the patient's future is intolerable, whatever his or her immediate past, we want our account to allow killing the patient. Obviously, then, it is the value of that patient's future which is doing the work in rendering the morality of killing the patient intelligible.

This being the case, it seems clear that whether one has immediate past experiences or not does no work in the explanation of what makes killing wrong. The addition the discontinuation account makes to the value of a human future account is otiose. Its addition to the value-of-a-future account plays no role at all in rendering intelligible the wrongness of killing. Therefore, it can be discarded with the discontinuation account of which it is a part. . . .

The purpose of this essay has been to set out an argument for the serious presumptive wrongness of abortion subject to the assumption that the moral permissibility of abortion stands or falls on the moral status of the fetus. Since a fetus possesses a property, the possession of which in adult human beings is sufficient to make killing an adult human being wrong, abortion is wrong. This way of dealing with the problem of abortion seems superior to other approaches to the ethics of abortion, because it rests on an ethics of killing which is close to self-evident, because the crucial morally relevant property clearly applies to fetuses, and because the argument avoids the usual equivocations on 'human life', 'human being', or 'person'. The argument rests neither on religious claims nor on Papal dogma. It is not subject to the objection of "speciesism." Its soundness is compatible with the moral permissibility of euthanasia and contraception. It deals with our intuitions concerning young children.

Finally, this analysis can be viewed as resolving a standard problem—indeed, *the* standard problem—concerning the ethics of abortion. Clearly, it is wrong to kill adult human beings. Clearly, it is not wrong to end the life of some arbitrarily chosen single human cell. Fetuses seem to be like arbitrarily chosen human cells in some respects and like adult humans in other respects. The problem of the ethics of abortion is the problem of determining the fetal property that settles this moral controversy. The thesis of this essay is that the problem of the ethics of abortion, so understood, is solvable.

Notes

1. I have been most influenced on this matter by Jonathan Glover, *Causing Death and Saving Lives* (New York: Penguin, 1977), ch. 3; and Robert Young, "What Is So Wrong with Killing People?" *Philosophy*, I.IV, 210 (1979): 515–528.
2. Feinberg, Tooley, Warren, and Engelhardt have all dealt with this problem.
3. I am indebted to Jack Bricke for raising this objection.
4. Presumably a preference utilitarian would press such an objection. Tooley once suggested that his account has such a theoretical underpinning. See his "Abortion and Infanticide," pp. 44/5.

6.2f   Responding to Marquis

Marquis's argument is very impressive indeed. It doesn't rely on the unhelpful concept of personhood; it doesn't depend on the claim that life is sacred; nor does it confuse what an entity actually is with what it only potentially is. And yet Marquis seems able to account for the intuition that there is at least *something* ethically significant about the fact that fetuses, if they are not aborted, are in principle capable of being born and growing up. Without resorting to peculiar redefinitions of ordinary words, it appears that he has succeeded in identifying an ethically significant property that full-fledged humans and fetuses have in common, and in virtue of which it would be wrong to kill fetuses in just the way that it would be wrong to kill full-fledged humans.

That property, of course, is "a future like ours." To concentrate on this property is to capture what is meant when people speak of the fetus's potential, but without putting oneself in the position of having to make the implausible claim that an entity should get now what is only due to it later. For the fetus already has a future like ours. Its future isn't something that it gets after it's been born: It has its future now (as we all do). Thus, if the possession of a future like ours is sufficient to make it wrong to kill an adult, it must, on exactly the same grounds, make it wrong to kill a fetus. I do not see how a critic might hope to undercut Marquis's position on this point. Marquis is surely right to say that depriving an adult of his or her future is at least part of what makes killing adults wrong. If so, then killing fetuses must be wrong for the same reasons. Indeed, it seems that Marquis's argument really does settle the question we have been asking for much of this part of the present chapter: the question "Do fetuses have lives that are deserving of our ethical concern?" The answer appears to be a solid Yes. If this is right, then Marquis's critic, whom we may assume to be a defender of abortion, can only hope to attempt a damage-limitation exercise. In other words, it seems that the critic will not be able to defeat Marquis's central point; but he or she may be able to moderate its impact. How might this be done? The answer lies in the scope of Marquis's conclusion.

Marquis appears to conclude, on the strength of his argument, that it must be exactly as wrong to kill fetuses as adults. But this, surely, can be contested. When Marquis is defending his position against objections, he seems to assume that alternative accounts of the wrongness of killing must either replace his, or else drop out altogether. That is, he argues as if there could only be *one* correct account of the wrongness of killing (his). But why should we believe this? Marquis may be correct to hold that part of what makes killing wrong is depriving an individual of his or her future, but there is no reason to think that that is the only thing that makes killing wrong. If there are other things that make killing adults wrong, the critic might suggest, and if these additional factors do not apply in the case of fetuses, then there may be some reason to think that killing fetuses, although wrong, is not *as* wrong as killing adults—in other words, that killing fetuses is not as wrong as Marquis claims. The advantage of this way of replying is that the critic does not need to show that his or her new reasons for the wrongness of killing are better than Marquis's reasons, or that they might replace Marquis's. Rather, the critic need only claim that these reasons have been neglected by Marquis, and that if they are taken into account the picture looks rather less clear-cut than Marquis would have us suppose.

Perhaps the best candidates for further reasons why killing is wrong are found in the *relationship* that an individual stands in to his or her future. For instance, you and I anticipate our futures, make plans for them, fear for them, dread them, and so forth. That is, we have certain attitudes toward our futures that give our futures meaning for us. If we had no attitudes at all toward our futures, our futures would be a matter of perfect indifference— at least to us. Now Marquis is no doubt right to insist that it would, even so, be wrong to deprive us of those futures. But the wrongness of doing so is not something that you or I, being indifferent to our futures, could possibly be brought to see. In other words, while killing us would wrong us, it wouldn't wrong us in ways that we were capable of caring about. Now the critic might suggest that this makes a difference. Suppose that two people are being killed. The first is as we have imagined you and me to be—quite without attitudes toward our own futures. But the second person has an enormous range of attitudes toward his or her future—hopes, dreams, plans, fears, expectations, and ambitions. To this person, the future is anything but a matter of indifference. Assuming that Marquis is right that depriving someone of his or her future is simply wrong, both killings are wrong. But surely the second killing is wrong in a way that the first killing is not. For the second person is not merely deprived of his or her future, he or she is also the victim of a gross act of disrespect for autonomy. The second killing, it would seem, is worse. Thus, the critic may claim, there is something else—the principle of respect for autonomy—that can make a killing wrong on top of the wrongness that comes from depriving an individual of his or her future. If this is right, then it cannot be as bad to kill a fetus as it is to kill an ordinary adult: For ordinary adults, unlike fetuses, have attitudes toward their own futures.

It is not open to Marquis to reply to this by saying that the wrongness of killing people against their autonomous wishes *depends* on the wrongness of depriving them of their futures. He may be quite right: In other words, it may be true that a person's autonomous attitudes toward the future are only of any importance because that future is itself of importance. But the critic is not denying this. Rather, the critic is aiming only to supplement Marquis's account of the wrongness of killing, not to replace it. Construed this way, the critic's position looks strong. It may be possible for the critic to extend this tactic, and to attempt to identify other factors that make the killing of ordinary adults wrong, and yet which cannot be held to apply in the case of fetuses. If successful, such a tactic will further reduce the relative wrongness of killing fetuses. But of course it will never be able to make the wrongness go away altogether. If Marquis's original argument is correct, as I'm pretty sure it is, there will always be some moral violation involved in the killing of a fetus. Or, to put it another way, if Marquis is right, the life of a fetus will always deserve (at least some) ethical regard.

But this certainly doesn't settle the abortion debate (as Marquis, I think, assumes it does). For while it may be true that fetuses have valuable lives, and while it may be true that killing them always involves doing something wrong, it may *even so* be justifiable to terminate a pregnancy by abortion. Admittedly, that justification may be a little harder to produce now than it would have been before we had a look at Marquis's position. But the defender of abortion still has some powerful arguments to call upon.

6.2g   The Interests of the Woman

One objection that is sometimes raised in the abortion debate notes that the debate tends to concentrate on the interests of the fetus to the almost total exclusion of the interests of the woman who is pregnant with it. The present discussion has doubtless been vulnerable to that objection, and it's time now to set the balance straight. This is not to say that the interests of the pregnant woman should have been considered earlier. For there would have been no point in doing that before we had some kind of answer to the question: Pregnant with what? If it had turned out that the answer to that question was "Pregnant with something of no value," then the debate could have been settled without further complication. However, the answer seems instead to be "Pregnant with a fetus whose life is of value." So now it is necessary to turn to that other life—the pregnant woman's life—with which the life of the fetus may come into conflict.

At least one thing that is often said in this context can be examined quickly. It is sometimes held that, if people have a right to determine what shall happen to their own bodies, it must be within a pregnant woman's rights to determine that her body shall no longer contain a fetus. "It's her body," people say, "she should decide." This claim is certainly plausible in many contexts. For instance, if a woman wishes to have her appendix or her tonsils out, it seems that no one has any business to object. But we have seen that a fetus cannot be regarded in the same light as an appendix or a tonsil.

The difference between a fetus and, say, a tonsil, is that the fetus has an independently valuable future, which the tonsil does not. Hence, if Marquis's argument is correct, it is wrong to remove a fetus prematurely from a woman's womb, so depriving it of that future, in a way that it is not wrong to remove a tonsil from a woman's throat. Thus the observation that we do, normally, have authority over our own bodies does not by itself show that abortion is justifiable. Like any of our freedoms, the freedom to pursue our interests (by, for instance, deciding what happens to our bodies) is limited by consideration for the legitimate interests of others (for instance, fetuses). Thus the slogan "It's the woman's body; she should decide," does not, as it stands, make a helpful contribution to the debate. (A much better version of the argument is presented by Judith Thomson in the next section.)

Another matter that can be dealt with quite quickly is that of *direct* competition between the life of the fetus and the life of the pregnant woman. In cases where one or the other, but not both, can hope to survive, it seems clear that the woman's life must take precedence, and that abortion is justifiable. The reason for this conclusion emerged during the discussion of Marquis's argument in the previous section. Both the fetus and the woman have valuable futures, of which it would be wrong to deprive them. But the woman, unlike the fetus, is also in a position autonomously to value her valuable future. This, if our earlier discussion was right, would make her death a greater misfortune than the fetus's death. This suggests that the wrongness of killing the fetus is more than outweighed by the interests of the mother, and hence that in such a case abortion would be justified. Many would also hold, on similar grounds, that abortion is justified whenever a continuation of pregnancy would threaten the woman with serious harm. Even those who normally oppose abortion are often prepared to go along with these conclusions. Indeed it is hard to imagine how they might not: It would take a pretty extraordinary argument, after all, to show that the life of a fetus is actually *more* important than the life of a woman.

This section has not, perhaps, given very much encouragement to the defender of abortion. But it has shown one thing that the defender of abortion should welcome—which is that the fact that the fetus's life is a valuable one does not rule out abortion altogether. The question now is whether the case in favor of abortion can be extended to cover situations in which the woman is not under any immediate threat of harm from her pregnancy.

6.2h   Defending Abortion: Thomson's Argument: "A Defense of Abortion"

In 6.2a, I suggested that a life might justifiably be taken if a person has somehow forfeited his or her right to remain alive. But I argued that this was irrelevant to the abortion debate since no fetus is capable of doing anything that would count as forfeiting that right. But we have just seen that the taking of a life may sometimes be justifiable on *other* grounds, as when a fetus is killed in order to preserve a woman from harm. Thus we have discussed two kinds of justification for killing: forfeiture and direct (if involuntary) threat to the life of another. According to Judith Thomson, professor of philosophy at the Massachusetts Institute of Technology, there may be another kind of justification that is relevant to the abortion debate.

A DEFENSE OF ABORTION
Judith Jarvis Thomson

Most opposition to abortion relies on the premise that the fetus is a human being, a person, from the moment of conception.[1] The premise is argued for, but, as I think, not well. Take, for example, the most common argument. We are asked to notice that the development of a human being from conception through birth into childhood is continuous; then it is said that to draw a line, to choose a point in this development and say "before this point the thing is not a person, after this point it is a person" is to make an arbitrary choice, a choice for which in the nature of things no good reason can be given. It is concluded that the fetus is, or anyway that we had better say it is, a person from the moment of conception. But this conclusion does not follow. Similar things might be said about the development of an acorn into an oak tree, and it does not follow that acorns are oak trees, or that we had better say they are. Arguments of this form are sometimes called "slippery slope arguments"—the phrase is perhaps self-explanatory—and it is dismaying that opponents of abortion rely on them so heavily and uncritically.

I am inclined to agree, however, that the prospects for "drawing a line" in the development of the fetus look dim. I am inclined to think also that we shall probably have to agree that the fetus has already become a human person well before birth. Indeed, it comes as a surprise when one first learns how early in its life it begins to acquire human characteristics. By the tenth week, for example, it already has a face, arms and legs, fingers and toes; it has internal organs, and brain activity is detectable.[2] On the other hand, I think that the premise is false, that the fetus is not a person from the moment of conception. A newly fertilized ovum, a newly implanted clump of cells, is no more a person than an acorn is an oak tree. But I shall not discuss any of this. For it seems to me to be of great interest to ask what happens if, for the sake of argument, we allow the premise. How, precisely, are we supposed to get from there to the conclusion that abortion is morally impermissible? Opponents of abortion commonly spend most of their time establishing that the fetus is a person, and hardly any time explaining the step from there to the impermissibility of abortion. Perhaps they think the step too simple and obvious to require much comment. Or perhaps instead they are simply being economical in argument. Many of those who defend abortion rely on the premise that the fetus is not a person, but only a bit of tissue that will become a person at birth; and why pay out more arguments than you have to? Whatever the explanation, I suggest that the step they take is neither easy nor obvious, that it calls for closer examination than it is commonly given, and that when we do give it this closer examination we shall feel inclined to reject it.

I propose, then, that we grant that the fetus is a person from the moment of conception. How does the argument go from here? Something like this, I take it. Every person has a right to life. So the fetus has a right to life. No doubt the mother has a right to decide what shall happen in and to her body; everyone would grant that. But surely a person's right to life is stronger and more stringent than the mother's right to decide what happens in and to her body, and so outweighs it. So the fetus may not be killed; an abortion may not be performed.

It sounds plausible. But now let me ask you to imagine this. You wake up in the morning and find yourself back to back in bed with an unconscious violinist. A famous unconscious violinist. He has been found to have a fatal kidney ailment, and the Society of Music Lovers has canvassed all the available medical records and found that you alone have the right blood type to help. They have therefore kidnapped you, and last night the violinist's circulatory system was plugged into yours, so that your kidneys can be used to extract poisons from his blood as well as your own. The director of the hospital now tells you, "Look, we're sorry the Society of Music Lovers did this to you—we would never have permitted it if we had known. But still, they did it, and the violinist now is plugged into you. To unplug you would be to kill him. But never mind, it's only for nine months. By then he will have recovered from his ailment, and can safely be unplugged from you." Is it morally incumbent on you to accede to this situation? No doubt it would be very nice of you if you did, a great kindness. But do you *have* to accede to it? What if it were not nine months, but nine years? Or longer still? What if the director of the hospital says, "Tough luck, I agree, but you've now got to stay in bed, with the violinist plugged into you, for the rest of your life. Because remember this. All persons have a right to life, and violinists are persons. Granted you have a right to decide what happens in and to your body, but a person's right to life outweighs your right to decide what happens in and to your body. So you cannot ever be unplugged from him." I imagine you would regard this as outrageous, which suggests that something really is wrong with that plausible-sounding argument I mentioned a moment ago.

In this case, of course, you were kidnapped; you didn't volunteer for the operation that plugged the violinist into your kidneys. Can those who oppose abortion on the ground I mentioned make an exception for a pregnancy due to rape? Certainly. They can say that persons have a right to life only if they didn't come into existence because of rape; or they can say that all persons have a right to life, but that some have less of a right to life than others, in particular, that those who came into existence because of rape have less. But these statements have a rather unpleasant sound. Surely the question of whether you have a right to life at all, or how much of it you have, shouldn't turn on the question of whether or not you are the product of a rape. And in fact the people who oppose abortion on the ground I mentioned do not make this distinction, and hence do not make an exception in case of rape.

Nor do they make an exception for a case in which the mother has to spend the nine months of her pregnancy in bed. They would agree that would be a great pity, and hard on the mother; but all the same, all persons have a right to life, the fetus is a person, and so on. I suspect, in fact, that they would not make an exception for a case in which, miraculously enough, the pregnancy went on for nine years, or even the rest of the mother's life.

Some won't even make an exception for a case in which continuation of the pregnancy is likely to shorten the mother's life; they regard abortion as impermissible even to save the mother's life. Such cases are nowadays very rare, and many opponents of abortion do not accept this extreme view. All the same, it is a good place to begin: a number of points of interest come out in respect to it.

1. Let us call the view that abortion is impermissible even to save the mother's life "the extreme view." I want to suggest first that it does not issue from the argument I mentioned earlier without the addition of some fairly powerful premises. Suppose a woman has become pregnant, and now learns that she has a cardiac condition such that she will die if she carries the baby to term. What may be done for her? The fetus, being a person, has a right to life, but as the mother is a person too, so has she a right to life. Presumably they have an equal right to life. How is it supposed to come out that an abortion may not be performed? If mother and child have an equal right to life, shouldn't we perhaps flip a coin? Or should we add to the mother's right to life her right to decide what happens in and to her body, which everybody seems to be ready to grant—the sum of her rights now outweighing the fetus's right to life?

The most familiar argument here is the following. We are told that performing the abortion would be directly killing[3] the child, whereas doing nothing would not be killing the mother, but only letting her die. Moreover, in killing the child, one would be killing an innocent person, for the child has committed no crime, and is not aiming at his mother's death. And then there are a variety of ways in which this might be continued. (a) But as directly killing an innocent person is always and absolutely impermissible, an abortion may not be performed. Or, (b) as directly killing an innocent person is murder, and murder is always and absolutely impermissible, an abortion may not be performed.[4] Or, (c) as one's duty to refrain from directly killing an innocent person is more stringent than one's duty to keep a person from dying, an abortion may not be performed. Or, (d) if one's only options are directly killing an innocent person or letting a person die, one must prefer letting the person die, and thus an abortion may not be performed.[5]

Some people seem to have thought that these are not further premises which must be added if the conclusion is to be reached, but that they follow from the very fact that an innocent person has a right to life.[6] But this seems to me to be a mistake, and perhaps the simplest way to show this is to bring out that while we must certainly grant that innocent persons have a right to life, the theses in (a) through (d) are all false. Take (b), for example. If directly killing an innocent person is murder, and thus is impermissible, then the mother's directly killing the innocent person inside her is murder, and thus is impermissible. But it cannot seriously be thought to be murder if the mother performs an abortion on herself to save her life. It cannot seriously be said that she *must* refrain, that she *must* sit passively by and wait for her death. Let us look again at the case of you and the violinist. There you are, in bed with the violinist, and the director of the hospital says to you, "It's all most distressing, and I deeply sympathize, but you see this is putting an additional strain on your kidneys, and you'll be dead within the month. But you *have* to stay where you are all the same. Because unplugging you would be directly killing an innocent violinist, and that's murder, and that's impermissible." If anything in the world is true, it is that you do not commit murder, you do not do what is impermissible, if you reach around to your back and unplug yourself from that violinist to save your life.

The main focus of attention in writings on abortion has been on what a third party may or may not do in answer to a request from a woman for an abortion. This is in a way understandable. Things being as they are, there isn't much a woman can safely do to abort herself. So the question asked is what a third party may do, and what the mother may do, if it is mentioned at all, is deduced, almost as an afterthought, from what it is concluded that third parties may do. But it seems to me that to treat the matter in this way is to refuse to grant to the mother that very status of person which is so firmly insisted on for the fetus. For we cannot simply read off what a person may do from what a third party may do. Suppose you find yourself trapped in a tiny house with a growing child. I mean a very tiny house, and a rapidly growing child—you are already up against the wall of the house and in a few minutes you'll be crushed to death. The child on the other hand won't be crushed to death; if nothing is done to stop him from growing he'll be hurt, but in the end he'll simply burst open the house and walk out a free man. Now I could well understand it if a bystander were to say, "There's nothing we can do for you. We cannot choose between your life and his, we cannot be the ones to decide who is to live, we cannot intervene." But it cannot be concluded that you too can do nothing, that you cannot attack it to save your life. However innocent the child may be, you do not have to wait passively while it crushes you to death. Perhaps a pregnant woman is vaguely felt to have the status of house, to which we don't allow the right of self-defense. But if the woman houses the child, it should be remembered that she is a person who houses it.

I should perhaps stop to say explicitly that I am not claiming that people have a right to do anything whatever to save their lives. I think, rather, that there are drastic limits to the right of self-defense. If someone threatens you with death unless you torture someone else to death, I think you have not the right, even to save your life, to do so. But the case under consideration here is very different. In our case there are only two people involved, one whose life is threatened, and one who threatens it. Both are innocent: the one who is threatened is not threatened because of any fault, the one who threatens does not threaten because of any fault. For this reason we may feel that we bystanders cannot intervene. But the person threatened can.

In sum, a woman surely can defend her life against the threat to it posed by the unborn child, even if doing so involves its death. And this shows not merely that the theses in (a) through (d) are false; it shows also that the extreme view of abortion is false, and so we need not canvass any other possible ways of arriving at it from the argument I mentioned at the outset.

2. The extreme view could of course be weakened to say that while abortion is permissible to save the mother's life, it may not be performed by a third party, but only by the mother herself. But this cannot be right either. For what we have to keep in mind is that the mother and the unborn child are not like two tenants in a small house which has, by an unfortunate mistake, been rented to both: the mother *owns* the house. The fact that she does adds to the offensiveness of deducing that the mother can do nothing from the supposition that

third parties can do nothing. But it does more than this: it casts a bright light on the supposition that third parties can do nothing. Certainly it lets us see that a third party who says "I cannot choose between you" is fooling himself if he thinks this is impartiality. If Jones has found and fastened on a certain coat, which he needs to keep him from freezing, but which Smith also needs to keep him from freezing, then it is not impartiality that says "I cannot choose between you" when Smith owns the coat. Women have said again and again "This body is *my* body!" and they have reason to feel angry, reason to feel that it has been like shouting into the wind. Smith, after all, is hardly likely to bless us if we say to him, "Of course it's your coat, anybody would grant that it is. But no one may choose between you and Jones who is to have it."

We should really ask what it is that says "no one may choose" in the face of the fact that the body that houses the child is the mother's body. It may be simply a failure to appreciate this fact. But it may be something more interesting, namely, the sense that one has a right to refuse to lay hands on people, even where it would be just and fair to do so, even where justice seems to require that somebody do so. Thus justice might call for somebody to get Smith's coat back from Jones, and yet you have a right to refuse to be the one to lay hands on Jones, a right to refuse to do physical violence to him. This, I think, must be granted. But then what should be said is not "no one may choose," but only "*I* cannot choose," and indeed not even this, but "*I* will not *act*," leaving it open that somebody else can or should, and in particular that anyone in a position of authority, with the job of securing people's rights, both can and should. So this is no difficulty. I have not been arguing that any given third party must accede to the mother's request that he perform an abortion to save her life, but only that he may.

I suppose that in some views of human life the mother's body is only on loan to her, the loan not being one which gives her any prior claim to it. One who held this view might well think it impartiality to say "I cannot choose." But I shall simply ignore this possibility. My own view is that if a human being has any just, prior claim to anything at all, he has a just, prior claim to his own body. And perhaps this needn't be argued for here anyway, since, as I mentioned, the arguments against abortion we are looking at do grant that the woman has a right to decide what happens in and to her body.

But although they do grant it, I have tried to show that they do not take seriously what is done in granting it. I suggest the same thing will reappear even more clearly when we turn away from cases in which the mother's life is at stake, and attend, as I propose we now do, to the vastly more common cases in which a woman wants an abortion for some less weighty reason than preserving her own life.

3. Where the mother's life is not at stake, the argument I mentioned at the outset seems to have a much stronger pull. "Everyone has a right to life, so the unborn person has a right to life." And isn't the child's right to life weightier than anything other than the mother's own right to life, which she might put forward as ground for an abortion?

This argument treats the right to life as if it were unproblematic. It is not, and this seems to me to be precisely the source of the mistake.

For we should now, at long last, ask what it comes to, to have a right to life. In some views having a right to life includes having a right to be given at least the bare minimum one needs for continued life. But suppose that what in fact *is* the bare minimum a man needs for continued life is something he has no right at all to be given. If I am sick unto death, and the only thing that will save my life is the touch of Henry Fonda's cool hand on my fevered brow, then all the same, I have no right to be given the touch of Henry Fonda's cool hand on my fevered brow. It would be frightfully nice of him to fly in from the West Coast to provide it. It would be less nice, though no doubt well meant, if my friends flew out to the West Coast and carried Henry Fonda back with them. But I have no right at all against anybody that he should do this for me. Or again, to return to the story I told earlier, the fact that for continued life that violinist needs the continued use of your kidneys does not establish that he has a right to be given the continued use of your kidneys. He certainly has no right against you that *you* should give him continued use of your kidneys. For nobody has any right to use your kidneys unless you give him such a right; and nobody has the right against you that you shall give him this right—if you do allow him to go on using your kidneys, this is a kindness on your part, and not something he can claim from you as his due. Nor has he any right against anybody else that *they* should give him continued use of your kidneys. Certainly he had no right against the Society of Music Lovers that they should plug him into you in the first place. And if you now start to unplug yourself, having learned that you will otherwise have to spend nine years in bed with him, there is nobody in the world who must try to prevent you, in order to see to it that he is given something he has a right to be given.

Some people are rather stricter about the right to life. In their view, it does not include the right to be given anything, but amounts to, and only to, the right not to be killed by anybody. But here a related difficulty arises. If everybody is to refrain from killing that violinist, then everybody must refrain from doing a great many different sorts of things. Everybody must refrain from slitting his throat, everybody must refrain from shooting him—and everybody must refrain from unplugging you from him. But does he have a right against everybody that they shall refrain from unplugging you from him? To refrain from doing this is to allow him to continue to use your kidneys. It could be argued that he has a right against us that *we* should allow him to continue to use your kidneys. That is, while he had no right against us that we should give him the use of your kidneys, it might be argued that he anyway has a right against us that we shall not now intervene and deprive him of the use of your kidneys. I shall come back to third-party interventions later. But certainly the violinist has no right against you that *you* shall allow him to continue to use your kidneys. As I said, if you do allow him to use them, it is a kindness on your part, and not something you owe him.

The difficulty I point to here is not peculiar to the right to life. It reappears in connection with all the other natural rights; and it is something which an adequate account of rights must deal with. For present purposes it is enough just to draw attention to it. But I would stress that I am not arguing that people do not have a right to life—quite to the contrary, it seems to me that the primary control we must place on the acceptability of an account of rights is that it should turn out in that account to be a truth that all persons have a right to life. I am arguing only that having a right to life does not guarantee having either a right to be given the use of or a right to be allowed continued use of another person's body—even if one needs it for life itself. So the right to life will not serve the opponents of abortion in the very simple and clear way in which they seem to have thought it would.

4. There is another way to bring out the difficulty. In the most ordinary sort of case, to deprive someone of what he has a right to is to treat him unjustly. Suppose a boy and his small brother are jointly given a box of chocolates for Christmas. If the older boy takes the box and refuses to give his brother any of the chocolates, he is unjust to him, for the brother has been given a right to half of them. But suppose that, having learned that otherwise it means nine years in bed with that violinist, you unplug yourself from him. You surely are not being unjust to him for you gave him no right to use your kidneys, and no one else can have given him any such right. But we have to notice that in unplugging yourself, you are killing him; and violinists, like everybody else, have a right to life, and thus in the view we were considering just now, the right not to be killed. So here you do what he supposedly has a right you shall not do, but you do not act unjustly to him in doing it.

The emendation which may be made at this point is this: the right to life consists not in the right not to be killed, but rather in the right not to be killed unjustly. This runs a risk of circularity, but never mind: it would enable us to square the fact that the violinist has a right to life with the fact that you do not act unjustly toward him in unplugging yourself, thereby killing him. For if you do not kill him unjustly, you do not violate his right to life, and so it is no wonder you do him no injustice.

But if this emendation is accepted, the gap in the argument against abortion stares us plainly in the face: It is by no means enough to show that the fetus is a person, and to remind us that all persons have a right to life—we need to be shown also that killing the fetus violates its right to life, i.e., that abortion is unjust killing. And is it?

I suppose we may take it as a datum that in a case of pregnancy due to rape the mother has not given the unborn person a right to the use of her body for food and shelter. Indeed, in what pregnancy could it be supposed that the mother has given the unborn person such a right? It is not as if there were unborn persons drifting about the world, to whom a woman who wants a child says "I invite you in."

But it might be argued that there are other ways one can have acquired a right to the use of another person's body than by having been invited to use it by that person. Suppose a woman voluntarily indulges in intercourse, knowing of the chance it will issue in pregnancy, and then she does become pregnant; is she not in part responsible for the presence, in fact the very existence, of the unborn person inside her? No doubt she did not invite it in. But doesn't her partial responsibility for its being there itself give it a right to the use of her body?[7] If so, then her aborting it would be more like the boy's taking away the chocolates, and less like your unplugging yourself from the violinist—doing so would be depriving it of what it does have a right to, and thus would be doing it an injustice.

And then, too, it might be asked whether or not she can kill it even to save her own life: If she voluntarily called it into existence, how can she now kill it, even in self-defense?

The first thing to be said about this is that it is something new. Opponents of abortion have been so concerned to make out the independence of the fetus, in order to establish that it has a right to life, just as its mother does, that they have tended to overlook the possible support they might gain from making out that the fetus is *dependent* on the mother, in order to establish that she has a special kind of responsibility for it, a responsibility that gives it rights against her which are not possessed by any independent person—such as an ailing violinist who is a stranger to her.

On the other hand, this argument would give the unborn person a right to its mother's body only if her pregnancy resulted from a voluntary act, undertaken in full knowledge of the chance a pregnancy might result from it. It would leave out entirely the unborn person whose existence is due to rape. Pending the availability of some further argument, then, we would be left with the conclusion that unborn persons whose existence is due to rape have no right to the use of their mothers' bodies, and thus that aborting them is not depriving them of anything they have a right to and hence is not unjust killing.

And we should also notice that it is not at all plain that this argument really does go even as far as it purports to. For there are cases and cases, and the details make a difference. If the room is stuffy, and I therefore open a window to air it, and a burglar climbs in, it would be absurd to say, "Ah, now he can stay, she's given him a right to the use of her house—for she is partially responsible for his presence there, having voluntarily done what enabled him to get in, in full knowledge that there are such things as burglars, and that burglars burgle." It would be still be more absurd to say this if I had had bars installed outside my windows, precisely to prevent burglars from getting in, and a burglar got in only because of a defect in the bars. It remains equally absurd if we imagine it is not a burglar who climbs in, but an innocent person who blunders or falls in. Again, suppose it were like this: people-seeds drift about in the air like pollen, and if you open your windows, one may drift in and take root in your carpets or upholstery. You don't want children, so you fix up your windows with fine mesh screens, the very best you can buy. As can happen, however, and on very, very rare occasions does happen, one of the screens is defective; and a seed drifts in and takes root. Does the person-plant who now develops have a right to the use of your house? Surely not—despite the fact that you voluntarily opened your windows, you knowingly kept carpets and upholstered furniture, and you knew that screens were sometimes defective. Someone may argue that you are responsible for its rooting, that it does have a right to your house, because after all you *could* have lived out your life with bare floors and furniture, or with sealed windows and doors. But this won't do—for by the same token anyone can avoid a pregnancy due to rape by having a hysterectomy, or anyway by never leaving home without a (reliable!) army.

It seems to me that the argument we are looking at can establish at most that there are *some* cases in which the unborn person has a right to the use of its mother's body, and therefore *some* cases in which abortion is unjust killing. There is room for much discussion and argument as to precisely which, if any. But I think we should sidestep this issue and leave it open, for at any rate the argument certainly does not establish that all abortion is unjust killing.

5. There is room for yet another argument here, however. We surely must all grant that there may be cases in which it would be morally indecent to detach a person from your body at the cost of his life. Suppose you learn that what the violinist needs is not nine years of your life, but only one hour: All you need do to save his life is to spend one hour in that bed with him. Suppose also that letting him use your kidneys for that one hour would not affect your health in the slightest. Admittedly you were kidnapped. Admittedly you did not give anyone permission to plug him into you. Nevertheless it seems to me plain you *ought* to allow him to use your kidneys for that hour—it would be indecent to refuse.

Again, suppose pregnancy lasted only an hour, and constituted no threat to life or health. And suppose that a woman becomes pregnant as a result of rape. Admittedly she did not voluntarily do anything to bring about the existence of a child. Admittedly she did nothing at all which would give the unborn person a right to the use of her body. All the same it might well be said, as in the newly emended violinist story, that she *ought* to allow it to remain for that hour—that it would be indecent in her to refuse.

Now some people are inclined to use the term "right" in such a way that it follows from the fact that you ought to allow a person to use your body for the hour he needs, that he has a right to use your body for the hour he needs, even though he has not been given that right by any person or act. They may say that it follows also that if you refuse, you act unjustly toward him. This use of the term is perhaps so common that it cannot be called wrong; nevertheless it seems to me to be an unfortunate loosening of what we would do better to keep a tight rein on. Suppose that box of chocolates I mentioned earlier had not been given to both boys jointly, but was given only to the older boy. There he sits, stolidly eating his way through the box, his small brother watching enviously. Here we are likely to say "You ought not to be so mean. You ought to give your brother some of those chocolates." My own view is that it just does not follow from the truth of this that the brother has any right to any of the chocolates. If the boy refuses to give his brother any, he is greedy, stingy, callous—but not unjust. I suppose that the people I have in mind will say it does follow that the brother has a right to some of the chocolates, and thus that the boy does act unjustly if he refuses to give his brother any. But the effect of saying this is to obscure what we should keep distinct, namely the difference between the boy's refusal in this case and the boy's refusal in the earlier case, in which the box was given to both boys jointly, and in which the small brother thus had what was from any point of view clear title to half.

A further objection to so using the term "right" that from the fact that A ought to do a thing for B, it follows that B has a right against A that A do it for him, is that it is going to make the question of whether or not a man has a right to a thing turn on how easy it is to provide him with it; and this seems not merely unfortunate, but morally unacceptable. Take the case of Henry Fonda again. I said earlier that I had no right to the touch of his cool hand on my fevered brow, even though I needed it to save my life. I said it would be frightfully nice of him to fly in from the West Coast to provide me with it, but that I had no right against him that he should do so. But suppose he isn't on the West Coast. Suppose he has only to walk across the room, place a hand briefly on my brow—and lo, my life is saved. Then surely he ought to do it, it would be indecent to refuse. Is it to be said "Ah well, it follows that in this case she has a right to the touch of his hand on her brow, and so it would be an injustice in him to refuse"? So that I have a right to it when it is easy for him to provide it, though no right when it's hard? It's rather a shocking idea that anyone's rights should fade away and disappear as it gets harder and harder to accord them to him.

So my own view is that even though you ought to let the violinist use your kidneys for the one hour he needs, we should not conclude that he has a right to do so—we would say that if you refuse, you are, like the boy who owns all the chocolates and will give none away, self-centered and callous, indecent in fact, but not unjust. And similarly, that even supposing a case in which a woman pregnant due to rape ought to allow the unborn person to use her body for the hour he needs, we should not conclude that he has a right to do so; we should conclude that she is self-centered, callous, indecent, but not unjust, if she refuses. The complaints are no less grave; they are just different. However, there is no need to insist on this point. If anyone does wish to deduce "he has a right" from "you ought," then all the same he must surely grant that there are cases in which it is not morally required of you that you allow that violinist to use your kidneys, and in which he does not have a right to use them, and in which you do not do him an injustice if you refuse. And so also for mother and unborn child. Except in such cases as the unborn person has a right to demand it—and we were leaving open the possibility that there may be such cases—nobody is morally *required* to make large sacrifices, of health, of all other interests and concerns, of all other duties and commitments, for nine years, or even for nine months, in order to keep another person alive.

6. We have in fact to distinguish between two kinds of Samaritan: the Good Samaritan and what we might call the Minimally Decent Samaritan. The story of the Good Samaritan, you will remember, goes like this:

> A certain man went down from Jerusalem to Jericho, and fell among thieves, which stripped him of his raiment, and wounded him, and departed, leaving him half dead.
>
> And by chance there came down a certain priest that way; and when he saw him, he passed by on the other side.
>
> And likewise a Levite, when he was at the place, came and looked on him, and passed by on the other side.
>
> But a certain Samaritan, as he journeyed, came where he was; and when he saw him he had compassion on him.

And went to him, and bound up his wounds, pouring in oil and wine, and set him on his own beast, and brought him to an inn, and took care of him.

And on the morrow, when he departed, he took out two pence, and gave them to the host, and said unto him, "Take care of him; and whatsoever thou spendest more, when I come again, I will repay thee."

(Luke 10:30–35)

The Good Samaritan went out of his way, at some cost to himself, to help one in need of it. We are not told what the options were, that is, whether or not the priest and the Levite could have helped by doing less than the Good Samaritan did, but assuming they could have, then the fact they did nothing at all shows they were not even Minimally Decent Samaritans, not because they were not Samaritans, but because they were not even minimally decent.

These things are a matter of degree, of course, but there is a difference, and it comes out perhaps most clearly in the story of Kitty Genovese, who, as you will remember, was murdered while thirty-eight people watched or listened, and did nothing at all to help her. A Good Samaritan would have rushed out to give direct assistance against the murderer. Or perhaps we had better allow that it would have been a Splendid Samaritan who did this, on the ground that it would have involved a risk of death for himself. But the thirty-eight not only did not do this, they did not even trouble to pick up a phone to call the police. Minimally Decent Samaritanism would call for doing at least that, and their not having done it was monstrous.

After telling the story of the Good Samaritan, Jesus said, "Go, and do thou likewise." Perhaps he meant that we are morally required to act as the Good Samaritan did. Perhaps he was urging people to do more than is morally required of them. At all events it seems plain that it was not morally required of any of the thirty-eight that he rush out to give direct assistance at the risk of his own life, and that it is not morally required of anyone that he give long stretches of his life—nine years or nine months—to sustaining the life of a person who has no special right (we were leaving open the possibility of this) to demand it.

Indeed, with one rather striking class of exceptions, no one in any country in the world is *legally* required to do anywhere near as much as this for anyone else. The class of exceptions is obvious. My main concern here is not the state of the law in respect to abortion, but it is worth drawing attention to the fact that in no state in this country is any man compelled by law to be even a Minimally Decent Samaritan to any person; there is no law under which charges could be brought against the thirty-eight who stood by while Kitty Genovese died. By contrast, in most states in this country women are compelled by law to be not merely Minimally Decent Samaritans, but Good Samaritans to unborn persons inside them. This doesn't by itself settle anything one way or the other, because it may well be argued that there should be laws in this country—as there are in many European countries—compelling at least Minimally Decent Samaritanism.[8] But it does show that there is a gross injustice in the existing state of the law. And it shows also that the groups currently working against liberalization of abortion laws, in fact working toward having it declared unconstitutional for a state to permit abortion, had better start working for the adoption of

Good Samaritan laws generally, or earn the charge that they are acting in bad faith.

I should think, myself, that Minimally Decent Samaritan laws would be one thing, Good Samaritan laws quite another, and in fact highly improper. But we are not here concerned with the law. What we should ask is not whether anybody should be compelled by law to be a Good Samaritan, but whether we must accede to a situation in which somebody is being compelled—by nature, perhaps—to be a Good Samaritan. We have, in other words, to look now at third-party interventions. I have been arguing that no person is morally required to make large sacrifices to sustain the life of another who has no right to demand them, and this even where the sacrifices do not include life itself; we are not morally required to be Good Samaritans or anyway Very Good Samaritans to one another. But what if a man cannot extricate himself from such a situation? What if he appeals to us to extricate him? It seems to me plain that there are cases in which we can, cases in which a Good Samaritan would extricate him. There you are, you were kidnapped, and nine years in bed with that violinist lie ahead of you. You have your own life to lead. You are sorry, but you simply cannot see giving up so much of your life to the sustaining of his. You cannot extricate yourself, and ask us to do so. I should have thought that—in light of his having no right to the use of your body—it was obvious that we do not have to accede to your being forced to give up so much. We can do what you ask. There is no injustice to the violinist in our doing so.

7. Following the lead of the opponents of abortion, I have throughout been speaking of the fetus merely as a person, and what I have been asking is whether or not the argument we began with, which proceeds only from the fetus's being a person, really does establish its conclusion. I have argued that it does not.

But of course there are arguments and arguments, and it may be said that I have simply fastened on the wrong one. It may be said that what is important is not merely the fact that the fetus is a person, but that it is a person for whom the woman has a special kind of responsibility issuing from the fact that she is its mother. And it might be argued that all my analogies are therefore irrelevant —for you do not have that special kind of responsibility for that violinist, Henry Fonda does not have that special kind of responsibility for me. And our attention might be drawn to the fact that men and women both *are* compelled by law to provide support for their children.

I have in effect dealt (briefly) with this argument in section 4 above; but a (still briefer) recapitulation now may be in order. Surely we do not have any such "special responsibility" for a person unless we have assumed it, explicitly or implicitly. If a set of parents do not try to prevent pregnancy, do not obtain an abortion, and then at the time of birth of the child do not put it out for adoption, but rather take it home with them, then they have assumed responsibility for it, they have given it rights, and they cannot *now* withdraw support from it at the cost of its life because they now find it difficult to go on providing for it. But if they have taken all reasonable precautions against having a child, they do not simply by virtue of their biological relationship to the child who comes into existence have a special responsibility for it. They may wish to assume responsibility for it, or they may not wish to. And I am suggesting that if assuming responsibility for it would require large sacrifices, then they may refuse. A Good Samaritan would not refuse—or anyway, a Splendid Samaritan, if the sacrifices that had to be made were enormous. But then so would a Good Samaritan assume responsibility for that violinist; so would Henry Fonda, if he is a Good Samaritan, fly in from the West Coast and assume responsibility for me.

8. My argument will be found unsatisfactory on two counts by many of those who want to regard abortion as morally permissible. First, while I do argue that abortion is not impermissible, I do not argue that it is always permissible. There may well be cases in which carrying the child to term requires only Minimally Decent Samaritanism of the mother, and this is a standard we must not fall below. I am inclined to think it a merit of my account precisely that it does *not* give a general yes or a general no. It allows for and supports our sense that, for example, a sick and desperately frightened fourteen-year-old schoolgirl, pregnant due to rape, may *of course* choose abortion, and that any law which rules this out is an insane law. And it also allows for and supports our sense that in other cases resort to abortion is even positively indecent. It would be indecent in the woman to request an abortion, and indecent in a doctor to perform it, if she is in her seventh month and wants the abortion just to avoid the nuisance of postponing a trip abroad. The very fact that the arguments I have been drawing attention to treat all cases of abortion, or even all cases of abortion in which the mother's life is not at stake, as morally on a par ought to have made them suspect at the outset.

Secondly, while I am arguing for the permissibility of abortion in some cases, I am not arguing for the right to secure the death of the unborn child. It is easy to confuse these two things in that up to a certain point in the life of the fetus it is not able to survive outside the mother's body; hence removing it from her body guarantees its death. But they are importantly different. I have argued that you are not morally required to spend nine months in bed, sustaining the life of that violinist; but to say this is by no means to say that if, when you unplug yourself, there is a miracle and he survives, you then have a right to turn round and slit his throat. You may detach yourself even if this costs him his life; you have no right to be guaranteed his death, by some other means, if unplugging yourself does not kill him. There are some people who will feel dissatisfied by this feature of my argument. A woman may be utterly devastated by the thought of a child, a bit of herself, put out for adoption and never seen or heard of again. She may therefore want not merely that the child be detached from her, but more, that it die. Some opponents of abortion are inclined to regard this as beneath contempt—thereby showing insensitivity to what is surely a powerful source of despair. All the same, I agree that the desire for the child's death is not one which anybody may gratify, should it turn out to be possible to detach the child alive.

At this place, however, it should be remembered that we have only been pretending throughout that the fetus is a human being from the moment of conception. A very early abortion is surely not the killing of a person, and so is not dealt with by anything I have said here.

Notes

1. I am very much indebted to James Thomson for discussion, criticism, and many helpful suggestions.
2. Daniel Callahan, *Abortion: Law, Choice and Morality* (New York, 1970), p. 373. This book gives a fascinating survey of the available information on abortion. The Jewish tradition is surveyed in David M. Feldman, *Birth Control in Jewish Law* (New York, 1968), Part 5; the Catholic tradition in John T. Noonan, Jr., "An Almost Absolute Value in History," in *The Morality of Abortion*, ed. John T. Noonan, Jr. (Cambridge, Mass., 1970).
3. The term "direct" in the arguments I refer to is a technical one. Roughly, what is meant by "direct killing" is either killing as an end in itself, or killing as a means to some end, for example, the end of saving someone else's life. See note 6, below, for an example of its use.
4. Cf. *Encyclical Letter of Pope Pius XI on Christian Marriage*. St. Paul Editions (Boston, n.d.), p. 32: "however much we may pity the mother whose health and even life is gravely imperiled in the performance of the duty allotted to her by nature, nevertheless what could ever be a sufficient reason for excusing in any way the direct murder of the innocent? This is precisely what we are dealing with here." Noonan (*The Morality of Abortion*, p. 43) reads this as follows: "What cause can ever avail to excuse in any way the direct killing of the innocent? For it is a question of that."
5. The thesis in (d) is in an interesting way weaker than those in (a), (b), and they rule out abortion even in cases in which both mother *and* child will die if the abortion is not performed. By contrast, one who held the view expressed in (d) could consistently say that one needn't prefer letting two persons die to killing one.
6. Cf. the following passage from Pius XII, *Address to the Italian Catholic Society of Midwives:* "The baby in the maternal breast has the right to life immediately from God.—Hence there is no man, no human authority, no science, no medical eugenic, social, economic or moral 'indication' which can establish or grant a valid juridical ground for a direct deliberate disposition of an innocent human life, that is a disposition which looks to its destruction either as an end or as a means to another end perhaps in itself not illicit.—The baby, still not born, is a man in the same degree and for the same reason as the mother" (quoted in Noonan, *The Morality of Abortion*, p. 45).
7. The need for a discussion of this argument was brought home to me by members of the Society for Ethical and Legal Philosophy, to whom this paper was originally presented.
8. For a discussion of the difficulties involved, and a survey of the European experience with such laws, see *The Good Samaritan and the Law*, ed. James M. Ratcliffe (New York, 1966).

6.2j   Responding to Thomson

What makes Thomson's argument so impressive is the way it begins by granting the opponents of abortion their most powerful claim—the claim that fetuses have valuable lives—and still manages to present an argument in favor of abortion. This way, the opponents of abortion cannot simply turn to Thomson and accuse her of ignoring their arguments. Indeed, so keen is Thomson not to allow herself an easy ride, she even agrees to assume that the life of a fetus is every bit as valuable as the life of an adult. We saw in section 6.2f that there is reason to doubt this assumption. But if Thomson can make her position stick even so, then her achievement will be all the more remarkable. Her argument comes in two main parts. The first part defends the abortion of fetuses conceived through rape. The second part defends the abortion of fetuses conceived through failed contraception. We'll discuss them in turn.

6.2j(i)   Rape   The first part of Thomson's argument is very persuasive. Indeed her example of the unwanted violinist has become a classic of the philosophical literature. I have found, however, that people are often reluctant to accept the relevance of this analogy. They say it's too way out, too unrealistic. But I'd side with Thomson on this one. The example is meant to parallel and to highlight the crucial moral features of pregnancy caused by rape, and it seems to me to be very successful in this. In both cases, we have the absence of the woman's consent; in both cases, the unwanted being with whom the woman is encumbered plays an entirely blameless role; in both cases, that being is a valuable being, whose continued existence depends on the woman's body. The analogy appears to be very well drawn. The sheer unexpectedness of it also serves a useful function: We are jolted out of habitual patterns of thought and forced to think about a familiar problem in a fresh light. Thomson contends, of course, that reflecting on the violinist analogy will persuade us that the abortion of fetuses conceived through rape is, if not exactly admirable or desirable, at any rate justifiable. If we agreed that it would be justifiable to unplug the violinist, we seem to be committed on the same grounds to agree that it would be justifiable to abort a fetus conceived through rape.

The subtlety of Thomson's position protects it against certain obvious objections. Her discussion of supererogation—acting beyond the call of duty— and of minimal decency makes her immune to the charge of seeing *nothing* wrong with killing a valuable, blameless being (such as a fetus). The good samaritan does more than she is required to do and wins our admiration for that—just as a woman who carries to term a fetus conceived through rape deserves our admiration. But no one can be required to be saintly or heroic. A plausible morality can only demand of us that we be minimally decent samaritans. Hence, although the absence of saintliness or heroism may be in some sense regrettable, a person cannot be blamed for doing no more than she is obliged to do. It is plausible to maintain that no one has the obligation to devote a significant portion of her life to nurturing another life that has been imposed upon her by violence. It would be nice if she did go through with it; regrettable if she didn't; but not actually *wrong* not to. In my view, only a morality that demanded the impossible—that is, only a morality that demanded saintly or heroic behavior from all of us all of the time—would condemn the decision to abort a fetus conceived through rape. What is imposed upon us entirely against our will cannot be entirely our responsibility. The first part of Thomson's argument, then, appears successful.

6.2j(ii)   Failed Contraception   The second part of Thomson's argument is a lot less compelling. Here her analogy seems to let her down. We have "people-seeds" floating around, open windows, and faulty mesh screens—which, between them, are supposed to persuade us that it is justifiable to abort fetuses conceived through contraceptive failures. But a critic might doubt that the analogy is persuasive. The problem with the analogy is not that it's too way out or unrealistic. It's that it fails to parallel and to highlight all the morally relevant features of pregnancy caused by failed contraception. In other words, a critic might agree that it would be justifiable, in a minimally decent way, to uproot unwanted people-seeds from the upholstery, and still deny that this has any interesting consequences for the abortion debate. Let's look at the analogy. People-seeds are probably a perfectly adequate parallel for sperm. Faulty mesh screens are fine for faulty condoms. The problem comes with opening your windows, which is obviously meant to stand in for having sex. Here the analogy is pretty awful. Thomson clouds the issue a bit by talking about open windows, bars, and burglars, the idea being that you are not responsible for a burglary if you have taken all reasonable measures against it (the bars) and go ahead and open your windows. This, clearly, is right (although an insurance assessor might disagree if you had the contents of Fort Knox inside!). But your *reason* for opening your windows here—that it's "stuffy"—bears no relation whatever to the activities of the burglar. You have one objective: fresh air. The burglar has another: your possessions. You and the burglar are up to completely different things, and the unfortunate coincidence of your desires and his desires results in your being burgled. I think it is right to say that you have no responsibility for the outcome in a case like this.

But in the case of failed contraception, it is no "unfortunate coincidence" of the woman's desires and her partner's that results in pregnancy. It is their collective desire to have sex that has this consequence. Thomson claims that the analogical woman opens her windows because it is stuffy. But this is a complete disanalogy. Stuffiness is, at least in this case, a private problem, and the analogous solution to it is also private—in other words, masturbation or a good film to take your mind off it. The truth is that the motives for "opening your windows" are not acted upon *despite* the fact that your possibly faulty mesh screen will be bombarded with people-seeds, but at least partly *because* it will be bombarded with them. In other words, given that having sex is essentially bound up with the intravaginal emission of sperm, it is misleading to produce an analogy that makes the emission of sperm somehow an irritating side-effect.

But this way of addressing the shortcomings of Thomson's analogy will not appeal to everyone: To some, no doubt, what I've said will seem unduly biological and mechanistic. The point, however, can easily be put differently. People have sex with each other for many reasons: for pleasure, for togetherness, for procreation, for fear of losing one another, for curiosity's sake, for a bet, for something to do, for fear of what might happen otherwise, for revenge, for a final mystical affirmation of love. And none of these is remotely analogous to Thomson's (essentially solitary) feeling of stuffiness. The people-seeds in all of these cases are integral to the *reason* for opening the window. Which suggests that if one had none of these reasons, one would be absolutely opposed to people-seeds getting in on the act at all, and one would keep one's windows closed accordingly. Mere stuffiness can be sorted out in the ways previously indicated. If this is right, then Thomson's analogy lends no support to the claim that it is justifiable to abort fetuses conceived through faulty contraception.

Someone might say that this misses the point of Thomson's analogy. It might be said that, even given there is no accidental coincidence of purposes in the failed contraception case, the fact that reasonable measures have been taken against conception nevertheless absolves the participants of responsibility—just as the female victim is absolved of responsibility in the case of rape. But Thomson's argument provides no warrant for this view. Once one has given the lie to the allegedly incidental role of people-seeds in the equation, Thomson's analogy is dead in the water. But even so, it might be said that with or without support from Thomson's analogy the fact that precautions have been taken at least reduces the responsibility of those whose sexual activity has resulted in conception. Perhaps the idea here is that by deliberately reducing the *probability* of conception (to about 1 percent, say) you correspondingly reduce your *responsibility* for conception should it occur. It's hard to know what to make of this. Two obvious criticisms do spring to mind, however. The first is that you have hardly reduced the probability of conception as far as you could have done: You could easily have got it down to 0 percent by refraining from sex altogether, or else by being sterilized. The second is that probability and responsibility do not always shadow each other in the way required. For example, if I load ninety-nine blanks and one live round of ammunition into a gun, and I don't know which the live one is, I am hardly only 1 percent responsible if I put the gun to your head, pull the trigger, and unfortunately blow your brains out. Surely I am fully responsible for killing you. If this is right, then it appears that I must also be fully responsible for a pregnancy against which I have taken 99 percent effective precautions.

This last point looks reasonably good. If it *is* good, then the case for aborting fetuses conceived through failed contraception must be rather weak. But perhaps the defender of abortion in such cases still has an avenue of response. It might go as follows. The gun analogy is flawed: there is no good reason for putting a gun to a person's head and pulling the trigger—whether or not you know the contents of its magazine. That is why you deserve to take the rap if something goes wrong. But we have already noted how many good reasons there are for having sex, and sexual activity may be valuable for any of those reasons (many of which include no reference to conception). Whereas the prank with the gun is straightforwardly irresponsible, then, engaging in sexual activity need not be, even if the reasons for doing so rule out a willingness to conceive. If this is a fair way of looking at the situation, the use of reliable—but not, inevitably, fail-safe—contraception is evidence of a responsible attitude toward the possible consequences of an activity engaged in for other, valuable, reasons. This might suggest that the value of those reasons, taken together with the fact that reasonable precautions have been taken, may be set against the responsibility one bears when those precautions fail. If so, then it may be appropriate to view those who find themselves in such a position as unwilling victims of misfortune— a little as a woman who has been raped is the unwilling victim of misfortune —rather than as the architects of their own bad luck.

I have to confess that I do not know how to evaluate this suggestion. I suspect that it captures most of what Thomson really wanted her people-seed analogy to achieve; but then I rather wonder whether it mightn't be vulnerable to much the same objections. What is clear, however, is that if it is granted that fetuses have lives that are worthy of ethical concern (and if Marquis's argument is correct, that *ought* to be granted), the task of justifying the abortion of fetuses conceived through failed contraception is certain to be an uphill struggle. Perhaps a convincing justification can be found. If nothing else, though, the discussion of the present section should have shown what difficulties lie in the way of such a justification—as well as posting a warning against the use of certain kinds of analogy. Indeed, my current suspicion is that no analogy will ever be able to do justice to the unique moral qualities of sexual intercourse between consenting adults.

6.2k   Recap: The Abortion Debate

Our discussion of abortion is almost at an end. Both defenders and opponents of abortion have some powerful arguments at their disposal—even if, as I suspect, the task of the opponents is slightly easier. But take the defenders' worst-case scenario: Suppose that it is morally wrong to abort fetuses except in certain very rare instances (such as fetuses conceived through rape). This would still not be sufficient to show that abortion on demand should be prohibited or criminalized. We saw in the opening paragraph in Chapter One that questions of legality are different from questions of morality. To argue that something is morally wrong is not to argue that it should be made illegal. Legislation needs sometimes to have a consequentialist or utilitarian character—in other words, the legislator needs to consider the likely results of a particular piece of legislation. That is why adultery and lying, although surely morally wrong, are not illegal: Laws against them would be unenforceable and self-defeating. The legislator would not be acting in the public interest were he or she to attempt to outlaw such behavior. A very similar argument is available to those who oppose the criminalization of abortion. Experience suggests that making abortion illegal would not make it go away, but would rather push it underground. Illegal, "back-street" abortions cannot be regulated, nor can proper professional and clinical standards be enforced under such circumstances. The consequence would be that many more women would die, or be seriously harmed, through incompetent or botched abortions—especially poor women, who could not afford the discreet and expensive clinics that would doubtless spring up to abort the fetuses of the wealthy. The overall result, then, would not be a reduction in the number of fetuses killed, but rather an increase in the sum total of human misery. Hence, it would be bad public policy to legislate against abortion.

This argument is very persuasive, and it may well persuade even some of those who are most convinced that abortion is, morally, wrong. But I am sure that most defenders of abortion would prefer a bit more than this. The state of the debate suggests that they have no reason yet to accede to the

worst-case scenario, and that they still have every hope of defending, not merely the legality of abortion, but also the morality of it. So this (you don't need me to tell you) is an argument that is set to run and run. But it will run much more productively than it has tended to in the recent past if the participants would agree to discuss the matter rationally and honestly. There has been far too much sloganeering and name-calling in the abortion debate, and far too much reliance on disreputable philosophical tactics that wouldn't survive for ten seconds in another context. If this part of the chapter has done nothing more than expose some of these, it has achieved its most important purpose.

Study Questions

1. Does the fact that IVF often leads to multiple pregnancies affect the ethical standing of IVF? Should steps be taken to *reduce* the likelihood of multiple pregnancies?
2. Are there any ethical reasons to withold IVF treatment from women over a certain age? Or from women whose economic circumstances will make it hard for them to raise children?
3. Could a justification be given for regarding a fetus conceived through rape as less valuable than a fetus not conceived through rape?
4. Suppose a woman gets pregnant by her partner and wants an abortion. Suppose her partner disagrees. How much weight should be given to the partner's preferences?

Related Cases in Crigger, *Cases in Bioethics,* Third Edition

"Reproductive Rights" (section 6.1) is represented by cases 15, which deals with an unusual, and even somewhat morbid, instance of potential AI, and 13, which questions a couple's decision to go through IVF despite the wife's cancer.

Most relevant to "Abortion" (section 6.2) are cases 14, 16, 17, 40, and 54. Cases 14, 16, and 40 concern the relative importance of the mother's preferences versus the fetus's interests; case 54 introduces the father into the picture (in an extraordinary way); case 19 is about abortion in the context of retarded mothers. The discussions following cases 17, 40, and 54 are especially helpful.

CHAPTER SEVEN

Death and Dying

INTRODUCTION

In Chapter Six, we investigated some of the ethical issues surrounding the beginning of life. Now we turn to the no less difficult issues surrounding the end of it. "Nothing in life is certain," the saying goes, "except death and taxes"—and of these two, the edge would go to death. Taxes, one gathers, can be evaded or avoided; but death can only, if one is fortunate, be postponed for a time. It is, then, the sole thing that we can guarantee will come to us all. This is why death is so often the subject of poetry: Of all subjects, it is the single one that is ensured of universal relevance. When the poet reflects on death, he or she is also, of course, reflecting on the life that leads up to it. Life, it is said, is but a preparation for dying—and the meaning of our lives lies partly in their inevitable end. If we were immortal, our lives would be not merely longer, but of an almost unrecognizably different character. None of our goals and ambitions would be pursued against the clock (or perhaps pursued at all); our desires would lose their urgency; our fears would be less acute; our need to come to terms with life, to mend fences, and to build bridges, would be far gentler. Much of the *problematic* character of existence would simply disappear. Ethics is sometimes defined as the study of, or the search for, the good life—a life that must end in death.

The value of life, then, from an ethical point of view, is essentially bound up with its finiteness, its brevity, its unavoidable conclusion. Were it not for death, the nature of ethics would be vastly different. Indeed, in the absence of death, it is doubtful whether we'd even *have* an ethics. Our understanding of death, then, forms a vital part of our ethical grasp on life. To live as though death were not real—to kid ourselves into thinking that the right diet, for instance, or the right exercise-regime will be sufficient to postpone it indefinitely—is to live blindly: It is to refuse to face up to the true nature of our own existence. And that refusal is an ethical failure. If we deny the nature of existence, we put aside our capacity to deal with it intelligently; we forfeit our capacity to understand the lives of others, to judge and to forgive them in the light of peculiarly mortal values. The denial of death, then, is the denial of ethics. If we get death wrong, or refuse to take the business of dying sufficiently seriously, we will get life wrong too. The present chapter, therefore, is important not only for the consideration of specifically bioethical issues, but also for the consideration of ethics—of the search for the good life—as a whole.

7.1   WHAT IS DEATH?

On the face of it, the question What is death? looks about as easy to answer as a question could be. It's the opposite of life, the final cessation of all function, the irreversible loss of everything that gives life value. It's the state that organisms are in when they give up moving around and eating and breathing and circulating blood and all the other things they did before. Death is the end. And once upon a time, the answer to the question was indeed about this simple. If people's hearts didn't beat, if their breath didn't cloud mirrors, if all the usual reflexes were absent, then they were dead. Moreover, not much swung on when *precisely* they were deemed to have died. They would be buried or cremated in due course, and very little depended on whether death was pronounced at five o'clock, say, or a quarter after. In one sense, at any rate, dying used to be simple. Now, however, our greater technological capacities have confused the picture. We can pick up the minutest trace of brain activity, which may be present even after respiration has stopped; we can monitor respiration and circulation separately, and both with great accuracy. In other words, the factors that together used to indicate death have now become separable, and it is no longer clear which of them should be taken as final.

Furthermore, there didn't used to be a distinction between spontaneous physiological function and any other kind: A person's physiological function was spontaneous or it was nothing. But now that we have life-support machines, functions that have ceased to take place spontaneously can be sustained artificially. So we have another pulling-apart of the traditional conception of death. These added complications matter for at least two reasons. First, they make it harder to know how the idea of death should be understood, and this, as noted earlier, is a matter of real ethical importance when it comes to making sense of the idea of life. Second, they make it harder to know just *when* a person may be treated as dead. This, nowadays, is crucial in a way that it didn't used to be. With our new abilities to transplant organs from one person to another, it has become vital to identify the precise moment of death: Fresh organs transplant better, and even moments can count. For all these reasons, many have felt that it has become necessary, in a sense that it never was before, to have a definition of death that is capable of making very fine discriminations between people who may appear, on the traditional model, to be in identical states.

7.1a   The Official Definition: The Argument of the President's Commission: President's Commission for the Study of Ethical Problems in Medicine and Biomedical and Behavioral Research

The increasing sophistication of our knowledge about the human body has had at least one quite striking effect on the way in which death is conceived. Whereas formerly the focus tended to be squarely on the loss of heart and lung function—on "cardiopulmonary" factors—the emphasis has tended to shift more and more onto the loss of brain function. In part this is due to our increased understanding of the role played by the brain in spontaneous cardiopulmonary function. In part it is due to the thought that what gives our lives their peculiarly human value is bound up with consciousness, which is itself—in ways that no one understands—somehow bound up with brain function. Thus is it that the President's Commission for the Study of Ethical Problems in Medicine and Biomedical and Behavioral Research comes out in favor of a *neurological* conception of death: A person is dead when his or her entire brain has ceased to function.

WHY "UPDATE" DEATH?
The President's Commission

For most of the past several centuries, the medical determination of death was very close to the popular one. If a person fell unconscious or was found so, someone (often but not always a physician) would feel for the pulse, listen for breathing, hold a mirror before the nose to test for condensation, and look to see if the pupils were fixed. Although these criteria have been used to determine death since antiquity, they have not always been universally accepted.

DEVELOPING CONFIDENCE IN THE HEART-LUNG CRITERIA

In the eighteenth century, macabre tales of "corpses" reviving during funerals and exhumed skeletons found to have clawed at coffin lids led to widespread fear of premature burial. Coffins were developed with elaborate escape mechanisms and speaking tubes to the world above, mortuaries employed guards to monitor the newly dead for signs of life, and legislatures passed laws requiring a delay before burial. . . .
. . . The invention of the stethoscope in the mid-nineteenth century enabled physicians to detect heartbeat with heightened sensitivity. The use of this instrument by a well-trained physician, together with other clinical measures, laid to rest public fears of premature burial. The twentieth century brought even more sophisticated technological means to determine death, particularly the electrocardiograph (EKG), which is more sensitive than the stethoscope in detecting cardiac functioning.

THE INTERRELATIONSHIPS OF BRAIN, HEART, AND LUNG FUNCTIONS

The brain has three general anatomic divisions: the cerebrum, with its outer shell called the cortex; the cerebellum; and the brainstem, composed of the midbrain, the pons, and the medulla oblongata. Traditionally, the cerebrum has been referred to as the "higher brain" because it has primary control of consciousness, thought, memory and feeling. The brainstem has been called the "lower brain," since it controls spontaneous, vegetative functions such as swallowing, yawning and sleep-wake cycles. It is important to note that these generalizations are not entirely accurate. Neuroscientists generally agree that such "higher brain" functions as cognition or consciousness probably are not mediated strictly by the cerebral cortex; rather, they probably result from complex interrelations between brainstem and cortex.

Respiration is controlled in the brainstem, particularly the medulla. Neural impulses originating in the respiratory centers of the medulla stimulate the diaphragm and intercostal muscles, which cause the lungs to fill with air. Ordinarily, these respiratory centers adjust the rate of breathing to maintain the correct levels of carbon dioxide and oxygen. In certain circumstances, such as heavy exercise, sighing, coughing or sneezing, other areas of the brain modulate the activities of the respiratory centers or even briefly take direct control of respiration.

Destruction of the brain's respiratory center stops respiration, which in turn deprives the heart of needed oxygen, causing it too to cease functioning. The traditional signs of life—respiration and heartbeat—disappear: the person is dead. The "vital signs" traditionally used in diagnosing death thus reflect the direct interdependence of respiration, circulation and the brain.

The artificial respirator and concomitant life-support systems have changed this simple picture. Normally, respiration ceases when the functions of the diaphragm and intercostal muscles are impaired. This results from direct injury to the muscles or (more commonly) because the neural impulses between the brain and these muscles are interrupted. However, an artificial respirator (also called a ventilator) can be used to compensate for the inability of the thoracic muscles to fill the lungs with air. Some of these machines use negative pressure to expand the chest wall (in which case they are called "iron lungs"); others use positive pressure to push air into the lungs. The respirators are equipped with devices to regulate the rate and depth of "breathing," which are normally controlled by the respiratory centers in the medulla. The machines cannot compensate entirely for the defective neural connections since they cannot regulate blood gas levels precisely. But, provided that the lungs themselves have not been extensively damaged, gas exchange can continue and appropriate levels of oxygen and carbon dioxide can be maintained in the circulating blood.

Unlike the respiratory system, which depends on the neural impulses from the brain, the heart can pump blood without external control. Impulses from brain centers modulate the inherent rate and force of the heartbeat but are not required for the heart to contract at a level of function that is ordinarily adequate. Thus, when artificial respiration provides adequate oxygenation and associated medical treatments regulate essential plasma components and blood pressure, an intact heart will continue to beat, despite loss of brain functions. At present, however, no machine can take over the functions of the heart except for a very limited time and in limited circumstances (e.g., a heart-lung machine used during surgery). Therefore, when a severe injury to the heart or major blood vessels prevents the circulation of the crucial blood supply to the brain, the loss of brain functioning is inevitable because no oxygen reaches the brain.

LOSS OF VARIOUS BRAIN FUNCTIONS

The most frequent causes of irreversible loss of functions of the whole brain are: (1) direct trauma to the head, such as from a motor vehicle accident or a gunshot wound, (2) massive spontaneous hemorrhage into the brain as a result of ruptured aneurysm or complications of high blood pressure, and (3) anoxic damage from cardiac or respiratory arrest or severely reduced blood pressure.

Many of these severe injuries to the brain cause an accumulation of fluid and swelling in the brain tissue, a condition called cerebral edema. In severe cases of edema, the pressure within the closed cavity increases until it exceeds the systolic blood pressure, resulting in a total loss of blood flow to both the upper and lower portions of the brain. If deprived of blood flow for at least 10–15 minutes, the brain, including the brainstem, will completely cease functioning. Other pathophysiologic mechanisms also result in a progressive and, ultimately, complete cessation of intracranial circulation.

Once deprived of adequate supplies of oxygen and glucose, brain neurons will irreversibly lose all activity and ability to function. In adults, oxygen and/or glucose deprivation for more than a few minutes causes some neuron loss. Thus, even in the absence of direct trauma and edema, brain functions can be lost if circulation to the brain is impaired. If blood flow is cut off, brain tissues completely self-digest (autolyze) over the ensuing days.

When the brain lacks all functions, consciousness is, of course, lost. While some spinal reflexes often persist is such bodies (since circulation to the spine is separate from that of the brain), all reflexes controlled by the brainstem as well as cognitive, affective and integrating functions are absent. Respiration and circulation in these bodies may be generated by a ventilator together with intensive medical management. In adults who have experienced irreversible cessation of the functions of the entire brain, this mechanically generated functioning can continue only a limited time because the heart usually stops beating within two to ten days. (An infant or small child who has lost all brain functions will typically suffer cardiac arrest within several weeks, although respiration and heartbeat can sometimes be maintained even longer.)

Less severe injury to the brain can cause mild to profound damage to the cortex, lower cerebral structures, cerebellum, brainstem, or some combination thereof. The cerebrum, especially the cerebral cortex, is more easily injured by loss of blood flow or oxygen than is the brainstem. A 4–6 minute loss of blood flow—caused by, for example, cardiac arrest—typically damages the cerebral cortex permanently, while the relatively more resistant brainstem may continue to function.

When brainstem functions remain, but the major components of the cerebrum are irreversibly destroyed, the patient is in what is usually called a "persistent vegetative state" or "persistent noncognitive state." Such persons may exhibit spontaneous, involuntary movements such as yawns or facial grimaces, their eyes may be open and they may be capable of breathing without assistance. Without higher brain functions, however, any apparent wakefulness does not represent awareness of self or environment (thus, the condition is often described as "awake but unaware"). The case of Karen Ann Quinlan has made this condition familiar to the general public. With necessary medical and nursing care—including feeding through intravenous or nasogastric tubes, and antibiotics for recurrent pulmonary infections—such patients can survive months or years, often without a respirator. (The longest survival exceeded 37 years.)

CONCLUSION: THE NEED FOR RELIABLE POLICY

Medical interventions can often provide great benefit in avoiding *irreversible* harm to a patient's injured heart, lungs, or brain by carrying a patient through a period of acute need. These techniques have, however, thrown new light on the interrelationship of these crucial organ systems. This has created complex issues for public policy as well.

For medical and legal purposes, partial brain impairment must be distinguished from complete and irreversible loss of brain functions or "whole brain death." The President's Commission, as subsequent chapters explain more fully, regards the cessation of the vital functions of the entire brain—and not merely portions thereof, such as those responsible for cognitive functions—as the only proper neurologic basis for declaring death. This conclusion accords with the overwhelming consensus of medical and legal experts and the public.

Present attention to the "definition" of death is part of a process of development in social attitudes and legal rules stimulated by the unfolding of biomedical knowledge. In the nineteenth century increasing knowledge and practical skill made the public confident that death could be diagnosed reliably using cardiopulmonary criteria. The question now is whether, when medical intervention may be responsible for a patient's respiration and circulation, there are other equally reliable ways to diagnose death. . . .

7.1b Responding to the Commission

The commission certainly gives good reasons for accepting the "whole brain death" standard for the determination of death, and it also explains very clearly why new technologies have had such a impact on the question. Criticism of the commission's position seems likely to come from two main directions: from those who favor a brain-death standard of death, but do not believe that it is necessary for the entire brain to have stopped functioning; and from those who favor a definition of death that does not refer to the brain alone (or even at all). We will treat these positions in turn.

Advocates of a partial brain-death definition of death normally wish to count as dead those in whom all higher neurological functioning has ceased. On this account, a person is dead if his or her cerebrum has stopped functioning; the fact that his or her brain stem may still continue to function is regarded as irrelevant. What reasons might someone have to prefer this way of defining death to the commission's way of defining it? The main reason, I think, lies in the motivation for concentrating on the brain at all. The supporter of a higher-brain death definition might argue as follows. We, like the President's Commission, regard the brain as *the* crucial organ. Why? Because the brain is responsible for all of those functions that make human life distinctive and valuable. Without the brain, there is no possibility of loving or loathing, of hoping or fearing, of pride, fulfillment, or regret. It is in virtue of the brain that we are autonomous beings; it is in virtue of consciousness, for which the brain is somehow responsible, that we are capable of the experiences that give our lives their meaning. This is why we concentrate on the brain. But notice: Every one of these capacities is a higher capacity. Each of them depends, not upon the brain as a whole, but on the cerebrum. Thus the definition of death should make reference to the loss of cerebral function specifically, and not to the loss of all brain function. Which means that the commission's insistence on a "whole brain death" standard is inappropriate. A person should be regarded as dead, not when all brain function is irreversibly lost, but when cerebral function is irreversibly lost.

There is something quite plausible about this alternative to the commission's position. Indeed, if it is true that the brain should be regarded as *the* crucial organ, and if it is true that the brain is privileged in this way because of the value we place on consciousness, then it does seem that the commission has, as suggested, gone astray. If the irreversible loss of consciousness is what counts, a higher-brain death standard is more appropriate than a whole-brain death standard. This claim creates some real difficulties for the official definition. But one immediate counterargument, at least, is available. People who have lost all higher brain function, but in whom the brain stem still functions, remain capable of spontaneous cardiopulmonary activity: They will keep breathing and their hearts will continue to beat. Such people, surely, are not dead. To update the definition of death, so as to take account of technological advances, is one thing. But if the updated definition departs too far from an ordinary, commonsensical conception of death, it becomes quite unclear whether we are still talking about the same concept. On the higher-brain death model, after all, it would be perfectly appropriate to pronounce dead, and therefore to bury or to cremate, a warm, breathing person, about whose body the blood continues to be pumped by a perfectly healthy heart. Common sense tells us that no definition that has this consequence can possibly be a definition of death. Any plausible new definition needs to be a definition of the *same* concept; and the concept of death, however it is understood, certainly rules out the burial of breathing people.

This counterargument seems to me to be an unanswerable reply to the advocates of a cerebrum-death standard. However important consciousness might be to our conception of life, and hence however important its loss to our conception of death, it seems that consciousness cannot be the only factor to be taken into account. But this hardly gets the commission, and the official definition of death, off the hook. For although the proposed alternative to the official definition seems to be a failure, the criticisms of the commission's account, upon which the alternative account was founded, remain unanswered. If you're not going to focus on consciousness, after all— and hence on the higher brain—then what is the point of concentrating on the brain *at all?*

It is at this juncture that criticism of the commission's position from the second direction—from those who believe that it is wrong to focus exclusively on the brain when defining death—begins. Such a critic will no doubt applaud the fact that the commission's definition rules out the burial of people with spontaneous cardiopulmonary function. This, as noted above, would simply fly too hard in the face of common sense. But notice what the commission's position doesn't rule out. A person whose entire brain has died loses spontaneous cardiopulmonary function. But that function can be maintained (for between "two and ten days") by a ventilator. So now we have someone else who is breathing, whose heart is circulating blood around his or her body, and who nevertheless becomes a suitable candidate for burial or cremation. Again, this is not so much a fine-tuning of our ordinary conception of death, as a near-reversal of it. Imagine: If ventilators were extremely cheap, compact, and battery-operated, it would, on the commission's account, be perfectly appropriate to bury a person who was still hooked up to one and breathing (although I daresay the coffin would need modifying!). It is hard to see what might persuade one to accept this.

Perhaps the commission might respond by reemphasizing the fact that a person whose entire brain has died is no longer capable of spontaneous cardiopulmonary function. The sort of breathing that someone on a ventilator does is not, it might be suggested, *real* breathing. But this emphasis on spontaneity is very questionable indeed. The commission itself points out that a "heart-lung machine [may be] used during surgery," presumably for the purposes of keeping someone alive who, without the machine, would die on the operating table. Such a person enjoys no spontaneous cardiopulmonary function, and yet is clearly not dead. Nor is the person whose cardiac function is maintained only with the aid of a pacemaker. Loss of spontaneous function appears to be quite insufficient for death. The suggestion, then, that people whose entire brains have died, and who require a ventilator in order to breathe, are not "really" breathing—because they are not spontaneously breathing—looks doomed to failure. On the commission's account, it still comes out that people who are breathing may appropriately be buried.

By this time it is quite unclear what the virtues of concentrating exclusively on the brain are meant to be. Whether one opts for a whole-brain definition of death or a higher-brain definition it seems that one inevitably ends up in a position that advocates the burial or cremation of people who are, on any ordinary conception of death, not dead. Nor, a critic might say, does the President's Commission offer any compelling reasons for its exclusive concentration on the brain. Indeed the commission's assertion that the whole-brain death conception "accords with the overwhelming consensus of medical and legal experts and the public" will repay a moment's reflection. The part about the public would surely be false if the public were aware of the unorthodox burial arrangements that the commission's conception implicitly licenses. The parts about the medical and legal experts, however, are almost certainly true. But this, it might be suggested, is not because the official definition provides a particularly convincing account of death; rather, it is because it provides a particularly convenient one. The increasing success of transplant technology has led to an increasing demand for transplantable organs, which, in the best case, are taken from donors who still have cardiopulmonary function. From a medical point of view, then, the ideal organ donor may well be one whose cardiopulmonary function is maintained by a ventilator; from a legal point of view, it is obviously preferable if such a donor can be regarded as "dead," so as to avoid the complex legal problems that killing people raises. Thus the official definition is understandably popular among those with an interest—a generally praiseworthy interest, too—in making transplantation as efficient and as successful as possible. The only problem, a critic might conclude, is that the official definition of death fails to capture what we mean by "death" when we are not pursuing an interest in transplantation. Which suggests that the official definition is not really a definition of *death* at all.

7.1c   The Traditional Conception

Those who doubt, for some of the reasons given in the previous section, that a definition of death should concentrate so exclusively on the brain as the President's Commission's definition does, may wish to urge a return to a more traditional conception of death. Indeed, the sheer intuitive oddness of defining death in such a way as implicitly to endorse the burial or cremation of breathing people suggests that cardiopulmonary criteria of death may be altogether more appropriate than neurological criteria. We have already seen that no cardiopulmonary criteria could insist on the loss, merely, of spontaneous cardiopulmonary function; rather, because no one wants to count people fitted with pacemakers as dead, such criteria would have to insist on the irreversible loss of heart and lung function *however maintained.* So construed, a cardiopulmonary conception of death would at least be sure of avoiding the counterintuitive conclusions about burial practices that the neurological conceptions are prone to. Moreover, the cardiopulmonary conception is intuitively far better at describing what, in some cases, is actually going on. Take the President's Commission's own example: A person has suffered whole-brain death, and yet his or her heart and lung functions are being artificially sustained by a ventilator. According to the commission, he or she is already dead, and cardiopulmonary function cannot be expected to continue for longer than ten days. So what does the commission say has happened when it does stop? The person is, after all, *already* dead in the commission's view, so we are presented with the bizarre notion that a person can suffer cardiac arrest several days after he or she has died. Surely it is more plausible to say that the person is alive, or on the brink of death, for the period during which his or her cardiopulmonary function is being maintained by the ventilator, and to say that he or she has only died when the final and inevitable cardiac arrest has happened (or when the ventilator is switched off). It seems to me that our intuitions are all in accord with this way of describing the event.

Are there any good reasons to reject the traditional, cardiopulmonary definition of death? The fact that normal heart and lung function depends on the brain stem does not by itself show that the brain should be the proper focus of our attention. The facts, after all, can be reversed: Normal brain function depends on heart and lung function. Nor does the fact that we can now monitor brain function independently of cardiopulmonary function show anything very important, for the reverse is just as true. Indeed, it seems that the main motivation for rejecting the cardiopulmonary conception of death must lie in its comparatively inconvenient consequences for transplantation. On the cardiopulmonary conception, after all, the brain-dead person on a ventilator is alive, and removing his or her heart, for example, in the hope of transplanting it elsewhere, would cause him or her to die. And this seems a very different thing from removing the heart of a person who is already, conveniently, classified as dead. The question arises, then, whether this objection to cardiopulmonary criteria of death should be regarded as decisive.

Some will wish to say that it should. Admittedly the alternatives, such as that advocated by the President's Commission, involve *altering* our conception of death, rather than merely fine-tuning it in the light of new knowledge about the human body. But this, it might be said, is a comparatively small price to pay for the benefits of recent advances in transplantation technology. If we replace our commonsense conception of death with a purely technical conception, we will permit useful and valuable clinical procedures to be undertaken in a far more efficient way. And that is something we should all welcome.

Others will be less convinced. Indeed, some will argue that it is possible to retain an intuitively plausible conception of death, such as the cardiopulmonary conception, and still allow transplantation to proceed in the ways envisaged by those who favor the counterintuitive, official conception. This, it might be said, could be done as follows. We'll regard the brain-dead person on a ventilator as alive, but we'll allow him or her to be killed if his or her organs could benefit someone else by transplant. The idea here is that, although such a procedure would, strictly speaking, cause a person's death, it would not do so wrongly, or unjustly. In other words, the mere fact that someone is, literally, alive does not by itself show that it would be wrong to kill them. The challenge, it might be argued, is not to define the problem away by tinkering with the concept of death (as the President's Commission, for instance, seems willing to do); it is rather to think more carefully about what makes life valuable (when it is), and about what makes killing wrong (when it is).

7.1d   Recap: Defining Death

We have seen that there are competing conceptions of death, and also disagreements over how and whether recent advances in our technological abilities should affect the way we think about death. The official view is that those advances should indeed affect our thinking about death, and that it is now appropriate to define death in exclusively neurological terms. The traditionalists hold that there is no need substantially to revise our conception of death, and that an essentially cardiopulmonary account, rather than a neurological account, captures and makes sense of our intuitions better. I have suggested that a good part of the reason for officially redefining death is found, not in any genuinely new conceptual difficulties that that word raises, but rather in the practical, and possibly legal, consequences of *not* redefining it, now that our transplantation technologies are so advanced. It has become convenient to classify a certain class of potential organ donor as dead. Many will think that this need justifies the somewhat counterintuitive consequences of the official definition of death. Others will think that what is required is a reevaluation, not of the concept of death, but of the value of life. In the second part of this chapter we will discuss issues directly relevant to this latter suggestion. (For further discussion of organ transplantation, see 10.2.)

7.2   EUTHANASIA

One of the most widely discussed issues in contemporary bioethics is euthanasia—literally, "a good death," or, as it is often called, "mercy killing." Our increased ability to keep people alive long after they would ordinarily have died raises crucial questions about the justification for keeping people alive. Many people feel that there is no justification for keeping certain people alive at any cost just because we happen to be able to; such people are likely to be in favor of euthanasia in certain cases. Others—perhaps especially health care professionals—believe that it is the primary duty of the professional to do whatever is in his or her power to stave off death or harm to patients; from this perspective euthanasia will most likely seem wrong. The question whether we should seek to sustain life at any cost is an enormously complex and difficult one. So is the question whether we should ever deliberately end a life that seems, to the person whose life it is, to be worse than death. But perhaps we can make a start by comparing euthanasia to two other ways of causing death, in an effort to map out the ethical terrain more clearly. For euthanasia, whatever else might be said about it, certainly *is* a matter of causing death. And we'll need to get at an idea of when the causing of death is (and is not) justifiable. In the following two sections, then, we will compare euthanasia to suicide; in the section after that, we'll compare it to murder.

7.2a   Suicide

Defenders of euthanasia often say that euthanasia is really a form of suicide. If this is true, and if suicide is (at least sometimes) justifiable, then euthanasia must also be (at least sometimes) justifiable. In effect, this claim depends upon imagining an unbroken progression from ordinary suicide at one end, through assisted suicide, to euthanasia at the other end, with every stage having essentially the same ethical character as ordinary suicide. In many ways, the picture looks plausible. Imagine that you have a friend who is terminally and painfully ill; she has nothing to look forward to other than a lingering and still more painful death. She injects herself with an overdose of morphine—she commits suicide. Few people would say that she was wrong to do that. Now suppose, however, that she is unable to obtain the morphine: She asks you to obtain it for her. Nothing in the example has changed, it seems, except that your help is now required. Surely if it is okay for her to kill herself when she can obtain morphine without help, it must be okay for her to kill herself with morphine obtained by someone else; if so, it must surely be okay to agree to obtain the morphine for her. The fact that you have assisted her in her suicide does not appear to alter the ethical situation in any important respect. If her suicide would have been justifiable when committed unassisted, it must, by the same token, be justifiable to assist her in the committing of it. Now imagine a final alteration to the example. Not only is your friend terminally and painfully ill, she is also too weak and incapacitated to administer an injection to herself: She asks you to inject the morphine for her. This is now a full-fledged case of euthanasia, but the essential ethical character of the situation does not appear to be very different from the case in which your friend commits suicide unaided. If her unassisted suicide would have been justifiable, and if it would have been justifiable to assist her in her own suicide (by providing her with morphine), it must surely also be justifiable to assist her in the act that directly causes her death. If so, then euthanasia of this kind really is no different, ethically, from ordinary, unassisted suicide. Cooperating with someone in their desire to die appears ethically justifiable when that desire is itself justifiable. Under those circumstances, then, euthanasia appears to be (at least sometimes) justifiable. Euthanasia under circumstances such as these—where the person in question expressly wishes to die, but requires or requests assistance in order to do so—is usually called *voluntary* euthanasia.

An opponent of voluntary euthanasia might react to this argument in one of two ways. He or she might admit the parallel between suicide and voluntary euthanasia, but claim that suicide itself is unjustifiable. That is the claim we will investigate in this section. Or he or she might claim that there *is* an important difference between your friend killing herself and your doing the deed for her; we'll look at that claim in the next section.

Here, then, our question is this: Is suicide morally justifiable? If the answer is that suicide is never morally justifiable, then no defense of voluntary euthanasia can be mounted on the strength of the parallels between the two. If the answer is that suicide is sometimes or always morally justifiable, then the defense of voluntary euthanasia can go ahead. So what reason might someone have for claiming that suicide is always wrong? I suppose there might be a religious reason, but religious reasons are only persuasive to one's co-religionists. There is also the muddled claim that suicide is an unnatural way of dying. But we saw in 6.1a that mere unnaturalness doesn't amount to an ethical problem: It isn't "natural" to be cured of breast cancer, either. Indeed, the case against suicide is extraordinarily difficult to maintain. One may object to the reasons for it in particular cases because such reasons may seem trivial or ill thought-out. In particular cases, too, one might feel that the person in question has given insufficient thought to the interests of others, such as his or her dependents. But to move from some perhaps quite justifiable objections to specific acts of suicide to a *general* condemnation of suicide is extremely difficult. The primary harm, if it is a harm, inflicted by people who commit suicide is to themselves; it is a decision that they make in what they believe to be their own best interests. These facts pose a real challenge to anyone who wishes to argue that suicide is always, in itself, morally wrong.

Perhaps the best nonreligious case against suicide is found in the state of mind of the person who has given up on life, but has not yet departed from it. In this state of mind, a person might well become indifferent to all of the people, things, and feelings that would normally be held dear. For instance, I might, having elected suicide, just not *care* about the effect that my death might have on others; I mightn't care about anything but myself. Yet to care about nothing but oneself is to step outside the bounds of value, to lose all sense of what is justifiable and what is not. A person in this state is not merely, as we might say, "dead to the world" but dead to the *moral* world, and a person who is dead to the moral world may be a terrible and threatening sight to those still "alive" to it. A sense of that threat can perhaps be gleaned from the behavior of suicide bombers, who simply do not care about the lives that will be lost along with their own; or perhaps from the feeling, which most of us will have experienced, that it would scarcely matter if the whole world were to come to an end at the moment when we ourselves die. The dreadfulness of this moral indifference is not hard to see; I suspect that it is with something of this sort in mind that people occasionally say that the real sin in suicide is the sin of despair (of indifference to life, of being dead to the world). If so, there *is* a sort of general case to be made against suicide, at least inasmuch as the decision to die renders a person dead to the world before he or she is actually, clinically, dead within it.

How far this point might be pushed, I don't know. It is easy to imagine someone simply denying that people who have decided to kill themselves must inevitably become dead to the world in this sense; nor is it obvious that someone who does enter that state can be blamed for it in the way that people normally can be blamed for doing things that are morally wrong. In other words, this case against suicide—although it may be the best general case available—is not one that it is easy to maintain in the face even of some quite obvious objections. Most of us, I guess, will conclude that there is no compelling general case to be made against suicide. If that is so, then the way is open for a defense of voluntary euthanasia based on a parallel with suicide. For if suicide cannot be shown to be always wrong, then it must on occasion be justifiable. If voluntary euthanasia can be shown to be relevantly similar to suicide, then it, too, must on occasion be justifiable. The question now is whether voluntary euthanasia can indeed be shown to be relevantly similar to ordinary cases of suicide.

7.2b   Voluntary Euthanasia and Suicide

What differences are there between ordinary suicide and voluntary euthanasia? The most obvious difference is the involvement in the second case, but not in the first, of another person. The opponent of voluntary euthanasia may claim that this difference is crucial. He or she might try to argue like this: when, in the example mentioned earlier, your friend commits suicide by herself, it is her own life that she is taking, and she is directly responsible for its loss. No one else is implicated, and no one else ends up dead; moreover, there is no one now left to blame for her death if her suicide should be judged to have been a mistake. But when you inject the morphine for her, even at her own request, you become responsible for causing a death that is not your own. You take someone else's life and must also take the consequences. This argument is not very persuasive, however. The emphasis on taking the blame or the consequences seems particularly misplaced: If your friend's suicide would have been justifiable, then nothing in the counterargument shows that it would *not* be justifiable to assist her in any way up to and including euthanasia. Furthermore, the question of who actually performs the act that causes death is not obviously as crucial as the objection assumes. If, for example, I put out a contract on my bank manager, and pay you for doing the actual killing, then I am surely morally responsible for causing my bank manager's death—even though it was your finger that was on the trigger. In other words, the issue of who, precisely, is the direct cause of death does not by itself settle the important ethical question, at least not in the way that the present objection to voluntary euthanasia appears to suppose. The mere fact that you and not your friend administers the morphine is not enough to make your act more or less problematic than hers when she is the one to administer the morphine. This objection is not well enough focused to establish any important moral difference between suicide and voluntary euthanasia.

An altogether better attempt in the same direction is available, however. Assuming that suicide is sometimes justifiable, what makes your friend's unassisted suicide ethically acceptable? Presumably a combination of (at least) the following factors: Her condition is incurable and will lead to her death; her condition is also very painful; she feels she has nothing to look forward to except more pain, and perhaps a death less dignified than it might be; and she has *chosen* to die now rather than live on. In other words, her own assessment of her position, together with her assessment of her own best interests, has led to the conclusion that it would be better for her to end her own life now. Her decision to commit suicide is a fully autonomous decision. Assuming that no one else's interests are as vitally affected as her own, this autonomous decision, like any other autonomous decision, deserves to be respected. Most would say that she is justified on these grounds in killing herself. But she, of course, is in a very different position from the one that you are in when she asks you to inject the morphine for her. You can understand her reasons for not wishing to live; you can share her assessment of where her own best interests lie; but you cannot share her autonomous decision. You can never be completely sure that she means what she says—that your action in injecting her with morphine really does conform with her own deepest wishes. She may merely be making a plea for attention, or acting dramatically, or suffering from a temporary fit of depression. This fact, it might be concluded, is enough to show that there genuinely is a moral difference between suicide and voluntary euthanasia. It may show, moreover, that voluntary euthanasia cannot be justified in the same way as suicide (perhaps) can be.

This is a much more powerful objection to voluntary euthanasia than the previous one, and in pointing up the uncertainty of our conclusions about the true desires of others, it also serves to highlight the care required whenever we attempt to act in other people's interests. But the defender of voluntary euthanasia does have a promising line of reply. For the objection, surely, exaggerates the difference between suicide and voluntary euthanasia. After all, the suicide case may not itself be all that clear cut. Suppose your friend tells you what she means to do, giving you her reasons as before. I don't imagine you'd simply hear her out, say "Fine," and leave her to it. Surely you'd discuss her decision with her, try to make certain that her decision really was the one she wanted, really did conform with her interests and her wishes; you'd want to be sure that she wasn't temporarily out of her senses, or pleading for attention, or acting dramatically. In other words, you'd want to be sure that her decision to die really was a fully autonomous decision. If you weren't sure of this, I guess you'd probably try to dissuade her or to prevent her from killing herself. You might stay with her to keep an eye on her, or arrange for others to do so; you might even, in an extreme case, seek to have her taken into care. None of this, surely, would count as an unjustifiable interference in her autonomy. Rather, it would show a proper concern for her *as* an autonomous agent. Your concern would be to make certain that in allowing her to act in accordance with her apparently autonomous wishes, you were allowing her to act in accordance with her genuinely autonomous wishes also. If you were certain of this, and if her assessment of her situation and her interests were convincing, then it would be plausible to say that your (no doubt reluctant) decision not to interfere with her decision to kill herself would be justified.

But this, of course, is exactly similar to the case of voluntary euthanasia. Just as you'd have to be utterly convinced that your friend meant it in order to be prepared to refrain from interfering in her suicide, so you'd have to be utterly convinced in order to be prepared to assist her (by, for example, providing her with morphine), or in order to be prepared to inject the morphine for her. The differences between allowing someone to commit suicide and performing voluntary euthanasia on them are not, the defender of voluntary euthanasia might conclude, morally significant. Allowing someone to go ahead and commit suicide is not a less serious matter than administering the lethal dose yourself: Both are immensely serious, and both require the utmost care for the autonomy of the person whose life is at stake. But if one of these courses of action—allowing someone to commit suicide—is sometimes justifiable, so must the other—voluntary euthanasia—be justifiable.

This conclusion might be bolstered by considering another kind of example. Suppose you witness the following harrowing scene. An automobile accident leaves a driver trapped in the burning wreckage of his car. The flames are moving closer to him and there is no prospect of rescue. He is just able to reach into his glove-compartment and retrieve the gun he keeps there. He shoots himself. No one could do anything to stop this. Nor, surely, would anyone seriously wish to stop it, given that the driver cannot be rescued and that he will certainly burn to death otherwise. This appears to be as clear a case of justifiable suicide as one could hope for. Suppose, however, that the driver hasn't got a gun, but that you do, and the driver yells desperately for you to toss it to him through the smashed window. What reason could you possibly have to refuse? To throw the gun to him would surely be justifiable. And if, finally, the driver's arms are trapped and he yells to you to shoot him because he can't use a gun himself, could anyone really blame you if you agreed to and did? Indeed, to put it more strongly: Wouldn't it be a terrible cruelty to refuse? The driver's desires are clear, comprehensible, and surely well-warranted. So what compelling reason could you offer for ignoring them? Of course, you might be squeamish and refuse on that count. But squeamishness isn't a *reason;* later, having refused to shoot him, and watched him burn to death instead, you might surely conclude that you had decided wrongly. If this argument is convincing, it strongly suggests that the moral differences between allowing someone to commit suicide and performing voluntary euthanasia on them are not great, and that in cases where the one would be justifiable, so would the other be.

We saw in the previous section that it was difficult to maintain the claim that suicide is always morally wrong. In this section we have seen that it is no easier to maintain a hard and fast moral distinction between suicide and voluntary euthanasia. If these conclusions are acceptable, it appears that voluntary euthanasia may be justifiable on exactly the grounds that allowing someone to commit suicide may be justifiable. This places the hurdle quite high. For unless one is firmly and rationally convinced that the decision of the person in question is a fully autonomous one, based on a full and persuasive assessment of his or her interests, one has no business to be doing either. Indeed, the opponent of voluntary euthanasia has a last point to enter at this stage. He or she may suggest that, even if voluntary euthanasia *may* sometimes be morally justifiable, it is nonetheless a good idea to keep it illegal. The stakes, after all, are very high, and if the person who is contemplating performing voluntary euthanasia is aware that he or she might face prosecution, he or she is likely to make really sure that such an action accords with the truly autonomous interests of the sufferer before going ahead and doing it. This would at least make sure that people played safe. And, if prosecutions were rare, it might also mean that those cases in which voluntary euthanasia *is* justifiable would, in effect, be allowed to go ahead. But then perhaps that means that it ought to be illegal to allow people to commit suicide too.

7.2c Nonvoluntary Euthanasia and Murder

In the previous two sections, we have investigated some of the arguments for and against voluntary euthanasia by comparing it to suicide. In this section we turn to nonvoluntary euthanasia, in other words, to the "mercy killing" of people who have *not* requested their own deaths (I leave aside discussion of those who have made such requests in the form of "living wills" until 7.2g, below). A person is the subject of nonvoluntary euthanasia, then, when the decision that it would be in his or her best interest to die is taken by somebody else. Obviously, it is this crucial decision taken by the second person that invites the comparison between nonvoluntary euthanasia and murder: Murderers, after all, decide that others should die, normally without consulting their victims first.

An opponent of nonvoluntary euthanasia is liable to regard nonvoluntary euthanasia as a form of murder (much as supporters of voluntary euthanasia regard that as a form of suicide). If it is true that nonvoluntary euthanasia is a form of murder, then it is clearly going to be very hard to claim that nonvoluntary euthanasia can ever be justifiable: Murder is surely a central example of an unjustifiable kind of action. But what makes murder unjustifiable? We have already looked at this question in another context, when discussing abortion (see 6.2), and we can carry over our conclusion from there. Assuming that we are not dealing with cases of self-defense, legitimate warfare, and so on, killing people is wrong when it goes against their autonomous preferences, when it contravenes their best interests, and/or when it robs them of a "future like ours." Thus if I am killed by a mugger, his or her action is immoral in virtue of at least the following facts: I would strongly prefer not to die; all of my current interests would be far better served by my staying alive; and my future will be taken away from me if I am killed. Any of these facts by itself would be sufficient to make my murder wrong. But all of them together make it about as wrong as an action could be.

This allows us to see at once why at least some categories of nonvoluntary euthanasia must be wholly unjustifiable. The program adopted by the Nazis before and during the last war of killing handicapped and mentally incompetent people, though described by them as "euthanasia," was clearly murder. There is no reason to suppose, and every reason to doubt, that the majority of handicapped and incompetent people's preferences and interests would best be served by their being killed. It would be an extraordinary piece of arrogance to claim that such people were not, by being killed, also being deprived of futures of much the same value as anyone else's. In other words, if we can all agree that the mugger would be wholly wrong to murder me, we can agree, on exactly the same grounds, that a nonvoluntary "euthanasia" program such as the Nazis' would be wholly wrong too. We can also agree, again on the same grounds, that there is no possibility of justifying the killing of *any* patient who is able to conceive and to express a preference in the matter without consulting him or her first. Of course, as soon as consultation takes place, is taken seriously, and the patient requests your help in the matter, we are back in the territory of voluntary, and not nonvoluntary, euthanasia.

No one, I think, seriously wants to recommend nowadays any clearly murderous "euthanasia" program that involves killing people against their will. That is not where the debate over nonvoluntary euthanasia is centered. The cases posing the problems now largely concern, not handicapped or incompetent people, but people, such as those in persistent vegetative states (PVS), who have irreversibly lost consciousness—people who cannot be consulted about, or express, any preferences whatsoever. Obviously there is no possibility of voluntary euthanasia here. The question is whether it is ever justifiable to decide that a person who is, as it were, beyond preferences should die. When we call this "nonvoluntary" euthanasia, then, we clearly do not mean to say that a patient is being killed against his or her will (which would plainly be wrong); we are talking instead about killing a patient for whom the very idea of will, and the expression of will, are no longer possibilities, and never will be possibilities again.

The defender of killing in cases such as this will naturally be keen to point out the differences between the nonvoluntary euthanasia of PVS patients and murder. None of the factors that make murder wrong, it might be claimed, are present in the nonvoluntary euthanasia case. The patient, being irreversibly comatose, is incapable of any autonomy whatever, and so cannot have his or her autonomy contravened; nor does he or she still have any interests; nor can he or she be robbed of a "future like ours," since the future in question just isn't there to be taken away. If this is right then it would seem that central cases of nonvoluntary euthanasia cannot be wrong for any of the reasons that make central cases of murder wrong. If so, this constitutes a powerful defense of nonvoluntary euthanasia in cases where a patient has irreversibly lost all possibility of consciousness.

How might an opponent of nonvoluntary euthanasia respond? I guess that the first line to suggest itself would be an insistence on our *ignorance.* For all we know, the patient in a PVS is indeed beyond having preferences. But how can we be sure? Given our total ignorance of the relation between the mind and the brain, how confident can we be that a flat brain scan indicates a total absence of consciousness? How can we say, either, that we *know* that the patient's condition is irreversible? The completely unexpected sometimes happens, doesn't it? If so, how can we prove that the patient hasn't a future of which he or she might be unjustifiably deprived? The opponent of nonvoluntary euthanasia will argue that the impossibility of arriving at perfectly certain answers to these questions shows that we have no business acting as if such answers were available. There is room for doubt, and that alone should be enough to dissuade us. This oppositional strategy is stronger than it might look. For the thought upon which it is based is that killing (of which euthanasia is surely a form) is, on the face of it, far more likely to be wrong than right; hence it is up to the supporters of euthanasia to demonstrate that nonvoluntary euthanasia is an exception to the general rule. By raising these doubts, then, the opponent of nonvoluntary euthanasia hopes to put the ball squarely back into the defender's court.

How successful is this strategy? It can't be denied, I think, that the burden of proof does indeed lie with the defenders of nonvoluntary euthanasia. But it isn't hard to imagine their countermove. After all, if the merest shadow of a doubt were enough to stop us from doing things, we'd never do anything at all. We can't be perfectly certain, for instance, that rocks don't have preferences, interests, and valuable futures, yet no one seriously doubts the morality of quarrying. Nor can we be absolutely sure that lettuces are unconscious, but this doesn't stop us from eating salads. The sheer weight of evidence suggests that those diagnosed as irreversibly unconscious are indeed irreversibly so; nor do we have any evidence to suggest that mental processes ever continue in the absence of higher brain function. In other words, the defender of nonvoluntary euthanasia may claim that, while complete certainty is not available, the very best—and that's the *very* best— guess we can make is good enough. And this claim might be reinforced by widening the scope of discussion somewhat. For given the evidentially warranted nature of the guess (that the patient's condition is hopeless, empty, and irreversible), what positive justification might be offered for the continued expense and inconvenience of keeping the patient alive? This sounds hard-hearted, but it needn't be. Families can be bankrupted by the medical bills incurred in keeping a PVS patient alive indefinitely. More importantly, families can be inhibited from getting on with their own lives and their own futures by the almost certainly illusory hope that their persistently vegetative relation or loved one may, after all, have a future. The balance of doubt, now, is surely turned back against the opponent of nonvoluntary euthanasia.

The whole problem of what may and may not be done with PVS patients has been brought about by technological advances. We are now capable of keeping alive, almost indefinitely, people who would certainly have died before. Both the opponents and the defenders of nonvoluntary euthanasia in such cases agree that this possibility raises important new difficulties. The disagreement between them really swings on how great a moral risk we are prepared to run, with regard both to the (possible) interests of the patient and to those of the patient's family and loved ones. This has led some to try to exploit a number of gray areas surrounding the issue in order to produce a more harmless-sounding defense of nonvoluntary euthanasia than the forthright defense we have considered so far.

7.2d   Killing and Letting Die: Rachels's Argument: "Active and Passive Euthanasia"

Much of the difficulty about nonvoluntary euthanasia seems to be caused by the generally quite proper taboo on killing. Killing is usually wrong, and if euthanasia is a form of killing then it, too, will usually be hard to justify. But if certain forms of euthanasia can be redefined so that they don't *count* as killing, then much of the problem will evaporate. This, not surprisingly, is a tactic much favored by those likely to be most closely involved in the actual mechanics of euthanasia: by health care professionals, in other words. It would, after all, be comforting to feel that what one was involved in was not a killing (however justifiable), but . . . something else. The well-known distinction between "active" and "passive" euthanasia springs from this desire for comfort, with "passive" euthanasia (for example, doing nothing for a patient so that he or she starves to death) regarded as altogether preferable to "active" euthanasia (for example, administering a lethal dose of morphine, or unplugging the ventilator). But according to James Rachels, professor of philosophy at the University of Alabama in Birmingham, the distinction between active and passive euthanasia is a false one.

ACTIVE AND PASSIVE EUTHANASIA
James Rachels

The distinction between active and passive euthanasia is thought to be crucial for medical ethics. The idea is that it is permissible, at least in some cases, to withhold treatment and allow a patient to die, but it is never permissible to take any direct action designed to kill the patient. This doctrine seems to be accepted by most doctors, and it is endorsed in a statement adopted by the House of Delegates of the American Medical Association on December 4, 1973:

> The intentional termination of the life of one human being by another—mercy killing—is contrary to that for which the medical profession stands and is contrary to the policy of the American Medical Association.
> The cessation of the employment of extraordinary means to prolong the life of the body when there is irrefutable evidence that biological death is imminent is the decision of the patient and/or his immediate family. The advice and judgment of the physician should be freely available to the patient and/or his immediate family.

However, a strong case can be made against this doctrine. In what follows I will set out some of the relevant arguments, and urge doctors to reconsider their views on this matter.

To begin with a familiar type of situation, a patient who is dying of incurable cancer of the throat is in terrible pain, which can no longer be satisfactorily alleviated. He is certain to die within a few days, even if present treatment is continued, but he does not want to go on living for those days since the pain is unbearable. So he asks the doctor for an end to it, and his family joins in the request.

Suppose the doctor agrees to withhold treatment, as the conventional doctrine says he may. The justification for his doing so is that the patient is in terrible agony, and since he is going to die anyway, it would be wrong to prolong his suffering needlessly. But now notice this. If one simply withholds treatment, it may take the patient longer to die, and so he may suffer more than he would if more direct action were taken and a lethal injection given. This fact provides strong reason for thinking that, once the initial decision not to prolong his agony has been made, active euthanasia is actually preferable to passive euthanasia, rather than the reverse. To say otherwise is to endorse the option that leads to more suffering rather than less, and is contrary to the humanitarian impulse that prompts the decision not to prolong his life in the first place.

Part of my point is that the process of being "allowed to die" can be relatively slow and painful, whereas being given a lethal injection is relatively quick and painless. Let me give a different sort of example. In the United States about one in 600 babies is born with Down's syndrome. Most of these babies are otherwise healthy—that is, with only the usual pediatric care, they will proceed to an otherwise normal infancy. Some, however, are born with congenital defects such as intestinal obstructions that require operations if they are to live. Sometimes, the parents and the doctors will decide not to operate, and let the infant die. Anthony Shaw describes what happens then:

> . . . When surgery is denied [the doctor] must try to keep the infant from suffering while natural forces sap the baby's life away. As a surgeon whose natural inclination is to use the scalpel to fight off death, standing by and watching a salvageable baby die is the most emotionally exhausting experience I know. It is easy at a conference, in a theoretical discussion, to decide that such infants should be allowed to die. It is altogether different to stand by in the nursery and watch as dehydration and infection wither a tiny being over hours and days. This is a terrible ordeal for me and the hospital staff—much more so than for the parents who never set foot in the nursery.[1]

I can understand why some people are opposed to all euthanasia, and insist that such infants must be allowed to live. I think I can also understand why other people favor destroying these babies quickly and painlessly. But why should anyone favor letting "dehydration and infection wither a tiny being over hours and day"? The doctrine that says that a baby may be allowed to dehydrate and wither, but may not be given an injection that would end its life without suffering, seems so patently cruel as to require no further refutation. The strong language is not intended to offend, but only to put the point in the clearest possible way.

My second argument is that the conventional doctrine leads to decisions concerning life and death made on irrelevant grounds.

Consider again the case of the infants with Down's syndrome who need operations for congenital defects unrelated to the syndrome to live. Sometimes, there is no operation, and the baby dies, but when there is no such defect, the baby lives on. Now, an operation such as that to remove an intestinal obstruction is not prohibitively difficult. The reason why such operations are not performed in these cases is, clearly, that the child has Down's syndrome and the parents and doctor judge that because of that fact it is better for the child to die.

But notice that this situation is absurd, no matter what view one takes of the lives and potentials of such babies. If the life of such an infant is worth preserving, what does it matter if it needs a simple operation? Or, if one thinks it better that such a baby should not live on, what difference does it make that it happens to have an unobstructed intestinal tract? In either case, the matter of life and death is being decided on irrelevant grounds. It is the Down's syndrome, and not the intestines, that is the issue. The matter should be decided, if at all, on that basis, and not be allowed to depend on the essentially irrelevant question of whether the intestinal tract is blocked.

What makes this situation possible, of course, is the idea that when there is an intestinal blockage, one can "let the baby die," but when there is no such defect there is nothing that can be done, for one must not "kill" it. The fact that this idea leads to such results as deciding life or death on irrelevant grounds is another good reason why the doctrine should be rejected.

One reason why so many people think that there is an important moral difference between active and passive euthanasia is that they think killing someone is morally worse than letting someone die. But is it? Is killing, in itself, worse than letting die? To investigate this issue, two cases may be considered that are exactly alike except that one involves killing whereas the other involves letting someone die. Then, it can be asked whether this difference makes any difference to the moral assessments. It is important that the cases be exactly alike, except for this one difference, since otherwise one cannot be confident that it is this difference and not some other that accounts for any variation in the assessment of the two cases. So, let us consider this pair of cases:

In the first, Smith stands to gain a large inheritance if anything should happen to his six-year-old cousin. One evening while the child is taking his bath, Smith sneaks into the bathroom and drowns the child, and then arranges things so that it will look like an accident.

In the second, Jones also stands to gain if anything should happen to his six-year-old cousin. Like Smith, Jones sneaks in planning to drown the child in his bath. However, just as he enters the bathroom Jones sees the child slip and hit his head, and fall face down in the water. Jones is delighted; he stands by, ready to push the child's head back under if it is necessary, but it is not necessary. With only a little thrashing about, the child drowns all by himself, "accidentally," as Jones watches and does nothing.

Now Smith killed the child, whereas Jones "merely" let the child die. That is the only difference between them. Did either man behave better, from a moral point of view? If the difference between killing and letting die were in itself a morally important matter, one should say that Jones's behavior was less reprehensible than Smith's. But does one really want to say that? I think not. In the first place, both men acted from the same motive, personal gain, and both had exactly the same end in view when they acted. It may be inferred from Smith's conduct that he is a bad man, although that judgment may be withdrawn or modified if certain further facts are learned about him—for example, that he is mentally deranged. But would not the very same thing be inferred about Jones from his conduct? And would not the same further considerations also be relevant to any modification of this judgment? Moreover, suppose Jones pleaded, in his own defense, "After all, I didn't do anything except just stand there and watch the child drown. I didn't kill him; I only let him die." Again, if letting die were in itself less bad than killing, this defense should have at least some weight. But it does not. Such a "defense" can only be regarded as a grotesque perversion of moral reasoning. Morally speaking, it is no defense at all.

Now, it may be pointed out, quite properly, that the cases of euthanasia with which doctors are concerned are not like this at all. They do not involve personal gain or the destruction of normal, healthy children. Doctors are concerned only with cases in which the patient's life is of no further use to him, or in which the patient's life has become or will soon become a terrible burden. However, the point is the same in these cases: the bare difference between killing and letting die does not, in itself, make a moral difference. If a doctor lets a patient die, for humane reasons, he is in the same moral position as if he had given the patient a lethal injection for humane reasons. If his decision was wrong—if, for example, the patient's illness was in fact curable—the decision would be equally regrettable no matter which method was used to carry it out. And if the doctor's decision was the right one, the method used is not in itself important.

The AMA policy statement isolates the crucial issue very well; the crucial issue is "the intentional termination of the life of one human being by another." But after identifying this issue, and forbidding "mercy killing," the statement goes on to deny that the cessation of treatment is the intentional termination of life. This is where the mistake comes in, for what is the cessation of treatment, in these circumstances, if it is not "the intentional termination of the life of one human being by another"? Of course it is exactly that, and if it were not, there would be no point to it.

Many people will find this judgment hard to accept. One reason, I think, is that it is very easy to conflate the question of whether killing is, in itself, worse than letting die, with the very different question of whether most actual cases of killing are more reprehensible than most actual cases of letting die. Most actual cases of killing are clearly terrible (think, for example, of all the murders reported in the newspapers), and one hears of such cases every day. On the other hand, one hardly ever hears of a case of letting die, except for the action of doctors who are motivated by humanitarian reasons. So one learns to think of killing in a much worse light than of letting die. But this does not mean that there is something about killing that makes it in itself worse than letting die, for it is not the bare difference between killing and letting die that makes the difference in these cases. Rather, the other factors—the murderer's motive of personal gain, for example, contrasted with the doctor's humanitarian motivation—account for different reactions to the different cases.

I have argued that killing is not in itself any worse than letting die; if my contention is right, it follows that active euthanasia is not any worse than passive euthanasia. What arguments can be given on the other side? The most common, I believe, is the following:

"The important difference between active and passive euthanasia is that, in passive euthanasia, the doctor does not do anything to bring about the patient's death. The doctor does nothing, and the patient dies of whatever ills already afflict him. In active euthanasia, however, the doctor does something to bring about the patient's death: he kills him. The doctor who gives the patient with cancer a lethal injection has himself caused his patient's death; whereas if he merely ceases treatment, the cancer is the cause of the death."

A number of points need to be made here. The first is that it is not exactly correct to say that in passive euthanasia the doctor does nothing, for he does do one thing that is very important: he lets the patient die. "Letting someone die" is certainly different, in some respects, from other types of action—mainly in that it is a kind of action that one may perform by way of not performing certain other actions. For example, one may let a patient die by way of not giving medication, just as one may insult someone by way of not shaking his hand. But for any purpose of moral assessment, it is a type of action nonetheless. The decision to let a patient die is subject to moral appraisal in the same way that a decision to kill him would be subject to moral appraisal: it may be assessed as wise or unwise, compassionate or sadistic, right or wrong. If a doctor deliberately let a patient die who was suffering from a routinely curable illness, the doctor would certainly be to blame for what he had done, just as he would be to blame if he had needlessly killed the patient. Charges against him would then be appropriate. If so, it would be no defense at all for him to insist that he didn't "do anything." He would have done something very serious indeed, for he let his patient die.

Fixing the cause of death may be very important from a legal point of view, for it may determine whether criminal charges are brought against the doctor. But I do not think that this notion can be used to show a moral difference between active and passive euthanasia. The reason why it is considered bad to be the cause of someone's death is that death is regarded as a great evil—and so it is. However, if it has been decided that euthanasia—even passive euthanasia— is desirable in a given case, it has also been decided that in this instance death is no greater an evil than the patient's continued existence. And if this is true, the usual reason for not wanting to be the cause of someone's death simply does not apply.

Finally, doctors may think that all of this is only of academic interest—the sort of thing that philosophers may worry about but that has no practical bearing on their own work. After all, doctors must be concerned about the legal consequences of what they do, and active euthanasia is clearly forbidden by the law. But even so, doctors should also be concerned with the fact that the law is forcing upon them a moral doctrine that may well be indefensible, and has a considerable effect on their practices. Of course, most doctors are not now in the position of being coerced in this matter, for they do not regard themselves as merely going along with what the law requires. Rather, in statements such as the AMA policy statement that I have quoted, they are endorsing this doctrine as a central point of medical ethics. In that statement, active euthanasia is condemned not merely as illegal but as "contrary to that for which the medical profession stands," whereas passive euthanasia is approved. However, the preceding considerations suggest that there is really no moral difference between the two, considered in themselves (there may be important moral differences in some cases in their *consequences,* but, as I pointed out, these differences may make active euthanasia, and not passive euthanasia, the morally preferable option). So, whereas doctors may have to discriminate between active and passive euthanasia to satisfy the law, they should not do any more than that. In particular, they should not give the distinction any added authority and weight by writing it into official statements of medical ethics.

Note

1. Shaw A.: 'Doctor, Do We Have a Choice?' *The New York Times Magazine,* January 30 ,1972, p. 54.

7.2e   Responding to Rachels

Rachels's argument is an extremely compelling one: There is nothing no-
ticeably compassionate about so-called passive euthanasia, and both active
and passive euthanasia seem to be clearly designed to cause the deaths of patients. Rachels's claim, then, that there is no essential moral difference between the two—except, perhaps, that active euthanasia may sometimes be
preferable—looks very hard to refute.

What might a defender of the active/passive distinction say in response?
The only thing I can think of is the claim that, in choosing passive euthanasia
over active, one allows a little more scope and time for the patient to show
signs of unexpected recovery. A lethal injection would kill the patient right
off, whereas merely withdrawing treatment, although almost certainly resulting in the patient's death, at least leaves a door open. Thus it seems
worse to ensure someone's death through active euthanasia than to cease
acting and passively allow events to take their course—a course which
might conceivably not be the expected one. But this is a very lame counterargument. Rachels would surely reply that if you've any realistic doubt *at all*
that the patient's case is hopeless, you shouldn't be contemplating euthanasia of *any* kind. Yet if you don't have such doubts, why insist on "leaving a
door open"?

In other words, this objection to Rachels's position misses the point. The
only time when euthanasia should be contemplated is when one is as certain
as one could possibly be that the patient's condition is irreversible. If one is
still prepared to believe that the unexpected, or the miraculous, needs to be
taken into account, then one isn't certain, and one shouldn't even be thinking about withdrawing treatment. It's a bit like setting a mouse-trap. Someone might claim that setting a trap was quite different from clubbing a
mouse to death with a broom. Setting a trap, after all, is a passive kind of
thing, in which one merely puts something in place and then waits as matters take their course; whereas the broom approach actually involves *killing!*
But if you don't want to kill mice, you don't set a trap in the first place. The
mere possibility that no mouse will walk into it makes you no less of a
mouse-killer when a mouse does, in fact, walk into it.

This objection fails, then. But, unless I've missed something, no other
objection can hope to fare any better. Rachels's argument appears simple, direct, and conclusive. My own view is that we should accept his position and
agree that there is no essential moral difference between active and passive
euthanasia: Both are undertaken in the absolute conviction that the patient
will die as a result, so both are forms of killing. If the AMA insists that involvement in killing is utterly incompatible with the ideals of the medical
profession then it should condemn passive euthanasia as well as active. If, on
the other hand, it feels that certain cases of euthanasia may be justifiable, it
ought to shift its emphasis: Instead of highlighting the professional duty to
save, and not to take, lives, it should concentrate on the professional duty to
act in the best possible interests of patients. For it might be claimed that a patient's interests may sometimes be served best if he or she is killed, whether

that is done "actively" or "passively." What the AMA cannot do is seek to remove the dilemma by pretending that the deliberate withdrawal of treatment from a patient is not a way of deliberating causing the patient's death. Euthanasia kills, and we should remember that.

7.2f   The Doctrine of Double Effect

Another attempt that is sometimes made to soften the fact that euthanasia involves killing is expressed in the "doctrine of double effect." According to the proponents of this, it would be wrong for me intentionally to bring about someone's death—for instance, euthanasia would be wrong. But it *may* be justifiable for me to act in a way that has the effect of killing someone, and even to foresee that it will have that effect, so long as that effect is not the one towards which I am aiming. So, for example: You are terminally ill, in pain, and delirious or barely conscious. I want to ease your pain, but believe that it would be wrong to do so through an act of euthanasia. Instead, I inject you with a nonlethal dose of morphine and hope that this will be sufficient to ease your pain. But it isn't. I increase the dose a little, and still it isn't enough. Finally I reach the point at which I recognize that, if I am to realize my intention of easing your pain, I will have to inject you with a dose of morphine large enough to kill you. Suppose I go ahead and do this, and you die. According to the doctrine of double effect, my action may be justifiable—even though an identical action, performed as an act of euthanasia, would not be justifiable. The difference is supposed to be this: In the case I have described, I *aim* at the alleviation of your pain—that is the effect I intend to bring about—and there is nothing wrong with the intention to alleviate pain. (As a side-effect, of course, foreseen but not intended, you die.) In a case of euthanasia, by contrast, I aim directly at your death, and that is not a justifiable intention. According to those who hold this doctrine, then, euthanasia is always wrong. But giving people lethal doses of morphine— doses that you know will kill them—needn't be wrong (needn't be acts of euthanasia) so long as the reason for the injection is the desire to relieve pain. Pain-control is the intended effect; death is a foreseen but unintended side-effect.

This is a very odd doctrine. Indeed, it looks as if the main point of it is to give people a way out of a moral dilemma. I knowingly inject you with a lethal dose of morphine, but since I'm trying to relieve your pain rather than trying to kill you, I needn't feel quite so bad about the fact that what I'm doing causes your death. I needn't, that is, justify the fact that I'm killing you, since that isn't what I've set out to do. But surely this isn't convincing. I do, after all, foresee that the injection will kill you and, having foreseen it, go ahead and give it to you anyway. Moreover, the discovery that nonlethal doses of morphine are insufficient to ease your pain is tantamount to the discovery that the conditions of easing your pain are identical to the conditions of causing your death. Therefore I cannot any longer (at least not if I'm thinking clearly) take steps deliberately to end your pain without taking steps deliberately to end your life. In other words, the distinction which the doctrine of double effect tries to trade upon—the distinction between aiming at one effect (someone's death) and aiming at another effect (pain-relief) in a way that foreseeably involves the first effect—doesn't seem to stand up to scrutiny.

Take the same point from another direction. Suppose that you are otherwise healthy, but have a mild, nagging pain that responds to no known form of treatment. As your physician, I've tried everything. Now suppose that, in my desire to rid you of the pain, I decide to give you a lethal dose of morphine: Nothing less will do the trick. I then seek to justify my action by appealing to the doctrine of double effect. My intentions, I say, were honorable (pain-relief). But in order to realize my intentions I had to act in such a way as foreseeably to cause your death—even though this wasn't my aim. Therefore, since my intentions were justifiable, I must have been justified in what I did. But no one, surely would be impressed with this as a line of defense. The disproportion between the pain and the measures taken to alleviate it is so extreme that only a madman would regard my action as ethically defensible. What this shows is that the desire to alleviate pain isn't self-justifying and oughtn't be unconditional: Pain-relief must be *worth* it. And what this means is that giving you a dose of morphine that I know to be lethal can only conceivably be justified in cases where the evil of your death is outweighed by the evil of your continued suffering. In other words, I would have to judge that you'd be better off dead *before* the administration of lethal doses of morphine even becomes an option for me. So again, the distinction, essential to the doctrine of double effect, between justifying the alleviation of pain in a death-causing way and justifying the actual causing of death, simply collapses. One ought never seek to justify the former unless one is also prepared to justify the latter.

If these points are sound, there cannot be any moral difference between an act of euthanasia, deliberately undertaken as such, and an act of pain-relief that foreseeably results in death. Therefore if you think that euthanasia is wrong (perhaps because it involves the intentional taking of life) you ought also to condemn the foreseeable loss of life that results from extreme forms of pain-control. It is easy to understand, of course, why people would *like* there to be a moral difference here: Few of us, presumably, would want to be held directly responsible for killing someone. But the fact that we would like a let-out clause, perhaps along the lines of the doctrine of double effect, doesn't show that there is one, and the shortcomings of that doctrine show just how difficult to concoct (and probably how implausible) any such let-out clause is likely to be. The truth, I suspect, is that there is no way to soften the fact that euthanasia is a form of killing and no way to portray the practice of lethal pain-relief as something different from euthanasia. If this is right, the doctrine of double effect represents an attempt to skirt around an issue that needs to be faced, not dodged. Foreseeably lethal pain-relief is a form of euthanasia; euthanasia is a form of killing; therefore foreseeably lethal pain-relief requires precisely the same kind and degree of justification that euthanasia, like any other form of killing, requires. You can't make the problem go away by redefining your (lethal) action as something else. And it would be irresponsible to seek to do so. This is an issue that demands moral courage of us, not moral cunning.

7.2g   Living Wills

So far I have assumed that a patient is either in a condition, here and now, to request euthanasia, or else is in no condition to request anything, so that the decision, if it is to be made at all, is made entirely by somebody else. But of course there is a kind of middle ground. In recent years people have taken increasingly to writing "living wills", in which they state the circumstances—for instance, falling into a PVS—under which they would like to be killed or allowed to die. These are usually written well in advance of any such circumstances, when the future patient is perfectly able to conceive and to express preferences, in the hope that, should those circumstances ever come about, the patient's recorded preferences will then be acted upon.

It is rather mystifying that living wills should be controversial, but they are. It is sometimes said that a healthy patient's predictions about what he or she would like to happen in the unfortunate event that he or she should, for example, fall into a PVS, are not reliable, and so do not deserve to be taken entirely seriously. But this misses the point. The person who writes a living will isn't making *predictions* about his or her future preferences: Someone in a PVS doesn't *have* any preferences. Rather, he or she is stating current preferences about the future, and in the absence of later, different preferences being expressed it is hard to see why such preferences oughtn't to be honored. In effect, the situation is identical to that when a person writes an ordinary will. In making my will, I'm not predicting what I'll want to happen to my possessions after I'm dead: Once I'm dead I'll be beyond wanting anything. No, I'm stating what I *now* wish to happen, my wishes taking effect only once I've died. It is difficult to understand why one's wishes about one's property, as expressed in an ordinary will, should be thought more weighty than one's wishes, as expressed in a living will, about oneself. I'd have imagined that if someone was prepared to take the former seriously, he or she ought to be more than prepared to take the latter seriously too.

The only really strong argument against living wills that I can see depends on the claim that euthanasia itself is wrong. For if euthanasia is morally wrong, then it would be morally wrong to honor a living will that demanded euthanasia (just as it would be morally wrong to honor an ordinary will that required the deceased person's assets to be handed over to a terrorist organization). But if one believes that euthanasia is at least sometimes justifiable, it seems that one ought to have no objection in principle to living wills. If one has a quarrel with some specific living will, then the appropriate measure would presumably be to go to court over it, as with any other kind of contested will.

7.2h   Recap: Mercy Killing

The issues raised by euthanasia are peculiarly grave ones. The decision to kill a person, even in what seems clearly to be his or her own best interests, and even at his or her own request, is as agonizing as it is possible to imagine a decision being. But the discussion here has tended to suggest that the decision may, in certain cases, be justifiable. It isn't hard to picture an instance of potential voluntary euthanasia in which it would be positively callous *not* to kill a person at his or her own request (think of the motorist in 7.2b). Nor is it hard to see arguments in favor of nonvoluntary euthanasia in cases where a patient's consciousness is irretrievably lost, or absent, and his or her continued life will be nothing more than a spiritual and financial drain on family and loved ones. But it is perhaps too easy to be seduced by the attractions of euthanasia. Killing people should always be the exception to the rule.

If we permit ourselves to be dishonest about the nature of euthanasia— by inventing a distinction between active and passive euthanasia, for example, or by cooking up something like the doctrine of double effect—then we risk falsifying the moral position. Killing people requires a stern justification; if we manage to convince ourselves that what we are doing is not *really* killing, we will soon find our standards of justification going down. It is altogether more honest, it seems to me, to stick with the intuition that killing is just wrong (for whatever reasons), and so to regard euthanasia as wrong, than it is to defend euthanasia by redescribing it as something else. If euthanasia is to be defended, then it must be defended as a justifiable form of killing. For my own part, I believe this is possible. But I hope the remarks in this part of the chapter have shown that such a defense, even if possible, will never be easy.

Study Questions

1. To what extent should advances in technology be allowed to alter our everyday concepts? Is the concept of death a special case?
2. Is there an ethically significant difference between withdrawing treatment so that a patient dies and withholding treatment so that a patient dies?
3. What is the best rule-utilitarian argument against euthanasia that you can think of? How might a critic respond to it?
4. Suppose you have made a living will stating that you would like treatment withdrawn in the event that you are diagnosed as persistently vegetative. Suppose you fall into a PVS and your family does not want treatment withdrawn. Whose preferences should prevail?

Related Cases in Crigger, *Cases in Bioethics,* Third Edition

None of the cases directly confront the issues discussed in the first part of this chapter, "What is Death?" But many of those issues can be discerned in the numerous cases that are relevant to "Euthanasia" (section 7.2). These cases cover many facets of the debate: Case 2 raises disturbing questions about the duties of health care professionals who become involved in euthanasia; cases 8, 25, and 41 deal with the role of family members in making decisions on behalf of potential euthanasia patients, and with the conflicts this can cause; case 53 deals with the death of an anencephalic newborn;

cases 24, 26, 27, and 30 raise complex questions about when a patient's request for euthanasia should be honored; case 21 concerns the concept of the "living will" (also touched on in case 27); and case 29 is about a dubious instance of nonvoluntary euthanasia. Many of the discussions are useful, but those following cases 28 and 29 are especially so.

CHAPTER EIGHT
Research with Living Subjects

INTRODUCTION

Our clinical and therapeutic capabilities today are beyond the wildest dreams of people living a hundred, fifty, or even thirty years ago. This is almost entirely due to experimentation. If we hadn't tried out things, and tried to find out things, the progress of our knowledge would have ground to a halt. Anyone who has ever benefitted from any medical intervention can be grateful to the designers and the subjects of the experiments that made it possible. From this point of view, medical experimentation is unquestionably valuable. But, although valuable, it is not unproblematic. Research subjects, after all, may be inconvenienced, harmed, or even killed by experiments, so it is important that we come to grips with the ethical consequences of these facts. In other words, even if almost everyone would agree that advances in medical knowledge are a good thing, we have to be sure that this good is not bought at too high a price. We need to have a clear idea of what makes a person an ethically suitable research subject; of what limits, if any, should be placed on the degree of harm that an experiment may inflict; of what we should do with the results of experiments that have been conducted without due regard for various legitimate ethical concerns. We need, that is, to be satisfied that the benefits we gain from medical research have been, and will be, secured in justifiable ways. Otherwise we risk living off the medical equivalent of immoral earnings. The first five sections of this chapter are devoted to issues surrounding experiments conducted on human beings. The final two sections also deal briefly with animal experimentation. The overwhelming majority of medical experiments are performed on non-human subjects, after all, and we must be sure that we're getting that right as well.

8.1a Drug Trials

It will be helpful to begin with a brief overview of the procedures involved in drug trials—probably the most common kind of medical experiment. In carrying out a drug trial, researchers standardly want to find out two things: first, whether the drug in question provides effective treatment for a given condition; second, whether the drug in question causes undesirable side-effects. In most cases, drug trials are conducted in at least three stages: on animals in the first instance; then, if the animal stage produces promising results, on a relatively small number of human volunteers; and finally, if results are still promising, on much larger numbers of human volunteers. If the results are sufficiently good after all three stages, the drug may be licensed and take its place in the standard pharmaceutical armory of the health care profession.

In order to discover a drug's efficacy as a form of treatment, it is clearly necessary that research subjects at each of the three stages should suffer from the relevant medical condition. This condition may be artificially induced (as it normally is in animals) or naturally arising. In order to discover what side-effects a drug has, by contrast, it is often possible to make use of a "normal," healthy population of research subjects. If such subjects are in a normal condition to begin with, then deviations from that condition upon treatment with the drug will count as side-effects of it—some of which may be undesirable. So far, then, so simple.

But if the results of these trials are to be convincing, more is needed. First, the population of research subjects at any stage must be selected in a way that is as nearly *random* as possible. The reason for this is that there is, strictly, no such thing as a normal way of suffering from a particular medical condition or a normal way of being healthy. Individuals differ from one another in a great variety of ways: All of us have our own medical histories, our own dietary preferences, our own genetic endowments, our own temperamental quirks, our own allergies, our own more or less unpredictable ways of being different from anybody else. This means that there can, in principle, be no single ideal research subject. What improves my condition might not improve yours (however "normal" we both seem); what gives me headaches mightn't affect you in the least. Therefore individual differences need to be balanced out; this can be done if the population of research subjects is large and selected at random. If the research sample is large, subjects will exhibit a wide array of individual responses to treatment—and since these responses will not always be in the same *direction*, they will tend to cancel one another out. If the research sample is random, it may be assumed that the ways in which these differences cancel one another out is not peculiar to one particular population of research subjects, but is representative of the species (animal, human) as a whole. Thus, by employing large, random samples of research subjects it is hoped that the results of a drug trial will not be biased by the peculiarities of any one, unrepresentative individual or group.

But this is not the only precaution that needs to be taken. We saw in 5.1e that many of us exhibit the so-called "placebo effect"; in other words, our condition may change, not because we are being treated with any chemically efficacious drug, but because we believe that we are. The placebo effect must clearly be guarded against in drug trials. A person suffering from a particular medical condition may participate in such a trial and show signs of improvement, yet this might mean only that he or she has faith in the drug's effectiveness, not that the drug is any good as a treatment. Similarly, a person participating in a trial to discover whether a drug has any undesirable side-effects may indeed experience side-effects as a result of believing that the drug is (potentially) dangerous rather than as a result of any actual dangerousness in the relevant chemical combinations. The way in which these problems are standardly overcome is to divide the research sample into two groups: one group is given the drug being tested while the other group, called the "control" group, is deliberately given placebos. Since neither group knows which is which, any placebo effect should—if the sample is large enough and random enough—be canceled out in the manner described a moment ago. This is known as "blind" testing, since research subjects are, as it were, kept in the dark about what they are taking. But the placebo effect can plague researchers as well as research subjects. If I am especially optimistic about the efficacy of a drug that I am testing I may be overkeen to detect improvements in the condition of my research subjects, or unduly reluctant to recognize side-effects. Or, if I am especially pessimistic about the drug, I may discount apparent improvements and exaggerate apparent side-effects. It is in an attempt to cancel out this sort of unintentional bias that so-called "double-blind" testing is now widely used. Research subjects are divided into two groups as before, neither group knowing which is the control. But now the division is managed in such a way that those who gather the results of the test don't know which individual belongs to which group either. In this manner, with both researchers and research subjects operating blind, it is hoped that *all* irrelevant psychological factors can be cancelled out from the eventual findings, so that the results of a trial are as reliable as possible. There are, of course, many further modifications and adjustments to trial procedures that may be used in particular cases or that may be more appropriate to certain kinds of trial than to others. But the overview in this section should have been sufficient to indicate the sorts of factors that need to be taken into account if trial-results are to be scientifically adequate. (It goes without saying that the knowing use of scientifically inadequate results is unlikely to be ethically defensible.)

8.1b   Selecting Human Research Subjects

Human research subjects, as we have seen, come in two main categories: the ill and the healthy. Some forms of medical research require subjects who suffer from particular conditions, so that new drugs or procedures can be tried out on them. Other forms of research require healthy subjects, who may either be made ill (for instance by being infected with a common cold) or who may be studied in order to discover what the normal responses of the human body to various chemicals, procedures, and stimuli might be. In both cases, the concept of informed consent is clearly crucial. No one is obliged to become a research subject. Therefore when a person does agree to become a research subject, it is important that his or her decision be made with at least as much care as would be required for any other kind of medical intervention.

We have already discussed informed consent in detail in 5.2. The points made there should be sufficient to suggest the kinds of safeguards that need to be borne in mind. Indeed, in the case of research subjects who are already ill, and who perhaps hope for a cure, or at least for some form of relief, from a new experimental procedure or treatment, it would seem that the situation is almost identical to that in which any other kind of treatment or procedure is proposed. The patient must be allowed to make an autonomous decision whether to participate in the research or not. That decision must be made in the light of the best information available—including, of course, an expert assessment of the risks that the patient runs if he or she agrees to participate. The only difference between cases in which an experimental form of treatment is proposed and cases in which an established form of treatment is proposed springs from the possibly mixed motives of the professional in the former case. Where an established form of treatment is proposed, it seems clear that the professional's overriding desire is to benefit the patient as much as possible. Where the treatment is experimental, on the other hand, it is possible that running alongside this desire, and perhaps even competing with it, is the desire to discover how efficacious the treatment is. Given this, it is essential that health care professionals who are engaged in medical research should be ruthlessly honest with themselves. Indeed, as we saw in the previous section, this honesty may sometimes take the form of deliberately *denying* themselves access to certain kinds of information, as in double-blind test trials.

The situation with healthy research subjects is more complex. Clearly it is vital that the highest standards of informed consent apply, and that a maximum of information be made available to any volunteer. But because no healthy person needs treatment, and because there are an almost limitless number of healthy people around, it is possible for researchers to be far more selective in their recruitment of healthy research subjects than is the case with ill ones. This introduces a new ethical dimension to the picture. For now it is reasonable to require that researchers behave ethically not only in their treatment of present research subjects, but also in their recruitment of potential ones. If you have a drug you need to test on a patient suffering from a condition that is comparatively rare, you will have to take whichever research subjects you can get. But if you need a healthy control group for testing another kind of drug, or for assessing the side-effects of a drug, then the majority of the adult population will meet your requirements. The fact that your choice is now so much wider places an obligation upon you to choose wisely.

What would a wise choice of research subject be? First, I suppose, the person would have to satisfy certain physiological criteria, so that the science of the experiment is not compromised. But this doesn't narrow the field much, since if your main criterion is that a person should be healthy, most people would satisfy it. It is at this point that the concept of informed consent becomes important once more. For no one doubts that some people are better able to be informed on certain subjects than others. If you were to try to explain to me what is wrong with my car, for instance, you'd have an uphill struggle on your hands. My mechanic, on the other hand, would understand you very easily. My mechanic, therefore, would be much better equipped to give informed consent to some imaginary automotive procedure than I would be. People vary widely in the knowledge and understanding they have, in their intelligence, in their capacity to absorb and to make sense of new information. This means that, although everyone is capable in some sense of giving consent, not everyone is equally capable of giving informed consent. In the routine course of medical practice this is a problem that needs to be handled flexibly and sensitively: After all, you can't only have intelligent, knowledgeable patients. But in the context of medical research on healthy subjects you do have that option. If you are concerned that your experiments are conducted to the highest ethical standards, you will surely prefer to recruit subjects who are able to give the most thorough kind of informed consent possible. To prefer less would be to settle for an unnecessary ethical compromise.

In light of this, it is not hard to see why many people object to some of the standard procedures for recruiting healthy research subjects. The most questionable of these is held to be the practice of offering payment. The reason why this is disturbing is that the prospect of payment may tempt some people to consent to an experimental procedure that they would not otherwise have chosen to do. You might say that that is their choice: No one, after all, is forcing them to take part. But the matter is a little more complicated. For there is no question that those tempted to take part in research by the prospect of payment are those who are least well off—those who need the money most. Nor is there any question that the poorest members of society also tend to be the least well-educated and knowledgeable. This means that the offer of payment will tend to ensure that research subjects are not recruited from those best able to give fully informed consent. In other words, the offer of payment involves exactly that compromise of the highest ethical standards that I mentioned a moment ago. Given that the potential pool from which healthy research subjects can be drawn is so large, it would appear to be a condition of ethical recruiting practice that the selection should not deliberately target those who are, statistically, least likely to be able to give consent with the fullest possible understanding of what they are letting themselves in for. This applies to other situations as well; it is for this reason that most of us would object to the nonessential use of child volunteers, for example.

Nor are other recruiting practices immune to doubt. The targeting of prisoners as research subjects, for instance, seems open to very similar objections. The prison environment is deliberately designed, after all, to *limit* the autonomy of its inmates—to restrict their freedom to pursue their plans and preferences. This makes the quality of consent liable to be obtained from prisoners somewhat ambiguous. For instance, prisoners may hope that by cooperating with medical researchers—and so demonstrating a desire to benefit those who suffer from certain illnesses—they may win remissions of sentence or gain other privileges. Outside of prison, such people might not dream of participating in trials. If not, then this suggests that their consent cannot be said to have been given entirely freely: Rather, it seems as if their consent is given against a background of (implicit) coercion, even if no one is directly forcing them to take part. Nor are the inmates of a prison likely to be among the better educated or more well-informed sectors of the population, which again casts doubt on the quality of consent that they are able to give. Indeed, it is hard to shake the suspicion that prisoners are sometimes targeted as research subjects because of a feeling that prisoners somehow matter less than other people, that they have not merely forfeited their freedom of movement, etc., but have also forfeited their right to be regarded as fully human. If this *is* one of the motives for targeting them—and, as I say, this is only a suspicion—then it is surely an indefensible one. Prisoners, through their doubtless well-deserved loss of autonomy, become exceptionally vulnerable to certain kinds of pressure. And—as a civilized society—we should be seeking to protect our more vulnerable members, not to exploit them. On the whole, then, it seems that the use of prisoners as research subjects is far from ideal practice: statistically, the informed consent gained from them is likely to be neither ideally informed nor ideally consenting.

In light of this, it has been suggested—and not as a joke, either—that research subjects should ideally be recruited from that part of the population which is best able to give fully informed consent. What part of the population is that? Health care professionals, of course. No one is in a better position than they to understand and to assess the information that is given them; no one's consent is ethically less compromised than theirs. The very best approach, then, would be for experts in the medical world to carry out experiments on each other. Doubtless this would prove somewhat impractical. But as an ideal, it makes some sense. In taking seriously the idea of informed consent, we commit ourselves to recruitment policies that attempt to ensure that the consent received is of the highest quality possible, whereas many current recruitment policies appear designed to achieve exactly the reverse. We have moved on, of course, from the early days of medical experimentation when, as in the story of Dr. Jekyll and Mr. Hyde, an experimenter could be his or her own research subject. Such procedures would lead to results that were not nearly rigorous enough by contemporary scientific standards. But Dr. Jekyll's heart was in somewhere near the right place. When we have a choice, we must choose wisely, and part of that wisdom will consist in selecting our research subjects in the most ethical manner we can.

8.1c Harm

How much harm ought a medical experiment to inflict? What risks can a fully consenting, informed, volunteer research subject choose to run? The most clear-cut answer would be to say that there is no upper limit: A person may, if he or she wishes, choose to participate in an experiment that is likely or certain to cause irreversible injury, or even death. After all, it might be argued, we do not prevent people from climbing mountains, from skiing down idiotic slopes, from boxing or from motor racing; we don't stop people from being stuntpersons, high-divers or shark-enthusiasts. All of these activities carry a substantial risk; moreover, none of them is either intended or likely to yield any long-term benefits for humanity at large. If these activities are permitted, then, what reason could we possibly have to prevent people from taking part in risky or damaging research projects if they wish to—especially when these projects are intended to yield long-term benefits for all of us?

This is a fairly powerful point. Indeed, many will be persuaded that there should be no fixed upper limit on the amount of harm that an experiment may inflict, or on the amount of harm that someone may volunteer to suffer. Others, however, will take a different view. Perhaps the best reason for believing that there *should* be an upper limit on the amount of harm or risk that an experiment should involve comes from reflecting, not on the decision of the volunteer to participate, but on the attitude of those who give the volunteer the opportunity to participate. The purpose of medical experimentation, after all, is to achieve results that may be used for beneficent purposes. Ethically, the justification for medical experimentation is that it furthers our interests as living beings, that it aims to promote better, happier, and fuller lives for us. Concern for the human, then, underwrites the morality of medical research. Given this, a strong case exists for saying that an experiment that deliberately inflicts significant harm on human subjects—even if those subjects are fully consenting volunteers—is at odds with the overall ethical character of medical research. This, it might be said, is not how we signal our concern for the human. If we wish to carry out research that is truly in the spirit of our enterprise, we will be careful to limit the amount of harm we are prepared to inflict on other human beings: We will respect the lives and the interests of those others, even if they do not respect them themselves. We will not, in other words, give anyone the opportunity to volunteer for an experiment that carries a risk or a certainty of causing serious harm.

This, too, is a persuasive position. Indeed, it is a position that deserves to be taken seriously by anyone who is not a fully paid-up act utilitarian (he or she, of course, will simply reply that good consequences in the long run are sufficient to outweigh any lesser amount of suffering in the short term). Certainly, a concern for human life is not normally signalled by the deliberate causing of death or serious injury, and there do seem to be good grounds for discouraging the performance of experiments that are likely to have that result. Fixing the level at which an injury counts as "serious," of course, is not going to be an easy task, nor will it be easy to decide just what level of risk is acceptable (2 percent? 5 percent? 25 percent?). But unless we are prepared to think sensitively and responsibly about these questions, and to review our thoughts on a case-by-case basis, we run the danger of losing touch with those ethical factors that give our research its legitimacy in the first place.

8.1d   Unethical Experiments: Ridley's Argument: "Ill-Gotten Gains"

The discussion in the two preceding sections suggests that we need to be very careful if our medical research is to be of an ethically acceptable character. We must certainly ensure that the subjects of our research consent to their participation in the most fully informed way possible. We must try to select those subjects wisely and responsibly; perhaps we must also be prepared to forego the performance of experiments that are likely to inflict a significant amount of harm. But these considerations do not tell us what we should do with the results of experiments that have not been conducted with sufficient heed for the ethical dimensions of research. This question has been widely discussed recently in the context of the criminal experiments carried out by Nazi doctors in the death camps of World War II. No consent of any kind was obtained; subjects were selected purely on the basis of racial and political prejudice; no kind of upper limit was set on the barbaric harms inflicted. Yet the results of some of these experiments have proved to be very useful: We know in some detail now about the effects of extreme cold on the human body; our airplanes are designed at least partly on the basis of Nazi research into the human consequences of very low atmospheric pressures. Everyone agrees that these experiments were of the worst possible ethical character. But there is significant disagreement about whether that fact should influence our attitude toward the *results* of those experiments. Nor is this question of interest only in the context of Nazi war crimes. Other barbaric experiments have been performed around the world, and plenty of post-war research in the West wouldn't withstand close ethical scrutiny. So there is a general problem about what we should do with the results of unethical experiments in medicine. According to one line of argument, we should refuse to use them.

ILL-GOTTEN GAINS
Aaron Ridley

I

I am concerned here with experiments which have the following characteristics: 1) the use of human research-subjects; 2) the use of procedures which may be expected to harm research-subjects; 3) the anticipation of long-term gains which are not expected or intended to benefit research-subjects directly or specifically; 4) the anticipation of long-term gains which are sufficient, in some sense, to outweigh the short-term costs incurred by research-subjects who are harmed by the experimental procedures employed. So, for example, an experiment which involves deliberately giving a group of human volunteers a nasty cold in order to test the effectiveness of an anti-cold treatment will fit the pattern that I have in mind. 1) The research-subjects are human (I focus on human research-subjects so as to avoid unnecessary discussion of animal rights, etc.: I also prefer to exclude from discussion questions about extremely young humans —e.g., embryos and foetuses). 2) The research-subjects will be harmed by the procedures involved (they will be given a cold which they would otherwise not have had; and there is a risk that the treatment may itself prove harmful). 3) If the experiment has useful results then these will not have been sought in order to alleviate the condition of the research-subjects specifically (although research-subjects may of course benefit subsequently, if the treatment proves to be effective, or if it goes on the market, if they catch a cold of their own, etc.). And 4) the prospect of a cure for the common cold is arguably sufficiently attractive—given how many people catch a cold each year, and how debilitating a cold can be—to justify the infliction of a certain amount of short-term discomfort upon a group of research-subjects: the discomfort of a few people in the short term is outweighed by the (anticipated) reduction of discomfort for large numbers of people in the long term. The insistence upon these four characteristics is intended to keep the argument of this paper as simple as possible; and the term "experiment" will be used hereafter to refer only to such experiments as have these characteristics.

It is clear, I think, that experiments of the type that I have in mind can be either ethically acceptable or ethically offensive. The experiment described above seems fairly innocuous. The research-subjects are volunteers; and a nasty cold is no worse than nasty. But there would be cause for disquiet if the same experiment were carried out on non-volunteer research-subjects, for instance, or perhaps if the condition with which the research-subjects were deliberately infected was more harmful or dangerous than a common cold. At one end of the scale, then, are experiments which seek gains at the cost of inflicting minimal amounts of harm upon fully informed, maturely consenting volunteer research-subjects: such experiments, I imagine, will usually be ethically justifiable. At the other end of the scale are experiments which seek gains at the cost of inflicting large amounts of harm upon uninformed or involuntary research-subjects: and such experiments, I take it, will rarely if ever be ethically justifiable. The notorious Willowbrook hepatitis experiments leap to mind in this latter context (as, in a more extreme way, and under certain interpretations, do some of the experiments conducted in the Nazi death camps). When human research-subjects are deliberately not told about the risks that they run, or are tricked, coerced or forced into taking part in experiments, most of us will judge the experiment to be unethical; some will also deem unethical any experiment which inflicts upon research-subjects a significant or lasting degree of harm, however informed or consenting the subjects who suffer that harm may be.

But it is not the intention of this paper to draw distinctions between ethical and unethical experiments. For my purposes it will be sufficient if it is acknowledged that at least *some* experiments which have the characteristics that I have outlined are unethical. The question to be discussed here will then be whether, given that some particular experiment *is* unethical, the results from it ought to be *used.* Ought one to use the results from an experiment which unethically inflicts harm upon human research-subjects? If such an experiment results in improved or successful treatment for a serious medical condition, would it be wrong to make the treatment available to people suffering from that condition? Does the ethical character of the means by which a result was obtained affect the ethical character of the use of that result for future therapeutic or clinical ends?

Many, I think, will have mixed intuitions about these questions. But I would guess that the majority of us would come down on the side of using the results from unethical experiments, especially if those results appeared likely to yield large benefits in human terms. An unethically developed cure for AIDS, for instance, would be a cure nonetheless for that, and very few would think it proper to suppress or to withhold it on account of its unethical provenance. Arguments in favor of using such results might include the following: that a piece of information (e.g., how to cure AIDS) is always ethically neutral, regardless of its provenance, and so there is no connection between the ethical character of the way in which a piece of information was obtained and the ethical character of the way in which it is used; that the use of results from unethical experiments to produce large human benefits prevents the victims of those experiments from having suffered in vain or for nothing; that it would be wrong to withhold from sufferers a beneficial treatment if its use now would harm no one. And doubtless there are other arguments. But those just mentioned are some of the commoner ones, and all of them have a fair degree of *prima facie* plausibility.

So are there any good reasons for dissenting from such arguments? Is there any reason to suppose that the results of unethical experiments in medicine should remain unused, or should be suppressed, even if their use might be expected to yield large human benefits? It is my contention that there is such a reason; and I will attempt in this paper to spell out what it is. It seems that our intuitions in favor of using results from unethical experiments are in one important way inadequate, and that some of the arguments offered in support of such intuitions are—at best—double edged. If the following account is correct then the use of results from unethical experiments in medicine will always pose at least a serious dilemma. And sometimes, the account will suggest, it will be straightforwardly wrong to make use of the results from such experiments, *especially* when the human benefits which are expected to accrue from the use of them are large ones. But this is beginning to sound paradoxical. We need to do some groundwork first.

II

I suggested a moment ago that our intuitions might be a little mixed over the question whether to use the results from unethical experiments. So what intuitions might we have against using them? I think that there are three main kinds, which might be expressed as follows: we ought not to use the results from an unethical experiment because to do so would be disrespectful to the victims of the experiment; or to do so would be to condone the unethical methods employed in the experiment; or to do so would be to encourage others to employ such methods. Are any of these claims compelling?

The first one doesn't look very powerful. It isn't at all clear that one fails to respect someone whenever one takes advantage of, or seeks to benefit from, the fact that that person has suffered unjustly. If someone is murdered, and this brings about a revision of police tactics that allows other people to live more safely, there need be nothing which indicates a lack of respect for the murder victim in the fact that other people are now, and as a result of that murder, leading safer lives. Of course these people may, as it happens, not respect the murder victim; but that is a contingent matter, and any lack of respect which

they might feel is quite separate in principle from their enjoyment of a more secure existence. Similarly, if somewhat more metaphysically, it is far from obvious
that a Christian who hopes for salvation through the suffering of Christ is
thereby guilty of a failure to respect Christ, or of a blasé attitude towards
Christ's suffering. Only if the beneficiaries of the murder or martyrdom relish the
fact that their good fortune was made possible by the unjust suffering of someone else is anything evidently repulsive going on: but then it is these people's attitude towards unjust suffering that is repulsive and not the (mere) fact that they
happen to be the beneficiaries of it. The intuition, then, that it would be wrong
to use the results of unethical experiments in medicine because to do so would
be to fail to respect the experiment's victims (an intuition which seems to be expressed most frequently in the context of the Nazi death camp experiments)
does not appear well-founded. There does not appear to be any reason why
someone might not be filled with a genuine reverence and respect for the victims of an unethical experiment while at the same time benefitting from its results, or attempting to benefit others by using those results. In this context, the
thought mentioned earlier—that the beneficial use of such results at least en-
sures that the victims of the experiment did not suffer for nothing—seems
closer to the mark. If there is anything wrong with using the results from ueth-
ical experiments in medicine, the reason must surely lie somewhere else.

The second suggestion holds that we would be wrong to use such results
because by using them we would be condoning the methods by which they
were obtained. The quick objection to this is: "Says who?" If I use the results of
an unethical experiment to benefit someone, and I hotly condemn the methods
by which the results were obtained, campaign stoutly for tougher laws and
guidelines to ensure that such methods will never be employed again, adhere
enthusiastically to guidelines which I would like to see made universal, report my
less fastidious colleagues to the authorities whenever their experiments seem
ethically questionable—then what grounds can there possibly be for claiming
that I *condone* unethical methods of research? None, surely. And this may be
true even in the absence of such splendidly thorough evidence to the contrary.
Suppose a murderer strikes by draining (all of) someone's blood into a bucket;
suppose I know that this is what the bucket contains, and how it came to be
there. If, finding myself suddenly ringed by flames and with only the bucket to
hand, I hurl its contents onto the fire and save myself from burning, it would
clearly be wrong to say that I condone through my action the murderous methods by which the bucket came to be filled with its useful contents. Nothing in
my behavior lends support to this imputation. Whether or not one person condones a second person's unethical action is a question which cannot be settled
merely by appealing to an isolated piece of the first person's behavior, even
when that behavior is made possible only by the unethical action of the second
person, and even when the first person knows this. In the absence of behavior
such as cheering, public commendation, warmly approbative comment and so
on, it will always be plausible to present the first person as *not* condoning the
second person's unethical action. Condoning something unethical, just like supporting something ethical, requires more than *simply* taking advantage of it.
Further proof is required (which is why those who would run sins of commission

and omission together always sound so wrong: whatever *prima facie* plausibility there is in holding someone partly responsible for the awfulness of famine, for instance, merely because they could help to alleviate it by giving to Oxfam, but choose not to, is diminished sharply when one imagines holding someone partly responsible for alleviating the awfulness of famine merely because they could firebomb Oxfam if they wanted to, but choose not to). By itself, then, this intuition—that to use the results of unethical experiments in medicine would be wrong because it would be to condone the experimental methods involved—doesn't stand up. One must do more than merely take advantage of another person's unethical behavior if one is safely to be presented as condoning it.

Let us turn to the third intuition: that using results from unethical experiments in medicine is wrong because it encourages the performance of further unethical experiments. I believe that this intuition is sound. But if we are to see why, we must make a distinction. I do not think the intuition is sound if by "encourages" is meant "consciously incites," "deliberately makes more likely," "intentionally promotes," etc. Understood thus the intuition is unsound for much the reason that the last one was unsound: it attributes to a person a view that he may or may not hold, a commitment to which is not established merely by the fact that he (knowingly) takes advantage of someone else's unethical actions. The intuition is sound, however, if "encourages" means "effectively incites," "effectively makes more likely," "effectively promotes," etc. In this sense, whether a person "encourages" or not (unlike, e.g., whether he "condones" or not) is to be settled by looking at what effects his behavior actually has or might be expected to have, rather than at what effects his behavior was meant to have, or at any other psychological facts about him. The "encouraging" nature of a person's behavior is to be found in its consequences, and not in its motives. So to claim that the present intuition is sound is to claim that it would be wrong to use the results of unethical experiments in medicine because to do so would effectively make more likely the performance of further unethical experiments in medicine. On the face of it this claim now looks like a close relative of the claims that are sometimes made about pornography and violent videos—that a certain type of product (or behavior) is undesirable because it effectively promotes a certain type of undesirable behavior. As such, one might expect the present claim to degenerate into the sort of pointlessness that the apparently parallel claims about pornography and videos often do. X causes Y, either directly or else by creating a milieu in which Y is more likely to come about: therefore X is a bad thing. But the causal relations asserted by such claims are notoriously questionable, and the evidence in favor of them has the habit of turning out to be either opportunistic or circular. If the present claim is like the claims made about pornography and videos, then it would probably better be left unentered.

But it isn't like those claims. For the sense in which I believe that the use of results from unethical experiments in medicine encourages the performance of further unethical experiments in medicine is not causal. Rather, my claim is that there is a *conceptual* connection between the use of such results and the performance of future unethical experiments. The case I wish to make does not, therefore, require the support of empirical research into the effects caused by the use of such results (any more than, for example, the claim that a sound understanding of arithmetic encourages the correct solution of problems in division requires empirical support). But why might there be thought to be a conceptual connection between the use of results from unethical experiments and the performance of future unethical experiments?

III

The reason is to be found in the nature of the experiments themselves, and in the rationale which might be offered for performing them. The experiments with which this paper is concerned, remember, are undertaken in the anticipation that the long-term benefits provided by their results will in some sense outweigh the harm which the experimental procedures themselves inflict upon research-subjects. Thus such an experiment will only be worth performing if the gains anticipated from its performance are worth the costs. There is therefore a rationale for performing experiments of this kind which is laid down by the nature of the experiments themselves, and which is intrinsic to them; and that rationale is immediately recognizable as utilitarian. Experiments will, according to their intrinsic rationale, be justified so long as the human benefits which they yield outweigh the human costs at which those benefits are bought. And it will be rational to perform such experiments if there are good grounds to suppose that the human benefits secured will indeed outweigh the human costs incurred.

We might now find it useful to imagine an Ideal Experimenter, whose sole function in life is to carry out experiments of the kind we have been discussing, and to do so in strict accordance with the rationale intrinsic to them. Such an Ideal Experimenter is a rather specialized kind of utilitarian, who is motivated wholly by the desire to maximize human happiness through the performance of medical experiments. Human happiness, of course, is the only value of an ethical kind which he recognizes, insofar as he is an Ideal Experimenter. (Other values, such as intelligence, conscientiousness, honesty and the love of truth, he will recognize in as much as that they are essential to the production of experimental results which are in fact happiness-maximizing, because reliable. He will recognize them for their instrumental value, but not as ends in themselves.) Thus the Ideal Experimenter, necessarily wedded to the utilitarian ethic constituting the rationale intrinsic to the experiments which he performs, will never, insofar as he is Ideal (and hence, being utilitarian, rational), perform an experiment which is, by his own lights, unethical. If the results of an experiment are productive of human happiness, then that experiment is, for him, justified. And if it reasonable to expect that an experiment will be more successful when, for instance, it is performed upon involuntary rather than voluntary research-subjects, then the use of involuntary research-subjects will also be justified (provided that the gains in human happiness can reasonably be expected to outweigh the additional costs in human suffering).

So the Ideal Experimenter will never, in his own view, perform an unethical experiment, however unethical his procedures may seem to someone who is *not* committed to a utilitarian ethic. The charge that certain experiments include elements (such as the use of involuntary research-subjects) which are always unethical, and are unethical regardless of their happiness-maximizing results, will cut no ice at all with the Ideal Experimenter. Such a charge can only be made by someone who is not a utilitarian. Such a charge, therefore, can only be made from a perspective radically different from that to which the Ideal Experimenter is necessarily committed. This means that the widely shared conviction that there is something obviously wrong with experiments such as Willowbrook (i.e., with any experiment conducted without the consent of its subjects) springs from concerns which are incompatible with those motivating the Ideal Experimenter —which are, indeed, incompatible with the concerns motivating *any* experimenter insofar as he is committed to the utilitarian rationale intrinsic to his activities (i.e., insofar as he is committed to those activities). And this incompatibility signals the danger of an ethical stand-off, or at any rate of an ethical cat-and-mouse game.

For how ought those who believe that medical research should observe certain non-utilitarian guidelines (which is to say most of us) respond to the indifference, to the *vocational* indifference, felt by those committed to experimentation (and hence to the rationale intrinsic to such experimentation) towards the values underlying *any* non-utilitarian guideline? Assertion and counter-assertion of incompatible values will clearly result in nothing better than stand-off. Yet an attempt by the majority, assuming that most people do think that an experiment can be unethical even though beneficial, to *impose* non-utilitarian guidelines upon experimenters—who, *qua* experimenters, are after all Ideal Experimenters—will only result in a more frenetic kind of stand-off. The majority, perhaps in legislative guise, will stipulate which experimental procedures are objectionable, and which punishable; while the Ideal Experimenter and his real-world counterparts, having no reason intrinsic to their activity to respect these stipulations, will attempt either to evade, to avoid or to ignore them. They would, by their own lights, be behaving irrationally if they did otherwise: for the consequence of following a non-utilitarian guideline must inevitably be to lessen the happiness-maximizing effects which an experiment will have. The Ideal Experimenter will therefore regard any non-utilitarian regulation as, essentially, a nuisance which—if it is backed by coercive measures—he will have to take into account when he does his cost/benefit analyses. He will have to regard the risk to himself of prosecution, imprisonment, disgrace, etc. as just another of the human costs which the beneficial results of an experiment will need to outweigh. The attempt to impose non-utilitarian guidelines, then, will succeed only when the penalties for breaking them are severe enough to weigh heavily in the utilitarian balance of consequences, and only when they are of the appropriate kind.

No Ideal Experimenter is going to be deterred from breaking a non-utilitarian guideline by—for instance—the threat of public rebuke. Even if the gains which he expects from his experiment are very minor, he is still likely to regard them as major enough to outweigh the human cost of a ticking off (or else he would hardly be bothering with the experiment in the first place). The threat of a fine, or of imprisonment, or of professional disqualification might be expected to work rather better. The Ideal Experimenter will not court these penalties unless the gains which he expects from contravening a non-utilitarian guideline are at least comparably great. But when those gains *are* at least comparably great, the Ideal Experimenter will break the guideline (while, of course, because he is rational, attempting to conceal the fact). And if those gains are very great indeed, then the Ideal Experimenter will not be deterred by any threat to himself whatever. For what, he will ask, is the life of one (more) man, such as himself, compared with—for instance—a cure for cancer? It is here, in the extreme case, that the essential futility of trying to coerce the Ideal Experimenter into behaving like a non-utilitarian by threatening his person is revealed. For, as a utilitarian, his own happiness is no more important to him than that of any of those whom he hopes to benefit through his work; and since, if his work is important, these will always be more of them than there are of him, this makes the Ideal Experimenter almost invulnerable to personal intimidation.

So how might the Ideal Experimenter effectively be persuaded to conform to non-utilitarian standards of experimental practice? The answer, I think, is clear. One has to give him a motivation which, as a utilitarian, he will recognize, and will be bound to take seriously. For the reasons just mentioned, the threat of personal disadvantage or unhappiness will not furnish him with a motivation of the right kind, or at any rate of the right intensity. What one needs instead is to threaten him where, as an Ideal Experimenter, he is most vulnerable: one needs to threaten the ends which he is striving to bring about, and which provide the justification for his activities. If one can persuade him that these ends will be frustrated, then one will have ceased to be merely a nuisance. One will have become a genuine threat to him, for one will be threatening his very *raison d'etre*. If the Ideal Experimenter can be brought to believe that any experimental result obtained in contravention of non-utilitarian standards will *not* be used to benefit anybody (i.e., will be suppressed, destroyed if possible, outlawed), then he will have been given a powerful reason to conform to those standards. He will have been given a reason which is relevant to him *as a utilitarian*. And that reason will be powerful in proportion as the Ideal Experimenter is convinced that the results of unacceptable experiments will be not be used *even when* the human benefits to be gained by using them are large.

Thus—and this is the moral of the tale—there is at least one good reason why we should refuse to use the results from unethical experiments, and why we should especially refuse to use them when the benefits to be expected from them are very large. For by using such results, or by showing a willingness to use them (through our attitude towards existing results which have been unethically obtained), we give a clear signal to the Ideal Experimenter. We give him good reason to believe that, however much we jump up and down, however much we deplore certain experimental methods, seek their criminalization, tighten up our coercively-backed non-utilitarian guidelines, prosecute those who break them, and so on, we will *still* use the results whenever it looks expedient or humane to do so. And that, of course, is all that the Ideal Experimenter *essentially* cares about. So long as he believes that a beneficial result will be used, however obtained, he has no real motivation to ensure that his own future results are obtained in accordance with non-utilitarian standards of experimental practice. If the beneficial outcome to which he is committed is brought about regardless then, if he has got his utilitarian calculation right, it will be worth his while to court (although he will try to avoid) whatever opprobrium or punishment is visited upon him in virtue of his methods. Therefore the readiness on our part to use unethically obtained results to achieve beneficial ends constitutes an unmistakable *encouragement* to the Ideal Experimenter to obtain results by unethical means, if those happen to be the most expedient.

This is why I suggested earlier that the arguments which might be offered in favor of using such results were double-edged. For however humane and reasonable such arguments might appear when regarded in the context of unethical experiments which have *already* been performed, they take on a different character as soon as that context is widened so as to include *future* unethical experiments. Such arguments are, after all, either explicitly utilitarian (e.g., the argument that we should use the results in order to prevent the experiment's victims from having suffered for nothing) or else highly congenial to the utilitarian (e.g., the argument that the ethical character of a result's provenance has no bearing upon the ethical character of its use). These arguments are not, of course, necessarily *bad;* nor does their utilitarian, or utilitarian-friendly, character show that there is something necessarily the matter with them. But in the present context these arguments do certainly give a hostage to fortune. For they buy in to the Ideal Experimenter's own peculiar scheme of things, through the side door as it were, and no doubt inadvertently, and end up by effectively encouraging anyone who hopes for great results through the performance of experiments whose methods are defensible on utilitarian grounds, but on no others. And one can imagine the Ideal Experimenter rubbing his hands in glee as he hears the case being made: we should use these results, argues someone who deplores the way in which they were obtained, because information itself is ethically neutral, because if we do so we will prevent the experiment's victims from having suffered for nothing, because it would be wrong to suppress a beneficial result if no one *now* is going to be harmed by its use; and so one. The Ideal Experimenter hears these arguments and quite rationally concludes that, on his own terms, he is being given a free hand. At the very worst he can benefit mankind at the price of personal disgrace, disqualification, imprisonment—even, if the coercion is very strong, execution. And these are prices he might well be willing to pay.

So my claim is this. The thought that it would be wrong to use the results from unethical experiments in medicine is a well-founded one, because the use of such results constitutes an effective encouragement to the Ideal Experimenter to conduct experiments which contravene non-utilitarian guidelines whenever it is expedient to do so. The kind of encouragement which the use of results from such experiments constitutes is not causal (i.e., the claim that I am making is not like the claims that are sometimes made about pornography and violent videos). Rather, it constitutes a conceptual encouragement: the prospect that his results will be beneficiently used no matter how they are obtained gives the Ideal Experimenter a *reason* to break non-utilitarian guidelines whenever it is expedient to do so—a reason which derives immediately from the rationale intrinsic to the activity in which he is engaged. Thus if one wishes to discourage the performance of experiments which are, from a non-utilitarian standpoint, unethical, one must attempt to deny to the Ideal Experimenter the reason which he requires in order to justify such experiments to himself: one must seek, in other words, to undermine his rational expectation that the results of a (successful) experiment will be used beneficently no matter how they have been obtained. And one will be able to do this only if one is prepared consistently to refrain from using the results of any unethical experiment; only thus will the Ideal Experimenter have grounds rationally to expect that his own results will not be used when they have been obtained in a manner which the non-utilitarian would regard as unethical. Only thus, in other words, will the Ideal Experimenter be given a reason, (which *he* will recognize as a relevant reason) to perform all of his experiments in a manner which conforms with non-utilitarian standards of experimental practice—*no matter how great* he might otherwise expect the benefits of contravening those standards to be. . . .

8.1e   Responding to Ridley

This argument makes an interesting, if somewhat extreme, case. Someone might agree, however, that the argument was sound, and that it would be a mistake in some sense to use the results from unethical experiments in medicine, and yet still deny that the argument yields any interesting practical consequences. After all, the objection might go, the argument is entirely concerned with the motivations, the actions, and the likely responses of the Ideal Experimenter, who is an abstraction, a figment of the imagination; there is no reason to suppose that what is true of the Ideal Experimenter will also be true of the real-world researchers whose results are the ones that we might or might not actually decide to use. The argument might be good, the objection concludes, if laboratories were manned only by Ideal Experimenters. But since they are in fact manned by real people who are motivated by many different considerations, behave in various ways, respond diversely, and so on, the argument cannot hope to establish what will or will not encourage the actual performance, by real people, of ethically acceptable experiments in medicine. The argument is much too abstract.

There is no question that this objection has some force. Perhaps is it true that in the real world most experimenters will be deterred most of the time from performing unethical experiments by the threat of personal penalties; perhaps it is true that most real-world experimenters are not idealists in the sense that the Ideal Experimenter is an idealist. But even so the objection is hardly decisive. For, in the first place, the comfort to be gained from the fact that only a small minority of real researchers will approximate to the full-blooded idealism of the Ideal Experimenter is actually very slight: For it is just these people who are most likely to perform unethical experiments in the first place, and it is just these people who are least likely to be deterred from doing so by the threat of personal penalty. In pointing, no doubt justly, to the *un*Ideal qualities of the majority of real experimenters, the objection misses entirely the danger posed by that minority of experimenters abut whose behavior there is most reason to be concerned. That is one response to the objection.

A second, less dramatic, response is perhaps further reaching. To be sure, it runs, the Ideal Experimenter is an abstraction, to whom it is likely that no real-world experimenter approximates tremendously closely. But insofar as it is correct to characterize the activity the Ideal Experimenter is engaged in as one which has its own intrinsic rationale (which is a *utilitarian* rationale), the activity engaged in by the Ideal Experimenter's real-world epigones also has that rationale. Thus to whatever extent real-world experimenters are genuinely committed to the activity in which they engage, they are necessarily, and to that extent, committed to the (utilitarian) rationale intrinsic to their activity. Therefore, unless there are no real-world experimenters who are remotely committed to performing experiments whose long-terms benefits are expected to outweigh their short-term costs—which seems most unlikely—there must inevitably be experimenters who are, to a greater or lesser extent, committed to a utilitarian rationale in virtue of their experimental activities. This means that the question of whether the results of experiments will be used, if obtained in a manner deemed unethical from a nonutilitarian standpoint, must be crucial and relevant to the minimally committed real-world experimenter in just the way and for just the reasons that it must be crucial and relevant to the Ideal Experimenter. The argument, then, if sound, applies to the real world of real experimenters every bit as much as it applies to the abstract world of Ideal Experimenters.

So the conclusion—that the results of unethical experiments in medicine ought not to be used, even, or especially, when their use may be expected to yield large benefits—might be taken as a practical recommendation. The recommendation is not restricted to a rarefied world inhabited by only Ideal entities, with no real-world counterparts. But it is now easy to imagine a second objection. Someone might agree that, at least in principle, it would be practically desirable to refuse to use the results of unethical experiments, while claiming nonetheless that the principle is impractical. After all, the objection might go, you can't force the genie back into the bottle once it's out. If someone has discovered something, by whatever means, then no power on earth can undiscover it, can return it to the realm of the unknown. The cat is out of the bag and the damage has been done. If a piece of information is known, it will be communicated. If the information is useful, then sooner or later it will be used. Thus, however desirable it might be to do so, it will in practice be impossible to prevent the use of a useful result. So Ridley's argument makes a practical recommendation which is in fact unrealizable, a fantasy.

Again, the objection has some force. But one needs to distinguish between knowing something and using what is known. Certainly it is true that what has been discovered cannot be undiscovered. Nor, usually, will it be possible to prevent the dissemination of knowledge discovered (although one can imagine at least a few extreme measures here). But the use of such knowledge is a different matter. This is something with which one might hope to interfere quite effectively. For instance, one might refuse to license, or to give legal countenance to, any treatment or procedure which has been developed in contravention of nonutilitarian standards of experimental practice (for example, to any treatment or procedure that has been developed through the use of results from experiments performed upon involuntary human research subjects; or from experiments that inflict more than a certain amount of harm upon research subjects, whether or not those subjects are volunteers). One might make the sale of unethically developed drugs illegal. One might threaten those—such as doctors, surgeons, hospital managers, etc.—who would actually *use* such treatments, procedures, or drugs with severe personal penalties. One might seek to block state and other funding for the development of any treatment, procedure, or drug which depends upon unethical research. And so on

The point is that one might reasonably hope, through the cumulative weight of practical measures such as these, if consistently (and indeed internationally) applied, to persuade any experimenter that the odds against the results from unethical experiments being used to benefit anybody are so long as to render the future performance of such experiments pointless. Which, after all, is all that the argument suggests is necessary. By making the use of results from unethical experiments awkward, and preferably impossible, then, one is not so much locking the stable door after the horse has bolted, as slamming the door on the potentially unlimited number of horses still milling about inside. The use of such results, by contrast, however hedged about with disclaimers and condemnations of their provenance, provides the remaining horses with just the incitement to bolt that they need. It seems, therefore, that the argument can survive the objection. The recommendation it yields is not only sound in principle, but it is also practicable. It suggests measures which might realistically be taken, and it gives reason to suppose that the taking of such measures will indeed, and in practice, be more effective in discouraging the performance of unethical experiments than any other method will be.

A final objection springs to mind, however, and this time perhaps a more powerful one. The anti-use position for which the article argues may indeed be sound. But isn't it also rather simple-minded? Specifically, doesn't the article just assume that the minute we have been shown a reason to deplore the use of unethically obtained results all other considerations simply drop out? Why *should* they drop out? This objection is rather like the one raised against Don Marquis's argument in 6.2f. There it was suggested that the fact that abortion could be shown to involve a moral violation did not show that abortion must always and everywhere be morally wrong. Other, outweighing factors might come into play (sometimes or always). In the present context, the objection comes to this: The argument about the Ideal Experimenter may be effective in explaining why the use of unethically obtained results involves a moral violation, but it cannot show that other factors never play an outweighing role. Thus it may be open to someone to accept the general thrust of the argument while still insisting that the use of unethically obtained results may sometimes be justifiable, and be justifiable despite the moral violation that such use would involve. In effect, the objection urges that there may be occasions on which the moral violation in not using the results of unethical experiments would be greater than the violation in using them: The article oversimplifies the alternatives, preferring a black-or-white conception of the problem to the subtler, more nuanced, and more difficult approach that issues such as this almost always call for. If our only priority is to discourage the performance of unethical experiments in medicine, perhaps the article's position is good enough. But if we have other priorities as well, for instance the priority to provide the best possible health care, that position is simply too crude to carry that day.

This objection is rather compelling. If sound, it shows that no argument about an Ideal Experimenter can hope to establish the absolute wrongness of the use of unethically obtained results. Sometimes it *may* be worse to refuse such results than to use them. But even if this conclusion is accepted (and I suspect it should be), the Ideal Experimenter argument still does two important things. It provides a principled explanation and justification of the widespread intuition that the use of unethically obtained results involves *some* moral violation, and it shows how serious competing considerations will need to be if, in particular cases, they are to succeed in outweighing that violation. The use of unethically obtained results may sometimes be justifiable, but the arguments in favor of using them in any particular case will have to be very powerful indeed.

8.1f   Animal Research: Regan's Argument: "The Case against Animal Research"

It was noted earlier that the majority of medical research is not carried out on human beings at all, but on animals. The question inevitably arises whether it is ethically acceptable to harm and kill members of other species, who can neither consent nor refuse to participate in experiments, in order to benefit our own species. In the view of Tom Regan, professor of philosophy at North Carolina State University in Raleigh, such research is not usually acceptable.

THE CASE AGAINST ANIMAL RESEARCH
Tom Regan

THE AUTONOMY OF ANIMALS

Autonomy can be understood in different ways. On one interpretation, which finds its classic statement in Kant's writings, individuals are autonomous only if they are capable of acting on reasons they can will that any other similarly placed individual can act on. For example, if I am trying to decide whether I morally ought to keep a promise, I must, Kant believes, ask whether I could will that everyone else who is similarly placed (i.e., who has made a promise) can act as I do for the same reasons as I have. In asking what I ought to do, in other words, I must determine what others can do, and it is only if I have the ability to think through and reflectively evaluate the merits of acting in one way or another (e.g., to decide to keep the promise or to break it). and, having done this, to make a decision on the basis of my deliberations, that I can be viewed as an autonomous individual.

It is highly unlikely that any animal is autonomous in the Kantian sense. To be so animals would have to be able to reason at a quite sophisticated level indeed, bringing to bear considerations about what other animals (presumably those who belong to their own species) can or ought to do in comparable situations, a process that requires assessing the merits of alternative acts from an impartial point of view. Not only is it doubtful that animals could have the requisite abilities to do this; it is doubtful that we could confirm their possession of these abilities if they had them. . . .

But the Kantian sense of autonomy is not the only one. An alternative view is that individuals are autonomous if they have preferences and have the ability to initiate action with a view to satisfying them. It is not necessary, given this interpretation of autonomy (let us call this *preference autonomy*), that one be able to abstract from one's own desires, goals, and so on, as a preliminary to asking what any other similarly placed individual ought to do; it is enough that one have the ability to initiate action because one has those desires or goals one has and believes, rightly or wrongly, that one's desires or purposes will be satisfied or achieved by acting in a certain way. Where the Kantian sense requires that one be able to think impartially if one is to possess autonomy, the preference sense does not. . . .

From this it is a short step to acknowledging that these animals are reasonably viewed as being capable of making preferential choices.

Two types of cases illustrate the propriety of viewing these animals in this way. The first involves cases where they regularly behave in a given way when given the opportunity to do one thing or another. For example, if, when Fido is both hungry and has not recently had an opportunity to run outdoors, he regularly opts for eating when given the choice between food or the outdoors, we have adequate behavioral grounds for saying that the dog prefers eating to running in such cases and so acts (i.e., chooses) accordingly. A second type of case involves situations where there is no regular behavioral pattern because of the novelty of a given set of circumstances. If Fido is hungry, if we place before him both a bowl of his regular food and a bowl of boiled eggplant, and if, as is predictable, Fido opts for his regular food, then we again have adequate behavioral grounds for saying that the dog prefers his normal food to the eggplant and so acts (i.e., chooses) accordingly. And this we may reasonably contend even if this is the only time Fido is presented with the choice in question.

When autonomy is understood in the preference sense, the case can be made for viewing many animals as autonomous. Which animals it is reasonable to view as autonomous will turn, first, on whether we have reasonable grounds for viewing them as having preferences, understood as desires or goals, and, second, on whether we find that how they behave in various situations is intelligibly described and parsimoniously explained by making reference to their preferences and the choices they make because of the preferences they have. . . .

We have, then, two senses of autonomy—the Kantian and the preference sense—each differing significantly from the other. . . . The Kantian interpretation of autonomy does not give us a condition that must be met if one is to be autonomous in any sense. It provides a condition that must be met if one is to be an autonomous *moral agent*—that is, an individual who can be held morally accountable for the acts he performs or fails to perform, one who can rightly be blamed or praised, criticized or condemned. Central to the Kantian sense of autonomy is the idea that autonomous individuals can rise above thinking about their individual preferences and think about where their moral duty lies by bringing impartial reasons to bear on their deliberations. These two ideas (that of individual preferences, on the one hand, and on the other, one's moral duty) are distinct. Just because I prefer your death or public shame, for example, it does not follow that either I or anyone else has a moral duty to terminate your life or bring about your public disgrace, and there are many things I might be morally obligated to do that I personally do not prefer doing (e.g., keeping a promise). Suppose it is agreed that one must be autonomous in the Kantian sense to have the status of a moral agent. . . . It does not follow that one must be autonomous in *this* sense to be autonomous in *any* sense. So long as one has the ability to act on one's preferences, the ascription of autonomy is intelligible and attributions of it are confirmable. Though normal mammalian animals aged one or more are not reasonably viewed as moral agents because they are not reasonably viewed as autonomous in the Kantian sense, they are reasonably viewed as autonomous in the preference sense.

THE RIGHTS OF ANIMALS

. . . The principle basic moral right possessed by all moral agents and patients is the right to respectful treatment. . . . [A]ll moral agents and patients are intelligibly and nonarbitrarily viewed as having a distinctive kind of value (inherent value) and as having this value equally. All moral agents and patients must always be treated in ways that are consistent with the recognition of their equal possession of value of this kind. These individuals have a basic moral right to respectful treatment because the claim made to it is (a) a valid claim-against assignable individuals (namely, all moral agents) and (b) a valid claim-to, the validity of the claim-to resting on appeal to the respect principle, . . . The basic moral right to respectful treatment prohibits treating moral agents or patients as if they were mere receptacles of intrinsic values (e.g., pleasure), lacking any value of their own, since such a view of these individuals would allow harming some (e.g., by making them suffer) on the grounds that the aggregate consequences for all those other "receptacles" affected by the outcome would be "the best." . . .

TOXICOLOGY

. . . Some humans are harmed . . . as a result of a variety of pathological conditions, and many more will be harmed if we fail to investigate the causes, treatments, and cures of these conditions. Indeed, some will today lose their lives as a result of these maladies, and many more will lose theirs in the future if we fail to investigate their causes and cures. Now, one thing we must do, it may be claimed, is reduce the risk that the treatment prescribed for the given malady will make patients worse-off than they otherwise would have been, and this will require establishing the toxic properties of each new drug before, not after, humans take them. Thus arises the need to test the toxicity of each new drug on test animals. If we do not test the toxicity of all new drugs on animals, humans who use these drugs will run a much greater risk of being made worse-off as a result of using them than they would if these drugs were pretested on animals. In the nature of the case, we cannot say which drugs are toxic for humans *in advance* of conducting tests on animals (if we could, there would be no need to do the test in the first place). Indeed, we cannot even eliminate all risks *after* the drug has been extensively pretested on animals (thalidomide is a tragic example). The best we can do is minimize the risks humans who use drugs face, as best we can, and that requires testing for their toxicity on animals.

The rights view rejects this defense of these tests. *Risks are not morally transferable to those who do not voluntarily choose to take them in the way this defense assumes.* If I hang-glide, then I run certain risks, including the possibility of serious head injury, and I shall certainly, if I am prudent, want to minimize my risks by wearing a protective helmet. You, who do not hang-glide, have no duty to agree to serve in tests that establish the safety of various helmet designs so that hang-gliders might reduce their risks, and hang-gliders, or those who serve the interests of these enthusiasts, would violate your rights if they coerced or forced you to take part in such tests. *How much* you would be harmed is not decisive. What matters is that you would be *put at risk of harm, against your will,* in the name of reducing the risks that others voluntarily undertake and so can voluntarily decide *not* to undertake by the simple expedient of choosing not to run them in the first place (in this case, by choosing not to hang-glide). That tests on you would make it possible for those who hang-glide to lessen the risk of being made worse-off goes no way toward justifying placing you at risk of harm. As hang-gliders are the ones who stand to benefit from participation in this sport, they are the ones who must run the risks involved in participating. They may do all that they can to reduce the risks they run, but only so long as they do not coerce others to find out what these risks are or how to reduce them.

It would be a mistake to suppose that what is true in the case of high-risk activity is not true in the case of low-risk activity. Whenever I plug in my toaster, take an elevator, drink water from my faucet or from a clear mountain stream, I take some risks, though not of the magnitude of those who, say, sky-dive or canoe in turbid waters. But even in the case of my voluntarily taking minor risks, others have no duty to volunteer to establish or minimize my risks for me, and anyone who would be made to do this, against her will, would have her rights unjustifiably overridden. For example, the risks I run when I drive my car could be minimized by the design and manufacture of the most effective seat belts and the most crash-proof automobile. But it does not follow that anyone else has a duty to take part in crash tests in the name of minimizing my risks, and anyone who was coerced to do so, whether injured or not, would have every reason to claim that her rights had been violated or if the test subject is incapable of making the claim, others would have every reason to make this claim on the subject's behalf. "No harm done" is no defense in circumstances such as these.

To minimize the risks humans who use new drugs would run by testing them on animals is morally no different. Anyone who elects to take a drug voluntarily chooses to run certain risks, and the risks we choose to run or, as in the case of moral patients for whom we choose, the risks we elect to allow them to run are not morally transferable to others. Coercively to harm others or to put others, whether human or animal, at risk of harm in order to identify or minimize the risks of those who voluntarily choose to run them, is to violate the rights of the humans or animals in question. It is not *how much* the test subjects are harmed (though the greater the harm, the worse the offense). What matters is that they are coercively used to establish or minimize risks for others. To place these animals at risk of harm so that others who voluntarily choose to run certain risks, and who thus can voluntarily choose not to run them, may minimize the risks they run, is to fail to treat the test animals with that respect they are due as possessors of inherent value. As is true of toxicity tests on new products, similar tests of new drugs on animals involve treating them as *even less* than receptacles, as if their value were reducible to their possible utility relative to the interests of others—in this case, relative to the interests humans who voluntarily take drugs have in minimizing their risks. Laboratory animals, to borrow an apt phrase from the Harvard philosopher Robert Nozick, "are distinct individuals who are not resources for others."[1] To utilize them so that we might establish or minimize our risks, especially when it is within our power to decide not to take these risks in the first place, *is* to treat them as if they were "resources for others," most notably for us, and to defend these tests on the grounds that animals sometimes are not harmed is as morally lame as defending fox hunting on the grounds that the fox sometimes gets away.

The rights view is not in principle opposed to efforts to minimize the risks involved in taking new drugs. Toxicity tests are acceptable, so long as they violate no one's rights. To use human volunteers, persons who do not suffer from a particular malady but who give their informed consent as a test subject, is, though possible, not generally to be encouraged. To tie the progress of pharmacology and related sciences to the availability of healthy, consenting human subjects itself runs significant risks, including the risk that some may use deceptive or coercive means to secure participation. Moreover, few, if any, volunteers from the affluent classes are likely to step forward; the ranks of volunteers would likely be comprised of the poor, the uneducated, and those human moral patients whose relatives lack sufficient "sentimental interests" to protect them. There is a serious danger that the least powerful will be exploited. More preferable by far is the development of toxicity tests that harm no one—that is, tests that harm neither moral agents nor patients, whether humans or animals. Even at this date promising alternatives are being developed.[2] To validate them scientifically is no small challenge, but it is the challenge that must be met if we continue to desire or require that new drugs be tested for their toxicity prior to being made available on the market. To test them on healthy human volunteers is dangerous at best; to test them coercively on healthy animals and human moral patients is wrong. The moral alternative that remains is: find valid alternatives.

A number of objections can be anticipated. One claims that there are risks and then there are risks. If we stopped testing new drugs for their toxicity, think of the risks people would run if they took them! Who could say what disastrous consequences would result? The rights view agrees. People would run greater risks if drugs were not pretested. But (a) the rights view does not oppose all pretesting (only those tests that coercively utilize some so that others may reduce those risks they may choose to run or choose not to run), and (b) those who had the choice to use an untested drug, assuming it was available, could *themselves* choose not to run the risks associated with taking it by deciding not to take it. Indeed, prudence would dictate acting in this way, except in the direst circumstances.

Of course, if untested drugs were allowed on the market and if people acted prudently, sales of new (untested) drugs would fall off, and we can anticipate that those involved in the pharmaceutical industry, people who, in addition to their chosen vocation of serving the health needs of the public, also have an economic interest in the stability and growth of this industry, might look with disfavor on the implications of the rights view. Four brief replies must suffice in this regard. First, whatever financial losses these companies might face if they were not permitted to continue to do toxicity tests on animals carry no moral weight, since the question of overriding basic moral rights is at issue. That these companies might lose money if the rights of animals are respected is one of the risks they run. Second, there is mounting evidence that these companies could save, rather than lose, money, if nonanimal tests were used. Animals are an expensive proposition. They must be bred or purchased, fed and watered, their living quarters must be routinely cleaned, their environment controlled (otherwise one runs the scientific risk of an uncontrolled variable), and so forth. This requires employing trained personnel, in adequate numbers, as well as a large and continued outpouring of capital for initial construction, expansion, and maintenance. Tissue and cell cultures, for example, are cheaper by far. So the economic interests of commercial pharmaceutical firms are not necessarily at odds with the changes that will have to be made, as the rights of laboratory animals are respected. Third, anyone who defends present toxicological practice *merely* by claiming that these tests are required by the involved regulatory agencies (e.g., the Food and Drug Administration) would miss the essential moral point: though these agencies have yet to recognize nonanimal tests as meeting their regulations, these agencies themselves do not require that any pharmaceutical firm manufacture any new drug. That is a moral decision each company makes on its own and for which each must bear responsibility. Fourth, appeals to what the laws require can have no moral weight if we have good reason to believe that the laws in question are unjust. And we have good reasons in the present case. Laboratory animals are not a "resource" whose moral status in the world is to serve human interests. They are themselves the subjects-of-a-life that fares better or worse for them as individuals, logically independently of any utility they may or may not have relative to the interests of others. They share with us a distinctive kind of value—inherent value—and whatever we do to them must be respectful of this value as a matter of strict justice. To treat them *as if* their value were reducible to their utility for human interests, even important human interests, is to treat them unjustly; to utilize them so that humans might minimize the risks we voluntarily take (and that we can voluntarily decide not to take) is to violate their basic moral right to be treated with respect. That the laws require such testing, when they do, does not show that these tests are morally tolerable; what this shows is that the laws themselves are unjust and ought to be changed.

One can also anticipate charges that the rights view is antiscientific and antihumanity. This is rhetoric. The rights view is not anithuman. We, as humans, have an equal prima facie right not to be harmed, a right that the rights view seeks to illuminate and defend; but we do not have any right coercively to harm others, or to put them at risk of harm, so that we might minimize the risks we run as a result of our own voluntary decisions. That violates their rights, and that is one thing no one has a right to do. Nor is the rights view antiscientific. It places the *scientific* challenge before pharmacologists and related scientists: find scientifically valid ways that serve the public interest without violating individual rights. The overarching goal of pharmacology should be to reduce the risks of those who use drugs without harming those who don't. Those who claim that this cannot be done, in advance of making a concerted effort to do it, are the ones who are truly antiscientific.

Perhaps the most common response to the call for elimination of animals in toxicity testing is the benefits argument:

1. Human being and animals have benefited from toxicity tests on animals.
2. Therefore, these tests are justified.

Like all arguments with missing premises, everything turns on what that premise is. If it reads, "These tests do not violate the rights of animals," then we would be on our way to receiving an interesting defense of toxicity testing. Unfortunately for those who countenance these tests, however, and even more unfortunately for the animals used in them, that premise is not true. These tests do violate the rights of the test animals, for the reasons given. The benefits these tests have for others are irrelevant, according to the rights view, since the tests violate the rights of the individual animals. As in the case of humans, so also in the case of animals: overriding their rights cannot be defended by appealing to "the general welfare." Put alternatively, the benefits *others* receive count morally only if no *individual's* rights have been violated. Since toxicity tests of new drugs violate the rights of laboratory animals, it is morally irrelevant to appeal to how much others have benefited.[3]

A further objection is conceptual in nature. "Animals cannot volunteer or refuse to volunteer to take part in toxicity tests," it may be claimed, "and so cannot be forced or coerced to take part in them either. Thus the rights view's opposition to using them is fatuous." Now it is true that, unlike *some* humans, animals cannot give or withhold their informed consent, relative to participation in a toxicity test. But this is because they cannot be informed in the relevant way. It is no good trying to inform them about pH factors or carcinogens. They *will not* understand because they *cannot* understand; but is does not follow from this that animals cannot be forced or coerced to do something they do not want to do. Because these animals are intelligibly viewed as having preference-autonomy, . . . we are able intelligibly to say, and confirm statements made about, what they want, desire, prefer, aim at, intend, and so forth. We can, therefore, give a perfectly clear sense to saying that they are being forced or co-erced to do something they do not want to do. Beyond any doubt, those ani-mals used in the LD50 test.* for example, are not doing what they want to do, and those who use them in these tests do so by means of force or coercion.

To establish the scientific validity of nonanimal toxicity tests is a difficult challenge certainly, one that can only be met by scientists. No moral philosophy can do this. What a moral philosophy can do is articulate and defend the morally permissible means of conducting science. If the rights view has the best reasons on its side, this is the view we ought to use to assess what is and what is not permissible in the case of toxicity testing. And the implications of this view are clear. *Toxicity tests of new products and drugs involving animals are not morally justified. These tests violate the rights of these animals. They are not morally tolerable. All ought to cease. . . .*

ANIMALS IN SCIENCE, UTILITARIANISM, AND ANIMAL RIGHTS

The fundamental differences between utilitarianism and the rights view are never more apparent than in the case of the use of animals in science. For the utilitarian, whether the harm done to animals in pursuit of scientific ends is justi-fied depends on the balance of the aggregated consequences for all those af-fected by the outcome. If the consequences that result from harming animals would produce the best aggregate balance of good over evil, then harmful ex-perimentation is obligatory. If the resulting consequences would be at least as good as what are otherwise obtainable, then harmful experimentation is permis-sible. Only if harmful experimentation would produce less than the best conse-quences would it be wrong. For a utilitarian to oppose or support harmful ex-perimentation on animals, therefore, requires that he have the relevant facts— who will be benefited or harmed, how much, and so on. *Everyone's* interests, including the interests of those who do the tests or conduct the research, their employers, the dependents of these persons, the retailers and wholesalers of cages, animal breeders, and others, must be taken into account and counted equitably. For utilitarians, such *side effects count.* The animals used in the test

---

*Tests in which 50% of the animals die due to the toxicity of the dose of a substance to which they are exposed.

have no privileged moral status. Their interests must be taken into account, to be sure, but not any more than anybody else's interests.

As is "almost always" the case, utilitarians simply fail to give us what is needed—the relevant facts, facts that we must have, given their theory, to determine whether use of animals in science is or is not justified. Moreover, for a utilitarian to claim or imply that there must be something wrong with a given experiment, if the experimenter would not be willing to use a less intelligent, less aware human being but would be willing to use a more intelligent, more aware animal, simply lacks a utilitarian basis. For all we know, and for all the utilitarian has thus far told us, the consequences of using such an animal, all considered, might be better than those that would result from using the human being. It is not *who* is used, given utilitarian theory, that matters; it is *the consequences* that do.

The rights view takes a very different stand. No one, whether human or animal, is ever to be treated as if she were a mere receptacle, or as if her value were reducible to her possible utility for others. We are, that is, never to harm the individual merely on the grounds that this will or just might produce "the best" aggregate consequences. To do so is to violate the rights of the individual. That is why the harm done to animals in pursuit of scientific purposes is wrong. The benefits derived are real enough; but some gains are ill-gotten, and all gains are ill-gotten when secured unjustly.

So it is that the rights view issues its challenge to those who do science: advance knowledge, work for the general welfare, but not by allowing practices that violate the rights of the individual. These are, one might say, the terms of the new contract between science and society, a contract that, however belatedly, now contains the signature of those who speak for the rights of animals. *Those who accept the rights view, and who sign for animals, will not be satisfied with anything less than the total abolition of the harmful use of animals in science—in education, in toxicity testing, in basic research.* But the rights view plays no favorites. No scientific practice that violates human rights, whether the humans be moral agents or moral patients, is acceptable. And the same applies to those humans who, for reasons analogous to those advanced in the present [essay] in regard to nonhumans, should be given the benefit of the doubt about having rights because of the weight of our ignorance—the newly born and the soon-to-be-born. Those who accept the rights view are committed to denying any and all access to these "resources" on the part of those who do science. And we do this not because we oppose cruelty (though we do), nor because we favor kindness (though we do), but because justice requires nothing less. . . .

Notes

1. Robert Nozick, *Anarchy, State, and Utopia* (New York: Basic Books, 1974), p. 33. Nozick does not have animals in mind when he says this.
2. Richard D. Ryder, *Victims of Science: The Use of Animals in Research* (London: Davis-Poynter, 1975); and Dallas Pratt, *Alternatives to Pain in Experiments on Animals* (New York: Argus Archives, 1980).

3. The benefit argument sometimes is advanced, especially by veterinarians, in defense of testing for the toxicity of drugs on some animals in the hope that *other animals* might benefit. It is true that some animals have benefited because these tests have been done on others, but this does not provide a moral justification of these tests. Just as animals used in the laboratory are not resources to be used in the name of obtaining *human* benefits, so they are not to be viewed as a resource to be used in pursuit of benefits for *other animals.*

8.1g   Responding to Regan

Regan's argument makes a very powerful case against research on animals. In particular, his claim that it is wrong to force on one individual to take risks in order to benefit other individuals is quite compelling—as is borne out by his hang-gliding example.

Many will agree that if other forms of experimentation were available and practicable, that required either human volunteers or else no living subjects at all, research on animals should cease. The question, essentially, is whether such research should continue until those alternatives are available (if, indeed, they ever do become available). Regan's answer is that it shouldn't.

How might a defender of animal research reply? One response would simply be to insist on the adequacy of act utilitarianism as an ethical theory (which would have little difficulty in justifying animal experiments), and leave it at that. But I'd like to explore some other, more interesting, lines of reply instead. The first of these might begin by looking at Regan's idea of "preference autonomy," from which his whole argument springs. A critic might agree with Regan that animals' behavior does indeed show that they have preferences, and hence that they are, to that extent, autonomous. But he or she might doubt whether that plus the principle of respect for autonomy is sufficient to establish that animals ought never to be harmed, as Regan suggests. Indeed Regan's suggestion seems to be not just that it would be wrong to harm animals, but that it would be exactly as wrong to harm them as it would be to harm human beings; hence that experimenting on animals (against their will) is exactly as wrong as experimenting on unconsenting humans. This is a large step from the observation that animals have preferences! Just how large can be seen when one reflects that insects, too, have preferences: It is because wasps prefer syrup to sulphuric acid that wasp-traps are baited with the former and not the latter. Yet no one, surely, is about to suggest on the strength of this that it's just as bad to injure an unconsenting wasp as it is to injure an unconsenting human being.

What's gone wrong here? The trouble seems to lie in Regan's assumption that the mere possession of preferences is sufficient to guarantee full moral value. You have preferences; a cat or a cockroach has preferences. Therefore you, the cat, and the cockroach are each entitled to full and equal moral regard. The idea here seems to be a) that the principle of respect for autonomy is an all-or-nothing affair; b) that the possession of any autonomy at all is sufficient to make that principle fully operative; c) that the right not to be harmed depends upon no other consideration than the principle of respect for autonomy. A critic might quarrel with any or all of these assumptions. But their shortcomings can be seen even without piecemeal analysis. First, as we have already noted, these assumptions, if correct, would confer an exactly equal right not to be harmed upon both you and an insect: clearly, that can't be right. Second, nowhere in Regan's assumptions is it recognized that different individuals and different species can have preferences of utterly different kinds, some of which may be more deserving of respect than others. Nor, seemingly, is it noticed that my legitimate reasons for not wishing to harm my family, for instance, might extend well beyond the fact that I respect their right to make their own choices.

Perhaps some of these considerations can be drawn together in an example. Take a cat with three kittens and a human mother with three children; suppose that someone kills a kitten and someone else kills a child. Which of these actions is worse? Which causes more harm? Regan would presumably say that both were equally harmful, and therefore that both were equally wrong. Both kitten and child have died (presumably in defiance of preferences deducible from their behavior), and both the cat and the human mother have been deprived of their offspring (again, in defiance of deducible preferences). But let's look a little harder at the mothers. The cat will no doubt show signs of distress, but she'll soon be licking and suckling the other two kittens, and a few days later it will be as if nothing had happened. The human mother, on the other hand, will go through a lifetime of mourning. She, clearly, has been harmed in ways that the female cat has not been, and moreover, could not be. The far greater complexity of human beings and of the relationships between them (and hence the far greater complexity of their preferences) render human beings vulnerable to harm in ways that cats and cockroaches are not. This, it would suggest to most people, is quite sufficient to show that the child-killer inflicted more harm, and acted more wrongly, than the kitten-killer did. (And that is to leave aside all the ways in which the human mother's friends and relations would be harmed. It is hard to imagine that the cat's friends and relations would be harmed.)

Perhaps Regan would agree, but add that this still doesn't make what the kitten-killer did morally acceptable. The rights of the kitten and its mother have still been violated, no matter what one says about the human child and his or her mother. This, surely, is a fair response. The fact that one thing is worse than another thing doesn't magically eliminate the wrong of the second thing. But the critic might now press a little harder, for the example has introduced a kind of wedge-shaped gap into Regan's position. Regan wanted to claim that animal research, just like research on unconsenting humans, was absolutely wrong. Yet we have seen that this is not so: Humans can be and are harmed in ways that animals can't be and aren't. Furthermore, these differing levels of harm can be and are inflicted by exactly the same actions (both the human and the cat mother were deprived of their offspring, after all). It follows from this that animal research is *less* wrong than research on unconsenting humans, for humans can be harmed more than animals can by one and the same experimental procedure; hence animal research is not absolutely wrong. If animal research is not absolutely wrong, it may at times be justifiable (only the absolutely wrong can never be justified). Therefore, to return to the original point, the mere fact that animals have preferences does not show that it is always wrong to use them as research subjects.

One reason why Regan may have concluded that if something is wrong it must be absolutely wrong is his reliance on the language of "rights." As mentioned in Chapter Two, depending on the language of rights will often lead to confusion. In particular, if one approaches matters from a rights perspective, one is liable to end up concluding that every right is absolute, and that all rights are equally important. If, on the other hand, one remembers that rights are the flip-side of obligations, this confusion is less likely to arise. For no one doubts that some obligations are more important than other obligations. Thus, if we all have an obligation to keep our promises, then we all have a right to have the promises made to us kept. But that right is not absolute or unconditional. For we have other obligations too, some of which may be more important than the obligation to keep promises. So, for instance, if I have promised you that I will meet you at noon, you have a right to expect me to keep my promise. But if a colleague suddenly and urgently needs to be driven to the hospital, my obligation to help her may take precedence over my obligation to honor my promise to you. By breaking my promise to you, I have violated your rights. But my doing so was, under the circumstances, reasonable and justifiable (as you'd probably agree). It is this simple truth—that rights may, on occasion, be justifiably violated—that those who regard rights as the most fundamental building blocks of ethics so often overlook. If Regan's argument about "preference autonomy" is correct, then he is of course correct to say that animals have a right not to be harmed. But how binding this right is, and what kinds of obligation might justify the violation of it, are not questions to be settled merely by noting that animals do have the right in question.

The discussion so far suggests that the right of animals not to be harmed is at any rate less binding than the right of human beings not to be harmed. The defender of experiments conducted on animals might attempt to make quite a lot of this. For while it may be wrong to harm animals, it may nonetheless be justifiable to do so in the interests of human beings (just as the wrongness of breaking a promise may be justifiable if some more weighty human interest is served as a result). If so, then it may be less wrong to harm animals by conducting experiments on them than it would be to sacrifice significant human interests by not conducting such experiments. Notice that a defense such as this doesn't involve the claim that animals lack the right not to be harmed. Rather, this defense agrees that they have that right. But it then suggests a type of circumstance under which that right may justifiably be violated. It is in this sense that animal experimentation might be defended as a "necessary evil."

The position that results from this defense is quite a moderate one. In granting that animals have the right not to be harmed, the critic is very far from opening the flood-gates to any and every kind of animal research. For the violation of an animal's right requires a *justification*. If that justification is to be provided in terms of human interests, and if the violation of the animal's right is a serious one, then clearly the human interests in question must themselves be serious. Thus, it is difficult to envisage a way in which the present set of considerations could be used to justify research into something trivial, such as cosmetics. Indeed, the defense of animal experimentation we have been considering would require that the infliction of serious harm on animals be considered only in cases where very substantial human interests are at stake. Moreover, this position, just like Regan's, provides a real moral encouragement for researchers to investigate alternative, non-harmful methods wherever possible. Animal research does violate an animal's rights, after all, and it would clearly be better if no rights were violated in any way—even justifiably.

In my view, Regan's argument performs the valuable service of reminding us of, and making us think about, the value of lives other than our own. Gone are the days when we could confidently assume that animals had been put on earth for our pleasure and convenience. Some will doubtless agree with Regan that the factors that make *our* lives and *our* preferences important are present in animals also, and hence that we should never treat them in ways we wouldn't treat a human being. Those taking this view will perhaps condemn the defense of animal research outlined here as "speciesist." Others, reflecting that the very idea of morality arises from distinctively human concerns, will question the equality of interest that Regan grants to nonhuman animals: Morality is a people's game, after all, and any extension of it to cover nonhuman players must be secondary at best. From this perspective, research involving animals, although regrettable, may nevertheless be justifiable, especially if our own primary interests are well served by it.

8.1h   Recap: Sacrifices

All research with living subjects involves the risk or the certainty of injury, or worse, to those subjects. In the short term, medical research is much more likely to be harmful to the individuals who are on the receiving end, than otherwise. Hence, performing any experiment involving living subjects requires a justification. Mere curiosity is unlikely to be sufficient. The wise course, one would think, would be to err on the side of caution. Perhaps in the case of patients who are gravely ill, and for whom an experimental treatment offers the only real hope, however slim, of improvement, this caution need not be overly exaggerated. In the case of healthy human research subjects, by contrast, a maximum of caution is surely required. The need for informed consent, in particular, should encourage reflection: We ought to be certain not merely that such consent is forthcoming, but also that it comes from those best able to give it. And we should be cautious about animal experimentation. Regan's argument shows that animals deserve our respect. If we harm them at all, we should be aware that our actions need a justification—and that such a justification may be rather difficult to provide. The fact that people are increasingly reluctant to buy unnecessary products, such as cosmetics, that have been tested on animals—thereby putting commercial pressure on producers to develop their creams, etc. in other ways—is an encouraging sign. We may have begun to get it right, morally speaking, when we are equally concerned about the ways in which all the other products we need or enjoy have been developed.

The ethical standards of research involving living subjects (of which research we are all, to varying degrees, the beneficiaries) have not, either historically or recently, been very edifying. Perhaps we should think harder about medical research, then, and be prepared, as nonsubjects, to make a few more sacrifices. It's not, after all, as if life as the majority of us in the West lead it now were exactly intolerable.

Study Questions

1. Suppose you wish to test a treatment for an illness that primarily afflicts children. What special measures might you need to take when selecting human research subjects?
2. In 1971, the artist Chris Burden had himself (nonfatally) shot as a piece of performance art. Does this show that it might be legitimate to inflict nonfatal gunshot wounds on human volunteers for research purposes?
3. If a researcher discovers a cure for breast cancer by testing drugs on patients who do not know that the treatment they are receiving is experimental, should the researcher be praised or blamed for finding the cure?
4. Is there any good reason to regard the life of a monkey, say, as more valuable than the life of a fish? Does it make a difference if the monkey or the fish belongs to a rare species? Do these questions have any implications for the value of human life?

Related Cases in Crigger, *Cases in Bioethics,* Third Edition

The issues in this chapter are very well represented. Cases 30 and 33 deal with the participation in research of human subjects who are ill with cancer and anorexia nervosa, respectively; case 31 concerns a patient who has a family history of breast or ovarian cancer. Each of these cases raises difficult questions about informed consent. Case 34 concerns the possibility of inflicting harm on a healthy, consenting patient; case 39 is about research on animals; and case 35 deals with the use of results from unethical experiments. A number of the discussions are useful, but the most useful are perhaps those following cases 34 and 35.

CHAPTER NINE

Mental Incompetence

INTRODUCTION

Much has been said in earlier chapters about informed consent, autonomy, and the importance of treating patients with the respect that is due to them. But of course not all patients are equally able to exercise autonomy or to give informed consent. Young children, for instance, may have too hazy an idea of their own interests or of how best to realize them to count as fully autonomous. Although they may be unable to understand information sufficiently well to be capable of giving informed consent to a proposed course of treatment, young children must still be treated with respect. Usually, of course, this is achieved by allowing parents or guardians to make decisions on the child's behalf. On the whole this creates no special problems; after all, a loving parent or guardian can usually be trusted to have the child's best interests at heart.

But there are other kinds of people, often of adult age, who may experience difficulty in pursuing their own best interests or in understanding the information given to them. Such people may be described as mentally incompetent. Incompetence may be due to mental illness, to brain injury, to retardation, or to other causes, and the condition may or may not be remediable. There are many vexing questions about how the mentally incompetent should be regarded, and a host of difficulties surrounding issues of treatment (most mentally incompetent people are not in the care of parents or guardians). Indeed many of these issues are highly topical. Until quite recently, it was normal practice to commit the seriously mentally incompetent to institutions (with or without their consent), in the belief that a controlled environment, separate from the mainstream of society, was the best place for them. But in the last thirty years or so this practice has been much less widespread.

It has been argued that the routine institutionalization of the incompetent is both an unnecessary waste of resources and an inappropriate way of trying to meet incompetent people's needs. The consequent move to a policy of deinstitutionalization has led to the release (with or without consent) of many mentally incompetent persons from mental hospitals into so-called community care, with results seen by anyone who has visited a large city recently. In practice, deinstitutionalization has often meant the wholesale dumping of the mentally incompetent onto the streets, the provision of largely imaginary care facilities, and a burgeoning population of bewildered people left to fend for themselves as best they can. Many believe that the policy has been a failure, and there is a lively debate about what should be done to rectify the situation and to mend the damage done. Of course, the policy itself may have been sound—in other words, it may be true that the most appropriate environment for many mentally incompetent people is not an institution, but the community (given proper provision of care and support). But in that case, there has been a tragic failure of implementation. Or it may be that the whole concept of deinstitutionalization is flawed, and that the needs of the community and of the mentally incompetent would be better served by committing the incompetent to institutions where they can be cared for in a controlled environment. Many questions surround the issue of institutionalization—questions to do with the nature of mental incompetence, with autonomy and the involuntary treatment of incompetent persons, with beneficence and paternalism—and it is the business of this chapter to investigate some of the most important and pressing of them.

9.1   THE NATURE OF MENTAL INCOMPETENCE

The concept of mental incompetence is an unclear one, and there is much disagreement about what is meant when it is said that a person is or is not mentally incompetent. For instance, some people hold that a person is mentally incompetent when, in virtue of a mental condition, he or she poses a threat to his or her own well-being. Others hold that mental incompetence is a matter of posing a threat to second parties. Still others hold that a person is mentally incompetent when his or her behavior is found offensive by the community at large, or when his or her behavior deviates markedly from whatever is the norm for that community. The seriousness of these disagreements is underlined when one reflects that, in the last of the views just mentioned, a person might become a candidate for commitment merely because he or she is unusual or eccentric. Such a criterion would surely be open to abuse. So it is important to try to clarify what ought to be understood by the concept of mental incompetence.

9.1a   Incompetent at What?

It is best to begin by ignoring the causes of incompetence. In other words, it is best not to worry for the moment whether a case of incompetence is due to a mental illness, to brain injury, to retardation, or to something else. Instead, we should ask what all cases of incompetence have in common, no matter how they have been caused.

All of us are incompetent to some degree. No one can do everything well, and most of us are markedly better at doing some things than we are at doing others. Some people are hopeless at arithmetic; others have difficulty with words, or with geometric problems, or find it hard to concentrate on intricate puzzles. Some people have a useless sense of direction. There are any number of things that many or most of us are remarkably bad at: incompetence, in this sense, seems to be a universal condition. This means that if we are going to pick out particular people as "mentally incompetent" we need to do so carefully, or else we're likely to end up with a classification that counts everyone as mentally incompetent and the concept will become useless. We need to distinguish, then, between the kind of mental incompetence which is a problem and the kind which appears to be part and parcel of the human condition. Simply being hopeless at certain things isn't enough.

So we need to identify something distinctive about problematic incompetence. This explains why many have been tempted to regard someone as mentally incompetent if he or she deviates markedly from normal levels of (in)competence. On this account, someone is construed as incompetent if he or she is hopeless at things in the same sort of way as, but to a significantly greater degree than, the rest of us are. There is doubtless something right about this way of thinking about the problem. But it does seem too crude. After all, a person may be abnormally bad at an abnormally large number of things without necessarily being problematically incompetent as a result. This suggests that we should look not so much at degrees of incompetence as at kinds of incompetence.

However bad someone is at arithmetic, or however miserable their sense of direction, neither deficit is sufficient to mark him or her as mentally incompetent in the sense that interests us. The person who is hopeless at math is unlikely to be a good accountant; the person without a sense of direction will make a disappointing navigator. But since no one is obliged to be either an accountant or a navigator, these forms of incompetence do not constitute a problem. And this gives us a clue as to what we are after. For if these deficits do not constitute a problem, then it seems to be because they are rather local and specific: They affect only a limited and perhaps a comparatively unimportant part of a person's capacity to function. The innumerate person may make a very satisfactory bodyguard, after all, and the person without a sense of direction may become a successful politician. There is nothing in these particular incapacities that need affect a person's overall ability to function. Problematic mental incompetence, by contrast, must involve some more *systematic* failure. A mentally incompetent person is not merely someone who finds this or that particular function difficult to fulfill. A mentally incompetent person is someone who finds a whole range of functions difficult to fulfill.

A sense of this can be gained by considering temporary mental incompetence as brought on, for example, by excessive drinking. When I am drunk, there isn't anything in particular that I am unable to do satisfactorily; I am temporarily unable to do anything satisfactorily. My driving, my conversation, my judgment, my balance, my arithmetic, my sense of direction, my sense of proportion, my sense of humor, my handwriting, my grip on reality, my lecturing, my social skills, my eating habits—all of them are impaired. When I am drunk I am afflicted with a systematic failure of function. I am a problem: I can't do anything satisfactorily, and the only thing for it is to go to bed and sleep it off. Mental incompetence, then, involves an inability to function that affects not merely some discrete portion of a person's life, but broad swathes of it, or perhaps all of it.

Drunk people are clearly mentally incompetent. But systematic failures of function may come in many other guises. Severely retarded people, for instance, exhibit a generally impaired level of intellectual function that affects every aspect of their lives. A person who cannot distinguish fact from fiction experiences an immense array of difficulties, not just in doing this or that, but in doing anything requiring true beliefs. A person who cannot conceive of other people as having inner lives—as having hopes, thoughts, feelings, and so on—finds relationships impossible, and is unable to bring off any but the simplest kinds of social interaction. A person who has only a short-term memory can do next to nothing. In each case, an impairment (either temporary or permanent) has a systematic effect on a person's capacity to function effectively.

Thus there is something right in saying that a mentally incompetent person is one who deviates from the norm of (in)competence. But mentally incompetent people aren't just more incompetent than other people: They are incompetent in a different way. Whereas "normal" kinds of incompetence may disbar a person from performing certain quite closely defined functions, "mental incompetence" has a systematically negative effect on a person's capacity to function in broad areas of his or her life. It is the systematic nature of mental incompetence, then, that also makes it problematic. For while no one is obliged to become an accountant, specifically, or a navigator, everyone is obliged to live in some way or another; and being incompetent across a broad spectrum of functions is bound to make that more difficult.

9.1b   A Conspiracy Theory: Szasz's Argument: "The Myth of Mental Illness"

I distinguished a moment ago between normal kinds of incompetence, and the kind of incompetence that someone who is mentally incompetent has. But this surely begs the question, unless we can say what is meant by normal. Also, it may be that a person whom we identify as mentally incompetent—because we believe that he or she suffers from a systematic failure of function—is someone who is merely different from us, and that his or her "failure" amounts only to a failure to be the same as us (which may or may not be a bad thing). Certainly these are criticisms that Thomas Szasz, professor of psychiatry at Syracuse, might be expected to raise.

THE MYTH OF MENTAL ILLNESS
Thomas Szasz

I

At the core of virtually all contemporary psychiatric theories and practices lies the concept of mental illness. A critical examination of this concept is therefore indispensable for understanding the ideas, institutions, and interventions of psychiatrists.

My aim in this essay is to ask if there is such a thing as mental illness, and to argue that there is not. Of course, mental illness is not a thing or physical object; hence it can exist only in the same sort of way as do other theoretical concepts. Yet, to those who believe in them, familiar theories are likely to appear, sooner or later, as "objective truths" or "facts." During certain historical periods, explanatory concepts such as deities, witches, and instincts appeared not only as theories but as *self-evident causes* of a vast number of events. Today mental illness is widely regarded in a similar fashion, that is, as the cause of innumerable diverse happenings.

As an antidote to the complacent use of the notion of mental illness—as a self-evident phenomenon, theory, or cause—let us ask: What is meant when it is asserted that someone is mentally ill? In this essay I shall describe the main uses of the concept of mental illness, and I shall argue that this notion has outlived whatever cognitive usefulness it might have had and that it now functions as a myth.

II

The notion of mental illness derives its main support from such phenomena as syphilis of the brain or delirious conditions—intoxications, for instance—in which persons may manifest certain disorders of thinking and behavior. Correctly speaking, however, these are diseases of the brain, not of the mind. According to one school of thought, *all* so-called mental illness is of this type. The assumption is made that some neurological defect, perhaps a very subtle one, will ultimately be found to explain all the disorders of thinking and behavior. Many contemporary physicians, psychiatrists, and other scientists hold this view, which implies that people's troubles cannot be caused by conflicting personal needs, opinions, social aspirations, values, and so forth. These difficulties— which I think we may simply call *problems in living*—are thus attributed to physicochemical processes that in due time will be discovered (and no doubt corrected) by medical research.

Mental illnesses are thus regarded as basically similar to other diseases. The only difference, in this view, between mental and bodily disease is that the former, affecting the brain, manifests itself by means of mental symptoms; whereas the latter, affecting other organ systems—for example, the skin, liver, and so on—manifests itself by means of symptoms referable to those parts of the body.

In my opinion, this view is based on two fundamental errors. In the first place, a disease of the brain, analogous to a disease of the skin or bone, is a neurological defect, not a problem in living. For example, a *defect* in a person's visual field may be explained by correlating it with certain lesions in the nervous system. On the other hand, a person's *belief*—whether it be in Christianity, in Communism, or in the idea that his internal organs are rotting and that his body is already dead—cannot be explained by a defect or disease of the nervous system. Explanations of this sort of occurrence—assuming that one is interested in the belief itself and does not regard it simply as a symptom or expression of something else that is more interesting—must be sought along different lines.

The second error is epistemological. It consists of interpreting communications about ourselves and the world around us as symptoms of neurological functioning. This is an error not in observation or reasoning, but rather in the organization and expression of knowledge. In the present case, the error lies in making a dualism between mental and physical symptoms, a dualism that is a habit of speech and not the result of known observations. Let us see if this is so.

In medical practice, when we speak of physical disturbances we mean either signs (for example, fever) or symptoms (for example, pain). We speak of mental symptoms, on the other hand, when we refer to a patient's communications about himself, others, and the world about him. The patient might assert that he is Napoleon or that he is being persecuted by the Communists. These would be considered mental symptoms only if the observer believed that the patient was *not* Napoleon or that he was *not* being persecuted by the Communists. This makes it apparent that the statement "X is a mental symptom" involves rendering a judgment that entails a covert comparison between the patient's ideas, concepts, or beliefs and those of the observer and the society in which they live. The notion of mental symptom is therefore inextricably tied to the social, and particularly the ethical, context in which it is made, just as the notion of bodily symptom is tied to an anatomical and genetic context.

To sum up: For those who regard mental symptoms as signs of brain disease, the concept of mental illness is unnecessary and misleading. If they mean that people so labeled suffer from diseases of the brain, it would seem better, for the sake of clarity, to say that and not something else.

III

The term "mental illness" is also widely used to describe something quite different from a disease of the brain. Many people today take it for granted that living is an arduous affair. Its hardship for modern man derives, moreover, not so much from a struggle for biological survival as from the stresses and strains inherent in the social intercourse of complex human personalities. In this context, the notion of mental illness is used to identify or describe some feature of an individual's so-called personality. Mental illness—as a deformity of the personality, so to speak—is then regarded as the cause of human disharmony. It is implicit in this view that social intercourse between people is regarded as something inherently harmonious, its disturbance being due solely to the presence of "mental illness" in many people. Clearly, this is faulty reasoning, for it makes the abstraction "mental illness" into a cause of, even though this abstraction was originally created to serve only as a shorthand expression for, certain types of human behavior. It now becomes necessary to ask: What kinds of behavior are regarded as indicative of mental illness, and by whom?

The concept of illness, whether bodily or mental, implies deviation from some clearly defined norm. In the case of physical illness, the norm is the structural and functional integrity of the human body. Thus, although the desirability of physical health, as such, is an ethical value, what health is can be stated in anatomical and physiological terms. What is the norm, deviation from which is regarded as mental illness? This question cannot be easily answered. But whatever this norm may be, we can be certain of only one thing: namely, that it must be stated in terms of psychosocial, ethical, and legal concepts. For example, notions such as "excessive repression" and "acting out an unconscious impulse" illustrate the use of psychological concepts for judging so-called mental health and illness. The idea that chronic hostility, vengefulness, or divorce are indicative of mental illness is an illustration of the use of ethical norms (that is, the desirability of love, kindness, and a stable marriage relationship). Finally, the widespread psychiatric opinion that only a mentally ill person would commit homicide illustrates the use of a legal concept as a norm of mental health. In short, when one speaks of mental illness, the norm from which deviation is measured is a *psychosocial and ethical* standard. Yet, the remedy is sought in terms of *medical* measures that—it is hoped and assumed—are free from wide differences of ethical value. The definition of the disorder and the terms in which its remedy are sought are therefore at serious odds with one another. The practical significance of this covert conflict between the alleged nature of the defect and the actual remedy can hardly be exaggerated.

Having identified the norms used for measuring deviations in cases of mental illness, we shall now turn to the question, Who defines the norms and hence the deviation? Two basic answers may be offered: First, it may be the person himself—that is, the patient—who decides that he deviates from a norm; for example, an artist may believe that he suffers from a work inhibition; and he may implement this conclusion by seeking help *for himself* from a psychotherapist. Second, it may be someone other than the "patient" who decides that the latter is deviant—for example, relatives, physicians, legal authorities, society generally; a psychiatrist may then be hired by persons other than the "patient" to do something *to him* in order to correct the deviation.

These considerations underscore the importance of asking the question, Whose agent is the psychiatrist? and of giving a candid answer to it. The psychiatrist (or non-medical mental health worker) may be the agent of the patient, the relatives, the school, the military services, a business organization, a court of law, and so forth. In speaking of the psychiatrist as the agent of these persons or organizations, it is not implied that his moral values, or his ideas and aims concerning the proper nature of remedial action, must coincide exactly with those of his employer. For example, a patient in individual psychotherapy may believe that his salvation lies in a new marriage; his psychotherapist need not share this hypothesis. As the patient's agent, however, he must not resort to social or legal force to prevent the patient from putting his beliefs into action. If his *contract* is with the patient, the psychiatrist (psychotherapist) may disagree with him or stop his treatment, but he cannot engage others to obstruct the patient's aspirations. Similarly, if a psychiatrist is retained by a court to determine the sanity of an offender, he need not fully share the legal authorities' values and intentions in regard to the criminal, nor the means deemed appropriate for dealing with him; such a psychiatrist cannot testify, however, that the accused is not insane but that the legislators are—for passing the law that decrees the offender's actions illegal. This sort of opinion could be voiced, of course—but not in a courtroom, and not by a psychiatrist who is there to assist the court in performing its daily work.

To recapitulate: In contemporary social usage, the finding of mental illness is made by establishing a deviance in behavior from certain psychosocial, ethical, or legal norms. The judgment may be made, as in medicine, by the patient, the physician (psychiatrist), or others. Remedial action, finally, tends to be sought in a therapeutic—or covertly medical—framework. This creates a situation in which it is claimed that psychosocial, ethical, and legal deviations can be corrected by medical action. Since medical interventions are designed to remedy only medical problems, it is logically absurd to expect that they will help solve problems whose very existence has been defined and established on non-medical grounds.

IV

The position outlined above, according to which contemporary psychotherapists deal with problems in living, not with mental illnesses and their cures, stands in sharp opposition to the currently prevalent position, according to which psychiatrists treat mental diseases, which are just as "real" and "objective" as bodily diseases. I submit that the holders of the latter view have no evidence whatever to justify their claim, which is actually a kind of psychiatric propaganda: their aim is to create in the popular mind a confident belief that mental illness is some sort of disease entity, like an infection or a malignancy. If this were true, one could *catch* or *get* a mental illness, one might *have* or *harbor* it, one might *transmit* it to others, and finally one could *get rid* of it. Not only is there not a shred of evidence to support this idea, but, on the contrary, all the evidence is the other way and supports the view that what people now call mental illnesses are, for the most part, *communications* expressing unacceptable ideas, often framed in an unusual idiom.

This is not the place to consider in detail the similarities and differences between bodily and mental illnesses. It should suffice to emphasize that whereas the term "bodily illness" refers to physicochemical occurrences that are not affected by being made public, the term "mental illness" refers to sociopsychological events that are crucially affected by being made public. The psychiatrist thus cannot, and does not, stand apart from the person he observes, as the pathologist can and often does. The psychiatrist is committed to some picture of what he considers reality, and to what he thinks society considers reality, and he observes and judges the patient's behavior in the light of these beliefs. The very notion of "mental symptoms" or "mental illness" thus implies a covert comparison and often conflict, between observer and observed, psychiatrist and patient. Though obvious, this fact needs to be re-emphasized, if one wishes, as I do here, to counter the prevailing tendency to deny the moral aspects of psychiatry and to substitute for them allegedly value-free medical concepts and interventions.

Psychotherapy is thus widely practiced as though it entailed nothing other than restoring the patient from a state of mental sickness to one of mental health. While it is generally accepted that mental illness has something to do with man's social or interpersonal relations, it is paradoxically maintained that problems of values—that is, of ethics—do not arise in this process. Freud himself went so far as to assert: "I consider ethics to be taken for granted. Actually I have never done a mean thing." This is an astounding thing to say, especially for someone who had studied man as a social being as deeply as Freud had. I mention it here to show how the notion of "illness"—in the case of psychoanalysis, "psychopathology," or "mental illness"—was used by Freud, and by most of his followers, as a means of classifying certain types of human behavior as falling within the scope of medicine, and hence, by fiat, outside that of ethics. Nevertheless, the stubborn fact remains that, in a sense, much of psychotherapy revolves around nothing other than the elucidation and weighing of goals and values—many of which may be mutually contradictory—and the means whereby they might best be harmonized, realized, or relinquished.

Because the range of human values and of the methods by which they may be attained is so vast, and because many such ends and means are persistently unacknowledged, conflicts among values are the main source of conflicts in human relations. Indeed, to say that human relations at all levels—from mother to child, through husband and wife, to nation and nation—are fraught with stress, strain, and disharmony is, once again, to make the obvious explicit. Yet, what may be obvious may be also poorly understood. This, I think, is the case here. For it seems to me that in our scientific theories of behavior we have failed to accept the simple fact that human relations are inherently fraught with difficulties, and to make them even relatively harmonious requires much patience and hard work. I submit that the idea of mental illness is now being put to work to obscure certain difficulties that at present may be inherent—not that they need to be unmodifiable—in the social intercourse of persons. If this is true, the concept functions as a disguise: instead of calling attention to conflicting human needs, aspirations, and values, the concept of mental illness provides an amoral and impersonal "thing"—an "illness"—as an explanation for problems in living. We may recall in this connection that not so long ago it was devils and witches that were held responsible for man's problems in living. The belief in mental illness, as something other than man's trouble in getting along with his fellow man, is the proper heir to the belief in demonology and witchcraft. Mental illness thus exists or is "real" in exactly the same sense in which witches existed or were "real."

9.1c   Responding to Szasz

It is important to notice that Szasz's argument applies only to certain kinds of mental incompetence. A person who is mentally incompetent because of brain disease or brain damage (or, in general, because of an organic deficit) falls outside the scope of his argument. For Szasz, both the problem and the potential cure in such cases are purely medical, and no issues are raised that are not common to the treatment of disease and injury in general.

The "myth" that Szasz is concerned to expose does not operate in the realm of disease and injury.

It operates instead in the realm of what Szasz calls "problems with living," problems that seem to have much in common with the systematic failures of function discussed in 9.1a, above. And much of what Szasz says is certainly compelling. There *is* something disquieting about our readiness to describe as an "illness" any pattern of behavior or attitude that conflicts with the social or ethical norms and ideals to which we are accustomed. First, such a description suggests that there is something that needs treatment. Second, it suggests that the appropriate response is a *medical* response—that is, that those in conflict with the social or ethical norms and ideals of a given society should receive medical treatment. A moment's reflection on the way in which dissidents in the former Soviet Union—in other words, those who failed to coincide with the social and ethical ideals of soviet communism— were committed to mental institutions for medical treatment should be enough to make one wary of both of these entailments. There are grave ethical dangers in the temptation to describe mere nonconformity as "illness."

Nor does one need to rake over the ashes of communism to see these dangers. In slightly more subtle form, the consequences of regarding nontypical patterns of behavior or attitude as symptoms of "illness" are evident today. My own favorite example concerns "self-esteem"—a quality that everyone nowadays is apparently expected to have in large quantities. Low self-esteem is increasingly regarded as a kind of mental illness. To have low self-esteem is to come into conflict with the social and ethical ideals of contemporary American culture, and those "suffering" from it are frequently encouraged to seek treatment, often of a medical nature. But it only takes a moment to see how inappropriate this way of talking is. Esteem, after all, is an attitude one takes toward something on the basis of believing it to be worthy or admirable (you cannot esteem what you believe to be contemptible). Your reasons for believing something to be worthy or admirable can be good reasons or bad reasons. A person who esteems a serial killer, for example, almost certainly has bad or mistaken reasons for believing the killer to be worthy or admirable. The esteem is almost certainly misplaced. And exactly the same is true when it comes to self-esteem. One can have good or bad reasons for believing oneself to be worthy or admirable. Insisting that a person *ought* to have high self-esteem, regardless of what he or she is actually like or has actually done, abolishes the distinction between having good and bad reasons for one's beliefs. In other words, it abolishes the distinction between fact and fiction; and to be unable to distinguish between fact and fiction, I have suggested, is to suffer from a species of mental incompetence. If someone is a dreadful person who has done dreadful things, his or her misplaced self-esteem is a symptom not of mental health but of a systematic failure of the faculty of judgment. If the faculty of judgment were in order, he or she would have *low* self-esteem—for excellent reasons—and proposing medical treatment for his or her low self-esteem would be wholly inappropriate. Indeed, it would be morally wrong. For recognizing that one has been a dreadful person who has done dreadful things—and hence that one has been neither worthy nor admirable—is the only cause likely to encourage one to become a better person. Thus the current trend towards regarding low self-esteem as an illness is dangerous for two reasons: It promotes the mentally incompetent view that there is no need to have good grounds for believing something (for instance, that one is worthy or admirable); and it devalues that capacity for self-criticism through which alone we can hope to become better people.

Whether or not Szasz would agree with this argument, it underlines quite well what is persuasive about his position. Mere deviation from social or ethical norms and ideals does not by itself constitute illness, and the tendency to think that it does can result in dangerous, inappropriate, and unethical countermeasures, often of a medical nature. A medicalized conception of "proper" attitudes and behavior can lead to real abuses. Sometimes, as in the former Soviet Union, those abuses are obvious and extreme; whereas at other times, as in the contemporary cult of self-esteem, they are quieter and more insidious. Whether quiet or extreme they clearly need to be guarded against.

One might go along with all of this, though, and still feel uncomfortable with Szasz's argument as a whole. A critic might point to two related reasons for this. First, Szasz's case for saying that mental illness is a "myth" rests partly on the claim that proper illnesses involve deviation from organic or physiological norms, whereas "problems in living" involve deviation from social or ethical norms. In a sense, this is clearly true. If I have a disease of the kidney, the cause of my problem is physiological, my symptoms are physiological, and any useful form of treatment is likely to be physiological too. Whereas if I have a problem in living my "symptoms" are behavioral— they involve, in other words, a departure from whatever are the relevant social or ethical norms of behavior. So far so good. But a critic might point out that nothing in this shows that when I have a problem in living the *cause* isn't physiological. That is, the fact that my symptoms are identified in social and ethical terms doesn't prove that the underlying problem involves no deviation from organic or physiological norms. If it does involve such a deviation, then surely my problem is an illness, and surely the appropriate response would be a medical one. Szasz's position appears to assume that where no physiological cause is known, none exists.

Second, Szasz seems to assume that all physiological defects can be identified in purely physiological terms. Again, this is true in a sense. If there *is* a physiological defect, then it can, in principle, be identified and described in purely physiological terms. But that is not the only way in which physiological defects can be identified. To take Szasz' own example: "a *defect* in a person's visual field may be explained by correlating it with certain lesions in the nervous system." Sure: But how do you know a person has a defect in his or her visual field to start with? The answer is behavioral. The person has problems seeing things; the person describes the appearance of things in nonstandard ways; the person experiences greater difficulty in getting about than most people do; and so on. Without clues of this kind there would be no reason to start looking for defects in the nervous system. In other words, the tip-off that someone has a physiological problem may very often lie in his or her behavior, and in the way it deviates from norms which are not, primarily, physiological or organic. Indeed, this point becomes still stronger when one considers the range of symptoms that a person with a brain tumor may exhibit: Many such symptoms consist in deviations from norms of a clearly social or ethical character. A critic might conclude, then, that Szasz has exaggerated the extent to which physiological defects are always identifiable in purely physiological terms.

The critic might then put these two points together. Between them, they seem to indicate that the distinction between physiological problems and problems in living is not nearly as easy to draw as Szasz would like. Indeed, any problem in living *may* have a physiological cause, and many physiological problems show up *as* problems in living. Thus, Szasz's claim that mental illness is a myth—where "mental illness" means "problem in living"—does not appear to have been demonstrated.

These criticisms are well-directed, I think. The fact that someone conducts themselves at variance with prevailing social and ethical norms may mean that they have a physiological problem requiring medical treatment. It may be the case, in other words, that someone who behaves weirdly is ill (it's then a matter of taste whether one says that such a person is "mentally" ill). Of course he or she may not be ill. Szasz is surely right to insist on this point. Weird behavior or attitudes are not enough by themselves to warrant the conclusion that a person is ill or needs treatment. One needs first to enquire whether there are plausible nonphysiological explanations for a person's (apparent) weirdness. For example, low self-esteem in a person who routinely behaves badly is plausibly explained by the fact that he or she is at least blessed with self-knowledge. Persistent failure to conform with the demands of soviet-style communism is plausibly explained by a legitimate difference of opinion. In cases such as these, the motivation to seek an underlying physiological cause should clearly be resisted as unnecessary (as of course should any resort to medical counter measures).

But of course the gray areas here are immense. Just how plausible does a nonphysiological explanation need to be? What are the limits of "legitimate" differences of opinion? For instance, does my neighbor's claim to be God signal a legitimate difference between his opinion and mine? Or is one of us ill? These questions are tremendously difficult to answer, and they probably need to be addressed on a case-by-case basis. I suspect that the nearest one can come to a general answer is to say that one should become progressively less reluctant to seek a physiological explanation for someone's weird behavior the weirder, or less explicable in nonphysiological terms, that behavior seems to be. But certainly Szasz is right to warn us against simply *assuming* that any deviance from social or ethical norms is attributable to illness. (For further discussion of Szasz's views, see Paul Chodoff's article, 9.2a, below.)

9.1d Incompetence and Autonomy

It still seems plausible to suggest that mental incompetence consists of a systematic failure of mental functioning—perhaps caused by physiological defect, perhaps not. If Szasz is right, not all cases of apparent mental incompetence are properly to be described as illnesses. For our purposes, however, little hangs on this question; nor need we worry too much about the operative causes in any particular case. What concerns us here is the nature of the problem that mental incompetence poses, however it has been caused, and however it is properly to be described.

The heart of the problem lies in questions about autonomy. Take again the example of temporary mental incompetence brought about by drinking. When I am drunk, I suffer from a systematic failure of function—there is next to nothing I can do well. Because my judgment is impaired, my assessment of my situation, and of the effects that my behavior is likely to have, is unreliable, and I may act unwisely as a result. My autonomy, in other words, is reduced: My capacity to order my life in accordance with my interests is diminished, and my capacity to respect the autonomy of others (in other words, to act with due consideration for *their* interests) is diminished also. In this condition, I become a problem for myself and for others. This captures precisely what is problematic about mental incompetence, whether or not it is temporary and whether or not it is caused by drinking. The mentally incompetent person may be abnormally careless of his or her own best interests, and he or she may be abnormally careless of the interests of others. Of course some competent people may be like this too, especially with regard to the interests of others. But competent people may be presumed to have a choice in the matter. Because they suffer from no systematic failure of mental function, it is open to them to spare more thought for the effects their behavior may have on others (or on themselves). If they decline to do so, the law offers appropriate remedies for the protection of others, and in a free society, the neglect of one's own interests is generally permitted, even if it is rarely encouraged. But where an abnormal degree of carelessness for one's own interests or the interests of others is due to a systematic failure of mental function—to mental incompetence, in other words—the scope for talk about choice is much narrower. In cases where I am responsible for my own incompetence (as when I get drunk), I am clearly responsible too for the effects that my incompetence has: I have, as it were, autonomously reduced my own autonomy. But where I am mentally incompetent through no fault of my own, it is precisely my deficit in autonomy that is at issue. Mental incompetence, then, is a problem when the systematic failure of function of which it consists is such that a person becomes abnormally neglectful of his or her own interests, or abnormally neglectful of the interests of others through being unable (autonomously) to respect other people's autonomy. (Were an incompetent person to be abnormally neglectful of no one's interests, it seems clear that no problem would arise.)

9.1e Recap: On Counting as Competent

There is no general agreement about the nature of mental incompetence. In large measure, this is due to the difficult question of norms: How should one define "normal"? How far out of line does someone need to be to count as *ab*normal? There is no getting out of these questions: The issue of incompetence is essentially a comparative matter. If everyone were endowed with exactly the same quality of mental functioning, the concept of incompetence would never have come into being. Szasz's argument highlights just how careful we need to be in response to behavior or attitudes that strike us as unusual. If we take too narrow a view of the behaviorally or socially "normal" we may easily find ourselves responding inappropriately—and perhaps unethically—to people who are merely offbeat or eccentric.

But this doesn't mean that we should simply stop making judgements that refer to behavioral or social norms (as Szasz perhaps thinks we should). For one thing, it is in virtue of such judgements, and of the norms that they presuppose, that a society is able to function at all. If there were no general agreement about what kinds of behavior are normal and acceptable, we would find ourselves in a state of anarchy. But more to the point for our purposes, appeal to such norms isn't confined merely to the vexed issue of mental incompetence: Social and behavioral norms play their part in the identification of physiological defects too, as we have seen (9.1c, above). Indeed, it may be argued that such norms play an irreducible part in the very meaning of concepts such as disease and illness. Were it not for the fact that people's health varies, and that some people are clearly less healthy than it is "normal" to be, it is unlikely that these concepts would have arisen. And the "normal" here cannot be defined in purely physiological terms, either. For physiological variations only count as "illnesses" or "diseases" when they interfere with a person's ability to function within a given set of behavioral or social norms.

This point is true even of the concept "injury," which on the face of it looks like a purely physical concept. But in a society in which people are "normally" injured in a certain way—for instance, in a society that routinely practices circumcision—the resultant injury is not, in that society, counted as an "injury." In a circumcising society, it is normal and proper to be circumcised. The point here is that the difficulty of defining norms of a social, ethical, or behavioral character is neither peculiar to the issue of mental incompetence, nor avoidable as long as we wish to continue to pursue and to benefit from the practice of any kind of medicine. Perhaps this difficulty is at its greatest in the *essentially* behavioral context of mental incompetence. But unless we are prepared to admit that some people are not merely "different" from the majority, but *abnormal,* we will do everyone a disservice.

I have suggested that issues of autonomy lie at the heart of the problematic character of mental incompetence. Autonomy is one of our highest values, and our respect or lack of respect for the value of autonomy will be signalled in the approach we take to questions posed by the systematic failure of mental function experienced by some, abnormal, people.

9.2 DECISIONS ABOUT TREATMENT

Some mentally incompetent people pose a threat to themselves. Some mentally incompetent people—although relatively few—pose a threat to others. Where such people are capable of recognizing their own incompetence, and perhaps are frightened or alarmed by it, they may voluntarily seek treatment for themselves. When this is so, their position is similar to that of any other patient who autonomously submits him- or herself to a course of medical care; the fact that a person is mentally incompetent in certain respects should not entail any significant differences in the way he or she is treated by health care professionals. The hard cases arise, of course, when a mentally incompetent person who is incapable of acting autonomously, either in his or her own best interests or with due regard for the autonomy of others, fails or refuses to seek such treatment as is available. These are the cases in which the possibility of involuntary treatment arises.

9.2a   Treating People against Their Will: Chodoff's Argument: "The Case for Involuntary Hospitalization of the Mentally Ill"

When a person does not want to be treated, this negative desire must be regarded as autonomous—even when, as in the case of many mentally incompetent people, his or her overall level of autonomy may be low. Autonomous preferences must of course be treated with respect, but they need not always be the last word. Children, for instance, have many autonomous preferences which any sensible parent thinks it justifiable to override; drunk people also have autonomous preferences which most of us would sooner see thwarted. Thus the preference that a mentally incompetent person may have to remain without treatment does not by itself show that it would be wrong to force treatment on him or her. It is possible that other factors may legitimately override that preference. Paul Chodoff, clinical professor of psychiatry and behavioral sciences at George Washington University School of Medicine, seeks to identify what those other factors might be. (It is worth noting that Chodoff's article was written at the height of the move to deinstitutionalize mental patients.)

THE CASE FOR INVOLUNTARY HOSPITALIZATION OF THE MENTALLY ILL
Paul Chodoff

I will begin this chapter with a series of vignettes designed to illustrate graphically the question that is my focus: under what conditions, if any, does society have the right to apply coercion to an individual to hospitalize him against his will, by reason of mental illness?

Case 1   A woman in her mid 50s, with no previous overt behavioral difficulties, comes to believe that she is worthless and insignificant. She is completely preoccupied with her guilt and is increasingly unavailable for the ordinary demands of life. She eats very little because of her conviction that the food should go to others whose need is greater than hers, and her physical condition progressively deteriorates. Although she will talk to others about herself, she insists that she is not sick, only bad. She refuses medication, and when hospitalization is suggested she also refuses that on the grounds that she would be taking up space that otherwise could be occupied by those who merit treatment more than she.

Case 2   For the past 6 years the behavior of a 42-year-old woman has been disturbed for periods of 3 months or longer. After recovery from her most recent episode she has been at home, functioning at a borderline level. A month ago she again started to withdraw from her environment. She pays increasingly less attention to her bodily needs, talks very little, and does not respond to questions or attention from those about her. She lapses into a mute state and lies in her bed in a totally passive fashion. She does not respond to other people, does not eat, and does not void. When her arm is raised from the bed, it remains for several minutes in the position in which it is left. Her medical history and a physical examination reveal no evidence of primary physical illness.

Case 3   A man with a history of alcoholism has been on a binge for several weeks. He remains at home doing little else than drinking. He eats very little. He becomes tremulous and misinterprets spots on the wall as animals about to attack him, and he complains of "creeping" sensations in his body, which he attributes to infestation by insects. He does not seek help voluntarily, insists there is nothing wrong with him, and despite his wife's entreaties he continues to drink.

Case 4   Passersby and station personnel observe that a young woman has been spending several days at Union Station in Washington, D.C. Her behavior appears strange to others. She is finally befriended by a newspaper reporter who becomes aware that her perception of her situation is profoundly unrealistic and that she is, in fact, delusional. He persuades her to accompany him to St. Elizabeth's Hospital, where she is examined by a psychiatrist who recommends admission. She refuses hospitalization and the psychiatrist allows her to leave. She returns to Union Station. A few days later she is found dead, murdered, on one of the surrounding streets.

Case 5   A government attorney in his late 30s begins to display pressured speech and hyperactivity. He is too busy to sleep and eats very little. He talks rapidly, becomes irritable when interrupted, and makes phone calls all over the country in furtherance of his political ambitions, which are to begin a campaign for the Presidency of the United States. He makes many purchases, some very expensive, thus running through a great deal of money. He is rude and tactless to his friends, who are offended by his behavior, and his job is in jeopardy. In spite of his wife's pleas he insists that he does not have the time to seek or accept treatment, and he refuses hospitalization. This is not the first such disturbance for this individual; in fact, very similar episodes have been occurring at roughly 2-year intervals since he was 18 years old.

Case 6 Passersby in a campus area observe two young women standing together, staring at each other, for over an hour. Their behavior attracts attention, and eventually the police take the pair to a nearby precinct station for questioning. They refuse to answer questions and sit mutely, staring into space. The police request some type of psychiatric examination but are informed by the city attorney's office that state law (Michigan) allows persons to be held for observation only if they appear obviously dangerous to themselves or others. In this case, since the women do not seem homicidal or suicidal, they do not qualify for observation and are released.

Less than 30 hours later the two women are found on the floor of their campus apartment, screaming and writhing in pain with their clothes ablaze from a self-made pyre. One woman recovers; the other dies. There is no conclusive evidence that drugs were involved (1).

Most, if not all, people would agree that the behavior described in these vignettes deviates significantly from even elastic definitions of normality. However, it is clear that there would not be a similar consensus on how to react to this kind of behavior and that there is a considerable and increasing ferment about what attitude the organized elements of our society should take toward such individuals. Every has a stake in this important issue, but the debate about it takes place principally among psychiatrists, lawyers, the courts, and law enforcement agencies.

Points of view about the question of involuntary hospitalization fall into the following three principal groups: the "abolitionists," medical model psychiatrists, and civil liberties lawyers.

THE ABOLITIONISTS

Those holding this position would assert that in none of the cases I have described should involuntary hospitalization be a viable option because, quite simply, it should never be resorted to under any circumstances. As Szasz (2) has put it, "we should value liberty more highly than mental health no matter how defined" and "no one should be deprived of his freedom for the sake of his mental health." Ennis (3) has said that the goal "is nothing less than the abolition of involuntary hospitalization."

Prominent among the abolitionists are the "anti-psychiatrists," who, somewhat surprisingly, count in their ranks a number of well-known psychiatrists. For them mental illness simply does not exist in the field of psychiatry (4). They reject entirely the medical model of mental illness and insist that acceptance of it relies on a fiction accepted jointly by the state and by psychiatrists as a device for exerting social control over annoying or unconventional people. The anti-psychiatrists hold that these people ought to be afforded the dignity of being held responsible for their behavior and required to accept its consequences. In addition, some members of this group believe that the phenomena of "mental illness" often represent essentially a tortured protest against the insanities of an irrational society (5). They maintain that society should not be encouraged in its oppressive course by affixing a pejorative label to its victims.

Among the abolitionists are some civil liberties lawyers who both assert their passionate support of the magisterial importance of individual liberty and react with repugnance and impatience to what they see as the abuses of psychiatric practice in this field—the commitment of some individuals for flimsy and possibly self-serving reasons and their inhuman warehousing in penal institutions wrongly called "hospitals."

The abolitionists do not oppose psychiatric treatment when it is conducted with the agreement of those being treated. I have no doubt that they would try to gain the consent of the individuals described earlier to undergo treatment, including hospitalization. The psychiatrists in this group would be very likely to confine their treatment methods to psychotherapeutic efforts to influence the aberrant behavior. They would be unlikely to use drugs and would certainly eschew such somatic therapies as ECT.* If efforts to enlist voluntary compliance with treatment failed, the abolitionists would not employ any means of coercion. Instead, they would step aside and allow social, legal, and community sanctions to take their course. If a human being should be jailed or a human life lost as a result of this attitude, they would accept it as a necessary evil to be tolerated in order to avoid the greater evil of unjustified loss of liberty for others (6).

THE MEDICAL MODEL PSYCHIATRISTS

I use this admittedly awkward and not entirely accurate label to designate the position of a substantial number of psychiatrists. They believe that mental illness is a meaningful concept and that under certain conditions its existence justifies the state's exercise, under the doctrine of parens patriae, of its right and obligation to arrange for the hospitalization of the sick individual even though coercion is involved and he is deprived of his liberty. I believe that these psychiatrists would recommend involuntary hospitalization for all six of the patients described earlier.

The Medical Model

There was a time, before they were considered to be ill, when individuals who displayed the kind of behavior I described earlier were put in "ships of fools" to wander the seas or were left to the mercies, sometimes tender but often savage, of uncomprehending communities that regarded them as either possessed or bad. During the Enlightenment and the early nineteenth century, however, these individuals gradually came to be regarded as sick people to be included under the humane and caring umbrella of the Judeo-Christian attitude

---

Editors' note: Electroconvulsive therapy (ECT) involves direct intervention into the brain. In ECT, electric currents applied to the front of the patient's head induce convulsions and unconsciousness.

toward illness. This attitude, which may have reached its height during the era of moral treatment in the early nineteenth century, has had unexpected and ambiguous consequences. It became overextended and partially perverted, and these excesses led to the reaction that is so strong a current in today's attitude toward mental illness.

However, reaction itself can go too far, and I believe that this is already happening. Witness the disastrous consequences of the precipitate dehospitalization that is occurring all over the country. To remove the protective mantle of illness from these disturbed people is to expose them, their families, and their communities to consequences that are certainly maladaptive and possibly irreparable. Are we really acting in accordance with their best interests when we allow them to "die with their rights on" (1) or when we condemn them to a "preservation of liberty which is actually so destructive as to constitute another form of imprisonment" (7)? Will they not suffer "if [a] liberty they cannot enjoy is made superior to a health that must sometimes be forced on them" (8)?

Many of those who reject the medical model out of hand as inapplicable to so-called "mental illness" have tended to oversimplify its meaning and have, in fact, equated it almost entirely with organic disease. It is necessary to recognize that it is a complex concept and that there is a lack of agreement about its meaning. Sophisticated definitions of the medical model do not require only the demonstration of unequivocal organic pathology. A broader formulation, put forward by sociologists and deriving largely from Talcott Parsons' description of the sick role (9), extends the domain of illness to encompass certain forms of social deviance as well as biological disorders. According to this definition, the medical model is characterized not only by organicity but also by being negatively valued by society, by "nonvoluntariness," thus exempting its exemplars from blame, and by the understanding that physicians are the technically competent experts to deal with its effects (10).

Except for the question of organic disease, the patients I described earlier conform well to this broader conception of the medical model. They are all suffering both emotionally and physically, they are incapable by an effort of will of stopping or changing their destructive behavior, and those around them consider them to be in an undesirable sick state and to require medical attention.

Categorizing the behavior of these patients as involuntary may be criticized as evidence of an intolerably paternalistic and antitherapeutic attitude that fosters the very failure to take responsibility for their lives and behavior that the therapist should uncover rather than encourage. However, it must also be acknowledged that these severely ill people are not capable at a conscious level of deciding what is best for themselves and that in order to help them examine their behavior and motivation, it is necessary that they be alive and available for treatment. Their verbal message that they will not accept treatment may at the same time be conveying other more covert messages—that they are desperate and want help even though they cannot ask for it (11).

Although organic pathology may not be the only determinant of the medical model, it is of course an important one and it should not be avoided in any discussion of mental illness. There would be no question that the previously described patient with delirium tremens is suffering from a toxic form of brain disease. There are a significant number of other patients who require involuntary hospitalization because of organic brain syndrome due to various causes. Among those who are not overtly organically ill, most of the candidates for involuntary hospitalization suffer from schizophrenia or one of the major affective disorders. A growing and increasingly impressive body of evidence points to the presence of an important genetic-biological factor in these conditions; thus, many of them qualify on these grounds as illnesses.

Despite the revisionist efforts of the antipsychiatrists, mental illness *does* exist. It does not by any means include all of the people being treated by psychiatrists (or by non-psychiatrist physicians), but it does encompass those few desperately sick people for whom involuntary commitment must be considered. In the words of a recent article, "The problem is that mental illness is not a myth. It is not some palpable falsehood propagated among the populace by power-mad psychiatrists, but a cruel and bitter reality that has been with the human race since antiquity" (12, p. 1483).

Criteria for Involuntary Hospitalization

Procedures for involuntary hospitalization should be instituted for individuals who require care and treatment because of diagnosable mental illness that produces symptoms, including marked impairment in judgment, that disrupt their intrapsychic and interpersonal functioning. All three of these criteria must be met before involuntary hospitalization can be instituted.

1. **Mental Illness**   This concept has already been discussed, but it should be repeated that only a belief in the existence of illness justifies involuntary commitment. It is a fundamental assumption that makes aberrant behavior a medical matter and its care the concern of physicians.
2. **Disruption of Functioning**   This involves combinations of serious and often obvious disturbances that are both intrapsychic (for example, the suffering of severe depression) and interpersonal (for example, withdrawal from others because of depression). It does not include minor peccadilloes or eccentricities. Furthermore, the behavior in question must represent symptoms of the mental illness from which the patient is suffering. Among these symptoms are actions that are imminently or potentially dangerous in a physical sense to self or others, as well as other manifestations of mental illness such as those in the cases I have described. This is not to ignore dangerousness as a criterion for commitment but rather to put it in its proper place as one of a number of symptoms of the illness. A further manifestation of the illness, and indeed, the one that makes involuntary rather than voluntary hospitalization necessary, is impairment of the patient's judgment to such a degree that he is unable to consider his condition and make decisions about it in his own interests.
3. **Need for Care and Treatment**   The goal of physicians is to treat and cure their patients; however, sometimes they can only ameliorate the suffering of their patients and sometimes all they can offer is care. It is not possible to predict whether someone will respond to treatment; nevertheless, the need for treatment and the availability of facilities to carry it out constitute essential preconditions that must be met to justify requiring anyone to give up his freedom. If men-

tal hospital patients have a right to treatment, then psychiatrists have a right to ask for treatability as a front-door as well as a back-door criterion for commitment (7). All of the six individuals I described earlier could have been treated with a reasonable expectation of returning to a more normal state of functioning.

I believe that the objections to this formulation can be summarized as follows.

a. The whole structure founders for those who maintain that mental illness is a fiction.
b. These criteria are also untenable to those who hold liberty to be such a supreme value that the presence of mental illness per se does not constitute justification for depriving an individual of his freedom; only when such illness is manifested by clearly dangerous behavior may commitment be considered. For reasons to be discussed later, I agree with those psychiatrists (13, 14) who do not believe that dangerousness should be elevated to primacy above other manifestations of mental illness as a sine qua non for involuntary hospitalization.
c. The medical model criteria are "soft" and subjective and depend on the fallible judgment of psychiatrists. This is a valid objection. There is no reliable blood test for schizophrenia and no method for injecting grey cells into psychiatrists. A relatively small number of cases will always fall within a grey area that will be difficult to judge. In those extreme cases in which the question of commitment arises, competent and ethical psychiatrists should be able to use these criteria without doing violence to individual liberties and with the expectation of good results. Furthermore, the possible "fuzziness" of some aspects of the medical model approach is certainly no greater than that of the supposedly "objective" criteria for dangerousness, and there is little reason to believe that lawyers and judges are any less fallible than psychiatrists.
d. Commitment procedures in the hands of psychiatrists are subject to intolerable abuses. Here, as Peszke said, "It is imperative that we differentiate between the principle of the process of civil commitment and the practice itself" (13, p. 825). Abuses can contaminate both the medical and the dangerousness approaches, and I believe that the abuses stemming from the abolitionist view of no commitment at all are even greater. Measures to abate abuses of the medical approach include judicial review and the abandonment of indeterminate commitment. In the course of commitment proceedings and thereafter, patients should have access to competent and compassionate legal counsel. However, this latter safeguard may itself be subject to abuse if the legal counsel acts solely in the adversary tradition and undertakes to carry out the patient's wishes even when they may be destructive.

Comment

The criteria and procedures outlined will apply most appropriately to initial episodes and recurrent attacks of mental illness. To put it simply, it is necessary to find a way to satisfy legal and humanitarian considerations and yet allow psychiatrists access to initially or acutely ill patients in order to do the best they can for them. However, there are some involuntary patients who have received adequate and active treatment but have not responded satisfactorily. An irreducible minimum of such cases, principally among those with brain disorders and process schizophrenia, will not improve sufficiently to be able to adapt to even a tolerant society.

The decision of what to do at this point is not an easy one, and it should certainly not be in the hands of psychiatrists alone. With some justification they can state that they have been given the thankless job of caring, often with inadequate facilities, for badly damaged people and that they are now being subjected to criticism for keeping these patients locked up. No one really knows what to do with these patients. It may be that when treatment has failed they exchange their sick role for what has been called the impaired role (15), which implies a permanent negative evaluation of them coupled with a somewhat less benign societal attitude. At this point, perhaps a case can be made for giving greater importance to the criteria for dangerousness and releasing such patients if they do not pose a threat to others. However, I do not believe that the release into the community of these severely malfunctioning individuals will serve their interests even though it may satisfy formal notions of right and wrong.

It should be emphasized that the number of individuals for whom involuntary commitment must be considered is small (although, under the influence of current pressures, it may be smaller than it should be). Even severe mental illness can often be handled by securing the cooperation of the patient, and certainly one of the favorable efforts. However, the distinction between voluntary and involuntary hospitalization is sometimes more formal than meaningful. How "voluntary" are the actions of an individual who is being buffeted by the threats, entreaties, and tears of his family?

I believe, however, that we are at a point (at least in some jurisdictions) where, having rebounded from an era in which involuntary commitment was too easy and employed too often, we are now entering one in which it is becoming very difficult to commit anyone, even in urgent cases. Faced with the moral obloquy that has come to pervade the atmosphere in which the decision to involuntarily hospitalize is considered, some psychiatrists, especially younger ones, have become, as Stone (16) put it, "soft as grapes" when faced with the prospect of committing anyone under any circumstances.

THE CIVIL LIBERTIES LAWYERS

I use this admittedly inexact label to designate those members of the legal profession who do not in principle reject the necessity for involuntary hospitalization but who do reject or wish to diminish the importance of medical model criteria in the hands of psychiatrists. Accordingly, the civil liberties lawyers, in dealing with the problem of involuntary hospitalization, have enlisted themselves under the standard of dangerousness, which they hold to be more objective and capable of being dealt with in a sounder evidentiary manner than the medical model criteria. For them the question is not whether mental illness, even of disabling degree, is present, but only whether it has resulted in the probability of behavior dangerous to others or to self. Thus they would scrutinize the cases previously described for evidence of such dangerousness and would make the decision about involuntary hospitalization accordingly. They would probably feel that commitment is not indicated in most of these cases, since they were selected as illustrative of severe mental illness in which outstanding evidence of physical dangerousness was not present.

The dangerousness standard is being used increasingly not only to supplement criteria for mental illness but, in fact, to replace them entirely. The recent Supreme Court decision in *O'Connor v. Donaldson* (17) is certainly a long step in this direction. In addition, "dangerousness" is increasingly being understood to refer to the probability that the individual will inflict harm on himself or others in a specific physical manner rather than in other ways. This tendency has perhaps been carried to its ultimate in the *Lessard v. Schmidt* case (18) in Wisconsin, which restricted suitability for commitment to the "extreme likelihood that if the person is not confined, he will do immediate harm to himself or others." (This decision was set aside by the U.S. Supreme Court in 1974.) In a recent Washington, D.C., Superior Court case (19) the instructions to the jury stated that the government must prove that the defendant was likely to cause "substantial physical harm to himself or others in the reasonably foreseeable future."

For the following reasons, the dangerousness standard is an inappropriate and dangerous indicator to use in judging the conditions under which someone should be involuntarily hospitalized. Dangerousness is being taken out of its proper context as one among other symptoms of the presence of severe mental illness that should be the determining factor.

1. To concentrate on dangerousness (especially to others) as the sole criterion for involuntary hospitalization deprives many mentally ill persons of the protection and treatment that they urgently require. A psychiatrist under the constraints of the dangerousness rule, faced with an out-of-control manic individual whose frantic behavior the psychiatrist truly believes to be a disguised call for help, would have to say, "Sorry, I would like to help you but I can't because you haven't threatened anybody and you are not suicidal." Since psychiatrists are admittedly not very good at accurately predicting dangerousness to others, the evidentiary standards for commitment will be very stringent. This will result in mental hospitals becoming prisons for a small population of volatile highly assaultive, and untreatable patients (14).
2. The attempt to differentiate rigidly (especially in regard to danger to self) between physical and other kinds of self-destructive behavior is artificial, unrealistic, and unworkable. It will tend to confront psychiatrists who want to help their patients with the same kind of dilemma they were faced with when justification for therapeutic abortion on psychiatric grounds depended on evidence of suicidal intent. The advocates of the dangerousness standard seem to be more comfortable with and pay more attention to the factor of dangerousness to others even though it is a much less frequent and much less significant consequence of mental illness than is danger to self.
3. The emphasis on dangerousness (again, especially to others) is a real obstacle to the right-to-treatment movement since it prevents the hospitalization and therefore the treatment of the population most amenable to various kinds of therapy.
4. Emphasis on the criterion of dangerousness to others moves involuntary commitment from a civil to a criminal procedure, thus, as Stone (14) put it, imposing the

procedures of one terrible system on another. Involuntary commitment on these grounds becomes a form of preventive detention and makes the psychiatrist a kind of glorified policeman.

5. Emphasis on dangerousness rather than mental disability and helplessness will hasten the process of deinstitutionalization. Recent reports (20, 21) have shown that these patients are not being rehabilitated and reintegrated into the community, but rather, that the burden of custodialism has been shifted from the hospital to the community.

6. As previously mentioned, emphasis on the dangerousness criterion may be a tactic of some of the abolitionists among the civil liberties lawyers (22) to end involuntary hospitalization by reducing it to an unworkable absurdity.

DISCUSSION

It is obvious that it is good to be at liberty and that it is good to be free from the consequences of disabling and dehumanizing illness. Sometimes these two values are incompatible, and in the heat of the passions that are often aroused by opposing views of right and wrong, the partisans of each view may tend to minimize the importance of the other. Both sides can present their horror stories—the psychiatrists, their dead victims of the failure of the involuntary hospitalization process, and the lawyers, their Donaldsons. There is a real danger that instead of acknowledging the difficulty of the problem, the two camps will become polarized, with a consequent rush toward extreme and untenable solutions rather than working toward reasonable ones.

The path taken by those whom I have labeled the abolitionists is an example of the barren results that ensue when an absolute solution is imposed on a complex problem. There are human beings who will suffer greatly if the abolitionists succeed in elevating an abstract principle into an unbreakable law with no exceptions. I find myself oppressed and repelled by their position, which seems to stem from an ideological rigidity which ignores that element of the contingent immanent in the structure of human existence. It is devoid of compassion.

The positions of those who espouse the medical model and the dangerousness approaches to commitment are, one hopes, not completely irreconcilable. To some extent these differences are a result of the vantage points from which lawyers and psychiatrists view mental illness and commitment. The lawyers see and are concerned with the failures and abuses of the process. Furthermore, as a result of their training, they tend to apply principles to classes of people rather than to take each instance as unique. The psychiatrists, on the other hand, are required to deal practically with the singular needs of individuals. They approach the problem from a clinical rather than a deductive stance. As physicians, they want to be in a position to take care of and to help suffering people whom they regard as sick patients. They sometimes become impatient with the rules that prevent them from doing this.

I believe we are now witnessing a pendular swing in which the rights of the mentally ill to be treated and protected are being set aside in the rush to give them their freedom at whatever cost. But is freedom defined only by the absence of external constraints? Internal physiological or psychological processes can contribute to a throttling of the spirit that is as painful as any applied from the outside. The "wild" manic individual without his lithium, the panicky hallucinator without his injection of fluphenazine hydrochloride and the understanding support of a concerned staff, the sodden alcoholic—are they free? Sometimes, as Woody Guthrie said, "Freedom means no place to go."

Today the civil liberties lawyers are in the ascendancy and the psychiatrists on the defensive to a degree that is harmful to individual needs and the public welfare. Redress and a more balanced position will not come from further extension of the dangerousness doctrine. I favor a return to the use of medical criteria by psychiatrists—psychiatrists, however, who have been chastened by the buffeting they have received and are quite willing to go along with even strict legal safeguards as long as they are constructive and not tyrannical.

References

1. Treffert, D. A.: "The practical limits of patients' rights." *Psychiatric Annals* 5(4):91–96, 1971.
2. Szasz, T.: *Law, Liberty and Psychiatry,* New York, Macmillan Co., 1963.
3. Ennis, B.: *Prisoners of Psychiatry,* New York, Harcourt Brace Jovanovich, 1972.
4. Szasz, T.: *The Myth of Mental Illness,* New York, Harper & Row, 1961.
5. Laing, R.: *The Politics of Experience,* New York, Ballantine Books, 1967.
6. Ennis, B.: "Ennis on 'Donaldson'." *Psychiatric News,* Dec. 3, 1975, pp. 4, 19, 37.
7. Peele, R., Chodoff, P., Taub, N.: "Involuntary hospitalization and treatability. Observations from the DC experience." *Catholic University Law Review* 23:744–753, 1974.
8. Michels, R.: "The right to refuse psychotropic drugs." *Hastings Center Report,* Hastings-on-Hudson, NY, 1973.
9. Parsons, T.: *The Social System.* New York, Free Press, 1951.
10. Veatch, R. M.: "The medical model; its nature and problems." *Hastings Center Studies* 1(3):59–76, 1973.
11. Katz, J.: "The right to treatment—an enchanting legal fiction?" *University of Chicago Law Review* 36:755–783, 1969.
12. Moore, M. S.: "Some myths about mental illness." *Arch Gen Psychiatry* 32:1483–1497, 1975.
13. Peszke, M. A.: "Is dangerousness an issue for physicians in emergency commitment?" *Am J Psychiatry* 132:825–828, 1975.
14. Stone, A. A.: "Comment on Peszke, M. A.: Is dangerousness an issue for physicians in emergency commitment?" Ibid. 829–831.
15. Siegler, M., Osmond, H.: *Models of Madness, Models of Medicine.* New York, Macmillan Co., 1974.
16. Stone, A.: Lecture for course on The Law, Litigation, and Mental Health Services. Adelphi, Md., Mental Health Study Center, September 1974.
17. O'Connor v Donaldson, 43 USLW 4929 (1975).
18. Lessard v Schmidt, 349 F Supp 1078, 1092 (ED Wis 1972).
19. In re Johnnie Hargrove, Washington, DC, Superior Court Mental Health number 506–75, 1975.
20. Rachlin, S., Pam, A., Milton, J.: "Civil liberties versus involuntary hospitalization." *Am J Psychiatry* 132:189–191, 1975.
21. Kirk, S. A., Therrien, M. E.: "Community mental health myths and the fate of former hospitalized patients." *Psychiatry* 38:209–217, 1975.
22. Dershowitz, A. A.: "Dangerousness as a criterion for confinement." *Bulletin of the American Academy of Psychiatry and the Law* 2:172–179, 1974.

9.2b   Responding to Chodoff

Chodoff's case against the "abolitionists" (such as Szasz) and the "civil liberties lawyers" is quite an impressive one. There *is* something unbeneficent about refusing to regard a severely disturbed individual as ill. And there *is* something narrow and dogmatic about raising the principle of liberty above any and every other important principle (for example, beneficence). Moreover, one does not need to be a committed paternalist to believe that it is sometimes justifiable to take responsibility for other people, even when that involves depriving them of their freedom. Many, then, will be persuaded by the essential humanity of Chodoff's position.

But Chodoff's position is not immune to criticism. A critic might sum up the case against him thus: Chodoff has done a good job of exposing some weaknesses in his opponents, but he has done very little to suggest when the preferences of a mentally incompetent person should be overridden, and that person involuntarily hospitalized. Chodoff's "medical model" of psychiatry, in other words, does little to answer the really hard question of when liberty and autonomy become less important principles than beneficence.

The critic would appear to be right about this. Chodoff does, admittedly, describe the "frustration" of the physician at being unable to treat a patient as a spur to one of the two undesirable extremes which have tended to polarize the debate—the extreme in this case being too much involuntary hospitalization. Yet it is not obvious what Chodoff is suggesting instead. The "medical model," after all, is meant to be an account of the *nature* of mental incompetence. It may well be a very good account. But to answer the question "What is mental incompetence?" is not to answer the question "How should mental incompetence be dealt with?" The two questions aren't unrelated, of course (if the medical model is accurate, for instance, then the "anti-psychiatrists'" case against involuntary commitment is greatly weakened). But they are distinct questions. If the adoption of a medical model of incompetence is supposed somehow to justify the involuntary hospitalization of some incompetent people even when they are dangerous to no one at all, which appears to be Chodoff's position, then it is up to him to explain why a medical model of other kinds of illness or disease wouldn't justify the involuntary hospitalization of some mentally *competent* people as well (for whatever maladies they refuse to have treated). If I suffer from a heart condition, but decline to seek treatment for it, then surely the undoubted fact that a medical model is the most appropriate model of coronary disease doesn't—couldn't—justify my being hospitalized for it against my will. Nor does the fact that my reasons for ignoring best medical advice are capricious or silly show that my desire to avoid treatment can itself be ignored. By the same token, then, the mere adoption of a "medical model" of mental incompetence cannot by itself justify the involuntary hospitalization of mentally incompetent people. Chodoff's argument is incomplete.

Chodoff is strongly opposed to "dangerousness" criteria for involuntary hospitalization. A critic might wonder why. After all, even if dangerousness is, as Chodoff insists, extraordinarily difficult to evaluate, it is at least clearly *relevant* to the issue of overriding people's preferences. Unlike the medical model, which offers no precedent or reason for overriding people's preferences, dangerousness is a criterion whose application in other contexts in which a person's autonomy may be overridden is not in doubt. No one questions that the dangerousness of certain criminals is sufficient to outweigh their understandable preference to stay out of jail, for instance. One person's dangerousness limits and threatens other people's autonomy. It is surely obvious, then, that in cases where a mentally incompetent person poses a foreseeable danger to others, he or she should be hospitalized, with or without consent. The medical model becomes redundant here.

Chodoff might concede this, while noting at the same time that he himself has said that dangerousness criteria may work well enough when a person poses a threat to others. But Chodoff claims, no doubt correctly, that advocates of dangerousness criteria have largely ignored the dangers that a person might pose to him- or herself. And he is surely right to insist that such cases also deserve our concern. But a critic might answer that there is no difficulty in principle here, even if supporters of dangerousness criteria have, in practice, neglected threat-to-self in their deliberations. Threat-to-self is a perfectly clear case of dangerousness, and it ought to be given its proper weight. Indeed, in conjunction with a different model from the medical model, threat-to-self might well constitute legitimate grounds for involuntary hospitalization. (We've already seen that the medical model provides no such grounds.) Adopting a "child model" of mental incompetence, for instance, according to which the mentally incompetent are viewed as deserving the protection due to a child, would clearly be sufficient to justify certain cases of involuntary hospitalization (children are involuntarily—but justifiably—hospitalized all the time). The benefit of combining these models will be especially clear when an incompetent person's autonomous preferences pose a substantial and foreseeable threat to his or her own well-being. This seems to me to be the critic's strongest positive counterargument.

But Chodoff would almost certainly reject it. After all, he explicitly denies that any tinkering with the dangerousness criterion would produce an acceptable solution. The critic has no option now but to stand firm, and ask: "What does Chodoff think *would* justify involuntary hospitalization?" With my critic's hat on, I can't detect an explicit answer to this in Chodoff's article. He talks about dealing with patients on a case-by-case basis, which is all well and good, but one still needs some guiding principle to do this. It looks increasingly as if Chodoff's guiding principle is really the "frustration" that a physician may feel at being unable to treat a patient when the patient might clearly benefit from treatment. Yet he himself acknowledges that this is the road to the undesirable, paternalistic extreme of too much involuntary hospitalization.

Perhaps an advocate of the medical model of incompetence who is also an opponent of dangerousness criteria for involuntary hospitalization has other argumentative options, but if so, I do not think those options are explained or explored in Chodoff's article. Chodoff's article is an excellent antidote to the unduly simplistic views of some of his adversaries: The medical model is a persuasive response to the anti-psychiatrists' debunking of the concept of mental illness. His discussion of the ethical issues strongly suggests that the principle of freedom-at-any-cost ought not to be allowed to have the last word. But his positive proposals seem less convincing. Indeed my own inclination, in line with the critical points discussed in this section, is to suspect that dangerousness criteria have a much more important role to play in the debate about involuntary hospitalization than Chodoff allows.

9.2c   Paternalism and Beneficence

The attitude that a society takes toward its more vulnerable members is one of the most revealing things about it. I take it as axiomatic that any society with pretensions to being civilized will regard the vulnerable with concern, at the very least. Adopting a policy of deliberately neglecting the vulnerable—of leaving them to fend for themselves with no assistance at all—would be a fair sign of barbarism. No one on any side of the debate about involuntary hospitalization is recommending the wholesale neglect of the mentally incompetent. Even the most ardent defenders of deinstitutionalization wish to see appropriate arrangements made for "community care"; even the most determined advocates of liberty approve of the availability of hospitalization for mentally incompetent people who *choose* to have treatment, or who can be persuaded voluntarily to seek it out. In other words, everyone recognizes the desirability of at least some beneficent provision for the mentally incompetent. Nor does anyone seriously doubt the legitimacy of hospitalizing some incompetent people against their will if they pose a substantial and foreseeable threat to the safety of others. This much, perhaps, is common ground. Disagreement arises when it is asked how interventionist beneficent provision should be. Should we intervene (against their will) to prevent incompetent people from harming themselves? Should we intervene (against their will) to prevent them from neglecting their own best interests? In other words, how paternalist should we be?

In the last section, I suggested that a child model of mental incompetence might be used to justify involuntary hospitalization. Clearly the thought behind this model is strongly (and literally) paternalist. It might be assumed that adopting such a model would justify all kinds of intervention. After all, we do not merely protect children from causing themselves direct physical harm (by stopping them from playing with matches, for instance). We also try to prevent them from damaging their own long-term prospects—for example, by insisting that they receive at least some education. The assumed inability of children reliably to exercise their autonomy in their own best interests is taken to justify a whole range of paternalist measures. If we agreed to regard the mentally incompetent as child-like, in this sense, then perhaps we would be justified not only in preventing mentally incompetent people from harming themselves directly, but also in preventing them from doing anything not in accord with their own long-term interests. This model might be expected to justify rather a lot of involuntary hospitalization and treatment.

Is there any reason not to adopt this model? One objection might be that it seriously undervalues freedom. But no one sensible objects to curtailing the freedoms of children, and if it is true that the mentally incompetent are appropriately to be viewed as child-like, then no one ought to object to curtailing their freedoms too. This is the heart of the matter. *Are* the mentally incompetent appropriately to be viewed as child-like? Let's ignore for a moment the fact that mental incompetence comes in many forms, only some of which literally resemble childhood. In other words, let's assume that the analogy is intended seriously. As such, it must be based on the observation that, like children, the mentally incompetent are standardly or often unable to exercise their autonomy in a way that accords with their own true interests. This observation appears sound. But another assumption is needed: We must suppose that, as in the case of children, the reduced autonomy of the mentally incompetent justifies others in taking at least some responsibility for them. This too seems defensible. After all, everyone agrees that a civilized society has at least some obligation to make beneficent provision for the incompetent. Construed in this way, the analogy looks good.

The stumbling block, however, comes at the next stage. For it is also necessary to assume that the true interests of the mentally incompetent can be assessed in essentially the same way as the true interests of children can be assessed. This seems to be altogether more questionable. I have distinguished between two categories of interest that a child may have, for the sake of which it might be legitimate to curtail his or her freedom to do as he or she pleases. The first is the interest to avoid direct physical harm; the second is the interest to avoid damage to what may be termed a child's life-prospects. The first category of interest is clearly shared by the mentally incompetent, and can presumably be assessed in the same way. Just as we would conclude that it was not in a child's true interests to douse him- or herself in gasoline, or to starve to death, so we would be justified in concluding that it was not in an incompetent person's true interests to do these things either. If this is right, then the child model of incompetence may be used to justify the involuntary treatment of mentally incompetent persons who pose a direct and serious threat to their own physical well-being.

But the second category of interest is almost certainly not analogous. A child's "life-prospects"—which it is in his or her true interests not to damage—are assessed by reference to social norms. In our society, for example, it is regarded as normal and desirable for a child to grow up, get a job, perhaps have a family, and to play a constructive role in the community. To these ends, it is regarded as justifiable to prevent a child from neglecting his or her education, to insist that he or she acquire at least a minimum number of social skills, even to arrange for a child's teeth to be straightened. The child may object to any or all of these measures at the time; but in the long run we can be reasonably confident that his or her own best interests will have been served; we can be fairly sure that the child will come to think so too. All of this is made possible—and indeed is justified—by the fact that the life-prospects of normal children in a society such as ours are relatively stable and predictable. Understanding those prospects, we can fairly claim to "know what is best." The life-prospects of the mentally incompetent, on the other hand, are a different matter entirely. The incompetent are picked out precisely by the fact that they are not normal. *Their* life-prospects are not predictable, and the course their lives will take is not assessable by reference to social norms in the way that is true of children's lives. This strongly suggests that paternalist intervention in the interests of the life-prospects of the mentally incompetent cannot be justified by appeal to the child model. The child model, that is, warrants no interference with the autonomy of the mentally incompetent except in cases of serious and foreseeable harm-to-self. Of course the incompetent can be encouraged or persuaded to seek treatment, but nothing in the child model suggests that they can be forced to have treatment in cases where they are not directly endangering themselves.

If this is right, then two things follow. First, the child model, if it is accepted, can be used to justify only a *limited* paternalism. Second, the criteria for involuntary hospitalization that the child model legitimates are dangerousness criteria. I have suggested that the child model, if it is properly understood, is indeed an appropriate model for mental incompetence—at least within a civilized society that recognizes the obligation to make beneficent provision for vulnerable people. If that is accepted, it follows that the proper criteria for treating incompetent people against their will must be that they pose a danger to others or that they pose a danger to themselves. If someone wishes to justify the involuntary hospitalization of the mentally incompetent on other, perhaps more paternalist criteria, then he or she will need to propose and defend a more sweeping model than the child-model.

9.2d Involuntary Sterilization

It is not uncommon practice to sterilize young, severely retarded women, with or without their consent. The rationale for this practice has nothing to do with the fear that the offspring of retarded people may themselves be retarded. If this were the rationale, then such sterilization would constitute an extreme form of gene therapy (see 10.3). Instead, the rationale is paternalist. The thought is that a retarded person who has the body of a woman, but the mind of a young child, may be particularly vulnerable to harm as a result of becoming pregnant. A severely retarded person may not understand what is happening to her or how it has come about; she may become distressed and frightened; she may suffer real emotional damage as a consequence.

Few people, probably, would object to sterilizing retarded people if fully informed consent for the procedure were obtained. But this is usually impossible, for obvious reasons. So the question is: Can we justifiably sterilize a retarded woman without her consent? Any out-and-out paternalist would clearly answer Yes. But out-and-out paternalism is always vulnerable to the charge of undervaluing autonomy. So if we wish to answer Yes to this question, we will probably do better to adopt a more balanced standpoint. The child model of incompetence, together with dangerousness criteria for involuntary treatment (see previous section), would appear to fit the bill. From this standpoint, the involuntary sterilization of the retarded might be defended by appeal to the criterion of harm-to-self. If it is true that there is a high likelihood that a severely retarded woman will suffer deep emotional distress at becoming pregnant, then it seems reasonable to say that unprotected sexual activity on her part constitutes a danger to her. If so, then the child model seems to warrant involuntary sterilization. Indeed this—or something very like it—is exactly the justification that is usually offered for such a procedure.

How good a justification is it? A critic might object on several grounds. First, there are empirical questions: Just how likely is a retarded woman to suffer extreme distress on becoming pregnant? In order for dangerousness criteria to be compelling, the likelihood would have to be very large. (Remember: Dangers must be "foreseeable.") Exactly how likely is a retarded woman to engage in sexual activity? Again, the answer would have to be "very likely." Any uncertainty in response to these questions would seriously undermine the attempted justification. Then there is a question about the *kind* of danger that a retarded woman's unprotected sexual activity is meant to threaten her with. Is "emotional distress" the right sort of harm—is it serious and substantial enough to warrant intervention? One can imagine someone answering No to this question, on the grounds that only physical harm is ever serious or substantial enough to warrant intervention. But this seems rather narrow: We all know how far from true the old saying that "Sticks and stones may break my bones, but words will never hurt me" can be. Most would agree that there are at least some emotional harms which, in terms of seriousness, far outweigh at least some physical harms. So that response won't do.

But the critic has a better point. Rather than say that emotional harm is not serious enough, the critic might suggest that emotional harm is not foreseeable enough. The effect of physical stress on someone's body is more predictable than the effect of emotional stress on someone's mind; when that person is mentally incompetent, our efforts at predicting mental effects may be still less reliable. In other words, the critic might argue that the nature of emotional harm, taken together with the fact that the potential subject of that harm is mentally incompetent, means that we should err on the side of caution: That is, that we should prefer the demands of autonomy in such cases to the demands of beneficence.

The defender of involuntary sterilization will not be convinced. If the empirical evidence is sufficiently strong, he or she will argue that the risks are high enough to justify intervention. Much hangs, then, on the empirical evidence. If the evidence of emotional distress is compelling, and if it is judged to be impossible or undesirable to prevent severely retarded women from entering into sexual relations, then the case for involuntary sterilization will appear quite strong. If the risks have been exaggerated, on the other hand, then only an out-and-out paternalist would think involuntary sterilization defensible. This issue, then, is one that will not be resolved until enough research has been done to justify confidence, one way or the other, that we know what harm a severely retarded, unsterilized woman might come to.

It has recently become feasible to use contraceptive implants in place of sterilization. It might appear that this development will itself settle the question by making sterilization obsolete, but a moment's thought suggests otherwise. It is true that the reversible nature of contraception means that involuntary contraception is less of an infringement of a retarded person's autonomy than involuntary sterilization. But this doesn't mean that it is *no* infringement of a retarded person's autonomy. And because forcing contraception on somebody is still an invasive medical procedure, and since the side-effects of contraceptive implants may be significant (no one really knows), it doesn't seem that this development settles or avoids any of the crucial issues raised by sterilization. The precise terms of the debate may change, but the underlying ethical difficulties remain the same.

9.2e   Recap: Helping the Helpless

If a person is mentally incompetent and we believe that he or she needs treatment, our first step should always be encouragement or persuasion. It is far better that a person should seek treatment of his or her own free will. Apart from anything else, a person will be more committed to a course of treatment if he or she has autonomously chosen it. Sometimes, however, it will be impossible to persuade a person to undergo treatment voluntarily. In these cases the possibility of *in*voluntary treatment arises. I have suggested that the mere fact that people might benefit from treatment is altogether insufficient to justify forcing it upon them. Otherwise any of us might be hospitalized against our will and treated in whatever way might be held to be "good for us." If it is wrong to treat competent people this way, then the mere fact that someone happens to be *in*competent cannot justify treating him or her that way, either. Nor, I suggest, is it good enough to hospitalize people involuntarily when it is believed that treatment would, in some broad sense, be in their interests, but they are held not competent enough to understand where their real interests lie. This is still too loose: It is easy, on these grounds, to imagine real abuses taking place in which the autonomy of people who are merely unusual, eccentric, or mildly retarded is seriously violated. (I suspect that the kind of approach that Chodoff proposes might lead to abuses of this kind.)

What is needed is a stricter criterion, together with an appropriate model of incompetence. Armed with these, we may hope to decide in a principled way which of a person's interests may be considered more important or fundamental than his or her autonomy, and when. My own suggestion is that it is appropriate to regard mentally incompetent people as being somewhat like children, in the sense that we owe them protection. I have argued in 9.2c, above, that this model of incompetence indicates the adoption of a "dangerousness" criterion for involuntary hospitalization. In this way, incompetent people become candidates for involuntary treatment when they pose a serious and foreseeable danger, either to others or to themselves. The difficulties in deciding what kind of danger counts as sufficiently serious or foreseeable have been highlighted in 9.2d. Many will disagree with my suggestion. Some will argue that it doesn't allow enough scope for genuinely beneficent intervention on behalf of extremely vulnerable people. Others will argue that it allows far too much interference with the legitimate freedoms of the incompetent. But whatever your conclusion, this chapter ought to have shown what kinds of argument are appropriate to the debate; some of the suggestions it contains may be useful, even if the majority are rejected.

Study Questions

1. Could a pattern of behavior that is normal in our society count as mentally incompetent in another society? How does your answer illuminate the concept of mental incompetence?
2. Should treatment decisions about people who have become mentally incompetent through senile dementia and about people who have been mentally incompetent from birth be made in the same ways? Does the fact that members of the first group have been competent in the past make a difference?
3. Can people truly be said to be harming themselves if they cannot be brought to see their treatment of themselves as harmful? What might "harm" *mean* in this context?
4. Of the child model and the medical model of mental incompetence, which do you think gives greater weight to the principle of beneficence?

Related Cases in Crigger, *Cases in Bioethics,* Third Edition

Questions of the kind discussed in "The Nature of Mental Incompetence" (9.1) tend to figure indirectly in the cases relevant to the issues discussed in "Decisions about Treatment" (9.2). Of these, the most interesting are: cases 37, 38 and 43, which deal with the involuntary treatment of incompetent or possibly incompetent adults; case 42, which is about the treatment of a retarded child; and cases 17 and 40, which concern the reproductive rights of incompetent women (also an issue in case 42). Mental incompetence in the context of euthanasia figures in case 9, and in the context of medical research in case 33. The most useful discussions are probably those following cases 37, 38 and 43.

CHAPTER TEN
Allocation and Health Care Policy

INTRODUCTION

So far in this book we have skirted around the wider political and social issues that the practice of medicine raises. But we shall do so no longer. Health is a matter of concern to everyone, and the structures and institutions that a society relies upon to promote its members' health are of enormous significance to everyone in that society. There is a lively political debate about these structures and institutions going on right now in the United States, and indeed in countries around the world, as the ever more complex and expensive business of health care comes under scrutiny. How should health care be paid for? How should its benefits be distributed? What lengths should we go to in order to improve our nation's health? What groundbreaking research and technologies should we be supporting?

There are many extremely difficult and extremely contentious issues here. Some of them are of a kind which philosophy can say almost nothing about. For instance, if you want to know how to get real value for money in your health care expenditure you'll be better off talking to someone who has the appropriate expertise, such as an experienced health administrator. Nor is philosophy well suited to assess the practicalities of revenue generation, for example, or the political impact of a policy proposal. But clearly there are other aspects to these issues—ethical aspects—to which philosophy can indeed make a contribution. When we ask how health care should be paid for, or how its benefits should be distributed, we raise questions not merely of efficiency, about which philosophy has little to say, but of principle. We want to know what would be ethically defensible answers to these questions, how we ought to pay for health care, how its benefits ought to be distributed. Similarly, when we raise issues concerning organ procurement or genetic engineering, there are purely practical questions here about which philosophy has little to say, but there are also ethical questions that philosophical methods can help us address. Such questions, then, are the subject of this chapter.

10.1 ALLOCATING SCARCE RESOURCES

We begin with questions about allocation. The first thing to notice is that allocation only poses an ethical *problem* when the resources to be allocated are scarce. "Scarce" here means "not unlimited." In this sense, then, a resource can be scarce even though there's quite a lot of it around. If a resource is not scarce in this sense, then there is enough of it to be allocated to everyone who wants or needs it; if this is the case, then there are no strictly ethical problems attached to allocation (though there may be plenty of practical problems). A scarce resource, by contrast, is one for which the demand outstrips the supply. In allocating a resource of this kind, inevitably some demands will not be met. This is why it is only the allocation of scarce resources that poses an ethical problem—the problem of how to decide which demands should be met and which should not.

10.1a Health and Wealth

Health is not a scarce resource. Indeed it is not a resource of any kind. Health may be a valuable or desirable state, or represent a valuable or desirable goal, but it is not the kind of thing that can be divided up, distributed, or redistributed. (Imagine someone deciding that I had too much health, and that some of mine should be reallocated to somebody else!) No, the scarce resource that interests us here is not health itself, but health *care.*

There is, as is often remarked, an almost limitless demand for health care. Every medical advance makes new techniques and procedures possible; the continual development of new techniques and procedures raises our expectations about the benefits that health care can deliver; these raised expectations result in an ever increasing demand for those benefits. The downside to the success of modern medicine—a success that *creates* the increased demand for care—is that better care costs more money. Sophisticated procedures for treating once incurable conditions are invariably more expensive than the cost of not treating those conditions. We can do more, and so we do do more; the more we do—the more we demand, and get—the more it costs. It would be possible for a wealthy country to bankrupt itself through health care costs and still not satisfy every demand. Thus health care is a scarce resource because its provision depends (at least in part) on wealth, which is itself a scarce resource. But wealth is not the only scarce resource upon which health care depends. Skilled and dedicated health care professionals, for instance, are not, and could not be, limitless in number. Nor does the supply of organs needed for modern transplant procedures come anywhere near to meeting the demand for them. On every side, then, the allocation of health care is limited by scarcity—as indeed it is bound to be, unless we miraculously become limitlessly rich in money, talent, and spare parts. This means that it is impossible for everyone who needs, or would like, or would benefit from a particular form of care to have it. How, then, are we to decide who gets how much of what? This is the ethical problem of health care allocation.

10.1b Rights

It is sometimes said that people have a right to health care. In fact, it is sometimes said that people have a right to health itself. But this can't be correct. We saw in Chapter Two that a right entails an obligation. So if someone had a right to health, this would mean that someone else—or all of us—had an obligation to provide it. But no one could have an obligation to provide health. Health, to put it crudely, is too much a matter of luck (of strength of constitution, of genetic predisposition, of chance bacterial encounters, etc.) for it to be possible to demand of anyone or everyone that they provide or guarantee it. Morality cannot require the impossible, and the elimination of good and bad luck from our lives is, simply, impossible. So it doesn't make sense to speak of a right to health itself.

We can, however, speak of a right to the means to become healthy, or to become healthier, or to suffer less from the pains of ill-health, wherever these means lie within the scope of human choice. Here at least we are speaking of a right that entails an obligation which someone could coherently be said to have. And it is a right of this kind that is being invoked when someone says that people have a right to health care. The idea is that there is something—health care—which some or all of us have the obligation to provide (or to contribute to the provision of), which gives others (perhaps all of us) an *entitlement* or a right to health care. This idea makes sense at a logical level, then. But it doesn't get us very far with questions about the allocation of health care. For health care is a scarce resource. Health care, given the limitations sketched out in the previous section, is something that is not possible to give everyone as much of as they might want, need, or benefit from. This means that the appeal to a right to health care is, as it stands, not enough to make any real headway with the matter at hand. We need to ask: What, if there is a right to health care, does such a right come to when health care is a scarce resource? And our answer to that will depend on the view we take about the ethics of the distribution of scarce resources. Traditionally, this question is a question about justice.

10.1c   Justice

Justice is a matter of giving people what is fair, due, or owed to them. When we consider the distribution of a scarce resource such as health care we must ensure that we decide fairly which demands are and are not met, so that everyone gets what is due to them or owed to them. In 3.5 we saw that justice requires that different ways of treating different cases must be justified by appeal to relevant differences between the cases. In the present context, this means that a fair or just distribution of resources depends upon identifying what differences count as relevant differences between the people competing for those resources. There isn't enough health care to go around. So we need to identify what factors might justify the allocation of differing levels of health care to different people. What factors qualify someone to receive health care? What sort of difference must there be between two people in order for it to be just to allocate health care to one of them and not to the other?

These are tough questions, but because health care is a scarce resource they need to be faced and answered. How one answers these questions will depend upon what one thinks are relevant differences between cases. Different theories highlight different differences. Here we will look at three ways of attempting to decide which differences matter—the utilitarian way, the libertarian way, and the egalitarian way.

10.1c(i)   Utilitarian Justice   The utilitarian approach is committed to promoting the greatest amount of happiness for the greatest number of people. A relevant difference between cases, for the utilitarian, must always boil down to a difference, in terms of maximizing happiness, between the consequences of treatment. If in one case a course of treatment will have happier consequences than it will in a second case, then this counts as a relevant difference between the two; it will be just, from the utilitarian perspective, to allocate health care in the first case but not in the second. Thus, for example, if I am much older than you (and so have a foreseeably shorter time left in which to be happy), or am much nastier than you (and so tend to produce more unhappiness in others than you do), or have a smaller circle of loved ones or dependents than you (and so matter to fewer people), or am far stupider than you (and so less likely to come up with life-enhancing ideas, objects, or technologies), then I am relevantly different from you in the utilitarian scheme of things. It will be just, from this perspective, to prefer you to me in the competition for health care. If we both need a kidney transplant, you get priority.

This is, as a matter of fact, the model that most closely approximates the way things are done in a publicly funded health care system. The experience in Europe of publicly funded health care systems is longer and deeper than it is in the United States, and that experience strongly suggests that priorities between cases are, in practice, settled by appeal to considerations of a broadly utilitarian character. Care for infants tends to take precedence over care for the elderly. Procedures with a high likelihood of success are preferred to experimental procedures, or to procedures with a patchy record of success. Interventions thought likely to produce significant improvement in quality of life enjoy priority over those thought less likely to do so. Economic calculation figures large. Time after time the question is: Given limited public resources, is *this* the best way to bring about the greatest balance of benefit over suffering? Difficult decisions have to be made. But on the whole it does seem that publicly funded health care systems are quite successful in achieving the broadly utilitarian goals set for them, and in delivering the results that the taxpayers who fund and use those systems expect from them. This fact suggests that there is at least something right about the utilitarian approach to the allocation of scarce resources.

But a purely utilitarian system would produce results that most people would shy away from. For instance, a utilitarian calculation could come out such that a miserable, unpleasant, unloved, uninnovative—yet sick—old man would receive no care at all, however great his need of it (there would always be someone more fruitful, in terms of happiness-maximizing, to allocate scarce resources to). I think most people would consider this unjustifiable. It is a widely shared intuition that a civilized society has some obligation to care for even the least prepossessing of its members, but this intuition finds no support in any strictly utilitarian approach to the just distribution of scarce resources. As we have already seen, then (2.3i), the relationship between utilitarianism and the principle of justice is a strained one, and this had led many to look elsewhere for a more satisfactory approach to the problems of allocation.

10.1c(ii)   Libertarian Justice   One alternative to the utilitarian approach is the libertarian approach. This, to all intents and purposes, is the approach to which the system in the United States has tended to approximate most closely. The libertarian believes in freedom of choice, so the relevant difference between people will boil down to a difference in their freedom to choose—which, in practice, means a difference in their ability to pay for what they want. If I am far richer than you then this fact will, from a libertarian perspective, constitute a relevant difference between us. My freedom of choice is greater than yours (I can afford a wider range of options) and hence, says the libertarian, it is fair and just that I should receive or have available to me a wider and better range of health care than you. If we both need an expensive operation, and I can pay for mine while you can't pay for yours, then it is just that I should have the operation and that you should go without.

It is important to notice that the libertarian position isn't simply the law of the jungle (although it can, at times, closely resemble the law of the jungle). For there *is* a principle at work in this position. That principle, of course, is respect for autonomy. According to the libertarian, respect for autonomy entails that it is wrong to seek to limit the freedom of others to make their own choices. If someone believes that it is unjust that the rich should receive better health care than the poor, then that person presumably also believes that it would be right to *prevent* the rich from exercising their economic freedoms in such a way as to obtain those superior benefits. In other words, an opponent of the libertarian position must be committed to limiting the freedom of choice enjoyed by the rich within a market-controlled health care system. The autonomy of the rich, such an opponent will claim, must be reduced (perhaps by taxing the rich in order to pay for care for the poor). To the libertarian, of course, this is unacceptable. Respect for autonomy is the libertarian's most cherished principle, and to attempt to restrict the autonomy of any particular group of people (for example, the rich) would, according to the libertarian conception of justice, be unjust. Taxing the rich to fund care for the poor would undermine the freedoms of the (rich) citizen.

As with the utilitarian conception of justice, something seems right about libertarianism. Respect for autonomy *is* an important ethical principle. Other things being equal, it does seem wrong to try to restrict the freedom of others to make their own personal choices (by, for instance, deciding what they must spend their money on). But there also seems to be something rather simplistic about the libertarian model. Are the freedoms of the rich really the only freedoms that matter? What about the autonomy of the less well-off? Is respect for autonomy really the only ethical principle that counts? What about beneficence? How can it be just that one person has full access to the priceless resource of health care, while another person, who differs from the first only in respect of his or her bank balance, is denied such access? I suggested a moment ago that it was the mark of a civilized society that it recognized some obligation to care for even the least prepossessing of its members. Surely the same point goes here: There must be some obligation to care for even the poorest and most unfortunate among us. If you agree with this, then it is unlikely that your sympathies will lie with any purely libertarian conception of justice. You will want to look elsewhere for an account of the way in which a scarce resource such as health care ought to be distributed between people. Libertarianism is perhaps just a bit too close to the law of the jungle to function persuasively as a *moral* picture of the way things should be.

To be fair, though, most people who would identify themselves as libertarians are prepared to water their position down—usually by recommending that some basic minimum of health care should be guaranteed to everyone, regardless of their ability to pay (the rich then being allowed to pay for as much on top of the basic minimum as they like). In the United States, the Medicare and Medicaid programs are the practical results of this watering-down of libertarianism. What is being injected into libertarianism here is a dash of *egalitarianism,* of the sense that at least some health care ought to be available to everyone.

10.1c(iii) Egalitarian Justice The egalitarian conception of justice insists on equality between people, such that from a moral point of view no person is worth more than any other person. Thus the egalitarian denies that a difference in happiness-maximizing potential constitutes a relevant difference between people (the utilitarian position); he or she also denies that a difference in economic freedom—ability to pay—constitutes a relevant difference between people (the libertarian position). Instead, the egalitarian holds that a scarce resource is allocated justly only when all who are competing for it are treated equally.

On the face of it, this position looks simple and compelling: Indeed, it seems to resemble much more closely our ordinary intuitive notions of justice than do either of the positions we have investigated so far. But we must tread carefully. For what, after all, is the egalitarian's answer to the question: Which differences between people count as relevant differences? If the answer is that there are no relevant differences between people (because everyone is of equal moral worth), then the egalitarian will have nothing of interest to say about the just distribution of *scarce* resources. When we say that a resource is scarce, after all, we mean that there isn't enough of it to go around; we mean that some people will have to be preferred over other people when we allocate it. In other words, what we are looking for is a principled way of deciding which differences between people do count as relevant, so that the scarce resource in question can be allocated as justly as possible. Therefore, if the egalitarian is to make a useful contribution to the debate he or she must be prepared to identify differences between people which justify the allocation of resources to certain people, and not to others. Otherwise the egalitarian will be guilty of ignoring the nature (and the difficulty) of the problem that the allocation of scarce resources poses.

There are two broad strategies open to the egalitarian here. Both begin with the thought that, in order to be "relevant," differences between people must be differences relevant to the scarce resource in question. So, for instance, the egalitarian denies that differences between people in happiness-maximizing potential or in bank-balance have anything to do with questions concerning the just allocation of *health care.* Differences in happiness-maximizing potential might be relevant to the just distribution of happiness (if happiness is something that can be distributed!), differences in bank-balance might be relevant to the just distribution of wealth. But neither is remotely relevant to the just distribution of health care. For that, the egalitarian claims, it is necessary to identify a difference between people that actually has a bearing on health care—on something directly relevant to the allocation of this particular scarce resource.

I said that there were two approaches open to the egalitarian. The first, and less plausible, is to pursue the parallel suggested by questions about the just distribution of wealth. The egalitarian usually deplores inequalities in wealth, and would like to see wealth redistributed in such a way that everyone ha a more or less equal amount of it. In other words, the egalitarian would like to achieve *equality of outcome*—an outcome where the (relevant) differences between the rich and the poor have been evened out. Perhaps this approach is indeed a worthy one in the context of wealth; but whether it is or not, it certainly yields nonsense when transferred to the context of health care. Equality of outcome? Presumably this means one of two things: Either that everyone should enjoy the same level of health—which, for reasons already discussed in 10.2b, is an unrealizable goal. Or else that everyone should receive exactly the same amount of health care; that health care should, literally, be distributed equally between us, so that the (relevant) differences between people—for instance, that the sick receive more health care than the healthy—will be evened out. Imagine what such a scheme would come to! We'd all have to have the same operations, whether we needed them or not. If anyone was given a blood-transfusion, we'd all have to be given a blood-transfusion. If one person received a wheelchair, then everyone would have to have one. What an incredible waste of scarce resources! Even discounting the pointless risks to healthy people, surely no one would think that such a scheme represented a sensible approach to the problem. Equality of outcome, then, cannot be the goal at which the egalitarian conception of justice aims—at least not in the context of health care.

The alternative, for the egalitarian, lies in the idea of *equality of access.* Here the thought is that health care should be equally available to all, but that those who actually receive it should do so only on the basis of *need.* Need for health care, then, becomes the decisive factor. If I need a particular form of treatment, and you do not, then that counts as a relevant difference between us, and it will be just that I should receive it and that you should not. In the next section we will discuss this more plausible version of the egalitarian approach in greater detail.

10.1d Care According to Need: Nielsen's Argument: "Autonomy, Equality, and a Just Health Care System"

Kai Nielsen, professor of philosophy at the University of Calgary, develops an explicitly egalitarian approach to the problem of the allocation of health care, arguing that justice requires that we allocate health care on the basis of need. Such an approach, he suggests, will actually increase freedom and autonomy, and not—as the libertarian might fear—diminish them.

AUTONOMY, EQUALITY, AND A JUST HEALTH CARE SYSTEM
Kai Nielsen

. . . An autonomy respecting egalitarian society with an interest in the well-being of its citizens—something moral beings could hardly be without—would (trivially) be a society of equals, and as a society of equals it would be committed to (a) *moral* equality and (b) an equality of *condition* which would, under conditions of moderate abundance, in turn expect the equality of condition to be rough and to be princi̹ ally understood (cashed in) in terms of providing the conditions (as far as that is possible) for meeting the needs (including most centrally the basic needs) of everyone and meeting them equally, as far as either of these things is feasible.

What kind of health care system would such an autonomy respecting egalitarian society have under conditions of moderate abundance such as we find in Canada and the United States?

The following are health care needs which are also basic needs: being healthy and having conditions treated which impede one's functioning well or which adversely affect one's well-being or cause suffering. These are plainly things we need. Where societies have the economic and technical capacity to do so, as these societies plainly do, without undermining other equally urgent or more urgent needs, these health needs, as basic needs, must be met, and the right to have such medical care is a right for everyone in the society regardless of her capacity to pay. This just follows from a commitment to *moral* equality and to an equality of condition. Where we have the belief, a belief which is very basic in nonfascistic modernizing societies, that each person's good is to be given equal consideration, it is hard not to go in that way, given a plausible conception of needs and reasonable list of needs based on that conception.[1] If there is the need for some particular regime of care and the society has the resources to meet that need, without undermining structures protecting other at least equally urgent needs, then, *ceteris paribus,* the society, if it is a decent society, must do so. The commitment to more equality—the commitment to the belief that the life of each person matters and matters equally—entails, given a few plausible empirical premises, that each person's health needs will be the object of an equal regard. Each has an equal claim, *prima facie,* to have her needs satisfied where this is possible. That does not, of course, mean that people should all be treated alike in the sense of their all getting the same thing. Not everyone needs flu shots, braces, a dialysis machine, a psychiatrist, or a triple by-pass. What should be equal is that each person's health needs should be the object of equal societal concern since each person's good should be given equal consideration.[2] This does not mean that equal energy should be directed to Hans's rash as to Frank's cancer. Here one person's need for a cure is much greater than the other, and the greater need clearly takes precedence. Both should be met where possible, but where they both cannot then the greater need has pride of place. But what should not count in the treatment of Hans and Frank is that Hans is wealthy or prestigious or creative and Frank is not. Everyone should have their health needs met where possible. Moreover, where the need is the same, they should have (where possible), and where other at least equally urgent needs are not thereby undermined, the same quality treatment. No differentiation should be made between them on the basis of their ability to pay or on the basis of their being (one more so than the other) important people. There should, in short, where this is possible, be open and free medical treatment of the same quality and extent available to everyone in the society. And no two- or three-tier system should be allowed to obtain, and treatment should only vary (subject to the above qualification) on the basis of variable needs and unavoidable differences in different places in supply and personnel, e.g., differences between town and country. Furthermore, these latter differences should be remedied where technically and economically feasible. The underlying aim should be to meet the health care needs of everyone and meet them, in the sense explicated, equally: everybody's needs here should be met as fully as possible; different treatment is only justified where the need is different or where both needs cannot be met. Special treatment for one person rather than another is only justified where, as I remarked, both needs cannot be met or cannot as adequately be met. Constrained by ought implies can; where these circumstances obtain, priority should be given to the greater need that can feasibly be met. A moral system or a social policy, plainly, cannot be reasonably asked to do the impossible. But my account does not ask that.

To have such a health care system would, I think, involve taking medicine out of the private sector altogether including, of course, out of private entrepreneurship where the governing rationale has to be profit and where supply and demand rules the roost. Instead there must be a health care system firmly in the public sector (publicly owned and controlled) where the rationale of the system is to meet as efficiently and as fully as possible the health care needs of everyone in the society in question. The health care system should not be viewed as a business anymore than a university should be viewed as a business—compare a university and a large hospital—but as a set of institutions and practices designed to meet urgent human needs.

I do not mean that we should ignore costs or efficiency. The state-run railroad system in Switzerland, to argue by analogy, is very efficient. The state cannot, of course, ignore costs in running it. But the aim is not to make a profit. The aim is to produce the most rapid, safe, efficient and comfortable service meeting travellers' needs within the parameters of the overall socio-economic priorities of the state and the society. Moreover, since the state in question is a democracy, if its citizens do not like the policies of the government here (or elsewhere) they can replace it with a government with different priorities and policies. Indeed the option is there (probably never to be exercised) to shift the railroad into the private sector.

Governments, understandably, worry with aging populations about mounting health care costs. This is slightly ludicrous in the United States, given its military and space exploration budgets, but is also a reality in Canada and even in Iceland where there is no military or space budget at all. There should, of course, be concern about containing health costs, but this can be done effectively with a state-run system. Modern societies need systems of socialized medicine, something that obtains in almost all civilized modernizing societies. The United States and South Africa are, I believe, the only exceptions. But, as is evident from my own country (Canada), socialized health care systems often need altering, and their costs need monitoring. As a cost-cutting and as an efficiency measure that would at the same time improve health care, doctors, like university professors and government bureaucrats, should be put on salaries and they should work in medical units. They should, I hasten to add, have good salaries but salaries all the same; the last vestiges of petty entrepreneurship should be taken from the medical profession. This measure would save the state-run health care system a considerable amount of money, would improve the quality of medical care with greater cooperation and consultation resulting from economies of scale and a more extensive division of labor with larger and better equipped medical units. (There would also be less duplication of equipment.) The overall quality of care would also improve with a better balance between health care in the country and in the large cities, with doctors being systematically and rationally deployed throughout the society. In such a system doctors, no more than university professors or state bureaucrats, could not just set up a practice anywhere. They would no more be free to do this than university professors or state bureaucrats. In the altered system there would be no cultural space for it. Placing doctors on salary, though not at a piece work rate, would also result in its being the case that the financial need to see as many patients as possible as quickly as possible would be removed. This would plainly enhance the quality of medical care. It would also be the case that a different sort of person would go into the medical profession. People would go into it more frequently because they were actually interested in medicine and less frequently because this is a rather good way (though hardly the best way) of building a stock portfolio.

There should also be a rethinking of the respective roles of nurses (in all their variety), paramedics and doctors. Much more of the routine work done in medicine—taking the trout fly out of my ear for example—can be done by nurses or paramedics. Doctors, with their more extensive training, could be freed up for other more demanding tasks worthy of their expertise. This would require somewhat different training for all of these different medical personnel and a rethinking of the authority structure in the health care system. But doing this in a reasonable way would improve the teamwork in hospitals, make morale all around a lot better, improve medical treatment and save a very considerable amount of money. (It is no secret that the relations between doctors and nurses are not good.) Finally, a far greater emphasis should be placed on preventative medicine than is done now. This, if really extensively done, utilizing the considerable educational and fiscal powers of the state, would result in very considerable health care savings and a very much healthier and perhaps even happier population. (Whether with the states we actually have we are likely to get anything like that is—to understate it—questionable. I wouldn't hold my breath in the United States. Still, Finland and Sweden are very different places from the United States and South Africa.)

It is moves of this *general* sort that an egalitarian and autonomy loving society under conditions of moderate scarcity should implement. (I say 'general sort' for I am more likely to be wrong about some of the specifics than about the general thrust of my argument.) It would, if in place, limit the freedom of some people, including some doctors and some patients, to do what they want to do. That is obvious enough. But any society, any society at all, as long as it had norms (legal and otherwise) will limit freedom in some way.[3] There is no living in society without some limitation on the freedom to do some things. Indeed a society without norms and thus without any limitation on freedom is a contradiction in terms. Such a mass of people wouldn't be a society. They, without norms, would just be a mass of people. (If these are 'grammatical remarks,' make the most of them.) In our societies I am not free to go for a spin in your car without your permission, to practice law or medicine without a license, to marry your wife while she is still your wife and the like. Many restrictions on our liberties, because they are so common, so widely accepted and thought by most of us to be so reasonable, hardly *seem* like restrictions on our liberty. But they are all the same. No doubt some members of the medical profession would feel quite reined in if the measures I propose were adopted. (These measures are not part of conventional wisdom.) But the restrictions on the freedom of the medical profession and on patients I am proposing would make for both a greater liberty all around, everything considered, and, as well, for greater well-being in the society. Sometimes we have to restrict certain liberties in order to enhance the overall system of liberty. Not speaking out of turn in parliamentary debate is a familiar example. Many people who now have a rather limited access to medical treatment would come to have it and have it in a more adequate way with such a socialized system in place. Often we have to choose between a greater or lesser liberty in a society, and, at least under conditions of abundance, the answer almost always should be 'Choose the greater liberty.' If we really prize human autonomy, if, that is, we want a world in which as many people as possible have as full as is possible control over their own lives, then we will be egalitarians. Our very egalitarianism will commit us to something like the health care system I described, but so will the realization that, without reasonable health on the part of the population, autonomy can hardly flourish or be very extensive. Without the kind of equitability and increased coverage in health care that goes with a properly administered socialized medicine, the number of healthy people will be far less than could otherwise feasibly be the case. With that being the case, autonomy and well-being as well will be neither as extensive nor so thorough as it could otherwise be. Autonomy, like everything else, has its material conditions. And to will the end is to will the necessary means to the end.

To take—to sum up—what since the Enlightenment has come to be seen as the moral point of view, and to take morality seriously, is to take it as axiomatic that each person's good be given equal consideration.[4] I have argued that (a) where that is accepted, and (b) where we are tolerably clear about the facts (including facts about human needs), and (c) where we live under conditions of moderate abundance, a health care system bearing at least a family resemblance to the one I have gestured at will be put in place. It is a health care system befitting an autonomy respecting democracy committed to the democratic and egalitarian belief that the life of everyone matters and matters equally.

Notes

1. Will Kymlicka, "Rawls on Teleology and Deontology," *Philosophy and Public Affairs* 17:3 (Summer 1988), p. 190.
2. *Ibid.*
3. Ralf Dahrendorf, *Essays in the Theory of Society* (Stanford, California: Stanford University Press, 1968), pp. 151–78 and G. A. Cohen, "The Structure of Proletarian Unfreedom," *Philosophy and Public Affairs* 12 (1983), pp. 2–33.
4. Will Kymlicka, *op cit.*, p. 190.

10.1e   Responding to Nielsen

Nielsen offers an attractive portrait of an egalitarian health care system, backed up by some interesting claims. His insistence that a decent society has an obligation to consider the needs of its members regardless of their importance or their ability to pay supports some of the remarks made above [in sections c(i) and c(ii)]; and his argument that we must, if we are to take morality seriously, be clear that each person matters, and matters equally, is very persuasive.

But there are features of Nielsen's account that an opponent might well take issue with. For instance, Nielsen appears to pay very little attention to the fact that health care is a *scarce* resource. He speaks as if there were no real problem in meeting everyone's needs—as if a condition of "moderate abundance" were sufficient to meet every legitimate claim for health care. But if this were true, it would be surprising that there had been so much debate about how health care should, in practice, be distributed. In reality, the expense of providing good or state-of-the-art health care to everyone who needed it would be prohibitive, and it is this fact that explains much of the reluctance—felt even in "decent" societies—to move to a fully egalitarian, socialized system of health care. (Indeed, in the time since Nielsen wrote this article, the Swedish system, which he greatly admires, has moved close to financial collapse.) An opponent might make quite a lot of this point. How much health care would it be realistic (in other words, affordable) to make available to everyone? Presumably only a limited amount—the limit being determined by how "moderate" a society's abundance is. This means that certain kinds of expensive health care might have to be withdrawn altogether. But as soon as one starts placing limits on the kinds of care available, one finds oneself in an uncomfortable position. For placing such limits will mean that some people will not receive the (expensive) treatment they need, even though the expertise and the technology to provide that treatment are, in principle, available. This, an opponent might urge, surely goes against the principle of beneficence as well as the principle of respect for autonomy. Further, under Nielson's proposed system it is unclear whether the motivation would exist for research into *improved* forms of treatment, since new treatments, especially if they are sophisticated, tend to be more expensive than the inferior treatments they were designed to replace. Again, the essential beneficence of Nielsen's ideas is called into question.

Or an opponent might focus instead on what Nielsen has to say about freedom. He claims that the overall amount of freedom enjoyed by the members of a society would be increased under his system. One can see that a society in which everyone has access to *some* health care will be freer, in the sense that its members will have more options, than a society in which many or most people have no access to health care at all. But this isn't to say much (after all, would the libertarian disagree?). Specifically, this argument doesn't appear to justify reducing the freedoms of particular individuals that Nielsen recommends. He is quite clear that on his model "no two- or three-tier system should be allowed to obtain"—in other words, he is clear that doctors and patients should not be permitted to enter into private, commercial arrangements for the provision of health care above and beyond what is available to everyone. These freedoms would disappear. But what is the justification for this?

According to Nielsen, the justification is simply that everyone living in a society under the rule of law accepts that their freedoms must be limited in certain ways; the present suggestion merely proposes one further limit to be placed on those freedoms. But an opponent of Nielsen's might object to this move. After all, our freedoms are usually limited only in order to protect the freedoms of others. We are not free to go around mugging one another because mugging people reduces their freedom to go about their business unmolested. But what freedom (whose freedom?) is protected by preventing people from improving the level of health care they receive if they wish to do so and can afford its costs? No one else would receive any *less* health care as a result. Indeed the only effect on health care that Nielsen's proposals seem likely to have would be to deprive certain people of access to the expensive and unusual forms of treatment that they need, are prepared to pay for, and that no one would be hurt by letting them have. In short, Nielsen's proposed system threatens to reduce people's autonomy without thereby protecting the autonomy of anybody else, and to do so in defiance of the principle of beneficence. Or so an opponent might argue.

If these criticisms are correct, then Nielsen needs to think again about his position, for his remaining arguments do not really support the kind of egalitarian system of health care allocation that he envisages. Rather, since his case against a two-tier system seems to be weak, what's left tends to support the watered-down variety of libertarianism mentioned at the end of 10.1c(ii): The health care needs of everyone ought to be met within certain limits (set by scarcity); those who wish to supplement their health care by paying for more should be free to do so. If Nielsen, or any egalitarian, wants to avoid this conclusion, then more arguments are needed: specifically, arguments showing that the restrictions on autonomy required by the egalitarian model are justified, and that the apparent costs of these restrictions in terms of beneficence are worth paying. The need for arguments of this kind highlights difficulties that many believe are unavoidable in the egalitarian position—difficulties that are often thought to prevent egalitarianism from being obviously or automatically preferable to utilitarianism or libertarianism. Again, we seem to have an approach that is less than ideal.

10.1f   Recap: Fair Shares

We have now looked at the three main approaches to the just allocation of health care. These might be summarized in the following slogans: Health care should be allocated according to happiness-maximizing potential (the utilitarian approach); health care should be allocated according to ability to pay (the libertarian approach); health care should be allocated according to need (the egalitarian approach). None of them, as we have seen, is without its problems. In attempting to identify the criteria by which certain people should be given preference over others in the competition for scarce resources, both the utilitarian and the libertarian approaches tend to promote a certain ruthlessness towards the less fortunate members of society—a tendency that many feel is the exact reverse of what it should be, given that these approaches are offered as *moral* solutions to a moral problem. This shortcoming is avoided by the egalitarian approach. But only at a price: The egalitarian seems to be committed to limiting the amount and the kinds of health care that people are allowed to have, so that the level of care made available is in fact lower than what is, from the point of view of technology and expertise, possible. Like the utilitarian and the libertarian, then, the egalitarian approach resolves the problem of allocating scarce resources only at the cost of raising as many ethical difficulties as it settles.

Is there no viable solution to the problem? My own hunch, for what it's worth, is that there isn't, if the solution we're after is to be an utterly consistent and principled one. My reason for saying this lies in the scarcity of the resource under consideration. If health care were an unlimited resource, I imagine that most of us would decide that the egalitarian approach matched our ethical intuitions best. But given the ever-increasing expense and sophistication of health care it seems unlikely, for the reasons suggested above, that the egalitarian approach would ever be sustainable or desirable in practice. The very complexity of the problem—and the constantly evolving nature of health care itself—both militate against clear-cut, principled solutions. It may be that the best we can do is to try to achieve a balance between the various concerns competing for our allegiance. If this is right, then the best solution is likely to be a rather messy, hybrid affair. For instance, it might lie in the kind of compromise between egalitarianism and libertarianism mentioned earlier (although if it does, I'd personally want the emphasis to be laid more squarely on the egalitarian side of the equation than it is, for example, within the system now operating in the United States).

The challenge posed by the complexities of allocation, and by the complexities of the scarce resource to be allocated, demand exceptional flexibility and intelligence from us. This highlights the difficulty of the ethical issues involved. If, as I suspect, the solution turns out to be a messy one, this doesn't lessen the need for scrupulous ethical reasoning. On the contrary: It is precisely when things get messy that our ethical reasoning needs to be at its most acute. The approaches surveyed here should, I believe, help us identify and avoid some of the pitfalls inherent in thinking about this topic. I hope that the principles invoked, and the arguments considered, will suggest some appropriate strategies for approaching the topic in the flexible and intelligent spirit it requires. It seems unlikely to me that any simple and straightforward reflection on the principle of justice will be sufficient to settle the matter.

10.2   ORGAN PROCUREMENT AND TRANSPLANTATION

We turn now to the ethical issues surrounding organ procurement and transplantation. Organs, such as hearts and kidneys, are clearly scarce resources: The demand for transplantable organs far outstrips the supply of them. So again we find ourselves faced with questions about allocation. But since the issues involved are much the same as those arising from the problem of allocating health care itself, I won't say anything more about them here. The material covered in the first part of this chapter should be sufficient to indicate the pitfalls to look out for and the useful strategies to adopt. Of course, some of the issues specific to procuring and transplanting bodily organs only arise because organs are a scarce resource. For instance, if organs were not scarce it is hard to imagine that anyone would be in the business of executing prisoners and selling off their body parts, as the Chinese are said to have done. But here we will take the scarcity of organs for granted, and concentrate on the kinds of question that are raised when any organ is procured from a donor and transplanted into a recipient. What qualities ought the donor to have? What qualities ought the recipient to have? Is it ever right to sell organs, or to "farm" them? These are the issues that will concern us here.

10.2a   The Donor

Until or unless we are able to manufacture fully functional mechanical or biological organs, every transplant will always require that someone (or some animal, but here I will concentrate on people) donates the organ in question. The organ is transferred from one human being to another. Until comparatively recently, this donation has been achieved in one of two ways: Either the organ is taken from a person who has very recently died (for questions about what counts as death, see 7.1); or, if the body-part is not 100 percent necessary for survival (such as one of a healthy person's two kidneys) or can be regenerated (such as a healthy person's bone marrow), it may be taken from the body of a living person. Nowadays it is also technically possible to "farm" organs, usually from the bodies of fetuses and damaged infants who are artificially kept alive for the purpose, but this is a matter we will discuss in 10.2e, below. For the moment, let's assume that the donor is not functioning as an organ farm.

What ethical problems are posed by organ donation? Let's look at dead donors first. One very down-to-earth response might be that dead donors pose no ethical problems at all. After all, it might be said, if someone's dead then none of his or her body parts can be of the slightest importance to him or her any longer, and if someone living requires those body parts in order to survive, or in order to lead a better life, both the principle of beneficence and the principle of respect for autonomy demand that those parts be transplanted (the living person benefits, the dead person is beyond harm, and only the living person has any autonomy to respect). Transplanting organs from dead donors, it might be claimed, is always and obviously justifiable. Is there anything to be said against this apparently very sensible position?

Perhaps there is. Imagine that some of my friends and I run a charity, and we decide that it would be an excellent fundraising stunt to take the organs from dead people and use them as targets in a shooting contest. Imagine that we're right and that we raise a great deal of money for a good cause. Surely, by analogy with the down-to-earth position outlined above, this stunt would pose no ethical problems: After all, the living will benefit, while the dead are beyond harm; and only the living have any autonomy to respect. But even more surely, most of us will want to reply, there must be at least *some* ethical question raised by this scheme. For one thing, it's in appalling taste. But more to the point, and underlying the question of taste, there seems to be something disrespectful—even sacrilegious—about using bits and pieces of dead people for target practice. What lies behind this intuition (which I suppose—hope!—that most of us would share)?

The answer is difficult to spell our properly. After all, it *is* true that the dead are beyond harm and that only the living have any autonomy to respect. But what I think we need to look at is the kind of relation that a person stands in to his or her body. There's something slightly misleading about the way we talk about our bodies: We talk of *my* kidney, *your* heart, *her* liver, and so on. This suggests that the relation we stand in to our bodies and body parts is rather like the relation we stand in to our material possessions—as when we mention *my* baseball bat, *your* video recorder, *her* back yard. But surely the two relations aren't the same at all. *My* body just *is* me: There isn't any me that stands apart from my body and somehow owns it (in the way that there is a me that stands apart from my baseball bat, and owns that). If my body goes out of existence, then *I* go out of existence; whereas if all of my possessions go out of existence, *I* am still left. What this shows is that it is a mistake to be kidded by our use of possessive language to refer to our body parts (*my* kidney, *your* heart, etc.) into thinking that our body parts are, literally, our possessions. Because they are not our possessions—they are *us*.

How does this relate to the matter at hand? Quite directly: The down-to-earth position we have been talking about—which holds that there just isn't any problem with plundering corpses for body parts—clearly gains whatever plausibility it has from the mistake of thinking that body parts are like possessions. If body parts *were* like possessions, then of course it would be true that the dead had no use for them any more, and that they might as well be used by the living to secure whatever benefits can be obtained from them—just as my nephew might as well gain whatever pleasure he can from the possession of my baseball bat if I die. But given that body parts are not like possessions, the questions raised by taking them from dead people are more complex than that. For if you die, then your dead body isn't simply some kind of possession that you've no further use for: it *is*, still, you—the dead you. If your dead body is then buried, *you* are buried. And if your dead body is recycled for use in transplantation (or for use in a shooting contest), it is *you* who is recycled and made use of. Of course, this doesn't show that it is wrong to take organs from dead people. But it does show that the matter is not nearly as simple as the down-to-earth position assumes. You might put it like this: By treating the body parts of dead people as possessions that they have no further use for, we misrepresent to ourselves the kind of thing that a person really is. We misrepresent the living as well as the dead, ourselves as well as our ancestors. It takes no great leap of the imagination to see that getting people wrong is a big step along the way towards getting our ethics wrong. If we don't understand what we're dealing with (people), our ethical judgements about how people should be dealt with will quickly come unstuck, possibly in some quite nasty ways. This is why it is important to pay heed to our intuition that there just *is* something vile about the idea of using dead people's organs as targets in a shooting contest, and, similarly, why it is important to resist the down-to-earth position on the transplantation of dead people's organs.

So there are reasons to think that we owe it to ourselves and to our conception of ourselves—the living—to treat the dead with respect, even though the dead are, literally, beyond harm. But of course treating the dead with respect doesn't necessarily mean that we ought never to transplant their organs into the living. Indeed, I can't think of any plausible argument to show that transplanting dead people's organs would *always* be wrong. But it does mean that if we do use dead people as organ donors, we are obliged to do so in a respectful way. This obligation explains why most people would think it questionable to take organs from a dead person without either some advance directive from that person (expressed, for example, by the fact that he or she carries an organ-donor card) or at least the permission of the dead person's loved ones. By requiring that permission be granted, we acknowledge the kind of value that a person has, whether living or dead. In many ways the issues here are similar to those that arise when euthanasia is in question (see 7.2b and 7.2g), although with the difference that the stakes for the potential organ donor are a lot lower than they are for the potential subject of euthanasia. This explains why we need more elaborate safeguards surrounding the use of living wills than we need in the context of organ-donor cards. The dead, after all, are already dead.

What about living donors? What ethical problems are posed by transplanting an organ from a healthy living person into a sick person? The first thing to say is that the organ must be something that the healthy person can do tolerably well without. It would be almost impossible to justify a procedure that meant that the healthy person was going to die—for instance, by having his or her heart transplanted into someone else. For one thing, such a procedure amounts to deliberately killing the healthy person, without this being done (as it might sometimes be done in cases of euthanasia) in that person's own best interests. We surely have an obligation not to do this. Such a procedure doesn't even add up from a utilitarian point of view: The healthy donor is certain to die, while the sick recipient is far from certain to survive. So it seems clear that transplanting essential organs from healthy donors is, ethically speaking, out of the question—and this conclusion looks safe even if the healthy donor happens to be perfectly willing to go through with the process.

So the organ in question must be one that the healthy donor can do tolerably well without, either because the organ is "spare" (a person can function with only one kidney) or else because, like bone marrow, it can be regenerated. Even in these cases, however, it is obvious that the procedure cannot be undertaken without some risk, suffering, and inconvenience to the donor. Indeed, the question arises whether a person could ever have a *duty* to become a living organ donor, given the risks and unpleasantness involved. In some cases, the answer might appear to be an obvious Yes. If, for instance, my son needs one of my kidneys and I can do without it, it would surely be monstrous for me to refuse it to him. But in other cases, where close family members or loved ones are not involved, the answer might be thought to be an equally obvious No. It may be praiseworthy, admirable, and noble for someone to make that decision, but they can never be required to make it. Indeed, it will be suggested, to become a living organ donor is to act above and beyond the call of duty—a classic example of supererogation. Why might someone argue in this way? One answer can perhaps be found in the considerations given a moment ago about our bodies and possessions. A possession is something that a person might justifiably be required to give up—as, for example, when he or she has pledged it against a debt that he or she cannot repay. But a body part is not properly to be thought of as a possession; when one gives up a body part for transplant one is giving up, not a possession, but a part of *oneself.* This, it might be suggested, is something that one could never be required to do, however heroic or saintly it might be of one to decide to do so voluntarily. Perhaps these reflections help explain why the gift of, for example, a kidney is felt to have a different kind of value from the value of the gift of any material possession. By giving someone one of your kidneys, you are investing your very self in that person's future. You are not merely transferring ownership of the kidney to somebody else.

Whether or not this is right, though, it is at least clear that a living, fully autonomous organ donor must consent to the procedure in question (the matter of nonautonomous living donors will be addressed in 10.2d, below). And once this is recognized, it becomes apparent that the issues involved are exactly the same as those that arise when a person's consent is required for any medical (or experimental) procedure. For discussion of these issues, see 5.2 and 8.1.

10.2b   The Recipient

Very little needs to be said about the recipient of a transplanted organ. Except perhaps in terms of the gratitude due to the donor, receiving an organ from a donor is no different in kind from receiving any other kind of implant, such as a pacemaker; the questions that arise are exactly the same as those attendant upon any and every other clinical procedure (see 5.2). Admittedly not all recipients of transplants have viewed the matter in this light. There is a famous story about a high-ranking officer who was severely wounded during a battle. Field surgeons replaced several yards of his intestine with intestine taken from the body of a soldier killed in the same action. When he found out about this, the officer was quite put out. "Good heavens, sir!" he is said to have exclaimed. "You've lumbered me with the bowels of a sergeant!"

I suppose it might be mentioned in the officer's defense that the situation was not one in which best clinical practice was likely to have been followed; for instance, it seems improbable that the field surgeons bothered to obtain anyone's consent. And I suppose, stretching it a bit, the officer's remark does suggest that he recognizes that the intestine is indeed a part of the sergeant, and not merely some possession formerly owned by the sergeant and now owned by himself. But I don't think we can do better for him than that. It is difficult, after all, to see how one might justify the response of a recipient who is simply prejudiced against the class to which, as it happens, the donor of the transplanted organ belongs. Rather than sympathize, we should probably tell him to think himself lucky to get any bowels at all.

10.2c   Organs for Sale

Recent years have seen a spate of cases in which organs have changed hands for money. Impoverished people in Central and South America and in the Middle East are said to have agreed to sell their organs (usually a kidney) to middlemen, in order that these might then be used for transplants. It is said that the Chinese authorities have sold body parts (usually corneal tissue) from people they have executed. These cases arouse strong feelings. They also raise the question whether it is *ever* appropriate that organs should be treated as commodities, to be bought and sold on the market.

It is easy to imagine how a utilitarian might defend the buying and selling of body parts. Take the case of a person who has been executed. This person's corneal tissue is no longer valuable in promoting his or her happiness. But it could be valuable in promoting someone else's happiness. If that someone else is prepared to pay for corneal tissue (a scarce resource, remember), then no one's happiness will be served by refusing to accept the money. On the contrary, since the recipient of corneal tissue will benefit from receiving it, and since the vendor of corneal tissue will benefit from supplying it, the greatest happiness principle demands that the sale should go ahead. Simple. The case is even simpler when one is talking about a poor person from a developing country agreeing to sell a kidney for transplant. The recipient will benefit in all the obvious ways, and the donor will receive a larger sum of money than he or she could possibly hope to raise by any other means (at the cost, if all goes well, of no more than a certain amount of discomfort and inconvenience). Surely, the utilitarian will argue, the pursuit of the greatest happiness for the greatest number of people requires that transactions of this sort be permitted, and even encouraged. It would be *wrong* to prohibit people from buying and selling organs. Indeed, in the case of the poor person, the utilitarian might go further, and appeal to the principle of respect for autonomy. Who are we, after all, to tell people what they may or may not do with their own bodies?

The utilitarian's case here looks quite strong—you don't even need to be utilitarian to recognize the force of the point about autonomy. For there *is* something rather questionable about the spectacle of comparatively wealthy people (like us) sitting around condemning the desperately poor for taking whatever measures are available to improve their lot, especially when those measures appear to involve harming no one but themselves. Indeed, it might be argued that such condemnation is entirely hypocritical unless it is complemented by a willingness to give material assistance to the desperately poor so that they no longer need to be tempted into such measures. These are powerful considerations, and the last point, I think, shows that this is an ethical problem that cannot be tackled in isolation. If one wishes to argue that poor people are morally wrong to sell their body parts, it seems that one must also be prepared to help such people attain a condition in which they will no longer find it expedient to do so. (This isn't like bribing people not to commit robbery, by the way: Robberies violate the rights of the robbed, and are wrong on that account. But it's not clear that selling one's left kidney violates anyone's right—even one's own. In fact, it's not clear that it's even possible to violate one's own rights.)

So the question can't be tackled in isolation. But how, bearing this in mind, might someone argue *against* the buying and selling of organs? The best approach, it seems to me, lies in the points raised in 10.2a, above. Possessions can be bought and sold: Indeed, they are exactly what is normally bought and sold. Yet body parts, I have suggested, are not properly to be seen as possessions. This is equivalent to saying that body parts are not properly to be seen as commodities. But "not properly"—what does that mean? The thought here is that conceiving of body parts in this way involves and encourages a false picture of the human person. It encourages a way of thinking of people as standing somehow apart from their own bodies—when, in fact, a person's body, for instance yours, just *is* you. This matters for the following reason: If we get into the bad habit of thinking of people as

being something different from their bodies, we will find it easy to begin mistreating people's bodies while claiming, at the same time, that we are not
mistreating *people*. Fairly obviously, to take an extreme example, a line of
thought like this could be used to defend torture (after all, it's only bodies
you're torturing, not people). It seems important, then, to resist this false
picture of the relation between people and their bodies. If this is right, then it
must also be important not to allow ourselves to begin thinking of body parts
as commodities. It is wrong to buy and sell body parts, this argument concludes, because doing so involves and encourages false and potentially dangerous conceptions of the human person.

I think this argument does help explain why many people believe that
there is something indecent about trading in human organs. The idea of an
organ supermarket would be distasteful to most of us.

But of course this does not by itself justify the outright condemnation of
those who part with their organs for cash. As mentioned earlier, there are
important questions of autonomy here; it does seem oversimplistic to ignore
the perhaps compelling reasons that certain people, particularly very poor
people, might have for exercising their autonomy in ways that disturb us.
There may be a sense in which an ideal world would not include sales of
human body parts. But this is not such a world. It may simply be that in the
real world we have to work out a tradeoff between competing, but equally
legitimate concerns. If so, then working out how that tradeoff should go will
require a great deal of tact and ethical good sense from us. I hope that this
section has indicated some of the factors that will need to be considered.

10.2d   Organ Farming

So-called organ farming occurs whenever an individual is kept alive, or
is conceived, solely for the purpose of becoming an organ donor. The individual might be an anencephalic newborn, for instance, being kept alive so
that his or her organs may be transplanted into other, less gravely defective,
newborns. Or the individual might be an embryo or fetus from which tissues
are to be obtained.

Let's begin by considering the first kind of case, where an individual who
has already been born is being artificially sustained so as to become an organ
donor. Clearly such an individual need not be an infant: Gravely ill adults,
too, can be kept alive for the sake of their organs. Is there anything the matter with this? Is there any reason to be disturbed by the idea of using people
in this way? I think it's clear that any opponent of euthanasia will find the
idea highly objectionable, for the upshot of these procedures is the deliberate
termination of the life of the donor. But suppose, for the sake of argument,
that one believes that euthanasia is sometimes justifiable. And suppose that
the individuals at the center of the present issue are individuals who might
justifiably be subject to euthanasia. Does farming organs from these people
pose any problems? Let's assume that nothing in the procedure causes the
individuals in question to suffer. Otherwise organ farming would clearly be
problematic: It would be very hard to justify inflicting pain on one person for
the benefit of another. But if no suffering is caused, it is unclear where any

special problems might be thought to lie. After all, the difference between cases of this sort and cases involving recently dead donors seem rather slight; it is tempting to conclude that, given respectful treatment of the sort appropriate to recently dead donors (see 10.2a), there is nothing wrong with sustaining hopelessly ill people for the sake of their organs.

A critic of this view might argue that the interests of the donor have not yet been given enough consideration. For there *is* an important difference between a recently dead donor and a potential donor whose life is being artificially sustained—and that is that the potential donor is still living, and so has interests in a sense that the recently dead donor has not. These interests, the critic might say, have been ignored. After all, how is it in the interests of the potential donor to be kept alive, without prospect of recovery, until a transplant is carried out? Or, to put it another way, how is it in the donor's interests to have the timing of his or her death settled at the convenience of the recipient? Surely the time at which a person beyond hope of recovery ought to die should be decided—if it is to be decided at all—only by reference to that person's own best interests (see 7.2). This point seems reasonable. But a plausible reply might be to ask whether the precise timing really does make any difference to the interests of the donor. If a person is, for example, anencephalic, or in a persistent vegetative state, it is hard to see how his or her interests are—or could be—affected one way or the other. So perhaps the earlier conclusion is slightly the more persuasive: Perhaps organ farming in cases of the kind we have been considering should be thought of in essentially the same way as cases in which the donor is recently dead. There is room for several views here, and we shouldn't forget the view of the opponent of euthanasia, either, for whom any clinical procedure that results in the deliberate causing of a death is unacceptable.

We turn now to cases involving embryos and fetuses, some of which may have been deliberately conceived in order to gain a supply of tissues or other body parts. Given that obtaining tissues or body parts from them will certainly result in the death of those embryos or fetuses, it seems clear that any opponent of abortion will also be opposed to farming organs from the unborn. But again, let us suppose for the sake of argument that one believes that abortion *is* sometimes justifiable. The question now is whether there is any substantive difference between abortion and farming organs from the unborn. Clearly we need to tread carefully here. For example, a person who believes that abortion is unacceptable except in cases of rape is unlikely to countenance organ farming in cases other than those arising from rape; similarly, a person who defends abortion only in cases where the mother's life is at risk is unlikely to relax his or her restrictions when it comes to organ farming.

So perhaps we need to look at this question from the perspective of people who believe that abortion should be available on demand, and ask whether they might then have any reasons to believe anything different about organ farming. On the whole, it would seem that they will probably not believe anything different. After all, if the person in question is a hardliner, who believes that abortion is fine because the unborn have absolutely no value, then it's pretty clear that the valuelessness of the unborn will, for this person, also justify organ farming. In the same way, if the person is rather more moderate, and believes that abortion is fine because the interests of the already born always outweigh the interests of the unborn, then again the conclusion that organ farming is acceptable will follow because the tissues or body parts of the unborn are being farmed for the benefit of the already born. In other words, it seems that one's beliefs about the ethics of most kinds of organ farming (from the unborn) will be determined by one's beliefs about the ethics of abortion (see 6.2).

There may be an exception, however. Take the kind of case in which an embryo or fetus has been deliberately conceived in order to farm tissues from it. Something new comes into the equation here. After all, it seems safe to say that embryos and fetuses are never deliberately conceived for the purposes of aborting them later, and it is this question of intention that may put a different complexion on the problem. Many would hold that there is a real distinction between conceiving an embryo or fetus with the intention of killing it later, and conceiving one with no such intention, or indeed any intention at all (even though, as a matter of fact, the pregnancy may, subsequently, be terminated). I don't suppose that this sort of distinction would trouble the hard-liner much: From that point of view, the unborn have no value whatsoever, so it hardly matters whether or not conception was undertaken for the purposes of organ farming. But the more moderate supporter of abortion, together with everyone else, may well take a different view. The more moderate line, remember, holds that the interests of the unborn are always outweighed by the interests of the already born. Thus the unborn, according to this point of view, do have interests—even if not very important ones. And this, of course, is to assign *some* value to the unborn. Hence the problem: is it acceptable deliberately to create something of value with the intention of destroying it later? An opponent of abortion will obviously answer that it isn't. And the moderate supporter of abortion may well agree. From this perspective, after all, although abortion is justifiable (because the interests of the already born take precedence over those of the unborn), it is nonetheless regrettable (because the unborn do have interests, which are overridden).

In the best of all possible worlds, then, the interests of the already born and the unborn would coincide, there would be no abortions, and there would be nothing to regret. The organ farming case, however, deliberately brings about the situation in which there is something to regret (the death of the embryo or fetus). Therefore the moderate supporter of abortion might conclude that it is wrong to conceive embryos or fetuses with the intention of killing them later. In other words, he or she might conclude that premeditated organ farming (as it were) is unacceptable. And I take it that only the hard-liner would think this conclusion obviously mistaken.

10.2e   Recap: You Stole My Heart Away

We have now surveyed a number of the most important issues surrounding the procurement and transplantation of organs. Not surprisingly, many of these issues overlap with those arising in the context of euthanasia and abortion, and issues of informed consent also figure large, again as one would expect. Perhaps the most important new issues are those concerning the relation between a person and his or her body. These are clearly particularly relevant to the question of organ transplants; but clearly, too, the way we think about persons and their bodies will have consequences for the whole of medical ethics. If we are to think carefully about the ethical issues that the practice of medicine raises, we need also to think carefully about the nature of the individuals upon whom medicine is practiced. This part of the chapter should have given us an idea of some of the misconceptions to be avoided.

10.3   GENE THERAPY AND GENETIC ENGINEERING

One of the areas of great scientific advance in the second half of this century has been the study of genetics. We are discovering ever more about heredity and about the ways in which our genes affect our lives. Indeed, with the progress of the Human Genome Project, we may soon possess a complete map of the smallest details of human genetic make-up. With this knowledge, of course, comes power. We are now able to detect certain abnormalities before they become manifest; we are able to assess the risks of certain conditions being passed on from one generation to the next; we may soon be able to cure certain conditions by altering or eliminating the genes responsible for them; we may even be able, through genetic engineering, to prevent the hereditary transmission of some conditions altogether; and perhaps we will one day be in a position to determine exactly what future generations will be like. If knowledge brings power, then power brings responsibility, and it is clear that these tremendous new possibilities require the utmost in responsible decision-making from us. Some of these possibilities have yet to be realized, of course. But no one doubts that they will be realized one day, and perhaps quite soon, which means that now is the time to start grappling with the ethical dilemmas we can be sure that they will raise. To be forewarned, after all, is to be forearmed.

10.3a   Choosing People

Our knowledge of genetics, together with the development of techniques such as amniocentesis and chorionic villi sampling, allows us to detect the presence of certain genetic diseases—such as Down's syndrome and spina bifida—in the first or second trimester or pregnancy. This, of course, means that there is the possibility of selective abortion. The position one takes on the issue of selective abortion will of course be influenced by the position one takes on abortion as a whole. It is hard to imagine a convinced opponent of abortion making an exception in cases where genetic disease is present; nor is it easy to see why a committed defender of abortion should suddenly decide to draw the line against abortions involving genetically diseased fetuses. But these common-sense observations shouldn't be allowed to obscure the fact that there *is* something different about abortion in the kind of case we are considering here. After all, in ordinary cases of abortion, it is not usually claimed (by either side) that it is in the fetus's own best interests to be aborted. But that claim might well be made in cases of selective abortion. Certain genetic diseases, it might be argued, are so debilitating and awful that it would be a kindness to prevent those afflicted with them from having to live the kind of life that such diseases bring; which means that abortion in these cases would be in the best interests of the fetus (or future person). Perhaps this argument is plausible. But many would not want to go all the way with it. For instance, one might wonder whether it's really true that a life with Down's syndrome or spina bifida is worse than no life at all. Even so, it would be hard not to agree that the incidence of these diseases does indeed lead to a markedly reduced quality of life. And insofar as this is true, there is surely a case for saying that the decision to abort a genetically diseased fetus may be made at least partly in the interests of the fetus itself. (This consideration brings the discussion of selective abortion into close contact with the issue of euthanasia.) The upshot, from the point of view of the abortion debate, is that some lines may, by some people, be redrawn (and redrawn with good reason). For instance, a person who is normally opposed to abortion on the grounds that it accords far too little weight to the interests of the fetus may take a different view when, as in the case of selective abortion, it can plausibly be argued that the fetus's interests really are being taken into account. So examples of this kind do need to be considered separately from other cases of abortion, or proposed abortion.

Before moving on, though, I want to look briefly at something that is quite often argued when selective abortion is discussed. It is common to hear people say: "Well *I* wouldn't want to have been aborted if *I* had Down's syndrome"; or "My cousin has Down's syndrome, and I'm glad *he* wasn't aborted"; or even "People with Down's syndrome don't wish *they'd* been aborted." At first sight, points of this kind do appear to offer quite powerful reasons for resisting selective abortion. But what, really, do they show? The first point, if you look at it, shows nothing at all; indeed it's not clear that it even makes sense. The differences in character and capacities between a person who has Down's syndrome and a person who hasn't are enormous; this makes it highly doubtful whether, as a non-Down's sufferer, you can say anything worthwhile about what your desires would be if you did have Down's syndrome. In saying "*I* wouldn't want to have been aborted if *I* had Down's syndrome," you are not simply reporting what you'd like to happen to you if things were slightly different; you are making a wholly unsupported claim about what your desires would be if you were a completely different kind of person (it's not clear, in other words, that the first "I" refers to the same person as the second "I"). Such a move will be found persuasive only by those who already agree with your conclusion, and don't much mind how it is backed up.

The second point—"My cousin has Down's syndrome, and I'm glad *he* wasn't aborted"—is uncompelling for rather different reasons. There's no problem here about imagining yourself into unimaginable situations. But there is a problem about what the claim is meant to be evidence for. If it's offered as evidence for the fact that you would *now* be unhappy if your cousin were to die or be killed, then fine. After all, you know your cousin, have a relationship with him, and you have reasons to value him as the person he is. But none of that is at issue here. In the case of selective abortion, you lack the relevant knowledge of or relationship with the person in question. Your good reasons for not wanting your cousin (now) to die or be killed are irrelevant to the question of the selective abortion of *other* individuals, whom no one knows, and with whom no one has the kind of relationship that you have with your cousin. This point, then, fails to engage with the issue.

The final point, however, is perhaps stronger. If it is true that people with Down's syndrome don't wish they had been aborted, then this fact would seem to count against the sort of claim, mentioned above, that selective abortion may be in the interests of those aborted. But it still wouldn't show that selective abortion on the grounds of genetic disease was *wrong*. For the fact that a certain measure is not in the interests of those it affects does not by itself show that the measure is unethical. For instance, it is no argument against the morality of taxation to point out that tax-evaders are glad not to be paying taxes. All this shows is that taxation is not always in the tax-payer's own best interests. And in any case—rather like the cousin example—no one is talking about killing anybody who *already* values the life that he or she is living. So this final point, too, is inconclusive.

I do not mean to suggest in this section that there are no good arguments against selective abortion. There are—and they're exactly the arguments that deserve respect in the context of abortion as a whole (see 6.2). But I do want to highlight the inadequacy of some of the arguments that are, very commonly, offered in this context specifically. This issue, it seems to me, is much too important to be left to the kind of emotive and irrelevant consideration we have been discussing.

10.3b   Avoiding People: Purdy's Argument: "Genetic Diseases: Can Having Children Be Immoral?"

There is a second sense in which our knowledge of genetics has allowed us to begin to "choose" people. We are now able to assess the risks that a particular genetic disease will be inherited by the offspring of a given pair of parents. Hence it is now possible for parents to decide not to have children because of those risks. This at once once raises a question: Is it ever wrong for parents to decide to go ahead and have children *despite* the risks? L.M. Purdy, associate professor of philosophy at Wells College, discusses this question in the context of the genetic disease Huntington's Chorea.

GENETIC DISEASES: CAN HAVING CHILDREN BE IMMORAL?
L.M. Purdy

I INTRODUCTION

Suppose you know that there is a fifty percent chance you have Huntington's chorea, even though you are still free of symptoms, and that if you do have it, each of your children has a fifty percent chance of having it also.

Should you now have children?

There is always some possibility that a pregnancy will result in a diseased or handicapped child. But certain persons run a higher than average risk of producing such a child. Genetic counselors are increasingly able to calculate the probability that certain problems will occur; this means that more people can find out whether they are in danger of creating unhealthy offspring *before* the birth of a child.

Since this kind of knowledge is available, we ought to use it wisely. I want in this paper to defend the thesis that it is wrong to reproduce when we know there is a high risk of transmitting a serious disease or defect. My argument for this claim is in three parts. The first is that we should try to provide every child with a normal opportunity for health; the second is that in the course of doing this it is not wrong to prevent possible children from existing. The third is that this duty may require us to refrain from childbearing.[1]

One methodological point must be made. I am investigating a problem in biomedical ethics: this is a philosophical enterprise. But the conclusion has practical importance since individuals do face the choice I examine. This raises a question: what relation ought the outcome of this inquiry bear to social policy? It may be held that a person's reproductive life should not be interfered with. Perhaps this is a reasonable position, but it does not follow from it that it is never wrong for an individual to have children or that we should not try to determine when this is the case. All that does follow is that we may not coerce persons with regard to childbearing. Evaluation of this last claim is a separate issue which cannot be handled here.

I want to deal with this issue concretely. The reason for this is that, otherwise, discussion is apt to be vague and inconclusive. An additional reason is that it will serve to make us appreciate the magnitude of the difficulties faced by diseased or handicapped individuals. Thus it will be helpful to consider a specific disease. For this purpose I have chosen Huntington's chorea.

II HUNTINGTON'S CHOREA: COURSE AND RISK

Let us now look at Huntington's chorea. First we will consider the course of the disease, then its inheritance pattern.

The symptoms of Huntington's chorea usually begin between the ages of thirty and fifty, but young children can also be affected. It happens this way:

Onset is insidious. Personality changes (obstinacy, moodiness, lack of initiative) frequently antedate or accompany the involuntary choreic movements. These usually appear first in the face, neck, and arms, and are jerky, irregular, and stretching in character. Contractions of the facial muscles result in grimaces; those of the respiratory muscles, lips, and tongue lead to hesitating, explosive speech. Irregular movements of the trunk are present; the gait is shuffling and dancing. Tendon reflexes are increased. . . . Some patients display a fatuous euphoria; others are spiteful, irascible, destructive, and violent. Paranoid reactions are common. Poverty of thought and impairment of attention, memory, and judgment occur. As the disease progresses, walking becomes impossible, swallowing difficult, and dementia profound. Suicide is not uncommon.[2]

The illness lasts about fifteen years, terminating in death.

Who gets Huntington's chorea? It is an autosomal dominant disease; this means it is caused by a single mutant gene located on a non-sex chromosome. It is passed from one generation to the next via affected individuals. When one has the disease, whether one has symptoms and thus knows one has it or not, there is a fifty percent chance that each child will have it also. If one has escaped it then there is no risk to one's children.[3]

How serious is this risk? For geneticists, a ten percent risk is high.[4] But not every high risk is unacceptable: this depends on what is at stake.

There are two separate evaluations in any judgment about a given risk. The first measures the gravity of the worst possible result; the second perceives a given risk as great or small. As for the first, in medicine as elsewhere, people may regard the same result quite differently:

> . . . The subjective attitude to the disease or lesion itself may be quite at variance with what informed medical opinion may regard as a realistic appraisal. Relatively minor limb defects with cosmetic over-tones are examples here. On the other hand, some patients regard with equanimity genetic lesions which are of major medical importance.[5]

For devastating diseases like Huntington's chorea, this part of the judgment should be unproblematic: no one could want a loved one to suffer so.

There may be considerable disagreement, however, about whether a given probability is big or little. Individuals vary a good deal in their attitude toward this aspect of risk.[6] This suggests that it would be difficult to define the "right" attitude to a particular risk in many circumstances. Nevertheless, there are good grounds for arguing in favor of a conservative approach here. For it is reasonable to take special precautions to avoid very bad consequences, even if the risk is small. But the possible consequences here *are* very bad: a child who may inherit Huntington's chorea is a child with a much larger than average chance of being subjected to severe and prolonged suffering. Even if the child does not have the disease, it may anticipate and fear it, and anticipating an evil, as we all know, may be worse than experiencing it. In addition, if a parent loses the gamble, his child will suffer the consequences. But it is one thing to take a high risk for oneself; to submit someone else to it without his consent is another.

I think that these points indicate that the morality of procreation in situations like this demands further study. I propose to do this by looking first at the position of the possible child, then at that of the potential parent.

III REPRODUCTION: THE POSSIBLE CHILD'S POSITION

The first task in treating the problem from the child's point of view is to find a way of referring to possible future offspring without seeming to confer some sort of morally significant existence upon them. I will call children who might be born in the future but who are not now conceived "possible" children, offspring, individuals, or persons. I stipulate that this term implies nothing about their moral standing.

The second task is to decide what claims about children or possible children are relevant to the morality of childbearing in the circumstances being considered. There are, I think, two such claims. One is that we ought to provide every child with at least a normal opportunity for a good life. The other is that we do not harm possible children if we prevent them from existing. Let us consider both these matters in turn.

A   Opportunity for a Good Life

Accepting the claim that we ought to try to provide for every child a normal opportunity for a good life involves two basic problems: justification and practical application.

Justification of the claim could be derived fairly straightforwardly from either utilitarian or contractarian theories of justice, I think, although a proper discussion would be too lengthy to include here. Of prime importance in any such discussion would be the judgment that to neglect this duty would be to create unnecessary unhappiness or unfair disadvantage for some persons.

The attempt to apply the claim that we should try to provide a normal opportunity for a good life leads to a couple of difficulties. One is knowing what it requires of us. Another is defining "normal opportunity." Let us tackle the latter problem first.

Conceptions of "normal opportunity" vary among societies and also within them: *de rigueur* in some circles are private music lessons and trips to Europe, while in others providing eight years of schooling is a major sacrifice. But there is no need to consider this complication since we are here concerned only with health as a prerequisite for normal opportunity. Thus we can retreat to the more limited claim that every parent should try to ensure normal health for his child. It might be thought that even this moderate claim is unsatisfactory since in some places debilitating conditions are the norm. One could circumvent this objection by saying that parents ought to try to provide for their children health normal for that culture, even though it may be inadequate if measured by some outside standard. This conservative position would still justify efforts to avoid the birth of children at risk for Huntington's chorea and other serious genetic diseases.

But then what does this stand require of us: is sacrifice entailed by the duty to try to provide normal health for our children? The most plausible answer seems to be that as the danger of serious disability increases, the greater the sacrifice demanded of the potential parent. This means it would be more justifiable to recommend that an individual refrain from childbearing if he risks passing on spina bifida than if he risks passing on webbed feet. Working out all the details of such a schema would clearly be a difficult matter; I do not think it would be impossible to set up workable guidelines, though.

Assuming a rough theoretical framework of this sort, the next question we must ask is whether Huntington's chorea substantially impairs an individual's opportunity for a good life.

People appear to have different opinions about the plight of such persons. Optimists argue that a child born into a family afflicted with Huntington's chorea has a reasonable chance of living a satisfactory life. After all, there is a fifty percent chance it will escape the disease if a parent has already manifested it, and a still greater chance if this is not so. Even if it does have the illness, it will probably enjoy thirty years of healthy life before symptoms appear; and, perhaps, it may not find the disease destructive. Optimists can list diseased or handicapped persons who have lived fruitful lives. They can also find individuals who seem genuinely glad to be alive. One is Rick Donohue, a sufferer from the Joseph family disease: "You know, if my mom hadn't had me, I wouldn't be here for the life I have had. So there is a good possibility I will have children."[7] Optimists therefore conclude that it would be a shame if these persons had not lived.

Pessimists concede these truths, but they take a less sanguine view of them. They think a fifty percent risk of serious disease like Huntington's chorea appallingly high. They suspect that a child born into an afflicted family is liable to spend its youth in dreadful anticipation and fear of the disease. They expect that the disease, if it appears, will be perceived as a tragic and painful end to a blighted life. They point out that Rick Donohue is still young and has not yet experienced the full horror of his sickness.

Empirical research is clearly needed to resolve this dispute: we need much more information about the psychology and life history of sufferers and potential sufferers. Until we have it we cannot know whether the optimist or the pessimist has a better case; definitive judgment must therefore be suspended. In the meantime, however, common sense suggests that the pessimist has the edge.

If some diseased persons do turn out to have a worse than average life there appears to be a case against further childbearing in afflicted families. To support this claim two more judgments are necessary, however. The first is that it is not wrong to refrain from childbearing. The second is that asking individuals to so refrain is less of a sacrifice than might be thought.[8] I will examine each of these judgments.

B   The Morality of Preventing the Birth of Possible Persons

Before going on to look at reasons why it would not be wrong to prevent the birth of possible persons, let me try to clarify the picture a bit. To understand the claim it must be kept in mind that we are considering a prospective situation here, not a retrospective one: we are trying to rank the desirability of various alternative future states of affairs. One possible future state is this: a world where nobody is at risk for Huntington's chorea except as a result of random mutation. This state has been achieved by sons and daughters of persons afflicted with Huntington's chorea ceasing to reproduce. This means that an indeterminate number of children who might have been born were not born. These possible children can be divided into two categories: those who would have been miserable and those who would have lived good lives. To prevent the existence of members of the first category it was necessary to prevent the existence of all. Whether or not this is a good state of affairs depends on the morality of the means and the end. The end, preventing the existence of miserable beings, is surely good; I will argue that preventing the birth of possible persons is not intrinsically wrong. Hence this state of affairs is a morally good one.

Why then is it not in itself wrong to prevent the birth of possible persons? It is not wrong because there seems to be no reason to believe that possible individuals are either deprived or injured if they do not exist. They are not deprived because to be deprived in a morally significant sense one must be able to have experiences. But possible persons do not exist. Since they do not exist, they cannot have experiences. Another way to make this point is to say that each of us might not have been born, although most of us are glad we were. But this does not mean that it makes sense to say that we would have been deprived of something had we not been born. For if we had not been born, we would not exist, and there would be nobody to be deprived of anything. To assert the contrary is to imagine that we are looking at a world in which we do not exist. But this is not the way it would be: there would be nobody to look.

The contention that it is wrong to prevent possible persons from existing because they have a right to exist appears to be equally baseless. The most fundamental objection to this view is that there is no reason to ascribe rights to entities which do not exist. It is one thing to say that as-yet-nonexistent persons will have certain rights if and when they exist: this claim is plausible if made with an eye toward preserving social and environmental goods.[9] But what justification could there be for the claim that nonexistent beings have a right to exist?

Even if one conceded that there was a presumption in favor of letting some nonexistent beings exist, stronger claims could surely override it.[10] For one thing, it would be unfair not to recognize the prior claim of already existing children who are not being properly cared for. One might also argue that it is simply wrong to prevent persons who might have existed from doing so. But this implies that contraception and population control are also wrong.

It is therefore reasonable to maintain that because possible persons have no right to exist, they are not injured if not created. Even if they had that right, it could rather easily be overridden by counterclaims. Hence, since possible persons are neither deprived nor injured if not conceived, it is not wrong to prevent their existence.

C Conclusion of Part III

At the beginning of Part III I said that two claims are relevant to the morality of childbearing in the circumstances being considered. The first is that we ought to provide every child with at least a normal opportunity for a good life. The second is that we do not deprive or injure possible persons if we prevent their existence.

I suggested that the first claim could be derived from currently accepted theories of justice: a healthy body is generally necessary for happiness and it is also a prerequisite for a fair chance at a good life in our competitive world. Thus it is right to try to ensure that each child is healthy.

I argued, with regard to the second claim, that we do not deprive or injure possible persons if we fail to create them. They cannot be deprived of anything because they do not exist and hence cannot have experiences. They cannot be injured because only an entity with a right to exist could be injured if prevented from existing; but there are no good grounds for believing that they are such entities.

From the conjunction of these two claims I conclude that it is right to try to ensure that a child is healthy even if by doing so we preclude the existence of certain possible persons. Thus it is right for individuals to prevent the birth of children at risk for Huntington's chorea by avoiding parenthood. The next question is whether it is seriously wrong *not* to avoid parenthood.

IV REPRODUCTION: THE POTENTIAL PARENT'S SITUATION

I have so far argued that if choreics live substantially worse lives than average, then it is right for afflicted families to cease reproduction. But this conflicts with the generally recognized freedom to procreate and so it does not automatically follow that family members ought not to have children. How can we decide whether the duty to try to provide normal health for one's child should take precedence over the right to reproduce?

This is essentially the same question I asked earlier: how much must one sacrifice to try to ensure that one's offspring is healthy? In answer to this I suggested that the greater the danger of serious disability, the more justifiable considerable sacrifice is.

Now asking someone who wants a child to refrain from procreation seems to be asking for a large sacrifice. It may, in fact, appear to be too large to demand of any one. Yet I think it can be shown that it is not as great as it initially seems.

Why do people want children? There are probably many reasons, but I suspect that the following include some of the most common. One set of reasons has to do with the gratification to be derived from a happy family life—love, companionship, watching a child grow, helping mold it into a good person, sharing its pains and triumphs. Another set of reasons centers about the parents as individuals—validation of their place within a genetically continuous family line, the conception of children as a source of immortality, being surrounded by replicas of themselves.

Are there alternative ways of satisfying these desires? Adoption or technological means provide ways to satisfy most of the desires pertaining to family life without passing on specific genetic defects. Artificial insemination by donor is already available; implantation of donor ova is likely within a few years. Still another option will exist if cloning becomes a reality. In the meantime, we might permit women to conceive and bear babies for those who do not want to do so themselves.[11] But the desire to extend the genetic line, the desire for immortality, and the desire for children that physically resemble one cannot be met by these methods.

Many individuals probably feel these latter desires strongly. This creates a genuine conflict for persons at risk for transmitting serious genetic diseases like Huntington's chorea. The situation seems especially unfair because, unlike normal people, through no fault of their own, doing something they badly want to do may greatly harm others.

But if my common sense assumption that they are in grave danger of harming others is true, then it is imperative to scrutinize their options carefully. On the one hand, they can have children: they satisfy their desires but risk eventual crippling illness and death for their offspring. On the other, they can remain childless or seek nonstandard ways of creating a family: they have some unfulfilled desires, but they avoid risking harm to their children.

I think it is clear which of these two alternatives is best. For the desires which must remain unsatisfied if they forgo normal procreation are less than admirable. To see the genetic line continued entails a sinister legacy of illness and death; the desire for immortality cannot really be satisfied by reproduction anyway; and the desire for children that physically resemble one is narcissistic and its fulfillment cannot be guaranteed even by normal reproduction. Hence the only defense of these desires is that people do in fact feel them.

Now, I am inclined to accept William James' dictum regarding desires: "Take any demand, however slight, which any creature, however weak, may make. Ought it not, for its own sole sake be satisfied? If not, prove why not."[12] Thus I judge a world where more desires are satisfied to be better than one in which fewer are. But not all desires should be regarded as legitimate, since, as James suggests, there may be good reasons why these ought to be disregarded. The fact that their fulfillment will seriously harm others is surely such a reason. And I believe that the circumstances I have described are a clear example of the sort of case where a desire must be judged illegitimate, at least until it can be shown that sufferers from serious genetic diseases like Huntington's chorea do not live considerably worse than average lives. Therefore, I think it is wrong for individuals in this predicament to reproduce.

V CONCLUSION

Let me recapitulate. At the beginning of this paper I asked whether it is wrong for those who risk transmitting severe genetic disease like Huntington's chorea to have "blood" children. Some despair of reaching an answer to this question.[13] But I think such pessimism is not wholly warranted, and that if generally accepted would lead to much unnecessary harm. It is true that in many cases it is difficult to know what ought to be done. But this does not mean that we should throw up our hands and espouse a completely laissez-faire approach: philosophers can help by probing the central issues and trying to find guidelines for action.

Naturally there is no way to derive an answer to this kind of problem by deductive argument from self-evident premises, for it must depend on a complicated interplay of facts and moral judgments. My preliminary exploration of Huntington's chorea is of this nature. In the course of the discussion I suggested that, if it is true that sufferers live substantially worse lives than do normal persons, those who might transmit it should not have any children. This conclusion is supported by the judgments that we ought to try to provide for every child a normal opportunity for a good life, that possible individuals are not harmed if not conceived, and that it is sometimes less justifiable for persons to exercise their right to procreate than one might think.

I want to stress, in conclusion, that my argument is incomplete. To investigate fully even a single disease, like Huntington's chorea, empirical research on the lives of members of afflicted families is necessary. Then, after developing further the themes touched upon here, evaluation of the probable consequences of different policies on society and on future generations is needed. Until the results of a complete study are available, my argument could serve best as a reason for persons at risk for transmitting Huntington's chorea and similar diseases to put off having children. Perhaps this paper will stimulate such inquiry.

Notes

1. There are a series of cases ranging from low risk of mild disease or handicap to high risk of serious disease or handicap. It would be difficult to decide where the duty to refrain from procreation becomes compelling. My point here is that there are some clear cases.
      I'd like to thank Lawrence Davis and Sidney Siskin for their helpful comments on an earlier version of this paper. . . .
2. *The Merck Manual* (Rahway, N.J.: Merck, 1972), p. 1346.
3. Hymie Gordon, "Genetic Counseling," *JAMA,* Vol. 217 No. 9 (August 30, 1971), 1217.
4. Charles Smith, Susan Holloway, and Alan E. H. Emery, "Individuals at Risk in Families—Genetic Disease," *J. of Medical Genetics,* 8(1971), 453. See also Townes in *Genetic Counseling,* ed. Daniel Bergsma, *Birth Defects Original Article Series,* Vol. VI, No. 1 (May 1970).
5. J. H. Pearn, "Patients' Subjective Interpretation of Risks Offered in Genetic Counseling," *Journal of Medical Genetics,* 10 (1973), 131.
6. Pearn, p. 132.
7. *The New York Times,* September 30, 1975, p. 1., col. 6. The Joseph family disease is similar to Huntington's chorea except that symptoms start appearing in the twenties. Rick Donohue is in his early twenties.
8. There may be a price for the individuals who refrain from having children. We will be looking at the situation from their point of view shortly.
9. This is in fact the basis for certain parental duties. An example is the maternal duty to obtain proper nutrition before and during pregnancy, for this is necessary if the child is to have normal health when it is born.
10. One might argue that as many persons as possible should exist so that they may enjoy life.
11. Some thinkers have qualms about the use of some or all of these methods. They have so far failed to show why they are immoral, although, naturally, much careful study will be required

before they could be unqualifiedly recommended. See, for example, Richard Hull, "Genetic Engineering: Comment on Headings," *The Humanist,* Vol. 32 (Sept./Oct. 1972), 13.

12. *Essays in Pragmatism,* ed. A. Castell (New York, 1948), p. 73.
13. For example, see Leach, p. 138. One of the ways the dilemma described by Leach could be lessened would be if society emphasized those aspects of family life not dependent on "blood" relationships and downplayed those that are.

10.3c   Responding to Purdy

I should probably begin by noting the scientific advances made since Purdy's article was written: A reliable "marker" for the Huntington's chorea gene has been found; as, more recently, has the gene itself. These developments mean that prenatal diagnosis of the disease is becoming easier, and the options open to potential parents who are carriers are becoming wider. Rather than simply going ahead and risking it, or refraining altogether from reproduction, parents may also have the option of selective abortion. But these advances and likely advances do not invalidate Purdy's position, for at least two reasons. First, there are other genetic diseases apart from Huntington's chorea, and prenatal tests for those may lie much further in the future. Purdy's arguments might then provide a model for thinking about any kind of genetic disease for which reliable prenatal tests are unavailable. Second, the option of selective abortion may well be regarded as unethical by some people. If so, then regardless of whether or not prenatal testing is possible, the issue will turn out to be exactly as Purdy describes it: Selective abortion will be out of the question (for ethical if not for scientific reasons), so the choice will come down to going ahead and risking it, or else refraining from reproduction altogether.

Given the issue as Purdy describes it, then, is it right to conclude that those at risk of producing offspring who suffer from a serious genetic disease, such as Huntington's chorea, *ought* not to have children? Purdy's case is undoubtedly a strong one; it is made stronger, if anything, by her refusal to mix up the ethical question with questions about the law. She does not argue that we should prevent certain people from reproducing; she argues only that it is wrong for those people to reproduce. It is wise to keep these matters separate. Not everything that is immoral is worth legislating against, after all (for example, it would be pretty pointless to try criminalizing adultery); it is only once the moral question has been settled that the legislative question ought even to arise. So this is a good tactic.

I don't imagine, either, that many will wish to quarrel with what Purdy says about the ethics of denying existence to possible children. It seems obvious that a non-existent entity (what entity?) cannot be harmed or wronged. A critic may be less happy, though, with Purdy's claim that parents in a given culture have a duty "to try to provide for their children health normal for that culture." This seems both too loose and too strict. It seems too loose because certain cultures may encourage practices which are known by members of those cultures to reduce the "normal" level of health. For instance, a culture may have religious reasons for refusing to permit certain kinds of medical treatment, even when culture-members know that those treatments would raise the "normal" level of health. Purdy's critic may well say that a parent within such a culture has a duty to do more than provide what is merely "normal": The parent has a duty to try to provide those (prohibited) forms of treatment that will make the child's health better than what is normal for that culture. In cases such as this, it seems that Purdy's formula doesn't demand enough. But in other cases it seems too strict. It appears to ignore the fact that some parents may occupy a seriously disadvantaged position within a given culture, which makes it altogether unreasonable to require that they try to provide a "normal" level of health. Ideally they will try to provide a level of health that is as good as their disadvantaged situation allows; but it may be unfair to criticize them if, as will almost inevitably be the case, that level falls short of what is the norm for the culture as a whole. In some quite advanced countries, for instance the United States, the most disadvantaged may not even know—because no one has made the effort to tell them—that such things as immunization programs exist, and you can't be blamed for not taking advantage of what you don't know is there. So a critic may want to suggest that this part of Purdy's argument needs to be reviewed. Her talk of "normal" levels of health is too superficial to be helpful.

More seriously, though, a critic may take issue with what Purdy says about the interests of parents. Perhaps she dismisses these interests a little too quickly. An important part of her reason for claiming that the desires of parents to have children should be overridden in cases where there is a risk that those children may suffer from Huntington's chorea lies in her "common sense" conclusion that the "pessimists" are right—that a life lived with Huntington's chorea is a blighted and terrible thing, and should be inflicted on no one. But a critic might argue that this is an exaggeration. An average sufferer from the disease can expect to live perfectly normally for between thirty and fifty years before symptoms become apparent. Surely, the critic might urge, this is not *such* a gloomy prospect. The critic might go further. Every child—whether it suffers from a genetic disease or not—is assured of death eventually, and quite likely of suffering too. Does this mean that *all* reproduction is ethically suspect? (After all, parents know that this will be their children's fate.) Or is Purdy saying that the extra thirty-five years or so that a person without Huntington's chorea might be expected to live somehow makes all the difference? If so, why? There seems to be a gap in the argument here (and it can't be plugged with Purdy's ideas about "normal" levels of health, since those ideas, as we have already seen, are not well enough worked out). So a critic might doubt whether Purdy's reason for overriding the interests of potential parents is really very convincing. A critic might also wonder about her quick dismissal of some parental desires. It may be true that the desire to see the genetic line continued "entails a sinister legacy of disease and death," but this is true of all reproduction. The only way to abolish human death and disease would be to abolish the human race. It may be true that reproduction doesn't secure immortality, but it is surely not *wholly* irrational to seek comfort in the thought that some part of you will live on after your death. In short, Purdy's critic may conclude that her case has not been established—that it has not been shown to be immoral to have children when there is a serious risk of genetic disease.

Purdy can no doubt reply to many of these criticisms, and her case that there is nothing immoral about deciding *not* to have children when there is a risk of genetic disease remains untouched. The issue is a complicated one, but this discussion should have indicated some of the factors that need to be taken into account.

10.3d   Curing People: Somatic-Cell Therapy

In the near future, it may well be possible to cure certain genetic diseases by genetic engineering—that is, by the manipulation of a person's genetic make-up. In the case of some diseases, this will occur by altering the genes located on an unborn person's sex chromosomes, in which event the alteration will be passed on to that person's descendants. This process is referred to as germ-line gene therapy (see 10.3e, below). In the case of other diseases (called autosomal genetic diseases), it will involve altering the genes of an unborn person's somatic cells: These alterations are not passed on to future generations. This process is referred to as somatic-cell gene therapy; such therapy will be the subject of the present section.

Somatic-cell therapy might be used to cure cystic fibrosis, a condition which normally kills its victims before the age of twenty. If it were possible to identify the gene responsible for cystic fibrosis early in pregnancy, and to eliminate it, would there be any good ethical reason not to? It is difficult to imagine what reason there might be. Surely such an intervention would not be different in kind from any other clinical intervention designed to effect a cure; so long as the risks were explained and informed consent properly obtained, somatic-cell gene therapy would seem to raise no new concerns. Of course, many people become uncomfortable whenever the possibility of altering someone's genes is raised. Genetic manipulation is felt to be deeply "unnatural," to be an improper interference with the basis of life itself. But the whole practice of medicine is unnatural in this sense, and no one—barring those with certain religious beliefs—thinks that the whole practice of medicine is wrong or improper. Indeed, where a genetic alteration is not inheritable—as with somatic-cell gene therapy—the interference involved appears not, in principle, to be any greater than that involved in the removal of an appendix. So it seems that somatic-cell gene therapy raises no special problems. There appears to be no good reason why research into such therapies ought not to be encouraged.

10.3e   Changing People: Germ-Line Therapy

People's worries about genetic engineering seem altogether more reasonable in the case of germ-line gene therapy—where the alterations brought about are passed on to future generations. This is disturbing partly because of its open-endedness. In somatic-cell gene therapy, the intention is to cure just one, present individual, and the effects of the therapy stop there. In germ-line gene therapy, by contrast, the effects stretch far into the future:

The genetic alteration will affect an indefinite number of future generations. Exactly why this is disturbing is brought out when one considers the consequences of something going wrong. If something goes wrong in somatic-cell therapy, the (perhaps tragic) results will directly affect only one person, the patient. But if something goes wrong in germ-line therapy, an indefinitely large number of people will be affected, and may continue to be affected far into the future. The stakes, in other words, are much higher. Additionally, it will rarely be clear what *other* results may be brought about by germ-line therapy, even when it is apparently successful in curing the disease it was meant to cure. For instance, the gene responsible for a genetic disease may also have as yet undiscovered beneficial effects; according to some people, the result of impoverishing the human gene-pool by germ-line therapy may be to rob future generations of potentially valuable genetic mutations. These considerations suggest that it is vital to discover not only enough about human genetics to be able to carry out the therapy in question, but also enough to be able to predict with some certainty what the long-term consequences of that therapy will be. We may be quite close to meeting the first condition, but we are nowhere near to meeting the second. This fact persuades many people that the risks are too high for it to be right, in our present state of knowledge, to go through with germ-line therapy.

A defender of germ-line therapy might argue that it would be simply wrong to withhold from people now a form of treatment that might help them, whatever hazy fears we may have about the future. Future generations can fend for themselves, it might be said; in any case, future generations are likely to know far more about human genetics than we do, and so will be well placed to rectify any damage we inadvertently cause now. This is certainly an optimistic response! But even if the optimism is well-warranted, it is still unclear that it would be right for us to bequeath such (potentially enormous) problems to our descendants. Don't we have *some* duty to try not to make things worse for future generations than we have to? My guess is that germ-line genetic therapy will continue to be thought disturbing, and properly so, until such time as we can be fairly sure that short-term beneficent results won't be bought at the price of much greater long-term disadvantages. This doesn't mean that germ-line genetic therapy is wrong. But it does mean that the burden of proof lies with those who would like to see germ-line therapy become widely accepted.

10.3f   Recap: A Better World?

We have now looked at a number of the issues raised by our increasing knowledge of human genetics. One issue I have not mentioned is that of nontherapeutic genetic engineering—the manipulation of genes with a view, not to curing people of certain conditions, but to enhancing them in some way (perhaps by making them smarter, or stronger). It is even possible to imagine parents being able to choose *exactly* what their offspring should be like.

I haven't discussed this issue because it falls somewhat beyond the scope of the present book; nontherapeutic genetic engineering poses questions, not so much of medical ethics, as of the broadest kind of social ethics. Neverthe-less, some of the questions we have addressed in this part of the chapter are unquestionably relevant to that broader question. Somatic-cell gene therapy might one day mean that no one will ever be born suffering from particular genetic diseases. Selective abortion and the avoidance of reproduction on grounds of genetic disease both indirectly contribute to an alteration of the human gene-pool; germ-line gene therapy would directly contribute to an alteration of the human gene-pool. Selective abortion and the avoidance of reproduction are already possible; somatic-cell and germ-line therapy will be possible before too long. The effect of all of these measures is (or would be) to modify in one way or another the kind of people that the world contains. The intentions behind such measures are (or would be) beneficent—there seems no real doubt about that. But the actual consequences of influencing the genetic make-up of human beings may diverge quite widely from what is intended.

This is not a point about gene therapy or genetic engineering being some-how "unnatural"; nor is it a warning against "playing God." Rather, it is a re-minder that however impressive our present state of knowledge might be, it is still, and will remain, imperfect. In such circumstances—where the potential, but as yet unknown, consequences of particular courses of action may be both significant and negative—it seems that the only ethically acceptable approach is one of caution. There may be nothing wrong with modifying the kind of people that the world contains. But we owe it to ourselves, and to our descen-dants, not to jump to that conclusion. And if this point holds good for thera-peutic forms of genetic intervention, where the underlying intention is clearly beneficent, it must hold doubly good for nontherapeutic forms of intervention, where the underlying intention may be very murky indeed.

Study Questions

1. Suppose the health of everyone in the population were, as a result of some intervention, improved by 10 percent. Would this be just? (Notice that the gap between the healthiest and the unhealthiest would be *in-creased* by this intervention.)
2. If it were proved that fewer people died and more people lived longer under a system in which poor people sold their kidneys to rich people, would this show that such a system was ethically desirable?
3. Does the fact that most of us would prefer not to suffer from genetic dis-eases show that the selective abortion of genetically flawed fetuses is ethically different from any other kind of abortion?
4. Is there an ethically significant difference between the following two po-sitions? (i) By engaging in germ-line gene therapy, we risk skewing the human gene-pool in ways whose consequences we cannot foresee: Therefore we shouldn't do it. (ii) By keeping alive until adulthood peo-ple who would otherwise die in infancy (and so by allowing them to reach reproductive age), we risk skewing the human gene-pool in ways whose consequences we cannot foresee: Therefore we shouldn't do it.

Related Cases in Crigger, *Cases in Bioethics*, Third Edition

The cases most relevant to "Allocating Scarce Resources" (section 10.1) are cases 45 through 50 and cases 52, 57, and 58. Cases 45, 47, 48, and 52 directly concern the just allocation of scarce resources—in the first instance, the question is which project should a hospital devote resources to; in the second instance, the resource is a bed in intensive care; in the third instance, the resource is a medical team; in the fourth instance, the resources are organs and the question is posed whether a person's nationality is relevant to deciding whether or not he or she should receive a transplantable body part. Cases 46 and 58 deal with decisions about care for the elderly based on consideration of cost, while case 56 addresses the cost of radical procedures that enable caregivers both to honor a Jehovah's Witness patient's refusal of blood transfusion and to save her life. Case 57 raises the issue of whether the state should meet the expense of treatment for AIDS; and cases 49 and 50 are about the duties of professionals to balance care against costs. The most helpful discussions are those following cases 45, 47, 50, 52, and 58.

Concerned with issues in "Organ Procurement and Transplantation" (section 10.2) are cases 36, 53, and 54. Case 36 is about the transplantation of animal organs into human beings; case 53 is about the ethical consequences of keeping an anencephalic newborn alive so that its organs can be transplanted elsewhere; case 54 presents a ghoulish scenario in which a fetus is to be conceived and then aborted, specifically in order to gain access to its organs. The discussion after case 54 is especially useful.

The issues in "Gene Therapy and Genetic Engineering" (section 10.3) is covered in case 12, which is about the consequences of Huntington's chorea, discussed by L.M. Purdy in this chapter.

Glossary

Artificial Insemination (AI)   A woman's egg is fertilized by a man's sperm, within her body, but not by means of sexual intercourse.

Autonomy, respect for   An ethical principle enjoining respect for the capacity of others to form and act upon their own plans, aspirations, and preferences.

Beneficence   An ethical principle stating that one should seek to benefit others.

Brain Death   The cessation of neurological function.

Cardiopulmonary   Pertaining to the heart and lungs; hence the cardiopulmonary conception of death specifies cessation of heart and lung function as the criterion of death.

Consequentialism   The view that the ethical value of an action depends upon its consequences.

Deinstitutionalization   The policy of replacing care for the mentally incompetent in mental institutions with care for the mentally incompetent "in the community."

Deontology   An ethical theory stating that one should act in accordance with one's duties and obligations.

Egalitarianism   The view that all people are of equal worth and deserve equal consideration or treatment.

Euthanasia   Mercy killing. **Active Euthanasia**   Acting so as deliberately to cause death (e.g., injecting a lethal dose of morphine). **Passive Euthanasia** Refraining from action so as deliberately to cause death (e.g., withdrawing nourishment and/or treatment).

Gene Therapy   The attempt to cure a disease by manipulating a person's genes. **Somatic-Cell Gene Therapy**   A form of genetic manipulation whose effects are not passed on to the patient's descendants. **Germ-Line Gene Therapy**   A form of genetic manipulation whose effects are passed on to future generations.

In Vitro Fertilization (IVF)   The fertilization of an egg outside a woman's body, the resultant embryo or embryos then being transplanted into her uterus.

Incommensurability   The mismatch of values—e.g., health and wealth—that cannot be measured along the same scale.

Justice   An ethical principle stating that one should give to people what is fair, due, or owed to them; differences in treatment must be justified by appeal to relevant differences between cases.

Libertarianism   The view that freedom is of paramount importance, and so that it would be wrong to interfere with the actions and preferences of others.

Paternalism   The view that it is legitimate to make decisions in the interests of others whether or not those decisions accord with their preferences.

Placebo   A treatment, typically a pill, that has no active ingredient relevant to the condition for which it is prescribed. Hence, **Placebo Effect**   The beneficial effect on some patients falsely believing that they have been prescribed a treatment with active ingredients relevant to the condition for which they are suffering.

Rights   Claims that one may legitimately make of others. A person who is owed an obligation by someone else has a right to expect or demand that that obligation be satisfied.

Supererogation   Acting above and beyond the call of duty.

Surrogacy   Bearing a child for someone else.

Utilitarianism   An ethical theory stating that one should seek to bring about the greatest amount of happiness for the greatest number of people.   **Act Utilitarianism**   A variant of utilitarianism according to which one should act, on a case by case basis, so as to maximize happiness   **Rule Utilitarianism**   A variant of utilitarianism according to which one should follow rules which, if generally adopted, would maximize happiness.

Index